JESUS

*An
Interview
Across
Time*

JESUS

*An
Interview
Across
Time*

A Psychiatrist Looks
at HIS Humanity

Andrew G. Hodges, M.D.

Village House Publishers
Birmingham, Alabama

To three women: Dorothy Smith Hodges, Mary L. Shirley Hodges, and Maymie Johnston Shirley

and

To four men: A. Gerow Hodges, C. S. Lewis, Francis A. Schaeffer, and Robert Langs

each of whom has affected my life in his own way

Second Edition

Unless otherwise identified, Scripture quotations in this volume are from the HOLY BIBLE, KING JAMES VERSION.

Scripture quotations marked NASB are from the New American Standard Bible, © The Lockman Foundation 1960, 1962, 1963, 1968, 1971, 1973, 1975, 1977.

Scripture quotations marked NIV are from the HOLY BIBLE: NEW INTERNATIONAL VERSION. Copyright © 1973, 1978, 1984 International Bible Society. Used by permission of Zondervan Bible Publishers.

Verses marked TLB are taken from THE LIVING BIBLE, copyright 1971 by Tyndale House Publishers, Wheaton, Illinois. Used by permission.

Library of Congress Cataloging in Publication Data

Hodges, Andrew G., M.D.
JESUS An Interview Across Time
Summary: A hypothetical interview with Jesus Christ.

ISBN 0–9617255–0–8

Copyright © 1986 by Andrew G. Hodges, M.D.
Published by Village House Publishers
Printed in the United States of America

Contents

THREE *Opposition and Confirmation*

FOUR *Instruction and Celebration*

FIVE *Crucifixion and Resurrection*

Introduction

John (the Baptist) held me under the water for a long time until my whole body was in pain from the lack of oxygen. John wanted me to feel that pain —it was so much like death—to let me know that he understood what this was costing me, that one day I would lie in a grave. Finally, he brought me up out of the water. I was gasping for air and he just stood there with his hand on me. It was a strong hand. After several seconds I finally caught my breath, and then it happened. I heard my Father's voice for the first time: "This is My beloved son in whom I am well pleased." I can still hear that rich, majestic voice. Heaven had opened. The door was no longer shut. I had heard my own Father's voice at last. I had waited 30 years . . . the impact on me was startling. All those years of preparation, of making sure, of waiting, of living on His written words, of keeping the faith, had been validated firsthand. For days afterward His voice kept coming back to me: "This is My beloved son." It was all I could think about.

It was such an overpowering experience that I wanted to be alone to savor it. I almost had to be alone to contain it. Before I went out into the world, I also wanted as intense an awareness of Him as possible. I knew from experience that the way to heighten my sense of Him was to be totally alone with Him and to fast. I had to go over with Him what I was to do and what I was to say. That knowledge could come only by waiting before Him. I felt that my Father was saying, "Before you go out into the world, go over My words one more time. Live on them. Fast for forty days to test yourself." So I did. He led me every step of the way. For forty days I wanted almost continually to eat. But I didn't.

Was this fast an encouraging time for you?

Fasting is a lot like seeing in the dark. At first, everything is black and all you can think about is pain and food. After a while, you begin to "see" things, to perceive things that you couldn't at first.

What became more clear for you?

Everything depended on me. Salvation by me and me alone. No one else could please God ultimately. No matter how hard they had tried, they had all failed and always would. But I would please Him. He had promised—I was His son.

His spirit was there in a new way. It was even more alive. You know how someone's personality can affect you when they are right there beside you talking. You can feel their spirit, their energy. I couldn't see Him but I could feel Him. His words had never been more alive. I was completely one with Him, and now I knew that my words would be His words. Everything I would say would have just as much authority as if He said it. Even better yet, He would be saying it through me when I spoke. At this particular time in the wilderness I was exhuberant. God had never been closer. He was right there beside me.

I had just finished the forty-day fast when Satan surprised me . . . As I was starting back to town I came around a boulder and suddenly a man appeared. He was a little on the short side, had a winsome smile, and seemed to be exceptionally gentle and kind. After a few minutes with him, I decided that he was perhaps the most striking person I had ever met. He radiated warmth. We began talking and it was obvious that he knew what I had been doing. As time went on, I began to think that this was perhaps one of my Father's ways of revealing Himself to me. After all, God had just spoken to me for the first time, and in the Old Testament angels had often appeared to various men.

I half-heartedly wondered if this were a trick, but he was the kind of person who dispelled doubt and put you at ease. Besides, I hadn't talked to another human being for forty days. We both laughed when he said "I don't suppose you are hungry." He volunteered, "I have been in the heavens with your Father, and I have come to talk to you. God wants you to use your power. He doesn't want you to suffer any longer. Go ahead. Use the power He's given you. You are hungry." And very unassumingly, in an encouraging way, he said, "If you are the son of God, turn those stones into bread." Things were really moving fast for me at this point. Was God, my Father, pushing me to trust Him more?

(Had something like this actually happened at the temptation of Jesus— the Son of God, the Holy One, God Incarnate, the worker of miracles? Was he truly tested? Did he actually become a man with all of man's limitations?

I wondered how Christ himself would answer these questions could He speak to us today. I went over the record of his life again. As I did so, this time as a psychiatrist specializing in the study of indirect verbal messages, the Scriptures astounded me, not only with their direct communications, but also with their consistently clear indirect coded messages. Thus, I came to the conclusion that the Scriptures give us many hidden clues to Christ's human development and the so-called "missing years."

The Scriptures themselves supported the idea that there was much more in them about Christ than we realize. As the 40th Psalm states prophetically about the Messiah, "Lo in the volume of the book is written of me" (Psalm 40:7).

Knowing that our Lord himself had studied the Old Testament Scriptures, and continuing to be amazed at the vastness of the Scriptures myself, I looked at the Gospel accounts of Jesus' life afresh. The personality of Jesus emerged in a new way, a personality that continually surprised me as I was freed from my preconceptions. How complex was this man. Demanding, but humble . . . Tender when I expected anger. Angry when I expected tenderness. Almost always doing the unexpected . . . the courage . . . the authority . . . the brilliance. He pre-dated by two thousand years what, in my opinion, remains the most important discovery in my field. He understood clearly the workings of the unconscious mind.

More and more, as I looked at the man and understood the context in which he lived out his life, I stood in awe. As a psychiatrist I have spent numerous hours listening to human beings. I have interviewed more than one person who thought he or she was the Messiah. This man Jesus reminded me of none of those. As Christ's personality became clearer to me, and as I listened to his powerful words speaking across the centuries, I could almost hear his answers to my questions echoing in my mind. That is how the story begins.

Much of the book is speculation, however biblically based, and obviously it is colored by my own personality as any other author's book would be. Therefore, I would admonish you to read the Scriptures, to separate fact from fiction, to "check it out."

Imagine that Jesus of Nazareth, Son of God, Son of Man, is telling his story. The One of whom it was said, "All the armies that ever marched, all the navies that ever sailed, all the parliaments that ever sat, all the kings that ever reigned, put together, have not affected the life of man on this earth as much as that one solitary life." He is the One on whom our calendar is hinged, the One whom the demagogues and dictators of Planet Earth have not been able to banish, the One who has promised to return "in power and great glory."

Imagine that this man has agreed to talk about how he came to his unique position in history, how he came to realize for himself who he really was, and what his thirty-three years on this earth were like.)

ONE

Preparation and Revelation

In the Beginning

God does not seem to be very popular these days.

Oh? I never had any trouble finding a great many people who were interested in God. In fact, I found people who would endure great hardships, walk miles, go without food, and actually knock your door down to learn about God if you presented Him for who He is. If God is not very popular today, it is not His fault. It is the people who tell His story. They are using the wrong version.

Which version is that?

The boring version.

I have always wondered how a story about someone who claims to be God and who acts like God—healing the sick, raising the dead, walking on water, taking on the establishment, allowing himself to be murdered and finally coming back from the dead just as he promised, returning to power and spreading his movement over the whole world to virtually every culture—I have always wondered how that could be boring.

If you tell that story over and over, in just the right way, you can make it boring. It is easy to forget that this story is by the same Creator who brings you the Grand Canyon, the Alps, Niagara Falls, and the Atlantic and Pacific Oceans, as well as the entire human race!

Let's get to your story. As I was reading about you recently, I came across the time you were speaking to a crowd and you told them, "I am the Light of the world." It made me wonder. Did an angel dramatically appear to you one day with an orchestra and bright lights and say, "You are God's son," or did you always know who you were?

Neither. An angel did appear to my mother without the orchestra, but I never heard my Father's voice aloud or saw an angel until I was thirty. Of course, on the night of my birth, some very special things happened. There was a very bright star in the East. Angels told some shepherds in Bethlehem about me. And wise men began a journey from the East to honor me with precious gifts. But it was a long time before I knew about those events and my unique relationship with God, although my mother and father knew.

Then how did you find out that you were the Chosen One, the Messiah? Did your mother tell you?

My mother would say such things as, "You are a very special child. One day when you get older, you will realize you were sent to serve God in a special way." But a lot of Jewish mothers say those things. As a young boy, I remember asking her, "How did you decide to name me Jesus?" and she, as if joking, always gave me the same answer: "An angel came down from heaven and gave us your name."

Which He did.

Exactly. But Mother never told me directly who I was as a child. Think about it. You are a mother and you are going to tell your child that he is not altogether your son, but is God's only Son—and that he has been appointed, despite all his humble surroundings, to be the Messiah, the Savior of the world! That's an unbelievable story to tell your child.

You've given birth to the most important person who's ever lived and how do you tell your son that fact without all the neighbors finding out and thinking you're a heretic, or even insane? Your mother could have been killed for telling what she knew to be true.

She would have been killed. So my mother did a very smart thing. She let my Father tell me.

Joseph?

No, my *Father.*

You mean your Father in heaven! How did He tell you?

My Father revealed who I was at just the right time. He was asking for enormous trust and faith from some very special people in order to carry out His plan and He made sure that none of us were alone in this plan by making it a "family matter." He first disclosed my coming to the prophets who came before me. Then, when the time was approaching, he told my mother and her cousin Elizabeth, older by many years, what was going to happen. He said that each of them would have a unique son.

　The circumstances were amazingly similar. Both women were childless. Both were told by angels that they would bear children miraculously. First, Elizabeth, who was so old that she was post-menopausal, was informed that she would bring forth a child. Then, six months later, my mother Mary, while still a virgin, was told that she was to have a baby without any help from a man!

I had never realized the striking similarities.

Both women were to have sons. Both were told by angels what to name their sons. Both were told what their sons would do. Even the sons had much in common, for they were long awaited and prophesied. Together these two men would turn the world toward God. One was a great prophet who would go before the other, serving him by announcing to the world that a great Light had come into its midst. That prophet was my cousin, John, known as the Baptist.

And the other was the Messiah, the Savior of the world. That's you.

Yes.

Why do you think it was such a sensitive thing to do to keep it all in the family?

It's a difficult to believe that you're a miracle or part of one. My Father knew that doubts could come to all of us. Could this really be true? When the doubts came, all we had to do was look at our own family, people we could immediately trust, and there were the miracles confirming the story. And He also mentioned us in the Scriptures so that everyone could know who we were. In fact, that's how my Father told me who I was. He left me written messages in the Scriptures which he confirmed to me with "circumstances."

Why didn't God just come out and tell you who you were by coming to see you Himself?

That would have changed everything that made my life important. Then I wouldn't really have been human like you. I would know nothing about trusting Him, about living by faith. How could I teach you about faith if I hadn't experienced it myself?

Still, the Scriptures seem a strange way for God to communicate, particularly with His only son.

On the contrary, the Scriptures were a brilliant idea. My Father was a genius in finding a way to communicate with all people everywhere over thousands of years. For people who, for the most part and for most of the time, never had a radio or television, a book was the only way to communicate. It was unforgettable, unchanging, and yet still alive—just as He was. He created that communication form so that a person could always check on what He had just said.

To communicate in a way that is fresh moment after moment to whoever listens and then to confirm a message with fulfilled prophecy—that's an astounding idea! He foretold the future in Scripture and it came to pass just as He predicted. It's also an incredible feeling to find yourself in the middle of the the Psalms and elsewhere in Scripture where He predicted what I'd be like and I was! That was very convincing for me.

Why did you trust His words?

Because they were true and because I realized ultimately they were my Father's words. It would have been harder not to believe them. All around me was the history Scripture talked about. I could see Jacob's Well, Solomon's partially rebuilt Temple, Jerusalem with her huge walls and gates, the same roads that King David had walked. David's city was there, Bethlehem, where I was born. The Jordan River my people crossed to get into the Promised Land —the very land in which I lived—was evident. Despite what some of your modern thinkers say, I think my ancestors were intelligent enough to recognize a miracle when it occurred. Moses, who wrote the first books of the Bible, was basically an honest man and an accurate reporter.

The reputations of many good men rest on these words. Besides Moses, look at who else wrote part of this book: Joshua, the man who replaced Moses as Israel's leader; Samuel, the prophet who anointed David; David himself—king and shepherd; his son Solomon, and other prophets, Isaiah and Jeremiah. All of these men were contributors to the Old Testament, which was the only part of the Scriptures that I had in my day. After I came along, I was quoted accurately in what is known as the New Testament by three of my disciples Matthew, Peter, and John, along with a physician by the name of Luke.* Later "on their own," Peter wrote two more books (First and Second Peter), and John wrote four more (First, Second, and Third John, and Revelation), and a talented writer, a man named Paul, wrote about fourteen books. Their writings constitute most of the New Testament. You have the word of some honest men on how things happened, besides having my Father's word. Another reason these words seemed so authentic was that they never covered up for their "heroes"—they reported everything just as it happened. Noah drank too much at times, Moses and David were murderers as was Paul in the New Testament, Abraham slept with his wife's servant, Jacob was a swindler, and Isaiah used profanity. Later on, the New Testament told the truth in the same way.

Did you ever consider that these words might just be myths?

I always considered it. But accurate, fulfilled prophecies destroy myths. They become facts. Facts are very convincing, particularly when you happen to be one of them.

When you read the prophecies about the Messiah—prophecies which had been there for centuries—did you begin to realize that you were the one who fit all those descriptions, particularly when you were told where the Messiah would be born —Bethlehem—where he would come from—Galilee—and which of the twelve tribes of Israel he would come from—Judah?

At first it was the furthest thing from my mind. Remember, my mother became pregnant with me during her engagement and then left town to go and tell her cousin Elizabeth. When she finally returned to Nazareth to be married, she was about three months pregnant. Nazareth was no different from any other small town. It didn't take the neighbors long to notice this fact and start the rumors flying. They continued my entire life.

Why do you think God arranged the circumstances in such a way that your mother and Joseph would have to endure such great suffering?

First of all, He was making a clear statement that I was virgin born and, characteristically, He went to a great deal of trouble to make things very plain. What people thought initially about my mother was not His first concern.

Why do you think He chose Mary to be your mother?

Because of her faith and her courage. Imagine the courage it took for her to wait three months at her cousin's house. All that time she was not married,

---

*Because the Book of Mark contains so much personal information about him, Peter is considered the disciple who provided most of the information and material for the book written by a younger disciple of Christ, John Mark, who was not in the original twelve. Peter was known to be John Mark's mentor, and the Book of Mark is commonly referred to as Peter's Gospel.

and realized that each passing day would only make the rumors about her "illegitimate child" worse. Really, she didn't know if she was to be married at all, because she didn't know what her fiancé Joseph would think about the situation. And, too, the angel Gabriel had promised her only a son. He hadn't promised her a husband!

Why do you think Mary stayed at Elizabeth's so long, then? Why didn't she return to Nazareth sooner and take care of business?

She wanted to be present at the birth of John. That was enormously comforting to her. I'm sure there were other reasons besides that one that led my mother to wait three months, but whatever they were, you can be sure she felt it was God's will. She was a woman of real faith. You know, God always pushes us to increase our faith. At the same time, in the middle of our trials, He repeatedly encourages us. At that time, my mother's cousin Elizabeth paid her the supreme compliment. She said, and Luke records it in his gospel,

> "You are favored by God above all women, and your child is destined for God's mightiest praise. What an honor this is that the mother of my Lord should visit me. When you came in and greeted me, the instant I heard your voice, my baby moved in me for joy! You believed that God would do what He said; that is why He has given you this wonderful blessing."[1]

That's a great tribute.

By causing my mother to wait three months after she was pregnant to get married, my Father was teaching me from the beginning of my life through the tough circumstances of my birth that I was to be identified with the sinners and unfortunates of the world. How many people have been born into circumstances that they would have liked to change? I can identify with the poor, the illegitimate, the crippled, and those with the "different colored" skin. How many people because of their sin have gotten themselves into circumstances filled with suffering which they later sincerely regretted having done? Although I was sinless, I was to be one with all of them in all of their pain. More than that, from the first second in my mother's womb, my Father was making known to me my role in this world. I was to be abused so that my people could be free. I was to be illegitimate so that they might be legitimate. My Father was preparing me to learn how to take suffering. When I got older I heard the taunts of some of my peers: "He doesn't know who his father is." "He doesn't know who his father is."

That must have hurt.

I also caught the ridicule of adults. Between my house and the synagogue was the town gate, where the businessmen gathered, and also the local drinking establishment. Occasionally as I walked to the synagogue, I would hear the snide comments of some of the men gathered at the gate, but the men at what you would call the "bar" were the worst of all. They made up a song about me where they would guess who my father was and name about five or six despicable characters. It became a game each day to add another name to the list, and then they would sing the same chorus and finally all of them would laugh. Every day there was that thought: "I'm a bastard." That's who they were telling me I was.

It got so bad that my half-brothers became ashamed of me and harrassed me, too. One of them, James, was later to write a New Testament book in which he addressed hypocrisy and true religion as opposed to false religion. He had a great deal to say about the true test of brotherly love, about looking past what people appeared to be on the surface. He had even more to say about how vicious the tongue can be and how hard a person must work to control it. After all was said and done, my brother had learned his lesson well. He never forgot how he had treated me and how self-deceptive human beings can be.

Another one of my brothers who harrassed me was Jude, who also later wrote a New Testament book. As you might have guessed, Jude wrote about heretics and those who lack faith.

It's amazing to me how many people mentioned in the New Testament Scriptures were once declared enemies of yours. They included people from all walks of life —The Pharisee, Nicodemus, the corrupt tax collectors, Zacchaeus and Matthew, the prostitute, Mary Magdalene, and the self-righteous Paul. And down through the ages in the history of the Christian church, the story is the same—Augustine had been a pagan womanizer, John Newton, the preacher and songwriter who wrote "Amazing Grace" had been a hardened slave-trader. But you and your Father specialized in winning these kinds of people over to your side.

If you're a follower of mine, you were once my enemy.

The Early Years

Years later, didn't the Pharisees use that rumor about your illegitimacy and accuse you of being illegitimate when you said that you were God?

They did. But it didn't bother me nearly as much as before. When you're a little boy ten years old, you know how much you love your mother—particularly if you've got a good one, and I had one of the best. They were calling her names and I was crushed. More than anything, I wanted to be devoted to God and to serve Him—for a true Jew there is no higher calling—but I felt like the worst sinner. Then I had the horrible thought that my mother must have been ashamed of me, too.

How did you handle your suffering?

I went to God. I didn't want to talk to my mother or my father Joseph about it right then. I wondered why God would allow this humiliation. Could he help me? Would he help me? I knew that David as a young shepherd boy alone tending his sheep had developed an enormous sensitivity to God and had written many of the Psalms. I thought that if David could find help from God I could, too. So many times, on the verge of tears, I prayed to Him and I read His Scriptures, particularly the Psalms.

You mean at first you read the Scriptures to find comfort and not to find out about the Messiah?

I rather "accidentally" found out who I was. There was a lot of talk about the Messiah because we were an oppressed people. God had promised us a Deliverer. As a Jew, I was interested in the Messiah and longed for Him, but I didn't see how He particularly related to me.

What did you read in this holy book that helped you?

One of my two favorite characters in the Old Testament was Joseph. As a young boy, he was betrayed by his older brothers and eventually sold into slavery in a foreign land, Egypt. Totally alone except for God, Joseph spent many years as a slave suffering one setback after another. But he always remained faithful to Jehovah God. God didn't forget about him, and one day, overnight, God made him second in command to the Pharaoh in Egypt—one of the most powerful kingdoms of that time. It was an absolute miracle—a foreigner becoming prime minister. There Joseph reigned for many years until his death.

I thought many times about Joseph, and I knew he must have been close to my age when he was kidnapped. I knew how alone he must have felt, how desperately he needed God and clung to Him and held on for years. Somehow, if Joseph could do it, I could.

So through this "old book," Joseph became a very real person to you?

There are all kinds of real people in the Book just waiting to meet people in similar circumstances. My second favorite character was David. Around the age of twelve, David became a national hero. This young shepherd boy challenged the giant Goliath, leader of Israel's enemy, face to face. Goliath was terrorizing Israel. Not one Israeli would stand up to him. Goliath was ten feet tall and would come down in the valley between the two enemy camps every day and dare anyone from Israel to fight him.

When David arrived on the scene to bring food to his older brothers, he couldn't believe anyone was talking this way to Israel when the Lord Almighty was their God. To David, Goliath was spitting in God's face! David became incensed and volunteered on the spot to fight Goliath in the name of Jehovah.

No one wanted him to go out, but David insisted. He took his sling shot, stopped at a brook, picked up five stones, and went after the huge warrior who was adorned in full armor. In the name of Jehovah, David charged him, dodged the profane giant's spear, and hit him directly between the eyes with his first and only shot, knocking him unconscious. With the giant's own sword he then cut off Goliath's head and carried it around all day. He was fearless! This happened right after David had been promised by God that one day he would be the King of Israel. But God made David wait about eighteen years to be king. During the latter part of those years, he lived in a barren wilderness sleeping in caves—running from King Saul, who didn't want David to be king. While he was being pursued, David had several opportunities to kill King Saul and to assume his throne, but he chose not to. He was waiting for God to give it to him.

What I began to see from the stories of Joseph and David was that "great men" suffered. Many of them suffered when they were young, like me. It was the suffering that enabled God to come to the rescue and that's how they came to love Him. What God was going to do for me at the time I didn't know. But I knew He would help me. By the way, David's writings in the Psalms touched me as much as the story of David's life.

Could you give me an example?

One night, I had come to my lowest point. I didn't think I could take the drunkards singing that song about me one more time. My zeal for God had burned hot within me. Now I felt utterly despised. My very presence was a stumbling block to those around me. I was convinced that I was a terrible sinner to deserve such a birth. As a sign of my mourning, I began to wear sack cloth, but that seemed only to make things worse and lead to more ridicule.

How could you feel guilty if you were God?

Just because I was God didn't mean that growing up I couldn't come to the wrong conclusions. I had to learn, too. I had a very sensitive conscience and I felt as if I had done something terribly wrong. You can imagine the relief I experienced when I "coincidentally" began to read the 69th Psalm which David wrote. There was a perfect description of me:

> "Shame covers my face. I am a stranger to my brothers, an alien to my own mother's sons . . . When I weep and fast, I must endure scorn; when I put on sack cloth, people make sport of me. Those who sit at the gate mock me, and I am the song of the drunkards."[2]

David had been through the same thing I had. I didn't know at the time that the 69th Psalm was a prophecy but I knew God wanted me to read that particular psalm on that particular night. You have to experience God's using the Scriptures in that way to see how sensitive He is. That night when I was ten years old, I began to understand that He knew everything about me, even though it took me years to appreciate just how well. Later on, I discovered that many experiences I was to have in the future had already been written in the Scriptures so that I would know who I was. My Father was communicating with me and preparing me. Already, I was learning how to suffer.

I learned something else from the experience. Sometimes you have to wrestle to find out which Scriptures are messages from God to you for a particular time. When I was ten, the 23th Psalm wasn't as comforting as the 69th Psalm, which went straight to my heart.

Life in the Family

I can't believe your mother and father watched you suffer at such a young age and never told you who you were.

At first they didn't know it was going on until my brothers started giving me trouble. Of course, they had known for years that the time would come when I would hear rumors about my birth. They understood to a significant degree that, for some reason, my real Father must have wanted me to face ridicule at an early age. As mother later told me, when I was a very young child of four or five, she and Joseph had talked about how they were going to handle it when I found out about my birth. Joseph in particular anticipated that I probably wouldn't find out in the kindest of ways, and he debated over whether they should say to me: "Something might come up about your birth." Yet, both my mother and father had experienced comparable pain because of the circumstances, a pain they both understood that God intended them to have.

They didn't understand entirely the purpose of this pain, that they were to learn how to handle it to teach me. They did understand in some way that God was telling them through the turmoil that surrounded my early life that my life was not going to be easy. The rumors about their marriage, the long journey they had had to make when my mother was eight and a half months pregnant, my life's being threatened by Herod when I was only a year old, and the sudden trip to a foreign land and being forced to live there for two years: all these things made them realize that God had His hand in these events.

Joseph always reminded my mother that Simeon, the old man in the Temple the day I was circumcised at eight days of age, had confirmed how much suffering I was to go through. Simeon blessed them but also told Mary,

> "A sword shall pierce your soul, for this child shall be rejected by many in Israel, and this to their undoing. But he will be the greatest joy of many others."[3]

My mother preferred to cling to the words of her cousin, Elizabeth, and to the words of the angel who told her she was pregnant with her son,

> "He shall be very great, and shall be called the Son of God. And the Lord God shall give him the throne of his ancestor, David. And he shall reign over Israel forever; his Kingdom shall never end.!"[4]

She had to cling to these words emotionally to get through her pregnancy. Afterwards, she had been upset by what Simeon had said, and naturally had wanted to push it out of her mind when it came up. She didn't want her son to suffer. Joseph always reminded her of that prophecy, however.

Both had a great respect for God's timing and sovereignty, a real sense of "God is setting the stage." They believed strongly that He should be the one to tell me who I was. After all, He was my Father, and He had been able to communicate with each of them. Because of this, Joseph decided that they would say nothing directly to me about my birth during my early years. Instead, he and my mother would continue to let God provide the circumstances, and they would be available to me whenever I needed them.

At the same time, Joseph made sure a lot was expected of me while growing up. They were rearing God's son, and he was going to make sure I had the toughness I needed, but they were also tender and loving.

When they found out what the townspeople and my brothers were saying to me, they comforted me. My mother and father would discipline my brothers when they heard their taunts. The day after I came home in sack cloth, Joseph took me aside and said, "There are some things you don't know yet, but one day you'll understand. Until then keep your head high and quit wearing that sack cloth. You've done nothing wrong. Nothing will appease those men. They just want somebody to ridicule because they have so little self-esteem." Joseph was right. I wore the sack cloth a few more days, and the men still didn't let up; so I quit. Soon after that was when I read the 69th Psalm.

When did you realize there was more in the Scriptures about you, and that you were the Messiah?

In reading the Scriptures I had come across the prophecies that the Messiah would be born in the City of David, Bethlehem; that He would be from Galilee, and that He would come out of the tribe of Judah. It was interesting to me that the Messiah and I would be born in the same place, from the same tribe, and the "same neighborhood." A coincidence, but nothing more than that, I thought. A short time later I came across another prophecy that stated that the Messiah would come out of Egypt. That struck me as strange—an Israelite to be born in Bethlehem and from Galilee—how could he also be from Egypt?

A week later—you'll see how God, the master director, blends in circumstances—my mother was sorting out the contents of an old trunk and there on the floor was a little cloth I had never seen before with an Egyptian design on it. I asked her, "Where did we get this?" and she said, "In Egypt." "In Egypt!" I stammered. She told me that she and my father had not wanted to frighten me, but just after I was born was a dangerous time for Jewish boys. Herod, the Roman Governor, had heard that the Messiah had been born and was executing all male children two years old and younger. She and Joseph had moved to Egypt to be safe for a couple of years.

Then I remembered something—huge faces of stone, rising from the ground, so overwhelming that they were frightening. I could see them in my mind just standing there surrounded by a barren land. Was it a dream? It seemed so real. Where had I seen them, those faces?

My mother saw my mind had wandered, and asked what I was thinking. I told her what was coming to mind and she said, "Those are the Great Pyramids of Egypt. We walked right by them on our journey there. You saw them. You were fascinated by them and kept pointing to them. I remember passing by them again as we were leaving Egypt, and your father and I talked about how much you had grown between the time we arrived in Egypt and when we left. You had just turned one on the first occasion that we saw them. When we left Egypt, you were nearly three years old."

Now I knew that, like Abraham, Moses, and Joseph, I had been to Egypt. And we had all seen the Great Pyramids. This discovery of my early journey to Egypt had followed on the heels of the powerful experience of reading the 69th Psalm. Both of these incidents got my attention. This is when I really began to study the Scriptures about the Messiah.

Your mother didn't tell you any more?

Not at that time. She seemed to be waiting for me. I didn't ask her any more questions but I surely did ask God! He seemed to be leading me and I wanted to find out from Him. Next, I came across a prophecy in the seventh chapter of Isaiah which said the Messiah would be born of a virgin. The whole issue of my birth was still on my mind and that caught my attention. I had already figured out that I was born less than nine months after my parents married. Naturally, I was hoping for an explanation. When I read that Scripture, that was the first time I had the thought that I might be the Messiah. I was almost embarrassed at such a thought.

It seemed preposterous, but I kept reading and certain memories began to come back. Years before, when John the Baptist's mother and father had been visiting us, I remember their whispering, thinking I was asleep in the next room, "Does he know how he got here yet?" "I wouldn't have believed it either if John's birth hadn't been so miraculous."

"And those gifts. Have you shown them to him yet?" "No, Joseph thinks we should wait for the right time." What gifts? What were they talking about? And those three wealthy men in their beautiful robes with their caravan, who just happened to be passing by Bethlehem the night I was born, the ones my parents kept mentioning from time to time. Who were they? Why would they stop and speak to a poor Jewish family?

Somehow, I knew there were things they weren't telling me, even though on many occasions my mother or father would relay the story of how, on a beautiful night, I was born, and suddenly, out of nowhere, three wealthy men came with their caravan, looking for a stable. When, after their long journey, they saw that a baby had just been born in that stable, they were surprised and thrilled. They came in, knelt down, and touched me. These men felt that I was probably a very special baby to be born in such rugged circumstances. They knew I would grow up to be strong and brave, and that one day many other people would think I was special, too. Even though they were so wealthy, they said that nothing was worth as much as a new baby, particularly one as healthy as I was.

Mother told me that God was making up for my being born in a stable. She always said that in a very serious way. So from early in my life, I had an image of a very great, kind God. I always wondered who these rich men were and what connection I had to a star.

What did you think about the Messiah as you read these prophecies?

The more I read, two things became clear. First, there was more in the Scriptures about the Messiah than people realized, and he was to be a great deal more important than the Jews were aware. They naturally wanted immediate deliverance from the Romans, but the Scriptures spoke of the Messiah as being the Savior to the whole world and reigning over it. Something else puzzled me—something which everyone including myself seemed to ignore. Not only was the Messiah to reign, but also to suffer. It was as if the Scriptures were talking about two men.

Another prophecy that had been set aside was that he would be a plain man, and not striking in appearance. In other words, he would be somewhat homely; certainly not handsome. I had no problem fitting that role and, once again, this was God's pattern. He always seemed to choose seemingly insignificant men for great tasks. Abraham, the founder of our nation, was an unknown farmer. Joseph, Jacob's son, had been a slave in Egypt before he became that country's prime minister. Moses, who led us out of Egypt after four hundred years of captivity, was the child of a slave. David was the youngest of his eight brothers, the most insignificant member of his own family. All these men—Abraham, Moses, Joseph and David—had no idea as children that they would one day be great leaders mightily used by God.

It occurred to me that God, if He operated the way He usually did, would fool everybody when He picked the Messiah just as He did when He chose David to be the King of Israel. The prophet Samuel had gone with instructions from God to go to the House of Jesse, David's father, where God would select one of Jesse's sons to be the next King of Israel. After the seventh and final brother had been presented, Samuel, almost in desperation, asked, "Are you sure there is not another son?"

They were all taken aback and told him, "Well, there is our little brother who is out in the fields with the sheep—he is very dirty and smells bad. All he does is play his harp. But if you really want to see him we can go get him."

His family forgot about him, but God didn't.

As you know, that little neglected shepherd boy became the greatest warrior and king in Israel's history. Just the mention of his name put the fear of Almighty God into Israel's enemies. Nobody ever protected Israel like David did. Of course, he had a little help.

And he had great preparation.

There is a lot of similarity in being a shepherd and in being a king. Before David killed Goliath, he had killed a bear and a lion with his sling shot while watching his sheep. He wasn't untested when it came to facing major challenges.

You often referred to yourself as the Good Shepherd. Did you identify strongly with David?

More than that, David's story was my story. It was a message to me from my Father. The Scriptures made a close connection between David and the Messiah. They would both come from the same tribe, Judah. The Messiah would be a direct descendant of David. As the Scriptures said,

"I will not lie unto David. His seed shall endure for ever."[5]

David was just a shepherd, and I was just a carpenter. Both of us were common laborers. Looking back, God was saying to me: "Often when I am talking about David, I am talking about you."

You seemed to comprehend a great deal for a young boy.

Remember, the Bible was our "television." These biblical characters were very real and I "went to school" every day from age five on to learn the Scriptures. School was demanding.

So you were coming more and more to the realization that you were the Messiah?

It came slowly, very slowly. It was an almost unbelievable thought, but I kept coming across these prophecies such as in the 72nd Psalm, which said that the son of David who will reign as king will have gifts brought to him by men from far away. Did that explain those gifts? My mother had said those wealthy men who gave me presents had been from foreign lands. Then there was another story in the Scriptures that intrigued me. David's son, Solomon, who succeeded him as King, had become world famous. Great rulers in other lands came long distances to bring gifts because of his greatness. Was God saying to me in another way, "Just so you don't miss it, I am repeating myself. The true king of Israel, the son of David, will have gifts brought to him from far away lands."[6]

As I began to hear the messages and to see what no one else had seen, it frightened me. I asked myself, "Do I understand what I think I do?" Once again, there was the prophecy about the Messiah in Isaiah:

"And the Spirit of the Lord will rest on him, the Spirit of wisdom and understanding, the spirit of counsel and strength, the spirit of knowledge and the fear of the Lord."[7]

I thought that was the reason I understood so much. He had given me special understanding. At that point I became aware of what David's son, Solomon, was famous for.

It was his wisdom, his understanding. So Solomon was a picture of you, too?

God was saying it directly and indirectly to make it clear. "Don't be surprised; I intended for you to have great understanding."

It seems strange that your Father communicates in a hidden, indirect form. Didn't that bother you? Some people say you can read things into the Bible that aren't there.

Don't you see that the two levels of communication tended to validate each other and serve as a check point? We all communicate indirectly every day. My Father is a genius at indirect communication but He always starts out directly so that there is no doubt about the indirect messages, "In the beginning, I created the heavens and the earth." That's direct. Certainly, the human being who is a follower of mine has to be very careful about what he is reading in the Scriptures on both levels. The indirect only confirms the direct. It never contradicts.

The greater danger is that antagonists of mine seek to deny the truth of both the direct and the indirect words of Scripture. That even goes back to Satan in the Garden of Eden. After my Father had specifically told Adam and Eve not to eat the fruit of one particular tree, Satan approached them, saying, "Did God really say not to eat the fruit of that tree?" That was a direct lie and an attack on the truth.

What else happened as you read the Scriptures?

As I was in the process of discovering who I was, there was something else going on inside me. I began to love God, His counsel and His ways. He actually "became" my Father. He comforted me many times with the Scriptures, particularly the Psalms. He loved me with these words; He taught me with them. When I was suffering tremendous abuse He lifted me above it with the Scriptures. I learned not to retaliate but to turn the other cheek, and from that I gained great respect from my fellowmen.

I was growing "in wisdom and in stature, and in favor with God and man." Because I had said nothing when the taunts were hurled my way, the "good" men in town, after watching how I handled what I was going through, silenced the songs at the bar and the town gate. More than ever I had a zeal to do what God wanted—if it meant being a carpenter like my father Joseph, a teacher, or the Messiah. I would do it. Whatever He wanted.

Then, shortly before my thirteenth birthday, which was right after Passover . . .

Wait. Passover is in the spring. I thought your birthday was in December.

To undercut a pagan Roman celebration, and to draw attention to me, the Pope at an early point in church history arbitrarily set the date of my birth. But I was born in the spring.

As I was saying, at twelve, I came across a well-known prophecy pointing out that immediately before the Messiah came there would be a forerunner—"a voice crying in the wilderness."

I rested comfortably in that, knowing that a prophet would appear prior to the Messiah's coming to announce to the world who the Messiah was. It didn't depend on just one person's thinking he was the Messiah.

Did you know much about John the Baptist at that point?

One evening a short time later, my parents spoke to me alone and told me that they had something important to tell me. They thought I was now old enough to know about my cousin, John, since I would soon legally be a man and since I would soon attend my first Passover in Jerusalem. They told me how an angel had appeared to John's father, Zacharias, telling him that he and his wife,

Elizabeth, were miraculously going to have a child in their old age. This son would be the prophet who would precede the Messiah and announce to the world his coming. When they finished, they asked me not to tell anyone. Then they asked me what I thought about the story. I just smiled and said, "I wonder why God couldn't have chosen me to do something like that?" They started to say something, and I saw them both catch themselves. Finally, Joseph said, "Perhaps he'll have a surprise or two for you."

That's as close as they ever came to telling you directly who you were?

Yes, until later. But what they had told me made my head spin. It was another piece of the puzzle. The forerunner of the Messiah was alive and that meant one thing—the Messiah was alive or soon would be. Now I had a chance to go to the Temple in Jerusalem where all the scholars were. And I had a great many questions. I knew that if I were the Messiah, confirmation would come in some way through the Scriptures and scholars. I couldn't wait to get there.

Journey to the Temple

So you journeyed to Jerusalem. That was the Passover the Scriptures talk about when you spent the whole week asking the scribes questions.

God's timing is superb. I was on the threshold of Jewish adulthood. My bar mitzvah was not far away, if everything went well. As all devout Jewish boys were to do, before being declared a man, I had to appear before the teachers of the Law in Jerusalem. There I would be examined regarding the Law and the Scriptures to determine whether I had come to a true understanding of God. Also, quite naturally, I began to wonder what was expected of one when he was "a man." Jerusalem was a seven-day journey away and I had a great deal to think about. During the entire journey there, one part of me was thinking, "This is preposterous; you're just a boy from Nazareth. Look at you —just one among thousands going to the Holy City—and you think you could be the Chosen One, above all these people?" At the same time, it was my first Passover, and I looked forward to seeing Jerusalem, where David had reigned, the city everyone always talked about. Jerusalem. The heart of Judaism. The heart of our nation. The site of the Temple where God met His people.

Several times on that journey one of my parents would tell me, "This is the same road you rode on twelve years ago, on that donkey when you were growing in your Mother's womb." Little did I understand at that time that I would ride down this same road on yet another donkey on a day that would eventually come to be known as Palm Sunday.

We walked for seven long days with thousands of other Jews. We sang with them over and over again the "Pilgrim Psalms." Those are the fifteen psalms which come immediately after the colossal 119th Psalm, the longest psalm in the Scriptures, the psalm which exalts like no other the fact that the Scriptures are the very words of God. Time after time in the Pilgrim Psalms, the people cry out for deliverance. Finally, in the 132th Psalm comes the promise:

"The Lord swore an oath to David, a sure oath that he will not revoke: 'One of your own descendants I will place on your throne . . . for ever and ever."[8]

On this, my first trip to Jerusalem that I could remember, I was faced again and again with God's great promise to David.

As His promise resounded through the crowds in the Psalms, the thought went through my mind, "Was it possible that in this caravan of Jews, hundreds of years after the promise of a Messiah, God was now fulfilling it?" Every time I heard that promise sung, it seemed to get louder and louder. So much was going on inside me.

My mother and father had told me that when the hills around Jerusalem first came into view, the people would immediately begin singing the 121st Psalm, and they did.

"I will lift up mine eyes unto the hills, from whence cometh my help. My help cometh from the Lord, which made heaven and earth."[9]

I felt as if I were walking back through history. Finally I was seeing Jerusalem. It was the most striking city in all the world, a city built on layered mountains. Although Nazareth was to the north, to get into Jerusalem we had to wind around the highest mountain in the region, the Mount of Olives, to enter Jerusalem from the south. Because the mountain was so high, the view of Jerusalem from that direction was completely blocked until you were almost upon it. As we came toward the top of the Mount of Olives, around a west bend there for the first time we saw Jerusalem. The first thing I could see on the west side of the city was Mount Zion, the Zion of the prophets. Sitting on top of it was Herod's palace—the site where David's palace had previously stood.

In my view of the rest of Jerusalem, everything to the east was blocked by the Mount of Olives. After our first glimpse of the city had momentarily disappeared I was overcome by a burst of indescribable reverance and antici-pation as we sang the Pilgrim Psalms while climbing that last hill. Suddenly the whole city came into view. And there it was! At the top of the magnificent tiered city on the right, three hundred and fifty feet away, directly across from Mount Zion on Mount Moriah I saw it—the Temple, the house of the Living God. Finally, I had seen it with my own eyes. With the pilgrims, I immediately began singing the 122nd Psalm,

"I was glad when they said unto me, Let us go unto the house of the Lord."[10]

That Psalm ended with,

"O Jerusalem may there be peace within your walls . . . for the sake of all my brothers and my friends."[11]

Were those my words? Was I to bring peace to my people? Was I the Prince of Peace? Indeed, as I was to discover later, the 122nd Psalm was telling me I was and the 22nd Psalm was telling me how I was going to do it.

What happened then?

As we walked down the Jerusalem side of the Mount of Olives, we were suddenly surrounded by flowers and the lush green canopy of trees that nature provided. There were orchards everywhere. Olive and fig trees mingled with pine and cyprus. The cool shade after our long dusty walk was a striking contrast. God had left a reminder of the Garden of Eden right outside His city. We made one more descent, then went across the Kidron Valley and up to Jerusalem, three hundred feet as the crow flies—three times as long by ground.

Descent and ascent, that's how you get into my Father's city. It's still that way. That's the road every believer must take, descent from pride, and ascent to glory. This was even more evident as I continued to be taken aback by a tiered masterpiece in front of me which kept rising, one level upon another, until it reached its crescendo in the golden-domed Temple. I couldn't wait to get there. I had a strange indescribable feeling that I was heading toward my goal.

Once one was inside the city, the most common route to the Temple was via a huge bridge from Mount Zion to Mount Moriah overlooking the Tyropoeon Valley. The bridge was mounted in places on columns of massive stone, some individual columns forty feet in length, with the valley two hundred and twenty-five feet below. It was three hundred and fifty feet across the fifty-foot wide bridge to the Royal Port, the most magnificent entrance to the Temple at the southwestern corner. There we walked through a striking triple colonnade arranged in four rows of forty pillars each with the central aisle being about fifty feet wide with gigantic white columns one hundred feet high on either side. The two outside aisles were thirty feet wide with the outside pillar being fifty feet high. This colonnade ran the entire length just inside the southern wall of the Temple proper and formed a "porch" along the edge of the first and outermost Temple courtyard. There were smaller porches along the other three walls of the Temple square, all forming natural classrooms in which I was to spend the next week with the rabbis and, in later years, where I was to teach on several occasions.

The view of the city and of the Temple had been unbelievable from the Mount of Olives, but now, as I went through that entrance and saw everything up close, my heart was in my throat. I had never seen the cities of the world, but surely there was nothing like this, so condensed and yet so awesome. With my parents, I walked all the way through those forty columns until we ran into the eastern wall where another porch seven hundred and fifty feet long started. At that corner it was four hundred and fifty feet from the top of the Temple wall to the Kidron Valley below. One day in the future, a very evil angel in disguise would urge me to jump from that spot. After we reached this corner, we walked out into the Temple courtyard, called the Court of the Gentiles. It was huge—six hundred and fifty yards in length. And there in front of me about three hundred feet away, in broad daylight running almost the entire length of the opposite wall from the Royal Porch, stood the Temple. It was surrounded by several terraces leading up to it. Everything seemed to get higher and bigger and more condensed. It was so massive it was frightening. And I hadn't yet even seen the inside of the Temple itself. Now I knew why everyone talked about Jerusalem and the Temple and why the Queen of Sheba had been so impressed.

The name of the first courtyard had an obvious meaning. Here Gentiles, properly respectful, could come. But they could go no further. Inside the courtyard, as one came near the Temple, was an exquisitely ornamented marble screen about five feet high with warnings to Gentiles, in both Latin and Greek, that to go any further meant death. It was as though God was saying to these Gentiles, "You can get a good look at some of my glory, but there's a great barrier between us." He would say the same thing inside the Temple to the Jews. At the time, I didn't know I would be the one who would eliminate both barriers.

Scattered about the courtyard were many large heavy tables with money changers and merchants selling animals at an exorbitant profit. One day I would have something to say about that!

There were nine gates into the Temple itself but by far the most magnificent one was the eastern gate also called the Beautiful Gate, the one generally entered for worship. This gate had massive double doors made of dazzling ornamental Corinthian brass. So tremendous were they that it took twenty men to open and close them.

The inside of the Temple consisted of three courts, each higher than the previous one, concluding with the Holy of Holies at the far (western) end. The first was the Court of Women, two hundred feet long by two hundred feet wide, so named because, except for sacrificial reasons, women could go no further. All around the walls in this room were thirteen chests into which the people brought their gifts and offerings, and where one day I would see a poor widow give away all the money she had. On another day yet to come, Judas Iscariot would also hurl thirty pieces of silver—blood money—at the Pharisees in this same room. My parents had brought me into the Temple on the first afternoon of our arrival in Jerusalem for the evening worship and I was spellbound. From the Court of Women inside the Temple, the next court was westward up fifteen steps and quite shallow—about seventeen feet—but extremely wide, running the entire two hundred-foot width.

You are rather precise about the size of things in your descriptions.

I was the son of a carpenter, and by this time in my life I had done a lot of measuring. My father Joseph had also taught me to observe carefully. And remember, everybody talked about the Temple. Every young Jewish boy knew all about it before he ever saw it.

Here in the Temple on this very narrow courtyard, the priests performed their sacrificial duties. There on the right side was the great altar of unhewn stone, forty-eight feet long and twenty-four feet high, with a ledge nine feet high all the way around where the priests on duty walked barefoot as they offered sacrifices in the fire which burned continually. They also poured drink offerings there. Slightly behind and to the left was an enormous laver where twelve priests could wash at the same time.

Behind the altar area was the Court of Priests, over two hundred fifty feet long by two hundred feet wide. In the center of the back or western wall stood the sanctuary itself, which contained the Holy places. Altogether, at one time this colossal Temple inside was twice the size of the Colosseum at Rome. It could accommodate 210,000 people for worship. Because of Passover, there was a crowd almost that size packed into God's house for the evening sacrifices. They were singing antiphonally the psalms and other liturgies they knew so well.

I looked down past the court where the altars were. There at the end of the Court of Priests up another series of steps, fourteen feet high, my attention was drawn like a magnet to the sanctuary. It was made from marble block roughly seventy feet high by ten feet wide, covered with gold and having a massive veil in front. I knew that behind that veil was the Holy Place, and behind that was the Holy of Holies—a small room, thirty feet by thirty feet —where once a year on Yom Kippur, the Day of Atonement, only one man, the High Priest entered. The chief priest of the day could be seen here in front of the sanctuary or Holy Place shortly before the daily offering of the lamb was made at the altar by another priest. The chief priest would be carrying a bowl of billowing incense on a chain which all the people could see as they faced him and the sanctuary. When he went into the Holy Place to offer the incense on the golden altar, all 200,000 people suddenly and impressively fell silent.

A few minutes later, public and private prayers were offered by the people. After the priest with the incense came out of the sanctuary, then the priest at the altar took the sacrifice in his hands and flung it onto the altar. Afterwards, he, along with the other priests, spoke the great Hebrew blessing to the people,

> "The Lord bless thee and keep thee; The Lord make his face to shine upon thee, and be gracious unto thee. The Lord lift up his countenance upon thee, and give thee peace."[12]

The people shouted back,

> "Blessed be the Lord God, the God of Israel, from everlasting to everlasting."*

Finally, one hundred and twenty priests with long silver trumpets gathered facing the people on the fifteen steps leading up to the altars, along with fifteen Levites who faced the sanctuary. Remember the number three. The priests and Levites would sing the song of the day, always in three sections, each one followed by three trumpet blasts, the people bowing and praying after

---

*Alfred Edersheim, *The Temple,* Wm.B.Eerdmans Pub.Co., Grand Rapids, Michigan, 1975, p.170.

each blast. Then the service officially ended, and at that time the people began bringing their sacrifices to the altar. So crowded was it during Passover that as many as five hundred white-robed priests were necessary to handle this part of the worship.

I can still remember that day—those huge terraced courts, the gleaming white columns, the trumpets blaring, the sacrifices. There were two hundred thousand people singing in unison or kneeling in total silence together, with incense, more sacrifices, and more trumpets. Who could ever forget his first Passover? God was there. After leaving the Temple that day all those experiences kept coming to mind. But what stood out for me was all those sacrifices. I had stayed after the official service was over and watched one person after another bring his young, unblemished animal to the altar—a ram or an ox. Each man was required to place his hand on the head of the living animal between the horns and to confess his sins for himself and his family. Then the animal's throat was cut, and the blood was caught by a priest who then poured it on the burning altar. Finally, the animal was cleaned and burned. One came right after another. I had never seen so much blood, and the animals seemed so helpless and afraid. I thought surely God has required much sacrifice, the shedding of much blood. I had no idea yet exactly how much and how personal that would be.

The Discovery

Was this the week you discovered who you were?

I stayed in the Temple the entire week and a few days more, particularly where the rabbis and scribes were. The whole atmosphere was mind-expanding. I was surrounded by the greatest minds in Israel. On the one hand, a whole new world was opening up for me, stretching my mind to see things I never had before. And yet, on the other hand, many times my own answers to questions amazed them—and me. When I realized that often I saw further than they did, I again thought of that promise to the Messiah in Isaiah,

> "The Spirit of the Lord will rest on him—the Spirit of wisdom and understanding."13

Was there much talk about the Messiah among these men?

Everybody including the scholars talked about the Messiah because we were so oppressed by the Romans. For over six hundred years, Israel had been under the heel of the four biggest boots the world had ever seen up to that time. Four great empires ruled the world from 600 B.C. until three hundred years past my death. All had come to power just as the prophet Daniel years before had said they would—Nebuchadneaazar and the Babylonians, Cyrus the Great and the Medo-Persians, Alexander the Great and the Greeks, and finally, the Romans. All are clearly mentioned by Daniel around 500 B.C., by the way. It was startling foresight for a Jewish eunuch in a foreign culture.

Let me tell you how accurate Daniel was with his prophecies. In 332 B.C., when Alexander the Great marched into Jerusalem, Jewish scholars met him at the city gate with the Scriptures and said, "We've known you were coming for two hundred years."[14] They showed him the Scriptures and he was so impressed that he knelt in Jerusalem and worshipped "the gods" and left the city unharmed.

For six hundred years the people of Israel had awaited the Messiah and for deliverance from one master after another. All the prophets of the Old Testament talked about the Messiah. The last one, Malachi, prophesied four hundred years before my coming. Then there were four hundred years of silence from God.

Your people endured six hundred years of waiting including four hundred years of silence. That's almost beyond comprehension.

In all this time, the cry in Israel for their Messiah got louder and louder. I told you my Father was a good director. He was making them wait, building their anxiety, highlighting the Scriptures.

David, the great warrior king of Israel, had an heir who was coming who would be even greater than he.[15] Israel's longing for the Messiah grew directly in proportion to their oppression. The stage was being set; the Messiah was to come in the fullness of time when the whole world cried out for Him.[16] Pagan Rome was beginning to crack at the seams, soon to be tried and found wanting by the world, just as the previous world empires had failed to bring peace and happiness.

For the Jews, Passover was a natural time to think about deliverance because that's how Holy Week had come to be. Passover looked back to the time (1200 B.C.) when God by His mighty power led His people out of Egypt across the Red Sea after four hundred years of captivity. From the time of the Passover when I was twelve, it was nearing the moment when another silent period of four hundred years—from the time of the last prophet, Malachi—would be broken by my cousin, John. But until then, it was a time of high anxiety that built with each succeeding Passover. It was a time for dreaming and hoping for the deliverer.

History records that you shocked the scribes with some of your questions and answers.

I asked them if it were not true as the prophet Isaiah had written, that the Messiah was to deliver the whole world. They acknowledged that prophecy, but seemed to downplay it. I asked them, "You say the Messiah is to reign, yet Isaiah says He is to be meek and mild. He will be broken as a reed and will not utter a word. Isaiah also says that by his wounds he will heal his people. Will he suffer as well as reign?" Just like the common people, most of the scholars wanted a hero and an immediate deliverer. They, too, ignored those prophecies that stood out so clearly about the Messiah's suffering.

In a way, it was natural because they had been oppressed so long that all they could see was a David on a big stallion. They had just seen Nebuchadnezzar, Cyrus the Great, Alexander the Great, and Julius Caesar. Israel wanted a mighty conqueror, too. I spent all my life confronting the misconception that the Messiah would come first as the warrior hero, even though one day he would be more than that. Now I was beginning to realize how my Father had prepared me to understand the Messiah's role and suffering through what I had already suffered up to this point in my life.

During that Passover I investigated all the prophecies I thought were Messianic. I asked the Rabbis how we would know someone was the Messiah. They talked about his being from the House of David, the Tribe of Judah, and they discussed his birth in Bethlehem, the City of David. They knew he would have some connection with Egypt and with Galilee, but more often than not, a scribe would try to explain away that fact because most expected him to come from Jerusalem. After all, that was God's city. But scholars did agree there would be a forerunner, a prophet to go before the Messiah announcing his presence. I asked them about two Scriptures which I felt were disguised prophecies. One was from Psalms and the other from Isaiah. Both concerned a new king being brought gifts. I wanted to know if those Scriptures could apply to the Messiah and His birth. There was debate, but the brightest two scholars whom I'll never forget, said, "Yes, the Scriptures were talking about the Messiah in those verses."

Then I asked them about the Scripture in Jeremiah where the coming of the Lord's king is associated with mothers grieving over the loss of their children.

You were thinking of Herod killing all those children when you were born?

Many were puzzled by my question, but again, one scholar said that that portion of the Book of Jeremiah was referring to the Messiah and it did seem to suggest that a grief-causing event for some Jewish mothers was connected with the Messiah's coming. Fleetingly, I thought, "The Messiah's life will be surrounded by suffering, from beginning to end." And it was.

Finally, I asked them, "The Scriptures say the Messiah will be a royal king, one who will reign mightily, and yet the Scriptures also say the Messiah will be a plain man about whom there is nothing striking." There were some scribes who had the integrity to say, "I don't know." One scholar said, "The Messiah may indeed be plain in a way and he may suffer—how we don't yet understand—but he will also be very special. I believe men will come from far away to see him and to bring him gifts. His birth, as the sixth chapter of Isaiah says, will be miraculous for he will be born of a virgin—the Almighty will father a child." Looking straight at me, he said, "You know, ten or twelve years ago, there was even a rumor around Bethlehem that the Messiah had been born. The story is still going around that an angel appeared to some shepherds one night and told them that the Savior had been born."

"They reportedly found him in Bethlehem. About a year later some wise men came on camels from the Far East bearing gifts for this alleged Messiah, inquiring where he might be. They said that the stars had led them to Bethlehem and had indicated a very special birth had taken place in that year. As you know, Herod became so frightened that he murdered all the young Jewish boys, two and under, around Bethlehem.

"No one knows what happened to that little boy then, or even if the whole story is true, but somewhere this Messiah could be alive today; and He could even be about your age."

Now it all came together in a hurry—being born in a stable but receiving those expensive gifts, moving to Egypt which explains the prophecy about grieving mothers. And now I had heard it from someone else. I understood what had happened to my mother. Even though she was a virgin, God had made her pregnant. At that moment I discovered my unique identity. I knew who I was. I was the Messiah!

At that great moment there were no angels, no burning bushes, no blinding lights, and no voices from heaven?

No, but there was all that and more going on inside me. He had taken the holiest book in the world and put me in the center of it. And talked to me through it. Burning bushes last only a moment, but the Word of God endures forever.

How did it affect you when you realized who you were?

One thought stuck in my mind, "The Almighty will father a child." He was actually my real father. I was His only son. It seemed incredible! And as that thought kept coming back, I became more curious. These men who had studied my Father—what else did they know about Him? What was He like? What was He trying to do here on this earth?

All the learned minds were there and one man would say, "The Lord is the Lord of Justice." Another would say, "The Lord is the Lord of Mercy. His mercies extend to the sky." Questions would come up. In a good man, why would God permit suffering? Why is He making us suffer now as a nation? After several more days of questioning, I began to understand what my Father was about—His complexity, the mystery of His plan. He intended to preserve justice eternally and yet simultaneously to save His people who would be destroyed by His justice.

You fulfilled over three hundred specific prophecies about the Messiah, yet the scholars, the ones who were supposed to teach the people what to look for in the Messiah, missed your appearance entirely. Why?

They didn't miss it. They chose to deny the truth, to keep it hidden away deep in their unconscious, hidden in their heart. That initial Passover was my first real association with Pharisees in great numbers, and their corruption was obvious. They had become self-righteous. They had turned Judaism into a religion of little rules which they themselves could keep and thereby exalt themselves. They were much more interested in quoting each other and what "some other brilliant scholars" like themselves had written, than in knowing my Father's words.

That's reminiscent of today's world and some modern theologians.

It is. And the reason that these Pharisees missed seeing who I was and why today's Pharisees have done the same thing is that they decided they would define the Messiah themselves. They would determine what he would be like, what he would do, regardless of what the Scriptures said. Their Messiah would be an immediate hero. He would conquer the Romans, establish his rule, and, of course, establish his beloved priests in places of honor. These Pharisees seldom paid attention to what my Father said. They were too busy talking.

And remember, it was an incredibly pagan world at the time. The other major Jewish religious group besides the Pharisees were the Sadducees. They were mostly wealthy, upper class men who advocated peace with Rome. While giving lip service to the Scriptures, they had essentially adopted a Roman lifestyle with all its comforts and materialism.

We were surrounded by paganism in its most overt and crude forms. Conquering soldiers in an oppressed country aren't on their best behavior, and Roman soldiers reflecting their motherland were the most corrupt of all. Besides that, I had always been disturbed by the degree of paganism in Nazareth. Worship of idols was still present.

Into the lost world that almost engulfed us, my Father sent His only son. Into one of the darkest times in history, truly the Dark Age, my Father sent The Light. Amazing timing, isn't it?

The Long Walk Home

Apparently you became so engrossed at the Temple that you forgot your departure time?

(Jesus burst out laughing when I brought that up. Laughing was something he did often.) Yes. My mother and father had walked for two days in the caravan back to Nazareth before they discovered I wasn't with them. The women walked together, starting out before the men who would catch up with them by the end of the day. When my mother and father got together at the end of the first day on the journey back, they discovered I was missing. Both felt certain I must be with another family. I was always responsible, being the oldest child. I had never given them any trouble, and after all I was the Messiah; nothing could happen to me. They decided to continue walking for another day. When there was no sight of me by the end of that day they immediately started back to Jerusalem in panic. This was the Messiah they had lost.

Similar things had happened before in Israel's history. Visions of the patriarch Joseph's being kidnapped as a boy come immediately to mind. They felt careless for trusting me so extensively. They had taken so much for granted.

The painful journey twelve years before on the same road when Mother had been nearly nine months pregnant with me had been nothing like this. This was a different kind of pain. Never in all she had gone through had my mother been this distraught. The whole way back to Jerusalem my father Joseph tried to reassure Mother, but his words had little effect. She had been charged with caring for the Messiah who was also her first-born son, and she had failed. Never had any mother anywhere loved a child more, or felt her responsibility more strongly.

The Scriptures record that they had to walk back to Jerusalem two more long days and it took them another three days of searching in Jerusalem before they found you in the Temple. I'm sure they were impressed when they saw you discussing questions with the teachers of the Law, amazing everyone with your understanding. Still, as parents, they must have been upset.

The reason I stayed so long at the Temple was that because of Passover, I couldn't really talk with the teachers in the depth that I needed to. I assumed that my parents, particularly since they knew I was soon to be an adult and also knew about my life's work, would know I was in the Temple. I figured that they were giving me the time I needed to work these things out. They had been so patient before. But I had tested them rather severely.

Upon finding me, my father Joseph, as usual, showed extraordinary restraint. Despite his frustration he waited to hear my answer. But my mother couldn't contain herself any longer and immediately scolded me,

"Son, why have you done this to us? Your father and I have been frantic searching for you everywhere."[17]

I told them, "Don't you know I must be about my Father's work? Didn't you know you could find me here in my Father's house?"[18]

Did they realize you had found out who you were?

It wasn't the first time nor was it the last I was to be misunderstood by my family. They didn't immediately appreciate my discovery. I have often looked back at that moment and thought, "Here you find out you are the Messiah, the Savior of the world, God's only Son, and the next minute you are an adolescent being disciplined by your parents."

And in a way, rightfully so. You were only twelve. Did you ever think that perhaps you were mistaken—that you had jumped to conclusions?

Certainly, I wondered. But don't forget, I had a mother and father and relatives who had told me some of the facts but never the whole story. At that point, I was confident they would confirm it.

As we made the long walk home, I also thought of all those other seven-day journeys to Passover in Jerusalem, the hot, tired, dusty but joyous crowds of thousands of Jews singing the Pilgrim Psalms together until they cried out in one voice for the Messiah. It was on the road toward home that

I began to think of myself as their leader and I remember saying to myself, "Your Messiah is here. This long, dusty walk is worth it. I know it's hard to believe, but he is here." They were going to be my sheep and I was going to be their shepherd. That was who God made me to be.

For the next eighteen years when I would enter or leave Jerusalem for Passover, I was always comforted by the thought of God's promise that one day the Messiah would enter Jerusalem with the people surrounding him, acclaiming him and proclaiming him king. That was almost more than I could imagine.

Many years would pass before that would happen. I got used to waiting. Palm Sunday was twenty-one years away. Even now, I've been waiting nearly two thousand years to come back in all my glory. God makes us all wait on our blessings, including myself.

On that walk back home, did you tell your mother and father what had happened to you and what you had learned?

Since the caravan had returned a week earlier to Nazareth, we had all our time together on our journey back. After a while, my parents calmed down. At one point when Mother and I were walking alone a little behind my father, I asked her, "Is God my real father?" She looked at me and asked me what I meant. I said, "As in the seventh chapter of Isaiah?" She stopped, looked intently at me and said, "I never knew a man before you were born."

She was a very poised lady. She didn't get flustered easily.

Not after what she'd been through. Do you remember the way she reacted when the angel Gabriel first told her she was going to have God's child? She was the same way then. Calmly and very humbly, as the gospel writer Luke records, she told Gabriel if that was what God wanted,

"Be it unto me, according to thy word."[19]

She also told God how honored she was.

"How I rejoice in God my Savior! For he took notice of his lowly servant girl, and now generation after generation forever shall call me blest of God."[20]

This was from Hannah's song in the Old Testament after she dedicated her young son Samuel to God at the Temple. My mother knew the Scriptures, too, and made sure I was reared on them.

Let's get back to her response to you on that road.

We walked along in silence for several minutes and then she asked me, "How did you find out?" I told her about my search and what had prompted it. Of course, she knew about my suffering and the name-calling. She was aware that I had been reading the Scriptures a great deal and I told her what I had found; the prophecies and all. I described all the questions that had come into my mind. I told her what had happened at Passover and asked her about the story the rabbi had heard.

She said, "That was about the way it happened." But before she continued, she called ahead to Joseph and told him there was something all three of us needed to talk about. He came back with us and all my mother said to him was, "He knows." She went back over the story I had heard several times —several hundred, probably. Growing up, I would often ask her to tell me the story about how upset and disappointed she was that her new baby, her first baby, was going to be born in a stable—a barn. And how God had made it such a special night. In the fresh air scented with the sweet smell of newly dried hay, a new baby cuddled next to her with the bright stars visible outside above the partial walls and through the open door. God had thought of everything in that stable.

She said, "But there were some things I had left out of that story. It was the clearest night you can imagine. The sky was all lighted up. There was a particular star—the brightest one in the sky. It seemed to be moving toward where we were. When it got to us it seemed to stop, and it covered us with the brightest but softest light. It was so peaceful.

"Suddenly, some shepherds were running toward us. They seemed confused, searching. And then the one who first saw you in the manger cried out, 'Here's the baby!' Immediately, they all came over, fell on their knees and praised God. They didn't even notice your father and me at first. Finally, after they had finished praising God, they looked up and realized that Joseph and I were there, too. One of them blurted out, 'We know who he is. You won't believe this, but we were in our fields, looking after our sheep and an angel appeared to us.' I told him I believed in angels.

"He went on, 'The first thing the angel said was

'Fear not.'

The angel waited for a few seconds until we could become more calm, and then he went on,

"for behold I bring you good tidings of great joy, which shall be to all people. For unto you is born this day in the city of David a Savior, who is Christ the Lord. And this shall be a sign unto you: ye shall find the babe wrapped in swaddling clothes, lying in a manger."[21]

At that point, the shepherd stopped and pointed towards your little wrappings, and your crib.

"Another shepherd volunteered, 'That's not all. Right after that, hundreds of angels surrounded us and sang the most beautiful chorus you have ever heard. The words were

"Glory to God in the highest and on earth, peace good will toward men."[22]

"Then the angels disappeared. We could hardly believe what we had just seen. We had to come find Him."

"Another one continued, 'We just left our sheep out there. We figured if God chose to tell us, He would look after our sheep for us tonight while we were gone.'

"Then the tallest shepherd asked me, 'He is the Messiah, isn't he?' And he quickly added, 'He is a boy, isn't he?'

"I said, 'Yes, He is a boy and He is the Messiah.' I told them that an angel had appeared to me, too, before I was married and said that I was going to have a child whose father would be God and who would be the Messiah, the Savior of the World. I told them the angel had instructed me what to name him. The shepherds asked what your name would be. I said 'Jesus', and they liked it.

"Then Joseph told the shepherds that an angel visited him in a dream shortly after the angel had spoken to me and that the angel had told him the same thing, including what to name the child—"Jesus," which means "Jehovah is salvation." The shepherds stayed for a while, and I asked them to tell us again the angel's song. They gladly repeated it. They couldn't quit talking about it. Finally, when they saw that I was getting very tired, they left.

"I lay there looking up at the wonderfully clear starlit sky. All those beautiful lights made me think of God's promise to Abraham when he had told Abraham to look at the millions of stars to see how many descendants he would have one day. I thought to myself, 'Three of those stars were for shepherds and the rest of them are for people who will one day be followers of my son. Everybody's going to have his own star one day.'

"Later I lay there with you beside me and told God how right he was for arranging your birth in a stable. You were meant to be born outside where everyone and all of nature could see you, for He had given you to the whole world. Just before falling asleep, I thanked Him for making the night so beautiful, for making it so special by sending the angels and the shepherds." I'll never forget what she said then. "Many times I have suffered because of the circumstances of your birth; the accusations, the slander; but I have always treasured the memory of that night. It has seen me through all the pain."

How did you feel after your mother told you that?

It made me love God more. I saw how well He had taken care of my mother. She continued with the story, saying, "God is so good, He didn't stop there. Eight days later, when we took you to the Temple to be circumcised, another significant event occurred. As we were walking into the Temple, a very old man named Simeon walked up to us. I'll never forget him. He was such a gentle man, but so alive and so excited. His eyes were filled with tears of joy. He told us that the Lord had promised him—just a humble, devout Jew, who had waited expectantly for the Messiah for years—that he would see the Messiah before he died. Simeon never told us how God had relayed that message, but he did tell us that on this particular morning he had sensed the strongest urge to go to the Temple. He knew that the Messiah would be there this day! God had placed it in his heart. He waited and waited for the right baby. When he finally saw you, he immediately knew you were the one.

"He looked at Joseph and then at me even more intensely as I was holding you and said, 'Do you realize that this child is the Messiah?' Your father and I just nodded. Simeon asked if he could hold you and we let him. Then he lifted up his eyes to heaven and said,

'Lord, now I can die content! For I have seen Him as you promised me. I have seen the Savior you have given to the world. He is the Light that will shine upon the nations, and he will be the glory of your people Israel![23]

Your father and I stood there in amazement."

She didn't tell me at that time that Simeon had also told her that a sword would pierce my mother's soul, for many in Israel would reject me, but that I would be the greatest joy of others. She saved that for later.

She finished telling me, "As Simeon was talking to us, an old prophetess named Anna came along. She was well over one hundred, and was famous in Jerusalem because she had never left the Temple for eighty-four years, ever since she had been widowed. She began thanking the Lord and telling everyone in the Temple that now the Messiah was here. By this time a crowd had gathered. As we went through the ceremony with everyone standing around, including Simeon and Anna, I looked around the huge, beautiful Temple and thought, "This is my son's room."

"There is one other event that you should know about," she said, "the gifts your Father sent you when you were born. We haven't shown them to you yet. We have been waiting for this moment. Do you remember the three wealthy men with their caravan who we told you visited you on the night you were born? They each brought you a very special gift on that night; however it took a year to get the gift to you. Actually, they visited you in Bethlehem when you were about a year old. Now you should know the whole story.

"The Magi, the three men who brought you the gifts, were scholars from the East who had studied the stars and the Scriptures. They told us that they were overwhelmed on the night of your birth by a magnificent star that appeared in the heavens. Never in all their years had they seen a new star appear with such gleaming brilliance. The other stars were as nothing in comparison. This star had a vast tail on it which flooded the heavens with light. It swept across the sky in regal fashion. If ever there was a king's star, this was it, they proclaimed.*

"These three men knew that the Scriptures pointed toward the Messiah being born in Bethlehem. Ours was the only religion which made such a claim of having been promised a Messiah. They knew that if the star were the sign of a king, it was to be the sign of the king of the Jews. They were so impressed with this message from God in the heavens that they began a journey of over two thousand miles. They knew it would take them over a year to find the Messiah.

"You should have seen them when they arrived in Bethlehem with their small caravan. Their servants went through the town inquiring about children who had been born the previous year on the same night that you had. They later told us that you were the only one they found. So one afternoon, suddenly these foreign men with their camels and servants and flowing robes showed up at the house in which we were staying. They were very mannerly as they began inquiring about you.

---

*Traditionally, stars in Jesus' day were often associated with the birth of royalty.

"After they told us what they had witnessed in the heavens that night, they wondered if we knew anything unusual about you. I could tell what they were thinking, because we weren't exactly overwhelming them with our wealth. Before coming to visit your father and me, they had talked with the Roman governor Herod. Expectation was all over their faces. 'Could this be the one?'

"Joseph told them we saw that same star on that same night. It seemed to stop right above your manger. Incredulous, they asked, 'Manger?' Your father explained to them that he and I were just two ordinary people. But Jehovah God had chosen us to be the earthly parents of His son. And, as Joseph put it, I was really your mother. God had honored us and prepared us by sending angels to tell us of His favor. They were sent not only to us, but also to the parents of your cousin John, who was to be the voice to go before you, crying in the wilderness. Finally he said that God had announced you to the shepherds on the night of your birth. I remember how bold Joseph was.

"Yes, even in the midst of the Magi with all their splendor he said to them, 'He is the Messiah. Praise be to God.' And he added, 'You know that God, our Father, must have quite a sense of humor. Last year, He sent shepherds to honor His son. This year He sends wealthy gentlemen like yourselves from far away. I guess He loves everybody.'

"Once the three men realized they were in the right place, they became very somber. Immediately they sent their servants for the gifts they had brought and asked if they could see you. You had been taking a nap and were still asleep when I led them inside our small dwelling. I'll never forget that moment as they bowed before you. Just as they knelt, you opened your eyes and tears ran down their cheeks. All those miles, all that waiting was worth it when they looked upon your innocence. Then they presented your father and me with three gifts we haven't shown you.

First, there is a gold box for a king. In that box was some very expensive, sweet-smelling myrrh* which symbolized your humanity. God has identified with His people, and you will continuously be a sweet smell to him." My mother didn't tell me at the time that the myrrh also symbolized my death. She went on, "The last gift in the gold box was frankincense, a picture of the incense used in the Holy of Holies as it drifts up to God, symbolic of the heavenly life you will offer to Him. You will be pleasing to Him with your life."

Then my mother related the wise men's warning about Herod whom the three of them had naively visited. She told me, "A few days later your father had a dream from God telling us to leave for Egypt immediately to escape the murdering sword of Herod. We obeyed! That was the reason we didn't tell you about the three wise men's coming when they did. We didn't want anyone possibly to suspect that you were the child Herod was looking for that year."

After my mother finished that part of the story, Joseph said they had saved those gifts for me and would give them to me when we got home. I could

---

*Myrrh was a scented gum used for a variety of purposes—perfumes, medicinal ointments, and particularly on burial linens.

read between the lines. I knew again why God had given me these two people for parents. Times were very poor economically in Egypt. But they had been determined not to sell all my gifts unless it was absolutely necessary to save my life, because they were my gifts. My own Father had given them to me. Nevertheless, as I was to be their Savior, too, they had to sell most of my frankinsence and myrrh to survive in Egypt.

By this time I couldn't believe what I was hearing. I was surprised and overwhelmed again by my Father, by how he had kept all these secrets as gifts for me until I could use them—until I understood the true meaning of Christmas.

My mother continued, "We've waited all these years to tell you these things. But we wanted you to find out first for yourself. We thought you would appreciate it best that way." She was so sensitive. So was Joseph.

You were really close to her, weren't you? Even on the cross you told John, your disciple, to take care of her.

She was very special. She was always open and honest with me. God couldn't have given me a better mother. All the years with the rumors and innuendoes flying, she never fought back, never got even, never even defended herself. She just waited until the right moment and told me exactly what had happened.

Do you think maybe God wanted you around that kind of person to prepare you for that one day on the cross when you would need not to defend yourself?

My Father picked the best possible teachers for me.

What occupied your mind the rest of the way to Nazareth?

I kept thinking that here I was on a long journey home in more ways than one. I thought about everything my mother had told me, particularly the journey of the Magi. The similarities were overwhelming. Three of them, through the leading of the Holy Scriptures, had left home to find a King in Israel. Three of them had made the same long journey back home now knowing who the king was. Now here were three of us; Mother, Joseph, and me, making the long seven-day trip back to Nazareth. Only now we knew who the king was, and we could talk about it. And like the wise men after their tiring journey and long-awaited discovery, we too had to wait for the king to grow up.

I also thought about the fact that every person who was to become a believer must make the same journey that the wise men and I made. How different "getting there" is from the trip home. On the way to Bethlehem, the wise men needed incredible faith. How many times they must have wondered whether or not they weren't doing something foolish. They undertook a year's journey with the hope of seeing a child whose name they didn't know, of whose birth they weren't sure. The trip was based solely on some ancient words and the testimony of nature. What a beautiful picture of faith they were, which is why my Father has honored them to this day.

That's the trip that all of us must make. One day we will all see God. Until then, we must all make our long journey. But listen to the wise men saying, "It's worth it; it's worth it." As these things passed through my mind, for the first time in my life I really appreciated Heaven. Blessings which are beyond belief, which we think will never happen, are much closer than we believe.

Back Home

What happened when you got home?

When we got back to Nazareth, my parents gave me the gifts my Father had sent on the night of my birth. I'll never forget seeing that gold box. I opened it and smelled the fragrant myrrh and frankincense. It was hard to believe that this was mine. I was in the process of learning my new identity. No longer was I just a carpenter's son from Nazareth. Now I was a king. Gold was for kings.

When I thought of gold, I always thought of Solomon, the richest as well as the most brilliant king who ever lived. I thought of the Passover I had just left, when I had amazed the priests and scribes with my wisdom. My Father was proclaiming, "See your wisdom. See your gold. You are Solomon; you are the king."

Solomon's father David came to mind. We both had faced a similar experience. I was in my own house just as David had been. I was approximately the same age. It was at the end of someone's journey—in his case Samuel's, in my case, Mary's and Joseph's. And, for the first time, I was being declared king. Even the feelings of awe and surprise I was having were implied in the Scriptures. David, I was sure, knew what it felt like to go from being a laborer to being a king overnight. At the same time, David had to learn to wait through tremendous sufferings before he sat on that throne, just as I would. It was as if my Father was saying to me, "See, there you are again in the Scriptures," a truth I saw over and over again in my life.

As I stood there holding that box, I saw once more how sensitive God is. He knows how hard it is to walk by faith. And for the first of many times, I saw that He always blesses us in a special way often with tangible events, just before great trials.

I was sure David never forgot what it felt like when he was a young boy, when the great prophet Samuel came to his home and personally annointed him as Israel's next king. I am sure that David could always remember that oil of annointing on his head, dripping down his face. The taste of it must have stayed with him, just as I would never forget holding that present of gold.

Did Joseph ever say anything more to you about your birth?

At first he simply confirmed my mother's story. Then he told me about his fear, after the wise men had come with their gifts and had related Herod's excessive interest in where this new Messiah was. He told me about the dream he had that night from God telling him to move us to Egypt. It was only a short time afterward that Herod massacred all the young males around Bethlehem.

A few weeks after our return from Passover, Joseph also told me about the doubts he had had about marrying my mother because she was pregnant. These doubts had even lingered to some degree after the angel appeared to him in the dream and told him that God had given Mary that baby and that he was to marry her. He knew how hard it was to believe something like that could happen, even though it was prophesied in the Scriptures and even though the angel had reminded him in the dream of that prophecy in Isaiah.

"Behold, a virgin will be with child and bear a son."[24]

He wanted me to know that it was true. He told me that my mother was a virgin until I was born. With great feeling he spoke of how much he revered my mother. When she was all alone at first in her pregnancy with me, and unmarried, he had not believed her story and had wanted to break the engagement. Yet she had never wavered in her faith, and told him to do what he had to do. She said she would understand. In the face of his grief, however, Joseph saw something special in my mother. He couldn't let her be killed, which would have been her fate according to Jewish Law. She would have suffered death by stoning for her sin. Joseph was quietly going to find my mother a place to live out of town to have her baby.

When the angel appeared to him and confirmed Mary's story, he had been both relieved and saddened. How alone she was; and he, the man she loved, had walked out on her. How pious he had been, how unbelieving. Then he told me something I should never forget . . . and I didn't. "Son, Jeremiah was right—the heart is deceitfully wicked, particularly when we think we are so pious. That's everybody's heart but yours. Only you will live your life without sin."

After he realized what he had done to Mary, he went back to her, and, although he knew he was supposed to marry her, he feared he had killed her love. He feared that she would marry him out of obedience and necessity; not love. He told her about his dream, and said that he wouldn't blame her if she couldn't forgive him, but he wanted her forgiveness more than anything. She just looked at him for a few seconds. To him it seemed like an eternity. And then she said, "Oh, Joseph," and put her arms around his neck. Then my father said one more thing to me that day, with tears in his eyes, "Your mother is a great woman." Those were the kind of parents I had.

What happened next in those "silent years?"

I don't think you could understand how much it affected me when I found out God was my father. He was my Father! Not just "my Father who art in heaven," but my Father. It was like finding out at twelve that I was adopted, but that my natural father happened to be God! All the way home, it kept going through my mind: "He is my real father, and He has been communicating with me all along."

That incident with the drunkard kept coming to mind. Now I knew that the 69th Psalm was written, in a way, especially for me, and I began to wonder how many more things in the Scriptures were just for me. I looked forward to that search with anticipation.

The Scriptures were now a letter from my Father, and in a real way, they were the only words I had from Him. They took on a new meaning for me. It was like a child having a father away from home fighting a long war. As he grows up, the only words the child has from his father are his father's letters. You can believe those letters would be read over and over again. In my case, they certainly were. In this singular, direct communication from my Father, He had a lot to say to His son. As I would find out, I was not only the King mentioned in the Scriptures, I was the King of the Scriptures.

What else did you find out about yourself as you began to go back over the Scriptures after your discovery of your Messianic identity?

Immediately there was confirmation from God about my birth. Two of the first characters in the Bible were pictures of me. Abraham's son, Isaac, was born miraculously when Abraham was one hundred years of age and his wife, Sarah, was ninety—a biological impossibility just as my birth. Moses, if you recall, was almost murdered right after he was born because, just as it was in my case, the monarch was killing all young Hebrew males. But God intervened miraculously and protected Moses, who eventually became the leader of Israel.

The Scriptures which had awed me before were now almost overwhelming me. They took me even further. They strongly hinted that Moses, who had had a unique beginning to his life, too, probably didn't find out who his real mother and father were until he was older. He may not even have discovered it until he was twelve or thirteen and on the verge of his official manhood.

Moses' parents were in the same situation as my parents. They could have been killed had their secret been revealed. After all, they had tricked the Pharoah who was killing Jewish male infants just as my parents had outsmarted the ruler Herod some years later. Good judgment would have demanded caution. If Moses' parents had told him everything too early in his life, it most likely would have gotten back to Pharoah, and Moses, the great liberator and leader of the Exodus, would have been killed.

Through God's amazing actions, Moses was saved and had come to live in Pharoah's own household. Moses probably grew up thinking that he didn't know his real parents, that he was just a Hebrew baby who had been abandoned by some couple in order to save his life. The Hebrew people who where helping to rear him were just some people whose daughter happened to be nearby, whose mother was still nursing because she had just lost a baby. Imagine how Moses must have felt, how relieved he must have been, when, as a young man the day came when his Hebrew "caretakers" told him, "We are really your mother and father." Like me, he never knew who his real father was for years.

Now I understood the prophecy I had always wondered about: why God had wanted the Messiah to live in Egypt for a period of time. That was the land where Israel's deliverers came from—Joseph, Moses, and now me. It was another sign that I was the Great Deliverer, the second Moses. We both made the same journey to deliver our people. The Scriptures were so sensitive to me. They were my Father's way of saying, "It happened just as your mother and father Joseph, said; I planned it that way."

David, Satan and Death

Besides Joseph and Moses, were there other Old Testament characters whose life mirrored yours?

David continued to have special meaning for me. David himself was promised by God that one of his descendants would sit on his throne and rule Israel forever. The Messiah was always referred to as a Son of David and was to be born in the City of David, Bethlehem. The Jews loved Moses and Abraham, but David was special. He was Israel's greatest king and greatest warrior. He was a tremendous poet whose writings influenced Jews daily. And I was to wear his shoes.

David's relationship with your Father has always been of special interest to me. God called him "a man after my own heart." David was the only man He ever said that about, and yet David committed some horrible sins. He had an affair with another man's wife, got her pregnant, and then murdered the man and took his wife. How could God feel so good about David?

David never denied who he was. He fully admitted to what he had done. I paid for David's sins, and that stripped them all away. Under that hardened crust of sin, my Father found a heart that wouldn't quit beating for Him. It takes a great man to repent.

It reminds me of something C. S. Lewis said that it takes a good man to repent, and we're all bad men.

I believe the three most difficult words to speak in the English language are, "I am sorry." But David did that, and that's the type of heart God wants in His people.

What other Scriptures vividly spoke to you about your Messiahship?

In the first book, Genesis, the third chapter, the Scriptures speak of a woman who will be given a child who will do battle with the evil one, Satan. Though the child will be injured, he will defeat Satan and deliver his people.

Did you understand all that the passage meant?

Not at the time, but I knew the Scriptures were talking about me and that somehow the Messiah would be hurt. I had already known that from Isaiah. It became more and more evident to me how much Moses, Job, David, Daniel and all the prophets, particularly Isaiah and Jeremiah, were pointing towards a great deliverance by this Messiah.

What kind of deliverance would it be? I was still puzzled. There were so many Scriptures on the theme of suffering and so many on the topic of deliverance. It was as if the Messiah were two separate men—the suffering servant and the Great Deliverer. And during this whole time, I was trying to decide what my "Father's work" was that I must be about.

I thought of the gifts my Father had meant for me. Strangely, I kept thinking of the myrrh, the gift which had most puzzled me. I couldn't get my mind off that great horrible 53rd Chapter of Isaiah.

> "He was wounded for our transgressions, he was bruised for our iniquities: the chastisement of our peace was upon him; and with his stripes we are healed."
> "Therefore, I will divide him a portion with the great, . . . because he hath poured out his soul unto death."[25]

Finally it occurred to me that my Father was trying to tell me about a different kind of suffering than I had visualized. I had thought that perhaps through a warrior's suffering I would lead my people to victory. But maybe now He was telling me, "You came into the world to die."

The first time I had that thought, my immediate reaction was, "No. The Scriptures can't mean that. I came to do His will, but they can't mean I came just to die. Dying is insane. Perhaps I will suffer, but not die." Who could do what he was asking? No one could look death in the eye and passively allow it. Most people couldn't even think about death. I could never do that, I thought, even if I were God's son. It seemed too impossible. That's when I asked the question, "Does God give that much courage?" I was going to have to find out the answer to that question if I understood what I thought I did.

As time went by, I finally was able to begin to consider the possibility that I had come into the world to die. But if that were true, I wondered, how would I reign? I continued to search the Scriptures and found more and more clues about Him and about me, until one day the Spirit opened my eyes and it all came together. I was to live twice.

This Holy Book which had told me all about my early life—my birth, my early years in Egypt, my suffering as a child and the prophet who would go before me—was indeed now telling me that one day I would be tortured and killed, most likely on a cross. My beard would be pulled out. I would be beaten beyond recognition. My side would be pierced. I was to respond to that persecution without protest. I was to allow myself to be murdered. I was to die for my people in their place as an atonement and then I would be resurrected. Once I saw the plan, I realized how obvious it was. It had been there all along. Atonement is at the heart of Judaism.

Yom Kippur is the Day of Atonement.

Not only were these Old Testament characters a picture of me, but the heart of the Jewish religion was the biggest picture of all—death as atonement for sin. On Yom Kippur a young, unblemished goat was sacrificed symbolically as punishment for the sins of the people. Immediately afterward the idea was repeated, as the priest would lay his hands on a second young goat, symbolically placing the sins of the people on him, and the goat would be sent off into the wilderness to "take away" the sins. That second goat was called the scapegoat. I would become the true scapegoat. I would deliver my people not for some enemy nation like Rome, but from themselves and from God and His justice. Then I was to deliver them to God.

The Scriptures were telling me this not only directly but indirectly as well. The first Jewish father-son relationship described in the Scriptures was that of Abraham and Isaac. Isaac had been a much-loved and long-awaited son who was born in a miraculous way. To test Abraham's faith, God later asked him to kill his only son. Abraham agreed to do it, even though he hated to carry out this command. But he was prepared to be obedient. At the final moment, God stopped him from going through with it but the message was there. The next time, a Father who greatly loved His only son would kill him. I was that son.

Then I thought of Joseph. As far as his father and family were concerned, Joseph was dead. But he "rose from the dead" as the Prime Minister of Egypt to save not only his own family—the future nation of Israel—but also Egypt and much of the pagan world from famine. When Joseph was "resurrected," he became second in command to the Pharaoh. I was second in command to my Father. The Scriptures were stunning in their portraits of me.

Even the final miracle four hundred years after Joseph that caused Pharaoh to let the Jews return to Israel was a picture of me. The death of the oldest son in every Egyptian family was the miracle that delivered Israel. I was to be the Passover Lamb. And I had even lived in Egypt, as had two other deliverers, Moses and Joseph.

Amazing "coincidences."

I also thought about David running down that hill to meet Goliath, charging him in the name of Jehovah God. If it was my job to die for my people, I wanted to do it charging, not retreating. But I wasn't ready to face Goliath yet. Sometimes I would get that myrrh and take it with me to the top of a hill just outside Nazareth. It was about five hundred feet high, and from it you could see to the west the beautiful Mediterranean Sea, to the east Mount Tabor, to the north the highest mountain in all of Israel, Mount Hermon. I could see a temple of Baal up there.

One day I would be transfigured on Mount Hermon, but for now I would tell my Father that if by my life I could bring that temple down and build His kingdom, I would do it. Then I would take that sweet-smelling myrrh out of my pocket, look at those hills all around me, and recall the 121st Psalm.

"I will lift up mine eyes unto the hills, from whence cometh my help."[26]

That first verse was the pagan's cry—mountain worship, nature worship. But the Psalm continues with my Father's magnificent answer—help would come not from nature, nor from Baal, nor from the sun or the water.

"My help cometh from the Lord, which made heaven and earth."[27]

I would need His help, too. Then I looked to the south of Nazareth where the vast wilderness and plains were including the valley of Armageddon, the valley that later impressed both Napoleon and Alexander because of its potential as a battle site.* It's ironic, isn't it, that the person who was to have the biggest internal battle in history grew up next to the place where the largest external battle in history will take place. Both battles were in the same land.

I spent many a day overlooking that plain. But little did I know about Armageddon then. Whenever I sought my Father, He was always there to meet me. Many times I spent hours with Him on that particular hill, often early in the morning. That was where I found my courage. So many times, He spoke to me there. I would look all around me and I knew if He could make all this, He could see me home.

Did it bother you that your own Father would allow you to die?

The closer I came to my death, the more it bothered me. I knew how angry He was. God's wrath had been stored up for centuries because of the sin of humanity, and I had to take it. It was a huge cup of fury. That's why later I asked my disciples if they thought they could drink from my cup.

It's very hard for us to imagine that God actually took out his rage on you.

Do you find it difficult to accept that my very own Father killed me? You must understand justice. His rage is righteous. He has to express it, or justice will be a sham. You see, atonement is really atonement, and God really does punish. At the same time, it hurt Him to punish me. It was the hardest thing He ever had to do. He was Abraham having to kill Isaac. His pain was greater than mine, because He had to do the killing. And do you think He's going to let anybody take His pain or mine lightly?

No one can ever imagine the cost of the pain because we love each other more than any two personalities ever have. And we had to voluntarily separate ourselves from one another. I "became evil" when the world put all its evil into me. And then He judged me. His whole plan was a catastrophe for both of us. But the plan was not ultimately fatal. It was successful because We had great power to bring me back to life, and We used it.**

You asked me if it bothered me. It did. But I was also "Isaac," and if you look at "the Script," Isaac went totally willingly. The same thing was true for Isaac's grandson, Joseph. As you know, Joseph suffered for years in a foreign country for the eventual good of his own country before suddenly

---

*Upon viewing Armageddon, Napoleon was once quoted as saying that all the armies of the world could do battle here.
**All three members of the Trinity participated in the resurrection. See *Afterword.*

becoming a hero. All the time he was suffering, Joseph never complained. He trusted God to work it out for good.

Did you ever stop and think, "Can this really be me the Scriptures are talking about?"

It took a long time to get over the difference in who I had been chosen to be and who I was. For twelve years I had been an average Jewish boy from a rather poor blue-collar family, not at all similar to someone who is to be the leader of the world. All of us were nobodies to start with.

That is the point of the gospel. We are all ordinary people who happen to be sons of the King. And one day we all will reign. As far as being surprised to find myself in the Scriptures, I was. All my followers should be equally surprised to find themselves there, too. If you believe in me, repeatedly the Scriptures talk about you. For example, in the Book of Hebrews, every one of my followers is called a joint heir. You will be a joint heir with me as Hebrews points out.

That's hard to believe.

I know.

So you learned about your death from Scripture. How did you find out about your resurrection?

As I continued to study the Scriptures, what eventually shocked me most was the fact that if I was going to reign over my people and if I was to die for them, it meant only one thing—resurrection.

Did it seem like a preposterous idea to you?

It did and it didn't. It always made sense to me that God could do it. He could do anything. By this time, I had such confidence in the way He was communicating with me through the Scriptures that once I knew I was to die, I knew the answer would be there—resurrection. And there it was. Moses, Job, David, and the rest of the prophets all looked forward to the resurrection. Never was it more precise than in David's 16th Psalm,

> "You will not leave me among the dead; you will not allow your beloved to rot in the grave."[28]

And there it was indirectly, too, in the story of Jonah, a perfect picture of death and resurrection. He spent three days in the deep, in the belly of a fish. I knew I would be three days in the grave, in the belly of the Earth, before I was resurrected. People have a hard time believing that story about Jonah, just as the most difficult thing for them to believe about me is that I was resurrected—the sign of Jonah. If you can't believe that God can save Jonah, can you believe that He would save me?

Creating a large fish and putting him in the part of the ocean where You want him to be is easy. The hard part is making a man. If You can create a person, You can do anything. It's creation that enables you to appreciate the resurrection. It helped me. More than anyone, I had to believe the resurrection. I was the one who was going to be in that grave. Yet initially it was hard to believe in a way, because it was such an incredible story.

It still is.

When I realized my task, one overriding question remained. Why? It was one I asked again many times, even in that Garden on the last night I was alive.

Why was it really necessary? Why couldn't God just forgive them and start over with another earth? Why did I have to atone for them, die for them? What was so redeeming about that? Why would He be so pleased with me as an atonement? I was only one person even if I was God's son.

You had all those questions going through your mind?

Naturally I was looking for a way out, and I asked every question you can think of about why suffering is necessary and why pain exists. One day as I was reading the Scriptures, I came to the 45th Psalm which was the key to me. That Psalm speaks of the Messiah, and in one place it says,

"Your throne, O God, is forever and ever."

I had my answer. For the first time it struck me: I was God, too! That is why I was so important. It might seem strange that I didn't know that yet, but it was an absolutely astounding realization that never ceased to amaze me. *I was God.* It was true that God was my Father, but I was God also.

Imagine standing around with a group of people at a party. Someone is pointing out the guests and she says, "The tall one, that's Bill. That's John on his right with the pipe. And the one next to him with the beard, that's God, and He goes by the name of Jesus."

It was hard to believe that I was to be alone on center stage, the one most important person in all of history! It took me a long time to get over being God. I felt so normal.

But the Scriptures took me even further. They told me that I had had a "previous life" with my Father for years, even before the earth was created. Listen to this: I had created the earth. You talk about having to have faith. Look what I had to believe! I had to believe I had another life I couldn't remember and in it I was God. And this was long before I performed any miracles and had the use of all my Father's power.

It was at this profound moment that I began to realize how great an identity I had. My Father continued to use the great personalities of the Scriptures to confirm what was happening and had happened in my life. It was like He was saying, "See, it's all really true. Remember Moses who was next in line to be the Pharaoh of Egypt? He gave that up at first to be just a plain Jew, just to identify with his people. That's a picture of you giving up your glory to come to earth to serve your people." One day, because of his sacrifice, Moses would become Israel's great leader.

God's promises to me were obvious. One day, because of my self-denial,

I would reign over all of Israel. I would taste a little bit of that now, He was saying to me. But the second time around, when I returned, I would get it all. My second coming was prophesied directly and indirectly. Indirectly, the idea of two distinct periods in someone's life was apparent. Abram, childless and unknown, became Abraham, the father of many nations. His grandson Jacob, a conniving young man, had his name changed by God to Israel later in life when he became the beloved father of the twelve tribes of Israel. Joseph, Moses, and David all had two different times of power in their lives. And in all these men, their greater recognition was in the second part.

Then there was Noah, the shipbuilder, the carpenter who saved the human race. What else is a carpenter but a creator? By my early trade as a carpenter like Noah, my Father was saying in yet another way, "If you will hear it, My son is the Creator, the very framework of this world."

I never ceased to be amazed at how rich the Scriptures were in their ability to communicate. It was like looking in a mirror.

Did you begin to experience a new responsibility to be God at this time?

Until this point, I never really understood that I hadn't sinned. Now I wondered. Could I go the rest of my life without sinning? I was a teenager. I had strong feelings of all kinds. Could I control them?

So you were not too different from us. You had to have faith and you had to wait. Do you think we can identify with you as a man?

I was a man. And my biggest stress was imminent death. The other constant stress I lived under was whether good could overcome evil. Most people throughout history would say that hate is stronger than love. My Father's way of love versus Satan's way of hate—that was the test. I was here to prove that love was stronger than any force that opposes it, that a person empowered with love will overcome a person motivated by evil, that "love never fails."

In one second my Father and I could have crushed Satan with our omnipotent power, but there was much more at stake here than physical power. We were going to see who had the best heart. My heart of love, my Father's heart, was to be tested. Would I give in to the destructive forces that surrounded me or would I be faithful to the truth? The whole plan hinged on the fact that good was never to lose to evil. Could I keep from taking my frustrations out on anyone, including my Father, particularly when I was tired?

I was particularly concerned about fatigue because it would have been so easy then to lash out. One of the things I did when I got weary was to be particularly careful. The other thing I did when fatigue hit was to push myself to be with my Father. I intentionally stretched myself when I was at the end so that I could clearly know He would sustain me. And He never let me down. I learned how strong that union with my Father made me.

Many times it would have been easy to gossip or to gratify myself inappropriately in a thousand different ways, not the least of which was sexual gratification. I fought the continual pressure every day of knowing that I could not deviate even once in my lifetime, that the destiny of the whole world was riding on whether I could overcome.

My final test would be the hardest of all. I had to offer myself as a sacrifice to take the world's evil and take it to the grave forever. In the process, my Father's absolute justice would be satisfied.

So this was the real contest. Did you ever wonder if you could make it through your suffering?

Until about five minutes before I gave up my life and died, I had these two sides warring within me. Humanly speaking, what He was asking me to do seemed impossible. I felt the weight of those doubts. On the other hand, I had His word that I would make it. When I wondered if I could carry it out, the strength of His promises sustained me. He was saying to me, "I've 'hand-picked' you for the job. I have been waiting for you for hundreds of years. You are My one and only begotten son. I promise that you will accomplish your mission and the joy that follows will make it more than worth it." Can you get a feeling of what kind of Father He was to me?

I think I'm understanding Him more.

There's no one who makes you as confident as my Father. But I had an internal battle raging that I had to win with His promises, just like you do. Our greatest enemy is ourself, especially our senses which insist that the material world is all there is. I came to the position in which I never stopped expecting a challenge from myself. That's why I could overcome it. I always expected that part of me would find it very difficult to get into the hidden world, the other world. That's why I worked so hard at it. That's why I got up early every morning to spend time with my Father.

Divine Limitations, Divine Rights

The traditional viewpoint has been that you were "fully God and fully man." If you were fully God and omniscient, how could you have been a man?

Even to begin to understand this very delicate area requires enormous sensitivity. I couldn't have been anything like a man if I hadn't had to learn things. I could not have been fully man without voluntarily, in a real way, laying aside —not using—some of my godly powers. Just as I veiled my presence, in my full identity I am omnipresent, I veiled my omnipotence and omniscience. Both my omniscience and my omnipotence were there, but veiled—latent, as far as my human nature was concerned.

One of the big hurdles I had to cross in realizing my identity was this issue. Would the Messiah have to learn who he was? Would he be that "ordinary"? The more I began to understand who I was, the more I asked the same question. If I were truly God, then where was my power? Certainly, I didn't experience myself as someone who was omniscient.

To my relief, the Scriptures answered that question, too. They prophesied that the Messiah would have to learn. The seventh chapter of Isaiah, speaks of the virgin-born Messiah who would have to learn right from wrong. Later the Scriptures report that the Messiah would teach himself many things by his deeds. That's why later the Gospel reporter, Luke, recorded about me:

> "And Jesus grew in wisdom and in stature, and in favour with God and man."[29]

That's one reason the Scriptures make note of my life at age twelve when I was asking many questions. Scripture can't be wrong. When it says I had to learn—I had to learn. What I learned was that my Father was omniscient and that I "had been," too. I learned too that I had had a "past life," and I'm not talking about reincarnation. My Father and I had co-existed before the beginning of time.

Progressively I also came to an awareness of my self-denial, of how much I had given up to come to earth. That discovery helped me immeasurably to understand who I was. That's why I was able later to withstand Satan's temptation to entice me to use my power. And that's why I was even more cautious about performing my first miracle even at my Mother's request.* It took me years to know how knowledgeable I was. That seems contradictory, but there's an exact picture in nature. For instance, recent psychiatric studies show that all human beings are brilliantly perceptive, recording and analyzing in great detail every event of their lives in their subconscious or subliminal minds. Yet a person must discover his own wisdom by working at self-understanding if he wants truly to know himself. It was the same for me. I had to work and study to know my own brilliance which was hidden.

There's no way I could have become fully human without some veiling of my omniscience. Otherwise it would have been impossible to be tempted. For example, if I would have known at 2:30 P.M. Thursday that at precisely 1:47 P.M. Friday I would be tempted by a beautiful woman, I could have avoided her and it would have been no temptation. Except for the cross, I did not know consciously what temptation was coming next. But I knew how I was going to react. To be fully human meant I had to live by faith and not by sight, just as you do. To be fully human meant I got tired and had to sleep. Do you think my Father or I ever got tired or slept before I came to this earth? As the prophet Isaiah says,

> "He who keepeth Israel shall neither slumber nor sleep."[31]

The New Testament declares that I was tempted in all ways, just as you are. That's possible only if I was vulnerable to the same temptations and uncertainties that you face—false guilt, provocation, unexpected attacks, unexpected seductions. If I allowed myself to know everything that was going to happen to

---

*At first Jesus refused to turn the water to wine and told his Mother, "Mine hour has not yet come."[30]

me or everything everyone was thinking, I would have had little pressure as a man. Therefore, my life would not have had the worth that it did.

The Book of Hebrews underscores why my life as a man had so much value.

> "Only as a human being could he die and in dying break the power of the devil who had the power of death."[32]

When I quoted Moses to Satan during the temptation in the wilderness, saying that

> "man shall not live on bread alone, but on every word that proceeds out of the mouth of God."[33]

Do you really think I didn't have to do that? Was my Father going to deny me the most precious experience a man can have—walking by faith in His words? The minute I had allowed immediate access to my full omniscience would have been precisely the moment that I wouldn't have needed the Scriptures and I wouldn't have had faith. Then I would have had absolute certainty and that would have contradicted the Scriptures. Read Isaiah. He tells you that I had to trust when he quotes the Messiah as one day saying,

> "I will put my trust in Him."[34]

To underscore the fact that Isaiah was describing me talking and stating that I had to have faith, the book of Hebrews in the New Testament quotes the identical verse.

This chosen self-limitation of becoming a man forced me into a mature, dependent relationship with my Father. God never intended for any person to have it any differently. He wants oneness with His people. My Father never let me get to the point of not having to walk by faith. To be tempted in all ways includes humanity's biggest temptation: not believing in God, doubting He's there. The first step in every sin is to think that God's not looking. That's why God was so angry with His people following His great deliverance of them at the Red Sea. They quit believing in Him. That's the same reason He's upset with so-called atheists who tell the biggest lie of all: "God's not there." My Father also wanted to make sure that I didn't miss out on the greatest adventure a person can have—putting all his weight on a God he can't see. That was the thing I initially feared, leaning on someone I couldn't see. But then that which I feared the most, I came to love the most. It was the challenge of obedience.

As a believer, you have knowledge of the future and of the present that others don't. You know how things will work out depending on the path you take. Yet the hard part is trusting that knowledge, or obeying.

What's the relationship between obedience and trusting?

Obedience is the heart of trusting. You're told the path to take and what will happen if you take it. Then the world calls from another way that at first seems brightly lit. You've got to decide which one to take—the loud, bright highway that becomes completely dark just around the next turn, or the quiet narrow road with just one light that gets brighter and brighter around each turn. It's a wonder anyone ever takes the narrow road. Whoever has the courage to take that road and not look back will find true pleasures that don't get old.

I'd like to read what the New Testament says you did in becoming human.

> "Have this attitude in yourselves which was also in Christ Jesus, who, although He existed in the form of God, did not regard equality with God a thing to be grasped, but emptied Himself, taking the form of a bond-servant, and being made in the likeness of men. And being found in appearance as a man, He humbled Himself by becoming obedient to the point of death, even death on a cross."[35]

That pretty well describes what I did. The passage you quoted goes on to say

> "Therefore also God highly exalted Him, and bestowed on Him the name which is above every name."[36]

That's why my Father valued so greatly what I did. He appreciated how difficult it was for me. If it were easy, it wouldn't be worth much. Fully utilizing my omniscience at all times would have made it too easy.

The whole issue of my divinity stirred my thoughts. I was often amazed when I wondered what I was really like before I limited myself. And what would I be like when I received my glory again? I had to wait for heaven, just like everyone else did, to see who I really was. Just as C.S. Lewis said, every person we encounter will one day be either the most glorious creature we can imagine or the most horrible demon.

We can talk about the mystery of my double identity until "doomsday." But many questions will have to be answered in heaven. Church councils have argued over the Incarnation for years, and often one is left where that early church saint, John of Damascus, was when he said "Oh, miracle surpassing all intelligence." One thing is certain, I was far enough from heaven to be fully human.

So your definition of a human being is someone who needs the Scriptures and who has to have faith. That's not very heroic at first glance.

Usually you don't see God or true heroes at first glance. As I looked at my life as a man, it took me some time to realize what I was to be about. Finally, I understood the challenge facing me, and why my death was so important. All of humanity was riding on my ability to be perfect, so they could be free —to do God's will at all times instead of Satan's. Nobody had ever done that before. They had failed at some point. I went back to the 10th Psalm.

> "Sacrifice and offering Thou didst not desire; mine ears has thou opened: burnt offering and sin offering has thou not required. Then said I, I come; in the volume of the book it is written of me—I delight to do thy will, O my God: and your law is within my heart."[37]

Here I was, speaking before I was born. You see why this is my script. I knew I could never give in. I had one purpose—to do His will—always! That was who I was. From that time on, whenever I was tempted to sin, I became increasingly aware of how much depended on me.

Wouldn't some psychoanalysts call you grandiose?

(He laughed especially heartily here.) Is God truly grandiose when He says He is God? That's like the person who says, "I can't believe in miracles." Well, what do you say to me when I am walking on the water? Would you say, "Hey, you can't do that"?

If I asked you what your Father was like as a personality, I would assume that one of the first things you would talk about would be His power.

The psychiatrists are right. God is grandiose. He is larger than life. But, of course, He ought to be; He's God. He didn't make his angels slow and unimpressive, but "swift as the wind, like flaming fire." Look how He expresses Himself in creation. The sun that He put in place is a light so blinding that you can't look at it directly. Nature commands you. All of nature is a picture of Him. The mountains and the oceans are monuments to His power and His peace. He made the earth tremendous and traveling 25,000 miles a day in space. The earth is a mere speck compared to the rest of the universe. That is another picture of the Almighty.

He sent His son into the world with courage, intelligence and power. God made mighty promises to His son in essence saying: "Your deeds will be so great all the people of the world will bow to you forever. All the Scriptures are about you."

He made all His creatures like me and like Himself. He made magnificent promises to my followers, like: "I will never forsake you. I, God, will be your strength. You therefore have nothing to fear. Whatever life brings, you can do all things through my Son who will strengthen you. You have all influence with me. Use it. Use my power."

The essence of my Father is passion, even in His judgment. If you study the Scriptures, you sense a Great Personality Who loves, Who loves to give. Go through the psalms, ten to fifteen of them at a time. In virtually every psalm you sense one of two things, often both. There is someone pleading for help, or a promise of rescue. My Father cries out for you to call on Him. He has a deep feeling toward anyone who trusts Him, and will give those who trust the help and "strength of His right hand." "Trust me, not yourself," is what He's saying.

Finally, even with all His powers, He is a humble God. He made every one of His children important enough to hurt His feelings. They could choose to reject Him and His ways. They could sin against Him.

Seldom do we think of God in terms of such an expansive personality.

You're right. But because I saw clearly this magnificent humble personality Who just happened to be my Father, I experienced a tremendous passion to give myself to Him completely. It was obvious to me that no one and no cause in this world alone was quite big enough.

Did knowing about your death and exactly what was going to happen to you make it any easier?

It made it both easier and harder. To be able to say one day, "I am the Light of the world,"[38] I had to have the manuscript. I had to know for sure that I was that light. At the same time, I was constantly reminded that I was to die. I saw it through the Scriptures, through the sacrifices of the lamb in the Temple, through the death of friends and particularly through other crucifixions I witnessed.

Here I was with a great double-edged discovery. On the one hand I found out that I was the Messiah, the Son of the Living God, and was myself God. On the other hand, because I was God, I was to die. I was to allow myself to be tortured and murdered. When you find that out as a teenager while everything in you calls out to live, it is disheartening. It becomes a load on your back.

Your Father knew how to keep you humble.

He knew it especially because I was His own son, but He made it as easy as He could. He put me in the center of the most important book in history, and had the world waiting for me for several thousand years. Who else had that advantage—Noah, Moses, Buddha, Mohammed?

You're making a distinction between yourself and other religious leaders.

Read what they say about themselves. They never made the claims I did. Some of their followers might have done so but they didn't and couldn't because they didn't have the authority I had.

Some people would say that you were a disturbed person reading yourself into the Scriptures.

Only a disturbed person would want to read himself into the role of the Messiah. I realized how they were to torture me—to beat my face beyond recognition, to flog my back with a whip, to pull my beard, to spit in my face, to mock me, to pierce my hands and feet, and to curse me as I hung on a tree. I knew it would mean that they would nail me to a cross. I had seen crucifixions. Most crucified people screamed in agony. They hung on a cross beam totally nude, eyes bulging, bones out of joint. Oh, I knew what was going to happen. I wondered how I was going to handle it. At fourteen, I thought that if they did that to me, it would be hard for me to keep from striking back or at least running. It was an impossible task. I knew I could never do it by myself.

Conversations with the Father

So you don't think you could have obeyed your Father and gone willingly to your death at fourteen like you did at thirty-three?

Fortunately, He never asked me to do that. He didn't ask me to go to the cross when I was two years old, either. He never lays on us more than we can bear. Ever. The Scripture said that he, the Messiah, would come in the fullness of time. For his part, that meant that the Messiah would be ready and mature. God was my manager. When I was fourteen, He knew I was still early in my training for the Big Fight. He was bringing me along.

But, I'll tell you, at that time I wanted to speak to Him directly in person more than at any other time in my life. I even wished an angel would bring me a message from Him. But the only way He was communicating with me directly then was through these words, the Scriptures. And so I continued to listen to them very carefully.

You trained for the fight on those words?

Once again I found out how great those words really are. As G. K. Chesterton put it, when you are reading the Bible you are "thinking God's thoughts after Him." There were, of course, some things in there I didn't like. Every time I read the 22nd Psalm which describes me on the cross, it took my breath away. Read some of it yourself:

> "My God, my God, why have you forsaken me? Why do you refuse to help me or even to listen to my groans? I am a worm, not a man, scorned and despised by my own people and by all mankind. Everyone who sees me mocks and sneers and shrugs. 'Is this the one who rolled his burden on the Lord? they laugh. 'Is this the one who claims the Lord delights in Him? We'll believe it when we see God rescue Him!' I am surrounded by fearsome enemies. They come at me with open jaws, like roaring lions attacking their prey. My strength is drained away like water, and all my bones are out of joint. My heart melts like wax; my strength is dried up like sun-baked clay; my tongue sticks to my mouth, for you have laid me in the dust of death. The enemy, this gang of evil men, circles me like a pack of dogs; they have pierced my hands and feet. I can count every bone in my body. See those men of evil gloat and stare; they divide my clothes among themselves by a toss of the dice."[39]

After I finished that psalm, I would read the next few psalms and then the answer would come. Do you think it's any accident that the most famous psalm and perhaps the most comforting, the 23rd Psalm, comes right after my annihilation is described in the 22nd?

> "The Lord is my shepherd; I shall not want. He leadeth me beside the still waters. Yea, though I walk through the valley of the shadow of death, I will fear no evil: for thou art with me."[40]

Can you sense what He was saying to me? He was with me?

Then came the 24th Psalm, which promised me I would be strong and mighty in battle and that one day I would reign and walk through those mighty gates in Jerusalem.

I thought of the day David had brought the ark into Jerusalem after recapturing it from the Philistines.* Thousands of people lined the road into Jerusalem surrounding the city gates, and thousands more sat on the city walls above looking down on David, who, ahead of the ark, danced alone before the people. And in one voice, as their king came into Jerusalem, these thousands of people sang the 24th Psalm.

"Lift up your heads, O ye gates; and be ye lift up ye everlasting doors; and the King of Glory shall come in."

Then the people on the wall would sing by themselves:

"Who is this King of Glory?"

And the crowd down below lining the road and following David and the Ark would reply,

"The Lord strong and mighty, the Lord mighty in battle."

Then they would all sing:

"Lift up your heads, O ye gates; and be ye lift up, ye everlasting doors; and the King of Glory shall come in."[41]

That day they sang the psalm over and over again as David came into Jerusalem. Years later I would tingle all over when after a seven-day walk with another crowd, we would sing that same song in the same place as we came into Jerusalem for Passover. Every year I would think of how David must have felt, and then I would know that they were really singing it to me—although they didn't know it at the time. One day I would feel what David had felt. And I'll feel it even more the second time I come. When I finished the 24th Psalm, I read the 25th Psalm.

"Let not my enemies triumph over me."[42]

The was my concern, too. But the 27th Psalm, my favorite, had the answer,

"The Lord is my light and my salvation; whom shall I fear? The Lord is the strength of my life; of whom shall I be afraid."[43]

He promised He would be my strength. And then came the end of that psalm,

---

*The ark was a moderate-sized golden box that contained three items: the Law—the tablets on which God had written the Ten Commandments; Aaron's rod—which Moses held when he delivered Israel from the Egyptians: and manna—the bread God had daily provided for his people for forty years. The ark was kept in the Holy of Holies, the forbidden territory where only the High Priest could enter once a year to be with God. The ark was a symbol of God's presence. Once David had recaptured the ark and placed it again in the temple, only the High Priest saw it and touched it one time a year on Yom Kipper, the Day of Atonement.

"Wait on the Lord; be of good courage, and he shall strengthen thine heart: Wait, I say, on the Lord."[44]

You can see what He was telling me. Wait. Wait. Have courage, for I will strengthen you. I will prepare you. So I learned to wait like He asked, and then He did what He said He would do.

There really is a tremendous flow to the Psalms.

These words didn't haphazardly fall together. At a glance it may not look like it, but there is a design to every page and the Author knew what He was doing. I can tell you that because I lived off them. That's why I could do what I did. Some people think of the Scriptures as disjointed, sixty-six different books by over thirty different authors. Nevertheless, there are consistent signs in each book bearing the mark of the true Author. As we discussed before, there are common themes. They include the men coming out of nowhere to be great— Abraham, Joseph, Moses, David; and the favorite son who always suffered— Isaac, Joseph, Benjamin, David, and the Messiah.

If you stand back just a bit from the Bible the consistency is overwhelming. The unity of the Scriptures is in itself a miracle. Of course, some people like to stand too close to the Scriptures and argue over apparent contradictions which have nothing to do with the essence of the Bible and which, in truth, are never contradictions. The Bible has a name for people like that. It calls them fools.

In Pursuit of an Identity

Let's get back to what went on inside you during those formative years.

There is a process of identity that takes place as you read the Scriptures. Watch how a family creates a child's identity. "Don't tell a story—you're not that kind of boy. Be fair; share your toys—you don't want to be selfish." Or, "Calm down; don't fuss. Everything is going to be all right; you can handle it." That's the way a family builds into a child truthfulness, fairness and self-control as long as the family is consistent with their words.

My Father did the same thing with me through the Scriptures. As I read them over and over, He was saying to me, "You are My only begotten son. I love you so much that I have written about you in the most important book in the world, and I have had the world waiting for you for hundreds of years. Before the foundation of the world, I begat you, shared My power with you, and you and I created this world, the universe. As I love you, you will love them. You—only you—have come to do My will. Mercy and justice will be your passions just as they are mine. So much will they be your passions; you will die for your friends to protect them from the death justice demands. You are like me, slow to anger, and you will not utter a word when they persecute you. You will overcome all fear because I am with you every minute. You and I are one. Your task looks impossible, but I promise you, you will make it because you have my strength. All that I have is yours. You will do it.

"After they murder you, I will resurrect you. I have your glory waiting for you at your place on my right hand where you will reign forever. Many will refuse the forgiveness and justice you bring, and they must live forever with their own justice and without you. For now, you're to turn over to me all judgment for your persecution. I am the Father; you are the son."

That's in essence who He was telling me I was. Of course, the process took years, but isn't that how a child develops? A little girl will play house and take care of her dolls for years so that one day she can take care of a real child. A basketball player will practice shooting baskets a thousand times so he can shoot well twenty times in a game. For me, I practiced on those words. I went over and over

"The Lord is the strength of my life; of whom shall I be afraid?"[45]

until He was my strength. I would read the verse:

"I sought the Lord and he answered me; he delivered me from all my fears."[46]

And I would seek the Lord continually until one day I could go out into the world as its Messiah, afraid of nothing—not the establishment, not demons, and not storms. A thousand times I meditated upon the verse

"He was led like a lamb to the slaughter . . . he did not open his mouth."[47]

Because I believed those words, ultimately one day I could go out and face death silently with courage. I read about how I loved to do His will until I did love to do it. The Scriptures taught me who I was.

Some people would call that brainwashing.

There is a difference between brainwashing and coming to believe the truth. You can imagine all day long that you are God; but when the test comes, you'd better be able to perform.

I believed these words until they became a part of me. I learned to keep from getting overwhelmed, to overcome fear, to be patient, and ultimately to check any insult. I learned to do the right thing, and often it was the most obvious thing to do.

When I was first learning how to use the Scriptures, I would find myself in the middle of a difficult situation and would begin to think about my Father's words that I had memorized.

"The Lord is on my side; I will not fear;"[48]
"I am with thee to deliver thee."[49]

It was like having a coach on the field, a teacher with me at all times. Finally, I reached the point that I had literally incorporated and shared His life. It was no longer memorization. I began to think like Him until His thoughts and His confidence became mine.

You were the Living Word.

It's a growth process. I was involved in the process for over thirty years.

Even God the man had to grow up to be truly himself. The process you went through reminds me of what your Apostle Peter wrote. He said that the primary goal in life was to share God's life. As he put it,

> "participate in the divine nature."[50]

One truth I've learned that has stood out in my mind is that all of life is a search for the Father who wants to share His life with us, and He's the best time of all because He has the best personality. He's the most fun. Think about it. This great God wants to share His life, His Personality, His power, His peace with you. When I shared His life enough to know that in every situation He absolutely prevailed, then I had His confidence and was ready to be the Savior of the world.

It must have been a strange feeling all those years to walk around with a great secret that no one knew.

Because they didn't know who I was, I got to see people for who they were. They didn't have time to put on their Sunday faces or tell the family, "Get ready, here comes the preacher."

Often I thought, "You wouldn't treat me like that if you knew who I was." Later on I realized many people would have treated me badly no matter what, and the only thing that would ever stop them was power.

But having this secret identity always gave me tremendous hope. Whenever I was mistreated or saw a hopeless situation, I thought, "It won't always be this way. One day I will make things right." I thought a lot about heaven. This world drives you to it.

Many people, particularly psychiatrists, would say that studying the Scriptures is neurotic—an escape from the real world.

You are who your friends are. There is sufficient evidence for that. Recent psychiatric findings indicate that we are continuously incorporating others all the time, much more than we thought. I fail to see how it hurts to be around God frequently. I used to tell my brothers and sisters when they were growing up, "Make sure you stay close to God." If you are often surrounded by a vindictive, selfish world and want life on a different plane, "a cut above," then God's the place to get it. He's the person from whom to get it.

Of course, all people come to God for mixed reasons. A person will spend a lifetime sorting out his or her good motives, sifting the truth from the bad motives, the lies. That's the Christian process.

Is that why you said that on Judgment Day you would say to some of your so-called followers,

> "I never knew you"?[51]

Some people go to church because they want power, because they want to think they are good, because they want to aggrandize themselves. Some church-goers actually use the church to judge others. Those who do that exclusively are not my true followers.

Some others come to church because they fear losing control of their sexual or aggressive impulses, as the Freudians say, and they feel the need for a sense of control. That's not a bad reason in and of itself, particularly if you become conscious of it. We are constantly identifying and "taking in," and the Scriptures and the church can be a good place to go. Nobody reads the Bible or goes to church for completely pure reasons.

But the Freudians don't understand that they are really on my side here. Read Jeremiah, the other prophets, and David. In the 139th Psalm, David did what Charles Spurgeon, the foremost British pastor of the nineteenth century called his most courageous act. David said to God,

> "Search me, O God, and know my heart: and see if there be any wicked way in me, and lead me in the way everlasting."[52]

David wanted to see his heart. Truly, what courage he had. It's astounding to realize that this "primitive man" from two thousand eight hundred years ago recognized the unconscious, which Freud "discovered" in 1899. David knew that all human beings have closets in which they are capable of hiding things, closets they can shut so tightly that they don't even know they are there.

The whole human race ought to have shuddered at what Freud discovered. For the most part they ignored it, as did Freud himself. Freud wasn't very much of a "Freudian," and this continues even to the present day with most of his followers, if you understand the current psychiatric literature. Now we can say to a conscious atheist or agnostic, "You don't know all of yourself, and that hidden part of you is no atheist." Read the first chapter of the Book of Romans where it speaks of

> "men who suppress the truth by their wickedness, since what may be known about God is plain to them, because God has made it plain to them."[53]

There ought to be a new commandment that says, "Fear thyself as thou fearest God." We don't honor ourselves enough and recognize our vast complexity. We think we are so simple, but we are made in the image of God.

Speaking of simplicity, some people say Christianity gives too simple an answer to the problems of modern day men and women.

I think they mistake profundity for simplicity. As we look at the state of affairs in the world today, couldn't we say that love and peace would be better than greed and hatred? The Christian message, the gospel, the "good news" is very brief: Jesus Christ, God's son, died for your sins which keep you from God. Let Christ change that for you. Trust in Him. Acknowledge your sin, and you will be one with God forever. He will start that relationship with you now. On the one hand, it is a very simple message which a child can understand. On the other hand, it is so complex that my followers will be discussing it forever.

No Ordinary Man

As you grew into manhood, did it amaze you that events were happening just as the Scriptures said they would?

It completely amazed me. The whole process captured me. From the shocking effect of fulfilled prophecy—"It's really coming true"—to the joy of becoming what I was meant to be—The Light of the world, all of it was amazing.

I enjoyed being that light. I had no hidden motivations. I never boasted, though I was tempted. I didn't envy. I was happy when someone received something good. When I was hurt, my first inclination was not to strike back. I didn't get angry as easily as others. I didn't delight when someone failed.

Some people—many people—would describe themselves just as you have. You often hear people say, "Can you believe people are like that?" They mean vindictive, angry, mean, or whatever. But they don't see those characteristics in themselves.

They should talk to their neighbors. Those who say that really don't believe they have any closets. They think they know all of themselves, and they certainly don't believe their Bibles at that point. Remember, and these are hard words, everybody you've ever met is "a criminal" who deserves capital punishment. We have a holy image of people like Daniel and John the Baptist among others. With all their great deeds, do you think of their hearts as deceitful, too? We can perhaps see it that way for David's, but what about Daniel's or the Baptist's? In this modern day and age, we discovered the closets even the "good people" have. We have discovered why I needed to die for Daniel and for John and for all the saints.

As the Scriptures make plain, you alone were the one human being without sin. There was a real difference in you and in all of the other people who have ever lived. When did you first realize that you were different?

I saw it when I was about eight years old. I had come to that age where one begins to become more aware of others, when children really begin to show who they are. It's the age when everybody wants to go first, but it's no longer cute.

The first time I noticed that I was different, I was in the synagogue being taught with all the other children, and I wondered why all of them wanted to be first. I wanted recognition, too, but I didn't have to be first. It seemed to me that everyone was selfish. I didn't pay much attention to that; I just tried to go on being who I was. Some time later, I was aware that my friends' humor that often turned to cruelty bothered me. I heard comments such as "girls are dumb" or "boys are stupid." I had sisters and brothers and a mother and a father whom I loved, and I didn't think any of them were stupid.

Another thing that occurred to me one day was that my parents had never disciplined me for intentionally disobeying them. I was unlike all my friends whose parents had. Later on this awareness was very important when I began to understand "why me?", why God was asking me to make such a huge sacrifice.

The Scriptures say that you learned obedience by the things you suffered. That almost sounds as if you had to do wrong, suffer the consequences, and learn the right way. It almost suggests that you would have disobeyed at one point.

I learned the cost of obedience my whole life and never more so than on the last day of my life. I had to learn to obey the rules of nature. If I ran too fast and fell down, it hurt. As I was growing up, if I didn't do a job properly, I had to do it over. I might forget to be home at a certain time and have to suffer the consequences, but I never once willfully disobeyed my parents.

Still, I never paid that much attention to my personality, until I was around ten and everyone started condemning me. I thought that I must be like everyone else—sinful and not able to see it. Later, after I realized who I was and that I hadn't sinned, the thing that was most apparent to me was that I didn't hate like the world did. It just wasn't in my nature to retaliate immediately. The first thing that I usually felt when someone was unkind to me was sympathy, I would wonder, "why is he so upset?" But I was no masochist, and sometimes I had to stop people from abusing me.

Did you ever have a fight?

I had one or two. Once when I was about eleven, I was walking home. The persecution about my birth had died down except for a few older boys who on occasion perpetuated the harassment. This particular day, these two older boys kept pushing me off the road every time I came near them. They weren't going to let me by, and finally I had to fight my way home.

Luckily, I was strong since I had been working in the carpentry shop, helping my father Joseph handle the heavy lumber. I got the better of them. Still, I was beaten up pretty well, too. On the way home, I felt like King David who defended himself against a lion and a bear. When Joseph saw me, he just looked at my bruises and the cut beneath my eye and said, "Who won?" I told him, "I did." All he said was, "Good!" My heavenly Father would one day ask me not to defend myself in a fight, but until that fight came, He never told me I couldn't stand up for myself.

You told your followers to turn the other cheek.

I did and I meant it. Always, always try to do that first, but that approach won't work every time. The Scriptures also say, "Love is not easily angered." They don't say that love is never angered. Again, Scripture says, "Love always protects." That includes one's self, as well as one's family and neighbor. I never taught the people that if a criminal wanted their house, wife, or property they should give it to him. I would have been condoning oppression.

Never forget that my Father and I will send people to a horrible, everlasting, ongoing death, where the fire never dies. It will be a death row, a cancer ward, and it will last forever. Although the doors to hell will be locked from the inside, and although, even in their misery, people will be unable to leave evil as it draws them like a magnet, nevertheless the doors will be locked from the outside, too. I was no pushover. Neither was my Father.

As far as being different from my fellowman, it was plain and simple: I alone could love perfectly because I was free to love. I didn't have "Adam's disease." My personality wasn't cluttered with hatred or competition. I was like my Father. He gave me His understanding. I could feel people's pain and share their dreams. I had His compassion, and despite all of humanity's flaws I could see my Father's image in every person. Let me quote the 13th Chapter of First Corinthians. You can see the best picture in Scripture of what my Father's like and how He begot me in that image.

> "Love is patient, love is kind. It does not envy, it does not boast, it is not proud. It is not rude, it is not self-seeking, it is not easily angered, it keeps no record of wrongs. Love does not delight in evil but rejoices with the truth. It always protects, always trusts, always hopes, always perserveres. Love never fails."[54]

My Father was letting me teach the world how to live, how to share. He was bringing me to the point as a teacher that I could say,

> "Heaven and earth shall pass away, but my words shall not pass away."[55]

Then as a true teacher, I was able to live out my words. Through my sacrifice which matched my words, one day we would all be brothers, sacrificing for one another. I would have an everlasting world-wide impact and bring about the greatest society in history. It would last longer than anything any dictator ever planned. This society would last forever because I had come to die for my country. Only my country happened to be the whole world.

The late John Lennon, the former Beatle, wrote a song called, *"Imagine."* He had the right idea, although he didn't understand at all how to make it happen. There's a line in there that goes something like,

> "Imagine there are no wars. Imagine all the people living life in peace, and the world could be as one."

That sounds like your teaching and your life.

I was going to do that. God had given me that role. For centuries my people had failed God, failed to keep their part of the agreement. Time after time they failed to keep their covenant with God. But I was going to fulfill that agreement and provide a new contract that they could keep. I was going to run that race and finish it, even though that last leg was almost unbearable. Can you see why He was such a great Father? He loved me, prepared me, sent me, and empowered me.

You get excited when you talk about your Father. The Scriptures say that you had more joy than any man who ever lived. The Psalmist described it as

"gladness above thy fellows."[56]

I had His spirit. With every passing day I could love more. To be able to love is a wonderful gift, *the gift.* It became more and more difficult to take that away from me, because I was learning the power of forgiveness. If you were hateful to me, you weren't going to make me hateful like you or make me hate myself. By mistreating me you couldn't change who I was, and you couldn't make me stop loving. Inside there was more and more peace, and more and more power. I was just like my Father.

That's what the Scriptures were doing to me. They were making me His kind of king for His kingdom. That's why I arose early every morning to listen to Him. Oftentimes after being along with my Father I would leave with my heart bursting. I had the privilege of bringing mercy to a merciless world. Think about it. Where today do you see symbols of mercy, of non-retaliation? The world is full of people who will say, "I showed them, didn't I," or, "Take that," or "In your face." In this century Gandhi and Martin Luther King were at moments symbols of mercy. Those kind of symbols are rare.

History records that both Gandhi and King were inspired clearly by your life. Who were your models of mercy besides your Father?

Both my parents were merciful people. I watched them live all the years in their community being labeled because of their oldest son. They heard the snide comments, the subtle putdowns. I also had many teachers who came from the Scriptures. Abraham was the first. He went to offer his son Isaac as a sacrifice not quite understanding why, but thinking that God had requested it for His people.

Joseph was another one of my models. He forgave his brothers for kidnapping him and selling him into slavery. Moses pleaded for his peoples' sins, offering his own life. David forgave Saul repeatedly for trying to kill him. Daniel never retaliated when they tried to kill him in a den of lions. The same thing went for Daniel's three cohorts, Shadrach, Meshach and Abednego.

Most of the prophets kept telling the people the truth despite being insulted, even at the risk of their own lives. Isaiah was sawed in two. Jeremiah continually wept for his people even as they destroyed his very words. I had some good models.

You meant it when you said, "Man shall not live by bread alone, but on every word that comes out of the mouth of God."

I had to have those words to live. I'll say it again. It was the only way I was going to do what I had to do.

From what you've said so far, you obviously think the Bible is a very effective means of communicating.

The Bible's words are powerful. They've changed the lives of millions of people, including my own. They have made terrible people into better people, made the proud humble, helped the rich to help the poor. To an unfair world they've brought fairness, and they've given hope over and over when all seemed lost. They've affected the destiny of nations. That's always been their legacy; and even this very minute, those words are alive, comforting and teaching millions of people around the world.

At the same time critics of the Bible say they've brought destruction and division. The Inquisition is always their favorite subject.

Any good gift is always distorted by people. Take drugs, sex, food, or power for example. Don't think that people haven't taken my Father's name in vain. Whenever they do, they're not true to those words. There is always a kernel of truth in every error. Even in the Inquisition, people were trying to tell their neighbors that salvation was a life-or-death matter. The message was accurate; the method of delivery was horrible.

The words are fixed. They're the same words to every person. How then does He make them personal?

First of all, He is talking to every person. Truth is truth. That helps. What often is overlooked is the enormous flexibility the Scriptures have.

On a particular day, at a particular time, my Father can get any message in His word through to anyone. That's how He does it—timing. It's how He makes it personal. Ask anyone who has ever listened to Him on a daily basis consistently for any length of time. That person will tell you that God's sense of timing is unsurpassed.

That's what went on with me during my private years, and it was quite an adventure. The exciting thing was that each day was different. I faced a fresh set of circumstances which forced me to seek Him anew. Every day I had to rediscover the secret way to Him, and usually it involved a "new" route with an "old" map. One day our possessions might be threatened, and, as head of the household, which I'll tell you about later, I really was concerned. In the midst of that the 16th Psalm would deliver His message to me.

"He guards all that is mine."[57]

One day I might be feeling very insignificant, not understood by anyone, and I would hear the 56th Psalm.

"You have collected all my tears and preserved them in your bottle!"[58]

Every morning I would read a certain portion of the Scriptures. But before I did, I would always pray that He would give me His eyes. More times than I could count, an event would happen that day which would fit exactly the portion of the Scriptures I had read that very morning. It was exactly what a good Father would have said to His son if He was guiding him and was truly interested in him. I remember one morning I read in the Book of Job,

"Acquaint now thyself with him, and be at peace: thereby good shall come unto thee."[59]

I read that on a morning when I had been tempted to get up early and work because my family really needed some extra money. But instead, I prayed. I had always set that time aside. It came to be a holy time for me. On this particular day I had honored my Father and had spent time with Him instead of going out early to earn money. God fulfilled the promise in Job by sending me some work that required the most skill and was the most costly that I did—a form of engraving. "Coincidentally," the man had his money with him and wanted to pay in advance. As I look back, my Father had been saying to me that morning, "You look to me and I will take care of your material needs. You trust me and rest."

I came to see that He knew every step that I would take and He was going ahead of me, anticipating my stresses. Often when I needed to wait, my Scripture reading for the day would be about waiting on Him. Many times when I was puzzled, my Scripture that day would be about enduring hard times and trusting Him. Sometimes it was something like,

"Weeping may endure for a night, but joy cometh in the morning."[60]

When something good happened as far as a material blessing, my verse for that day often would be about how all blessings come from Him. It was convincing to see Him use these words in so many creative ways. I began to look forward to my Scripture reading because it was guiding me and preparing me for what I needed that day. There was one other reason why my quiet times with Him were especially good: I was talking to my Father. That made it so real. I never got over the fact that my real Father was Someone no one could see.

There's a subtle interaction between God and His people that goes on for the whole of a person's life if one looks for it. God's timing is so perfect because He is such an aggressive, powerful God. Listen,

"Not by might, nor by power, but by my spirit, saith the Lord."[61]

or:

"He shall call upon me, and I will answer him: I will be with him in trouble; I will deliver him, and honor him."[62]

Repeatedly He reminds us, "I will deliver you."

I also learned to seek out His deliverance. When I needed patience, I would find His words telling me to wait joyfully. If I really wanted His encouragement, I knew where to go to hear Him tell me that He loved me. I began to see the Scriptures as a huge sanctuary divided into intricate meeting places with God speaking in all the rooms. I could choose what I needed to hear Him say that day as well as be surprised by Him.

He's so powerful, and the Bible is so magnificent, that you can take one verse and build your life on it. Everyone should have his or her favorite verses and build his or her life on them. The Scriptures should be full of places with warm memories for you.

When you look at a Bible it should remind you of your journey, of your stops along the way in the Word. They should be stops where you were comforted, just as Abraham and Jacob and all the great saints had geographical places where they had stopped, had heard God's voice and had built altars as reminders of how God had favored them. Over the years when they would pass by those places, they would be blessed by the memory of the day when God spoke to them.

For people today, the Scriptures should be full of "little altars"—places where God has spoken to them. One day you should be able to say about this whole Book, "It's mine!" For it is. It was written to you. That's why, ultimately, I could say what I did about those words. They are so real that you can live off of them.

You see the Bible as a great message carrier.

There is more about God in this Book than you can ever learn. There are hundreds of conversations, thousands of interactions you can have with Him through these messages. If you want Him to tell you that He loves you, He will do so anytime you want to hear it. If you need to be reminded of how secure you are, He will do that, too. If you feel tremendously hopeless and need encouragement, come to Him. If it's glory you want, then He will tell you how to get it. If you need peace above all else, He will guide you along the way to it. He will give you His peace.

"Cast your burden upon the Lord, and He will sustain you."[63]

Do you hear that verse when you are under stress?

Haven't you ever experienced the comfort of a friend, of a spouse? Have you never received an unexpected favor from another person? What we crave most when we're hurting is just to be understood, really understood. Don't we want sympathy or empathy? His powerful words are spoken by His Spirit. This Book is alive. If you want His Spirit to speak to you, open it. Learn to hear His voice.

It takes time, but the longer you listen, the better you become at hearing it. He left emotional treasures waiting for us any time we want them if we read the Bible the way He asks us to read it and if we believe in the power of those words.

Faith, then, makes it true.

No, faith honors the truth.

There will be a thousand moments in your life when God will use this Book to get personal messages through to you. He constantly tells you who He is and who you are. He tells you how to approach Him and what to expect. He instructs you when to wait, how to wait, and how to trust Him. Waiting is half the process because it teaches you who God is. Then you take Him with you out into the world.

Earlier in your life, you didn't listen to His words and you missed His actions. Now you begin to see that He's there, having gone before you and acting on your behalf. If you want to see God, to really know God, this is how you do it on this earth.

To find a way of reaching all men everywhere for all time requires a genius. The Scriptures are a miracle, and I never cease to be amazed at the beautiful creation with all its varied levels of communication He built into them. They are like a multi-story mansion with all kinds of secret rooms and beautiful hidden gardens.

As you describe them, the Scriptures remind me of some precious scrolls that an archeologist might find after years of searching in a foreign country which reveal unprecedented truths about a particular culture.

And all the time the people in that country have overlooked what was right under their noses. They are like the man who spends his whole life in poverty with an oil field or a gold mine underneath his feet. Many people in the West today are turning to the Eastern religions to find "the Truth," while the whole time it's hiding right there in their own houses in Bibles.

The biggest criticism of the Bible continues to be the accusation that it is dead, that these words are meaningless, or at best, fairy tales.

Until you're born again, they are. When you are born again, you become an archeologist.

Some scientists won't accept the Bible because it's not verifiable in a laboratory. They can't duplicate the findings and therefore have "no proof."

Science can be as big an idol as man has ever built. "Science says this and science says that;" is often cited, or better yet "Modern science says . . .": Some scientists appear to want to talk for God. If they limit their data only to what they can duplicate, then they have really created their own little boxes, their own little kingdoms. They're not very impressive kingdoms, because they have to outlaw history, archeology, sociology, and hence, ultimately reason.

Revelation—knowledge from a Higher source—is, of course, not even a possibility to be considered by most scientists. That tells you something about their "open-mindedness." They forget about their heritage. Copernicus, Keppler, Galileo, Sir Isaac Newton and Francis Bacon were all believers. In fact, as Alfred North Whitehead pointed out, it was their Christian mind-set, a belief that God was a God of order, which enabled them to make their discoveries.

Scientists who claim never to have an ounce of faith consistently take things on faith. Those scientists who say, "Only what I can duplicate is what I believe," are unwittingly taking a position based entirely on faith. They believe that only the information that they say is important is important. When a scientist does that, once again he lives out the Biblical truth: man wants to be God.

In their desperation, scientists often cling to a faith that won't stand up. Darwin was so in love with his theory that he believed it even though he himself realized it was utter foolishness when taken to the extremes that he took it. As he said, he couldn't believe that he had evolved from an ape. But, again, he stated that he couldn't trust his own mind because it had evolved from that of an ape.

As far as proof of Christianity goes, there's enough there if you want it. But you need to broaden your mind, break out of the trap of your own creation, and look at the evidence. There's usually a grain of truth in every error. Science talks about duplication—frequently finding the same occurrences— as a support for truth. Scriptural truth agrees entirely.

The Scriptures support their claims in every area. Wherever they touch on archeology, they are consistent with modern findings. Wherever they touch on history they are consistent. Wherever they touch on technical science they are consistent. And wherever they touch upon psychology they are true.

Approximately a third of the Scriptures is prophecy. Properly understood, prophecy is a form of duplication. How many scientists ever know that about the Scriptures, much less having examined them? Instead, they have simply stated that prophecies can't exist because they don't fit into their reality. That's "supernatural," and they don't want anyone above them. That's the problem. It's not that the Scriptures aren't true. Many modern scientists remind me of Pontius Pilate who, when I confronted him with the truth, cynically told me, "Who can know the truth?" In essence he was saying truth doesn't exist. In that way, Pilate was truly a modern man. Believe me, when you not only stand for the truth, but you and your Father also happen to be Truth, and someone indifferently calls you a liar, it's personally offensive.

I know that one of the objections to the Bible is that it's such an ancient book. How can a book so old have any relevance for my life? That's a question I've heard repeatedly.

That's the test. There's always a test to find the secrets. The same question regarding age occurs in our human development. Adolescents wonder how that old man, particularly their father, can know anything. He's so old. To be old, experienced, is exactly the idea. At first glance, one wonders what the Jews running around a small country thousands of years ago have to do with us. How can a poor Jew dying on an old dusty hill two thousand years ago really have something to do with the rest of mankind? He couldn't be that important.

On second glance, that one man has everything to do with you. If his life has no significance, yours doesn't, either. It won't be long before it's thousands of years from now, and your life will be meaningless. Mankind yearns for the crucifixion and resurrection, for one man to stand up and give all of us significance. Yes, the Scriptures are old, but check them out. Do they in any way sound like men and women today? Do they in any way answer humanity's basic problems?

At the same time your Father is almighty and all knowing, it says something to me about His character that He would choose a seemingly insignificant way to reveal Himself and to change the world. It is just one book, and a relatively small one at that. It's the same thing He did with you. He revealed Himself with only one person who, by most of the world's standards, was insignificant.

Well, I did a few significant things. You should have tasted the wine I made —and my fish.

The written word and the living word both came into the world seemingly in a small way. I was a plain man, a carpenter. The written word was first given to a small group of people. Hollywood would have done it differently. But my Father and I promise you one thing—an ending that Hollywood could never touch. I came first in humble circumstances. Later I'll be back with all my glory.

We talked about the grandiose part of my Father. There's also the other side, the restrained side. The way He keeps things hidden says that. For instance, because of who He is, there is a truth my Father implanted in the universe: You reap what you sow. Treasures must be sought after. That's never more true than in obtaining knowledge and wisdom. Understanding humbles you; it teaches you that once you were overlooking something. What you would now give your whole life for, you once considered of little value.

My Father had a purpose in making people learn things—humility. As I told you, He designed the marvelous universe to keep us humble.

It reminds me of what the Apostle Paul wrote in his letter to the Corinthians. He said that God chose the insignificant of the world to confound the wise. Some modern theologians say that since it has been so long since you were on the earth in person, we don't actually have your exact words or deeds; and, therefore, we can't trust the Bible.

How can you say that about me? They don't say that about Plato or Aristotle or Julius Caesar. And my followers went to a lot more trouble to preserve my works. The translators were expected to be exact to an extreme. God was behind the whole thing. If God is involved, do you think His power is small? If He can make a man or a woman, He can write a book.

Those are holy words. Think of all the people who have read those same words. I read them. So did John the Baptist, Paul, all the apostles. Even those who wrote the books of the Old Testament read some of their "co-authors' " works. Daniel read Jeremiah. Isaiah and Jeremiah read what David and Solomon wrote. Everybody read Moses.

But some people say that they get nothing out of reading the Scriptures.

Most people who say that have never read the Bible for longer than ten minutes. They want instant gratification. Have you ever found a treasure for which you didn't work? This book is full of treasures for anyone who wants to dig and can stand the brightness of the light. So rich are the Scriptures that there are still treasures left to discover, and there will always be until I return.

They will never be completely "mined." But first, you must be humble and ask God for "His eyes." He is Almighty God.

People who complain about the Scriptures don't understand the necessity of patience. God says, "I will take care of difficult situations," but usually you must wait a while. During the interim, however, He's right there with you helping you wait. My Father is saying through virtually all of life's experiences, "You must learn that you are a human being and I am God. If you wait, then you will know that I am God." Read the Old Testament. Over and over God says that He took a particular action that they may know that He is the Lord their God.

I ought to know something about that waiting process, because I had to learn about my Father that way, too. In modern terms, the spiritual world is like the business world, the stock market; you have to know how to wait.

People say this is a dead book, and yet I learned everything from it. Read what people like Augustine, John Donne, and even Napoleon thought about this book. Donne once said, "The Psalms foretell what I, what any, shall do and suffer and say." I learned from the Scriptures who I was, how I was born, and when I was to "come on stage." I found that I had to wait for my "announcer" to go before me. The Scriptures made plain that I would establish my authority by miracles, and even told me some of the ones I would do. I would heal the crippled, make the blind see, and there were even hints of others.

Many times I would find myself in a "familiar" situation, described in the Scriptures, and I would know how to react because many of my miracles had been done by prophets before me. When I walked into a man's house whose only child had died, I knew Elijah had raised an only child from the dead with my Father's power.

On another occasion, I found myself in the wilderness surrounded by five thousand families with only enough food for one person. I thought again of Elijah, who had fed a family for months with a smattering of grain, and of another prophet, Elisha, who kept pouring oil out of a little bottle and repeatedly filling large cisterns of oil. I also remembered my Father placing manna on the ground every morning for His people to eat for forty years when He led them out of Egypt to the Promised Land. I was to have power over nature, the same power that God had given Elijah when he stopped the rain for three years, and the same power that God had given Joshua who stopped the sun from going down for one entire day so that Israel could catch its enemy and defeat it.

There were so many things that Scripture told me that I would experience. They included Palm Sunday during the last week of my life, my betrayal by one disciple and the abandonment by the rest, and my death on the cross. It was a weird feeling, but it gave me a sense that nothing was too difficult for my Father, that He dominated and that I was to dominate.

In several scenes, I was actively to dominate—walk through the middle of a hostile crowd that was trying to kill me, stop a demon-possessed man from trying to harm himself, and walk on water when I wished. In another scene, the cross; I was not to dominate physically except by restraining myself. But I was to conquer spiritually by not retaliating, and thereby to overcome the forces of evil.

He wanted me to know exactly what I was to do. I think He wanted me to feel like the Messiah. Then I could teach my men that they were to dominate after I was gone from the earth physically.

So you meant what you said when you told them that you came so that they might have life and have it abundantly. [64]

Never forget that my Father made Adam, the first man, to have dominion over His creation. And he wants his children to dominate in His way today. God really did make them in His image. That means that you can handle whatever comes your way: poverty, disease, persecution, injustice, the death of a child or spouse, uncertainty, fear. You can overcome it all. You can love everybody else, even when they hate you. You can control the situation and not have the situation control you. That's dominance. That's how important His plan is.

But some people need doctors and, sometimes, even psychiatrists to help them face life. Then they feel guilty. They have failed to have enough faith. They haven't dominated in the way you just described.

The spiritual process involves bearing burdens and letting others bear your burdens. That's how He builds love into people—by letting them be loved. Sometimes a doctor, a psychiatrist, is the one to do that. My Father is always overcoming false pride. Remember, God is not so self-centered that He has left nothing for men and women to do. The Bible is not a textbook on psychiatry or nuclear physics or archeology. The Scriptures, where they touch any particular field, however, are always true.

As far as psychiatry in particular, there's tremendous compatability with the Scriptures. One of the fundamental tenets of both Christianity and analytical psychiatry is that humans don't know all of themselves; the goal is to find that out. A good therapist can help a patient unlock certain closets—the hidden motivations of the heart. You'll find a tremendous amount of agreement between my Father and Freud, for example, on what lies in the closets of the mind—fear, envy, greed, anger, lust. If you talk to a psychiatrist who isn't interested just in making people comfortable but in helping them discover the truth, he or she will tell you how hard most people fight their own personal truth. It is the same denial the Scriptures have talked about for years.

There's no problem between psychiatry and Christianity as long as the therapist doesn't try to be God and realizes that he or she's just there "to hold God's flashlight." Freud got in trouble when he thought he was the light. When he did, he began seeing things that weren't there and not seeing what was there. For example, man was not made for sex, but sex was made for man.

What turns history takes. One history-making Jew, the influential Freud, blasphemes another Jew, the founder of Christianity and the most important person in history.

There wasn't room enough on Freud's stage for any more than one person. In his blindness, Freud overlooked the many similarities between psychoanalysis and Christianity, particularly the scriptural emphasis on the unconscious which is called the heart. Freud "discovered" the secret way to the heart through a secret language which one unconsciously knows. One knows deep down that often when he or she is talking about his or her neighbor, one is actually talking about himself or herself. Freud called this projection. I had said the same thing nineteen hundred years before.

Is this what you meant when you said that the speck we see in our neighbor's eye is often a log in our own?[65]

Exactly. The second key to the heart or the mind is the coded language it uses —the second message hidden within the first. Freud overlooked the fact that I was using the second language long before he heard about it. So were the Scriptures. When I changed water to wine, I was primarily interpreting to the world that I was changing the way they were acceptable to God—before by their good deeds, now by my Atonement. The Old Testament story of Abraham almost slaying his son Isaac contains the much more important message that one day the Father would have to slay His only son.

I grew up understanding the hidden language—it was how I learned through the Scriptures who I was. Many of the prophets, including Ezekiel, Daniel, Jeremiah, and Zechariah, had visions which were nothing more than indirect or coded communications. Virtually the whole book of Revelation is in indirect language which, by the way, you had better understand if you want to be prepared for the future. There is nothing new, in many ways, about this twentieth-century discovery of Freud's. Similarities abound. Psychoanalysis, as I said, made plain the deep-seated, deviant motives of the heart. It was the same thing Jeremiah said years earlier;

"The heart is deceitfully wicked above all things, who can know it?"[66]

Freud keenly highlighted the universal conflict with authority that lies deep in the heart of every person, however disguised. Freud, however, denied the most basic power struggle of all—that between God and man—and he did it in the most classical way you can deny something. He said, "God is not there." What a nice rationalization it was.

Freud was like many other discoverers. Instead of bowing his knee in reverence when he made his partial breakthrough, he wanted to possess his discovery of the unconscious. By trying to do so, he allowed it to possess him, and he never really knew himself.

Freud and most of his legacies have ignored the fact that the Scriptures are constantly offering an interpretation to every person. If Freud had listened to them, he would have seen his pride. Nevertheless, psychoanalysis, whenever it comes in contact with the truth, is accurate. But like any other god, it's not big enough.

As C. S. Lewis said, science's job is only to observe. It can't possibly give ultimate answers.

It can't because it isn't the Creator. Only your Creator can tell you who made you, His purpose for your existence, and where you will end up after death. You can see the limitation of a religion like psychoanalysis which says, "Know yourself and you'll be free." Yet at the same time, apart from intellectual lip service, psychoanalysis ignores the ultimate terror—death—from which it has no power to deliver you. The psychoanalysts seldom talk about death because they have no answers. Their knowledge can't ultimately set you free; it can only cause you more pain. As the Psalmist said,

"Death is the shepherd of all mankind."[67]

However, my knowledge can set you free. My Father and I will be lords even over the mind—particularly over the mind. Do you think true psychoanalysis is not ours? Paul said it,

"Christ in whom are hidden all the treasures of wisdom and knowledge."[68]

The only words of hope for victory over death, the only interpretations to humans that can offer ongoing life, are hidden in me, in my mind. To really live again, one must accept the Freudian diagnosis of who men and women really are. Deep inside where the abscess of sin exists, the heart is selfish, powerhungry, ruthless, and lustful. Even "good people" have the disease. Wishing it weren't so can't change it. The murderous motives of one's heart usually manifest themselves for only brief moments, but then the Freudian cure, to forgive oneself, doesn't work. The problem is simply that one can't forgive himself or herself. That gospel has been tried and found wanting. It has failed to deliver on its promises to free humankind of suffering—a dream psychoanalysts shared at the beginning of the twentieth century.

There is one answer and one answer alone for the deepest level of humanity's guilt, and men and women won't rest until they get it. It is justice. Since a person's primary conflict in life is with my Father who made him or her a human being, that person is well aware that deep down God is the One whom he or she has really attacked.

Each person is keenly aware somewhere in his or her heart that until he or she settles with God he or she will be, however subtly, engulfed with guilt. You will hate yourself and won't be able to look God in the eye. Like Freud, you will even deny He has a face. Until you accept the treasure which only I possess—forgiveness—you will never be a free person. You will never have a Father in Heaven. That's the interpretation I made with my life from the cross. It was the most painful statement in history.

The few psychoanalysts who would acknowledge any of your credibility would say that you were a good, moral man, but that you failed to address adequately the real problems of mankind, particularly the vast unconscious with all its mixed motivations that haunt man's existence.

I hate to repeat myself, but they are looking at what appears to be a speck in my eye and have missed the big log in their own. That log has to do with meaning and purpose, life or death. If they have no answer for the Big Question in life, how can they speak with much authority? If the patient is dying of incurable cancer, is the question of whether or not to give him aspirin for his temperature really important?

What has happened in psychoanalysis is the same thing that has happened in virtually every field of endeavor. Through their knowledge humans attempt to exalt themselves above the Most High. Because a person has some knowledge, he or she mistakenly thinks that he or she has all knowledge. He believes he knows enough to speak like God. How many psychoanalysts have spoken for God; "Don't worry about your behavior—do what you want—God is not there."

You seem particularly hard on psychiatrists and also scientists.

Psychiatry, which includes psychoanalysis, and scientism, are two of the major religions of this day. Somebody ought to challenge the person who acts as if he or she is speaking for God and not telling the whole truth. I had to do the same thing when I was on this earth in bodily form.

Many psychoanalysts would say that they've helped people and even themselves with their own knowledge.

Wherever they have served the Truth, all of which is God's, it will help to some degree or another. Sensitive listening, compassion, self-control, non-retaliation, truthfulness—all these are my values, too. But the analysts' cures are far from perfect. Somewhere a person's unresolved guilt with my Father will manifest itself.

That's why, to a point, an analyst can be a good listener and therapist, and then go home and be a terrible father or husband or drink too much. Or worst of all, he can secretly think that he's a nice person, when deep inside he has the cancer that kills neighbors and causes wars. Of all people, psychoanalysts should have an appreciation for the unseen spiritual world. If they know what they're doing, they will have a look at a great unseen world—the unconscious—which few others have seen to the same degree. But then again, analysts can't see the spiritual world because they're blind.

A Role to Play

Did it bother you that your role was spelled out and that in a sense you were playing a part in a play?

There was a slight difference. The nails in this drama were real. It was a very difficult role to play, and the most difficult part of the script was the death scene, which, the more I read it, was unquestionably the clearest part. I knew down to the last detail how I would die. He made sure of that. I went over the Scriptures a thousand times. My face would be beaten beyond recognition. I would have forty lashes on my back. My beard would be pulled out. I would be nailed to a cross with my bones out of joint and with my mouth so dry that all I could taste would be dust.

How did you prepare for that?

He prepared me. There is some preparation in just knowing that you are going to be murdered. I remember that when I was older I used to pull my beard from time to time just to see what it felt like. One day my mother saw me doing it and asked me about it, and I told her, "You know what the 56th Chapter of Isaiah says." And she replied, "I don't want to think about it." Also, as strange as it may seem, there was a slight comfort in knowing that at least none of my bones would be broken. Not just my arms and legs, but also my nose and my jaw would remain intact.

Since you were the son of God, God Incarnate, many people will hold onto the idea that except for that last day, you were a "super human" being above it all. They would say that you knew everything that would happen, that life was so easy for you that all you had to do was to snap your fingers and you could do or have anything you wanted.

The people who think I was "Superman" make a mockery of the Incarnation. How was I going to teach people how to seek God, how to relate to Him when they couldn't see Him, and what to expect from Him, if I had never had to seek Him?

If all I had to do to find God was to open my eyes and see Him or snap my fingers and find Him there, I would know nothing about faith. If I'd used my omniscience, I would never have had to have an ounce of faith. Everything I taught, I learned firsthand.

What was one of the most difficult situations you had to face during these years?

When I was seventeen, my father Joseph became very sick. He and I were very close. I was his first child and oldest son and he taught me his trade, carpentry. To watch him work was an education. He was thorough and proud in the right sense. When a piece of furniture left his shop, it had his name on it. Around Nazareth he had quite a reputation for integrity and quality. I noticed the respect other men had for him. He would never think of doing a job just to make money. If something couldn't be repaired properly and wouldn't hold up, he would refuse to do the job even when his customers insisted and even when he needed the money, and even when he knew they could go down the street and get it done by someone else.

I remember when I was first learning the trade. As an eleven-year-old my work was not always, shall we say, perfect. He would take one look at a job I had done and all he would say was "do it over" or "finish the job." I heard those words a hundred times. "Finish the job." But I learned. He made sure of that, even if I was to be his Savior. And I needed to finish the task, because all of humanity was depending on my completing a greater task. One day I had to be able to say to the whole world, "It is finished."

I learned from him to observe small things about people and about nature. He was always asking me questions such as, "Did you see how that man didn't answer my question? He didn't want me to know that he doesn't have enough money. It hurts when you are poor." Or, just before spring when the trees and plants were still barren and the land gray, he would say, "Did you ever notice how, just before the trees are at their brightest, they are at their darkest? That's the way God works."

My earthly father knew how to raise a child, how to give him room to grow. Even though I always knew he was the authority in the home, I was comfortable with him. I enjoyed him. He was particularly good for a teenager because of his sense of humor. Another thing I enjoyed about him were his stories. He was a master storyteller. I can still hear my brothers and sisters after supper saying, "Father, tell us another story, tell us another story." Later on they were to call me a good teacher. I learned how from both my fathers. That's where I learned to teach in parables.

I saw Joseph's faults, too, but no son was ever closer to his father. I think because he knew who I was, he was more open with me. For over seven years we worked side by side every day, and then suddenly he became ill. I was frightened, concerned. I prayed and fasted for three days that God would heal him. But He did not. Joseph died early one morning after I had stayed up all night praying.

I had never felt so defeated. I was God's only son and He didn't hear me. Why would my Father do this to me? He knew I was to suffer enough and probably in the near future. Why did He add this to me? He knew how much I loved Joseph. And my mother was left with a house full of children and now no husband. Worst of all, my little brothers and sisters lost their father, Joseph, who had so much to give to them. It was almost more than I could bear.

At that moment I had a choice. I could have become angry with God and called Him a liar. "You are not my Father in heaven. You don't have any power; you don't care." But in my pain I was able to cling to His words,

"Many are the afflictions of the righteous: but the Lord delivereth him out of them all."[69]
"When you pass through the waters, I will be with you."[70]

He was there. I was finally able to say to Him, "I do not understand this. I hate it. I do not know why you allowed this to happen but you are still God Almighty with all your mercy and kindness, and you are still my Father."

I could not see into the future, but He could. He wanted me to be the most compassionate man who ever lived. And the price for compassion is pain. He was asking me to look death in the face and say to Him, "You are still a good God," just as years later when it came time for my own death, He would ask me to say the same thing to the whole world.

My Father was preparing me for the awesome test ahead when the temptation to renounce Him would be so much greater, when He would again have to say, "No," to my prayer on another night of, "Please let this cup pass from me." He was developing me into His son, a man of character, who in the face of adversity did not desert his friends or his Father. He wanted a son about whom He could say that He was well pleased.

At the moment Joseph died, it was the furthest thing from my mind that my Father was shaping me into the Savior of the world. The loss was so great that all I had was His word that He would work it out. But you have to be in a situation like that to understand the incredible comfort of my Father's words. They have always ultimately overcome pain of whatever type—fear, grief, poverty, and oppression. His words will always overcome the world.

In the middle of all my grief, I developed such a hatred for death that I thought I would be willing to go through death itself to destroy it. A tremendous hope began to grow. "So this—death—is what I am taking away. This is what I am going to do for the world." Now I desperately wanted to be the Savior of the world. When I looked at my brothers and sisters and my mother, I was more determined than ever to do what God was asking. That helped to ease the pain. Satan had really made an enemy.

What other events made your life hard?

It was all hard. As I told you, the older I got, the more I wanted to be a teacher —to show others who my Father really was. I had never forgotten that experience with the scholars in the Temple when I was twelve. That was when I really began to love teaching. But at the same time, at twelve I saw the high cost of being a teacher—experiencing the pain of life that teaches you. One of the reasons I had answered the scholars so well was because of the wisdom that my suffering had produced.

When my father Joseph died suddenly, I had to put aside my plans to be a teacher. But my Father worked it out. Although I was only seventeen I was the oldest son, and the responsibilities for our large family fell on my shoulders. I became the father. I took Joseph's place. I became the teacher for our family.

Money had never been plentiful, but after my father died, making a living became such a struggle that I had to sell the remainder of my gifts from the Magi. Even then, that just showed me how my Father in Heaven had prepared us for that moment by giving us savings to fall back on. Nevertheless, raising my brothers and sisters was very difficult. That was one reason I had to wait so long to be the Messiah. But, of course, my Father wanted me to experience the pressures of being a father myself.

It wasn't the most pleasant household in the world. My brothers in many ways didn't respect me. Have you tried to raise an adolescent lately who doesn't respect you? I was also under the same curse every other person had been under since the Fall. As the third chapter of Genesis states,

"From this day on, you shall earn your living by the sweat of your brow".[71]

More than once as I was carrying the responsibility for my family, I remember thinking, "Doesn't it ever get any easier?" And even after Joseph died, the rumors continued about my birth. Some neighbors spoke of Joseph's death as being "God's judgment on Mary." That hurt.

What good came from all this for you?

I remember facing the constant stress of not having enough to live on. I remember gradually selling what was left of my frankincense and myrrh to make ends meet. Finally they were gone, and then the day came when I had to take my gold box and sell it so I could put food on the table.

At first I was very sad. It was the only tangible gift I had left from my own Father. How many times I had sat there and looked at it, but my attitude changed. I realized how fortunate I was to be able to give my best for the people I loved, how fortunate I was to have a Father who had given me a precious gold box that I could use to buy bread. I could see that one day I would say to the world, "That Bread that you must eat in order to live is better than gold, because that Bread is the body of a King." So it was meant to be that my gold was sacrificed for my family's bread, just as my life was sacrificed for everyone.

There were countless other times when I learned His word was "as good as gold." It was better than gold, as a matter of fact, and I learned to live off that gift. If my Father's words were true, if He had promised comfort and certainty in an uncertain world, then I repeatedly had to find that certainty to diminish my stress. I made certain to spend enough time with Him that I had His mind on the matter. Eventually I spent enough time in the "other world" that this world wasn't frightening.

That was one of the beauties of fasting—I learned my vulnerability and it forced me to see I wasn't just "a strong, independent person," but someone with daily physical needs to be met. People who think they're autonomous, who hate even to take an aspirin for a headache should try giving up food and water and air, too, to test their own strength.

Another advantage to fasting for me was that I faced one of a human's basic fears, starving to death. I learned that if God allowed it, I could go through with it. With His strength I could do anything. I learned that His words were the ultimate reality, that they were greater than this world's "reality." Ultimately, I overcame my concern for not having enough food so much so that one day I could say, "I am the Bread of Life, all who come unto me shall never hunger." I could say that because my Father had taught me that He was my Bread. It was amazing how He worked all things out for good. His plan included even my pain. Particularly my pain.

TWO

*Baptism,
Temptation,
Selection*

The Announcement

Between the time when you were twelve and found out you were the Messiah, and when you were thirty, when you "went public," you had to wait for eighteen long years. Did you know exactly when you would begin your ministry or did you have to wait with some uncertainty?

I knew I had to wait for my "announcer." The "voice in the wilderness" about whom Isaiah spoke. But while I waited, I asked myself numerous questions. When would I start? What if the prophet showed up now? How would I begin? But with my new sense of responsibility from being head of the household, I began to get a sense of the process in which I was involved. I saw how my Father was preparing me.

It was always very clear to me that I had a lot left to learn about my Father. His personality was so varied that I could take one verse of Scripture and meditate on it for a month. God gave me the brightest mind in history and it still took me many years to know Him. I learned something new about Him every day until the day I died.

The Scriptures implied that the Messiah would come in the fullness of time. I felt that meant two things. The stage would not only be set historically but the Messiah himself would also go forward when He was ready. It was an historical and a personal "fullness of time." When I began to understand that my becoming the Messiah was a developmental process, I was led to a deeper awareness of my Father as someone who was in no hurry.

As time went on, David's life had new meaning for me. How long he had waited to be Israel's king! God promised him the throne when he was around twelve, but he was thirty years old before he got even a part of his kingdom. He was thirty-seven before he got the largest part, including the great city Jerusalem. David was special to me. His words had comforted me many times, and my Father had used his writings to tell me so much about myself that I began to wonder whether David's own life was paralleling mine even further. Both of us had found out about our royalty around the age of twelve. Was my Father now telling me that I would be thirty when I got part of my kingdom and that I would become the Messiah publicly at that time? Clearly I could see that the biography of David's life could be telling me, "When you do get your kingdom, you won't get it all at once. You will get most of your power later." I began to understand that when I returned the second time, I would completely rule and have much greater power. That part of David's life also matched perfectly with mine. Jerusalem and his greatest kingdom came in the second part of his reign.

The awareness that David had been thirty years old before he had become king occurred soon after my father, Joseph, died. I remember thinking that when I became thirty, my youngest sister—the youngest child in our family —would be fifteen and more than old enough to care for herself. As it turned out, that was exactly what the Scriptures were telling me. I was to be thirty years old when I announced to the world that I was the Messiah. But then, my Father taught us all to wait. I was no different. Abraham waited 100 years to have his first legitimate child, including twenty-five years after God promised him one. Joseph waited as a prisoner and a servant for about eighteen years before he became prime minister of Egypt. Moses waited forty years as a farmer and eighty years altogether before he became the leader of Israel.

The people of Israel had waited four hundred years since the last writer in the Old Testament, Malachi, had "signed off" in 400 B.C. Malachi had promised that, "the next voice you hear—the next prophet—will be 'the man from the desert,' the 'voice crying in the wilderness.' And the one following on the heels of the 'desert man' will be 'The Voice'."

When John finally came, the plan was being carried out at last, just as my Father had said. It was a very secure feeling. I was nearly twenty-nine when John the Baptist first came on the scene and began to attract attention, and I just chuckled to myself. I now felt very certain that my Father was telling me, "You're right. When you're thirty—that's the time."

Before you began your public life, you must have been thinking about what you were going to do as the Messiah and what you were going to say.

I wondered many times where I was to go. Would I be like John and stay mostly in one place, letting them come to me? Would I keep my job as a carpenter and teach, or would I go out and travel from city to city? Once again, the Scriptures were my guide. All of God's men had to go into the unknown, trusting Him alone. Abraham left his home. Moses went to a foreign land. Joseph had to live in another land. And David spent years in the wilderness. As the leading character, was I to do any differently? Would I have any less adventure than they?

The nation of Israel had trusted God for over forty years every day to lead them by a pillar of fire. There was something challenging about letting God lead me daily, about not planning, but letting Him plan. I was determined to present myself to the world as the Messiah in the Spirit of "Give, don't take. Trust, don't fear." Those words were at the heart of what I wanted to teach. And I was privileged to live those words as well as teach them. Although I didn't know exactly what I would say or do, I had confidence in the leadership of my Father.

You waited over a year after John the Baptist first appeared before you presented yourself. What made you finally decide to go forward? Were there any special signs directing you exactly when to declare who you were?

I had also wondered where and when I would start my career. Everything pointed towards Jerusalem. I had been born near there. I was circumcised there at eight days of age. That's where I discovered that I was the Messiah. David had reigned there. The Passover was held there—a time when everyone thought and talked about the Messiah. When John the Baptist began his ministry baptizing people in the Jordan River not too far from Jerusalem, I felt that was further confirmation that I would make one of my first appearances in Jerusalem. And I wanted to do it around the time of Passover, for I was the Passover Lamb.

My identity led me to think about Jerusalem as the place and Passover as the time. After John came, I realized even more how much authority my Father had given me. *I* was to pick the moment that I gave myself to the world just as later *I* was to select the moment I was to die.

As you said later, "No one takes my life from me, I give it."

That's right. For a few years, I'd waited as the Baptist prepared the way, bringing about a radical change in many people's minds. His message was simple: everyone was a sinner who needed cleansing, and the Lamb of God, the Messiah who would do it, was on the way.

One day about three months before Passover, after I'd finished all the work I'd promised my customers, I closed my part of the carpentry shop. I had turned all of my new business over to my brother. The last night at home, the night before I went out to be baptized by John, I remember praying, "Father, I know Your ways, I believe You are asking me to step out and trust that You have called me this far and that You will lead me on. Tomorrow, as the sign of my willingness to do what You have asked, I will go to the Jordan River to be baptized by John. Please confirm to me that now is the time for me to publicly declare I am the Messiah. So many times before You have answered me; I know You will again."

Why did you get baptized? You didn't need to repent of any sins.

Besides being a symbol of forgiveness, baptism is a picture of death and of resurrection. The body first goes under the water—"into the grave." I was saying to my Father and to the world that I accepted my death.

Your cousin, John, was a sight to behold, wasn't he?

At first glance he was frightening. He had a beard down to his waist and long, wild-looking hair. As a child he had taken the Nazarene oath and had never cut his hair nor his beard. He dressed in camel skins and lived in the wilderness eating wild honey and locusts. He had an incredible booming voice that sounded like thunder! He was a picture of God—awesome, bold. He looked like someone from another world—and yet, at the same time, he was very comforting.

Imagine God's turning someone like this loose on the world and saying to him, "Get them ready." Do you think my Father doesn't have a sense of humor! When He does something of this nature, He does it better than anyone. Think about having a "public relations" man like John.

John was unlike any preacher the people had ever seen or heard before. It was as if Ezekiel had just stepped out of the pages of the Old Testament. When John finally got a chance to use his voice, he wasn't shy about it. "You followers of the one true God of Israel, you chosen people, you're fat and lazy. You're not ready for the Messiah who is almost in your midst. You think you can rest on your heritage: Forget it! God can raise up followers out of these stones. I am the one Malachi talked about, the man from the wilderness, and I tell you, repent. Turn away from your sins, all of you. Come be baptized to show you mean it. Say it: 'I'm sorry. I'm sorry.' "

Far from being antagonized, the people were drawn to John like a magnet. They all wondered if he was not the prophet they had been waiting for. He told them he was not worthy to be the slave of the One who was coming soon. Repeatedly, he warned them that the Messiah was coming with a big stick, with "a life or death matter; with an ultimate choice" . . . "Take me seriously," John said. "He, the Holy One will separate wheat from chaff, and burn up the chaff with an eternal fire. Eternal. Eternal fire."

John was given such a strong message to deliver. He didn't understand I was going to show more mercy than he ever thought about. Even though he knew I was going to die, he thought I was going to come in like he did and take the world by storm in the same way—rightfully claiming that the world was mine and denouncing sinners immediately with judgment. Even though he didn't completely understand my role, he never backed off from his truth.

Since he was a teenager, he had spent his time almost exclusively in the wilderness alone with God. Imagine a man with that kind of fire and energy having to channel it all into one relationship—and, at that, with Someone whom he couldn't see. I had tremendous admiration for what John had done. I also had some idea of what it was like to wait before the Father when everything inside me was bursting with excitement to share, with conviction to teach. I knew what it was to be burning with truth yet having to contain it all.

There's something innately expansive about truth, as though it has a mind of its own and demands to be shared. And yet, at the same time, truth often demands self-denial and containment. Truth can create an unbelievable tension. It can be a terrible burden. John lived with that burden for years like I did—almost identically the same length of time. He went to the wilderness just after his bar mitzvah at thirteen, six months before I found out who I was. When his opportunity came, seventeen years later, John was ready. What a faithful man he had been; closer to my Father than any other human being had ever been besides myself. But who else in history had spent seventeen years alone with God? When my Father was preparing my prophet, He really prepared him. God didn't pick just anybody to deliver the message. He wanted someone with a heart that burned for Him to take the message to the people. It takes years to get a heart warm and even longer to get one burning hot.

(Jesus once said that there was never one greater among all the men who had ever lived than John the Baptist. Now I understood why he felt so strongly about John. John had walked where Jesus had walked, had traveled the same road of alienation, unbelieveable self-denial, and waiting —waiting—waiting, all for the Father. In the midst of his pain, John had nowhere else to turn but to God for the comfort a human being so desperately needs. There John drank deeply from the Living Waters of Scripture, of prayer, of meditation, like no one else had ever done except

one. Jesus and John had had the same Father, and both knew Him better than anyone else ever had.)

Day after day, John railed against the authorities of the time, screaming at the hypocrisies. The bigger they were, the harder he came down on them. Jew or Gentile—it didn't make any difference. That's what finally got him killed. He condemned Herod, the Governor appointed by Rome, the enemy who occupied Israel, for stealing his brother's wife. Yet John came down hardest on the Pharisees for teaching the people false religion. He was so genuine. He deeply loved God and was totally devoted to saying what God wanted him to say. He didn't care what others thought. That was one reason he had such strong personal appeal. John was a free man. He assured the people of the enormous blessings waiting for them if they turned from their sins. And they loved him. Everyone came from miles around to hear John preach. They were people from all walks of life—common people, teenagers, Roman soldiers—even some of the Pharisees. His fame had spread beyond Israel, and you've never seen anyone who could reach a crowd the way he could. After he preached, hundreds of people would line up to be baptized by John.

Most of all, the Baptist talked about me, telling them that a *Light* had come into their midst. The Messiah was here! John really did his job. He prepared the crowds for me.

According to the Gospel accounts, when you were standing in line to be baptized, it seemed that John didn't recognize you. That suggests that you had not seen your cousin in years. Did you think about telling him who you were?

John hadn't seen me in years. I thought about telling him. But my Father had been able to tell me who I was. I figured that He was just as capable of telling John.

It seems that your Father did a good job of informing John. The Scriptures record a very dramatic scene when John did recognize you.

Just before it was my turn to step into the water, a little dove landed on my shoulder and John startled me as he screamed to the crowd.

"Look, the Lamb of God, who takes away the sin of the world!"[1]

I can still hear his voice echoing across the water. After he said it, silence fell over the crowd. Later John told me that a voice from God had told him that the man upon whom the dove had just landed was the Messiah.

I recall thinking, "What a great appreciation for history my Father has. How well He knows how to communicate and how much trouble He goes to in order to do so. The dove was the symbol of hope, of new discovery, and most importantly, of peace. He showed me that He understood down to the last detail. As Isaiah had promised, I was to be the Prince of Peace. My Father's preparation was making sure that it would come true. That was enormously comforting.

What happened next?

What happened next was just as surprising as the dove. John didn't want to baptize me. He wanted *me* to baptize *him*. But I insisted that I be baptized. He paused for a moment, looked at me, and then finally baptized me in a way to let me know that he understood. He told me to take a deep breath, and then he held me under a very long time, much longer than anyone else who was baptized. It was so long that I started to get short of breath. I felt the panic that happens when you can't get enough air. I almost lost control until I realized what he was doing.

He wanted me to feel that pain so much like death to let me know that he understood what this was costing me. He knew that one day I would lie in a grave. Finally, he brought me up out of the water. I was gasping for air as he stood there with his hand on my shoulder. It was a strong hand. After several seconds, I finally caught my breath, and then it happened: I heard my Father's voice for the first time,

"This is My beloved son, in whom I am well pleased."[2]

God could have said anything, but listen to what He said to me, "This is My beloved son in whom I am well pleased." I can still hear that rich, majestic voice. Heaven had opened! The door was no longer shut! I had heard my own Father's voice at last!

After thirty years of waiting!

Many times I had wanted to hear His voice just as Moses and the other prophets had. Often I wondered why He hadn't spoken to me directly, especially if I were as important as the Scriptures and the world around me was telling me. But when I needed it most, He spoke. During the years I waited, I wondered what His first words to me might be. Would they be direct encouragement such as, "Keep fighting the battle," or "Never give up"? Would they be just a command as with Abraham: "Go to Jerusalem"? Would they be just a greeting of some sort: "This is your Father in Heaven."? I had always had a feeling that they would be very kind and special because His written words were like that. The impact on me was startling. All those years of preparation, of making sure, of waiting, of living on His written words, of keeping the faith, had been validated firsthand.

Another thought that had occurred to me after I had heard my Father's voice was that I should have expected it. When the Prophet Ezekiel was thirty, as the first verse in his book records, the "heavens opened" and God spoke to him for the first time. This happened just before God had asked Ezekiel to go publicly before Israel as a prophet and deliver His message to the people. Ezekiel was also from the Tribe of Judah, which "coincidentally" I was, too. As I had waited all those years to hear my Father's voice I had always wondered if He were telling me that I would be thirty years old when it would happen. Just before my baptism my mind was on other things and I had forgotten that message. I'm glad I did, because it was such a nice surprise.

For days afterward, His voice kept coming back to me: "This is My beloved son." It was all I could think about. It was such an overpowering experience that I wanted to be alone to savor it. I almost had to be alone to contain it. Before I went out into the world, I also wanted as intense an awareness of Him as possible. I knew from experience that the way to heighten my sense of Him was to be totally alone with Him and to fast. I had to go over with Him what I was to do and what I was to say. That knowledge could come only by waiting before Him.

That was when you went into the wilderness and fasted for forty days?

The time had come for me to go out into the world and I was faced with two extremely difficult tasks. I had to tell everyone, including strangers, "I am the most important person in your life because your ultimate destination, heaven or hell, rides on my shoulders." That wasn't easy. It was one thing for me to know that I was the Messiah. It was another to tell the world, "I've got a surprise for you. All those years you thought I was just a carpenter with some of you even questioning my heritage, I have been growing up among you as your Messiah, and my hour has now come." But if my Father could say to me I was the Messiah, I could say it to the world.

I was also going out into the world to die and I had total freedom to choose not to go. But He had said to me, "This is my beloved son." I would do anything for Him, even give up my life.

Did you plan to fast for as long as forty days when you went into the wilderness?

As I said, my experience at my Baptism was so intense, I had to get away. My desire to respond to my Father was so strong, I wanted to tell Him, "And You are my Beloved Father." I thought of Moses and Elijah both of whom had been so consumed by the Lord that they fasted for forty days and nights before Him. I wanted to do that, too. It was an overpowering feeling. Something or Someone was driving me to do that too; so I started toward the wilderness to be alone with God.

I also knew the rest of the script. Before a new beginning in Scripture, there were always waiting periods of "forty." To create a new world, it rained for forty days and nights. After the great flood, Noah's ark came to rest on the mountain and Noah waited forty days "in the mountains" after his great discovery before he opened the windows of the Ark and sent out a raven to explore the land. Moses waited forty years in the wilderness before he led the nation of Israel out of captivity in Egypt. The Israelites wandered for forty years in the wilderness before they went into the promised land.

The Scriptures led me even further. On one occasion, soon after Moses heard God's voice, he fasted without food or water for forty days and nights on Mount Sinai where God had called to him from the clouds. Years later, Elijah had also fasted, again without food or water, in the same place in the wilderness for an identical forty-day period. I wouldn't have tempted my Father and fasted without water, too, unless I had thought the Scriptures were clearly leading me. I felt that I needed a testing, something to prepare me for the big battle to come. I had to have a major battle with my flesh and defeat it if I were going to win the "big fight" at the end of my life when

I had to overcome all of my physical senses, when everything in me would call out to give up. As it turned out, He had a bigger test planned for me than I knew.

Once again, the Scriptures guided me clearly as I remembered what Moses said to the Israelites toward the end of their forty years in the wilderness,

> "Remember how the Lord your God led you all the way in the desert these forty years, to humble you and to test you in order to know what was in your heart, whether or not you would keep his commands. He humbled you, causing you to hunger and then feeding you with manna, which neither you nor your fathers had known, to teach you that man does not live on bread alone but on every word that comes from the mouth of the Lord."[3]

I felt that my Father was saying, "Before you go out into the world, go over My words one more time. Live on them. Fast for forty days to test yourself." I obeyed my Father. He led me every step of the way. For forty days I wanted to eat almost continually, but I didn't. I was practicing.

Was this fast an encouraging time for you?

Fasting is rather like seeing in the dark. At first, everything is black and all you can think about is pain and food. After a while, you begin to "see" things, to perceive things that you couldn't at first. When you don't eat, you quickly recognize how vulnerable you are, and I wanted to know that. Without leaning heavily on Him, I could never go through with it. Once again I went over my role, and my mission became more focused than ever—even after I had already thought that it was clear.

My Father had indeed filled me in a new way with his Spirit and I understood more in depth what I was about. It was just as the eleventh chapter of Isaiah had promised the Messiah:

> "And there shall come forth a rod out of the stem of Jesse, and a branch shall grow out of his roots: and the spirit of the Lord shall rest upon him, the spirit of wisdom and understanding, the spirit of counsel and might, the spirit of knowledge and of the fear of the Lord."[4]

You mentioned you became more focused. What became more clear for you?

Everything depended on me. Salvation would be by me and me alone. No one else could please God ultimately. No matter how hard they had tried, they had all failed and always would. But I would please Him. He had promised. I was His son. For those forty days, I went over and over His words spoken to me. When I wasn't thinking about food, I thought only of my Father and my role, and that experience took me to a new depth.

It became more and more clear that when I carried out this mission that I would be changing the face of an entire religion, affecting ceremonies that were embedded in a way of life. Soon there would be no need for animal sacrifices, altars, or ceremonial washing. Yom Kippur would not be celebrated in the same way and no more would the "Holy of Holies" be totally exclusive.

If I understood all that I thought I did, the social implications themselves were enormous. Never again would people have to bring animals to sacrifice so that God would continue to bless them, because by then *The Sacrifice* would have been made once and for all. The whole worship service would have to change its emphasis and everyone who was "sprinkled with my blood" would now be able to enter the Holy of Holies.*

The Pharisees would have a hard time with that one. No one likes to share power. My Father was making me into a "radical," even if I didn't want to be. Truth is a sword that cuts wide paths wherever it goes.

As all of this went through my mind. I realized how much my Father was asking of me. As is so characteristic of Him, whenever He asks much, He gives much in return. His Spirit was there in a new way, even more alive. You know how someone's personality can affect you when they are there beside you. You can feel their spirit, their energy. I couldn't see Him, but I could feel Him. His words had never been more alive. I was completely one with Him, and now I knew that my words would be His words. Everything I would say would have just as much authority as if He said it. Even better yet, He would be saying it through me when I spoke. As great as it was to hear my Father's voice, the experience in the wilderness and the oneness I shared with Him there was the greatest moment of my life. It was to be the central focus of my teachings. I never felt stronger than I did at that moment on the fortieth day of my fast. That's when "he" appeared.

He? You mean Satan? Did you know beforehand you were going to be tempted?

Not consciously. Unconsciously I knew everything. Consciously I knew that I could expect the enemy at some point.

But later on you were recorded as saying before you could take an enemy's house you had to defeat him. You clearly saw the world as Satan's house, didn't you?

That's what I learned when he tempted me. I didn't know exactly what Satan was going to do. I knew he would try to turn the people against me and I knew that death was waiting for me eventually. I also knew that he had tried to kill me as a baby and had tried to discourage me many times. In the back of my mind, I knew he would try to deceive me and, like a good soldier, I had always trained my mind to be prepared for an unexpected attack.

Like the time your own disciple Peter tried to discourage you from going to the cross and you snapped at him,

"Get thee behind me, Satan."[5]

*Only one man in all of Israel, the High Priest, could enter the sacred room in the temple called the Holy of Holies. And then he could enter on only one day of the year—Yom Kippur—the Day of Atonement. At that time, the High Priest would take the blood of a goat and sprinkle it on the mercy seat which was atop the Ark in the Holy of Holies. The blood represented a symbolic atonement for the sin of all the people of Israel. If God accepted the sacrifice that year, the Priest was allowed to live. It was a very solemn time, and the people waited outside while their High Priest went into that sacred room to meet with God. Every year there was a rope tied to the High Priest's leg so that if he offended God and the sacrifice was not accepted, then the people could pull him out it he were struck dead.

At this particular time in the wilderness I was elated. I had just heard my Father's voice. He was never closer. He was there beside me. I had just finished the forty day fast when Satan surprised me.

You said he just appeared.

It had been forty days. I was thinking I would finally be able to eat something. As I was starting back to town I came around a boulder and suddenly a man appeared. He was a little on the short side, had a winsome smile and seemed to be exceptionally gentle and kind. After a few minutes with him, I decided that he was perhaps the most striking person I had ever met. He radiated warmth. We began talking and it was obvious that he knew what I had been doing. As time went on, I began to think that was perhaps one of my Father's ways of revealing Himself to me. After all, God had just spoken to me for the first time, and in the Old Testament angels had often appeared to various men.

I half-heartedly wondered if this were a trick but he was the kind of person who dispelled doubt and put you at ease. Besides, I hadn't talked to another human being for forty days. He seemed to take delight in me and to revere me. I told him about my joy and he seemed to understand. He even brought up the fact that I would overcome the evil in the world. It crossed my mind that he might be the enemy, but he was so convincing. We talked some more about fasting and what a great experience it had been. We both laughed when he said, "I don't suppose you are hungry." I had not asked him who he was, but ever so gently he volunteered, "I have been in the heavens with your Father and I have come to talk to you."

That part was true about having been with God.

He said, "We both know your uniqueness, your special role, and how your Father wants to give you everything He has including His power." He said, "Read the Old Testament. The Messiah will make the blind see and the lame walk. He means that literally, He is going to give you that power by faith. All you have to do is believe Him." He continued, "God wants you to use your power. He doesn't want you to suffer any longer. He knows how hungry you are. Go ahead. Use the power He's given you. You are hungry." And very unassumingly, in an encouraging way, he said, "If you are the son of God, turn these stones into bread."

Things were really moving fast for me. Was God, my Father, pushing me to trust Him more? This man was so encouraging! It seemed exactly the right thing to do. I was starving. But there were two things that made me wait. One, I didn't really know this man, and there was just the slightest hint of urgency in his suggestion—of impulsiveness—of acting without thinking. And there was that one little word thrown in almost offhandedly—"if"—"*if* you are the son of God." More importantly, I knew the code—and the code was "wait." Abraham, Joseph, Moses, David—all the prophets had waited for God to put them in a place of power. Just as the Scriptures that had led me to fast for forty days said,

"He humbled you causing you to hunger and then feeding you with manna—which neither you nor your fathers had known, to teach you that man does not live on bread alone."

The Scriptures seemed to be saying to me that He would feed me; when He was ready He would send the manna. I had never done anything ahead of my Father's command. If I were to do something more, this man-angel, if that's what he was, would have to show me out of God's word something that I didn't know was there. Or I would have to hear it straight from God.

That's what the whole test for forty days had been about: to learn to put His words ahead of everything, my instincts included, just as the Scriptures had led me to do in the first place when I began to fast. Besides, I was here to use my Father's power for humanity's benefit, not mine; so I told Satan the same thing that Moses had just told me:

"Man shall not live by bread alone, but by every word that proceedeth out of the mouth of God."[6]

I really wanted to turn those stones into bread. I thought I had that kind of faith and that kind of deity.

How did Satan react?

He was cunning. He dropped the subject immediately and acted as if it didn't bother him one bit. That relaxed me. I recall thinking that perhaps I wasn't trusting God—maybe this was His way of communicating with me and I was not pleasing to Him.

And then the little man said, "Come with me." Just like that, he whisked me to the top of the Temple miles away, and that power frightened me. We were sitting on top of the magnificent Temple on the southeast corner with the Kidron Valley four hundred and fifty feet below. He began talking about the power that God had given to me and how it was God's will that I use it. He could understand my reluctance, he said, but he told me that God had sent him to teach me and that now was the time for me to live out my faith in God just as my mother had. Then he looked down at the ground and said that there was a message for me hidden in the Scriptures just as all the other secrets were. He said it was the same kind of message that had led me to fast for forty days without food and water like Elijah did. Then he quoted part of the 91st Psalm.

"For he will command his angels concerning you to guard you in all your ways; they will lift you up in their hands, so that you will not strike your foot against a stone."[7]

Satan said, "You can see that the Scriptures have prophesied this moment and are telling you to jump to the ground from here. The angels surrounding us will catch you. Listen to what your great, almighty Father says to you. He will guard you in all your ways. He really means your ways, whatever you want to do." Quietly, almost in a whisper, but firmly, he said, "Use your power!

Use it. Don't lack faith, believe! If you are the son of God, cast yourself down."

It was difficult for me to think. There was something daring in what he was saying. And I loved the challenge. This man-angel had taken me right to the Word of God. Was God reading my mind? Was my Father again going before me as the Scriptures had said He always would? On top of that, it seemed as if my every thought had been anticipated and the Scriptures seemed so specific for this moment. I had always wondered what that verse meant. There was a godlike power in faith, and nothing pleased my Father like our having faith in Him. It was a totally new world that was being opened to me and I wanted to experience His power in a new way. I wanted to jump! Could I fall from this building and be caught by angels? Is God that real? To be caught by God six inches before I was to be bashed to death. What a challenge! I needed that much confidence in Him to go out into the world to do what I had to do. After all, to be the Messiah was a supreme challenge of faith. Shouldn't I go ahead and use my power if I were really the Messiah?

I already knew that I would perform miracles to get the peoples' attention at some time in the near future. Prophecy told me that. Why not start now? I had always planned on making as bold an entrance as possible. After all, my Father was bold. He had sent my cousin, John the Baptist. He had chosen Solomon at one time to make a bold statement. David charged boldly down the hill to meet Goliath. Maybe that was a picture of me jumping down from this building. I wanted to jump. That challenge was within my power. My Father was greater than material power, greater than those rocks below.

My thoughts also went back to Moses' sermon to the Israelites just before they entered the Promised Land after wandering for forty years on a journey that should have taken them only about eleven days. It had been prolonged because the people didn't trust God. That part of Scripture was so fresh in my mind because it was about how the Jews were to handle their new blessing, their new land, after such a long wait. This was precisely what I had been thinking about. I needed to know how to handle my new role, my new power.

One of the things Moses told them was not to push God, not to demand or complain, but to accept what He had given to them. Here was Israel's great leader at the end of his life leaving them his final words even though he couldn't go with them because of his own disobedience. He had pushed God and demanded more than God had wanted to give. So Moses told his people,

"Ye shall not tempt the Lord your God."[8]

Moses had learned the hard way and, through Moses' example, I thought I had my answer to this man-angel's urgings. Moses' disobedience had come when he smashed a rock that he wasn't supposed to strike. It occurred to me that perhaps I wasn't to smash the rocks either.

This particular place on the Temple was also known as "blasphemer's corner" where the authorities on occasion pushed blasphemers to their death. Was this location a message from my Father saying, "Don't blaspheme me?" Quickly my mind flashed through the remainder of Scripture and immediately

I thought of David, my character. God had told him when he was twelve that he would be Israel's next king. This had come about because God was extremely displeased with the man who was then king, Saul. After David's anointing by the prophet Samuel, Saul made several attempts to kill David and David spent twelve years living in caves, hiding from Saul.

David had two specific opportunities to kill Saul, and he would have been justified in doing so. After all, Saul was attempting to kill him unjustly. But David decided if he were to be king, he would wait for God to make him king. Again the message was, "Wait." Even more specific was the message, "Wait for the power."

As I looked at this man-angel who was urging me to act, the same doubts flashed through my mind. The subtle word, "if," was a problem. What did it remind me of? What was it? Then I remembered! There was the same doubt in the first book in the Bible when Satan used doubt to deceive Eve as to what God had said. Satan had asked Eve, "Did God really say, 'Don't eat the fruit of that tree?' " when he knew very well that God had. Satan had urged Eve to eat something, too, like this man-angel had just urged me to eat minutes before.

Something else reminded me of that garden. The garden was a deserted place. Satan suddenly appeared out of nowhere and started talking. He had obviously been very charming. The confusion started to clear for me. Was this man really trying to push me just for my own good? This was the second time he had wanted me to act quickly. The first time he had wanted me to use my power. Now he wanted me to force my Father to use His power. There was just a hint of urgency, of manipulation. That had been Eve's mistake, and Adam's. They had been manipulated into action. "Watch out, think, don't act. Wait on the Lord," the Scriptures seemed to be screaming at me. David's answer to uncertainty had been wait on the Lord. I thought I had my answer, too.

It occurred to me that if I jumped, popularity would be mine. But then again, I knew I had not come to win a popularity contest. I knew I would do miracles, but somehow the idea of "jumping off a building" onto some rocks below seemed to draw more attention to me without having much value to others. The rocks themselves seemed to be images of deadness as I looked at them. Right then I also had the thought that surely God wouldn't believe that I would do anything without Him. "Surely this isn't that kind of test," I thought. "I haven't eaten in a long time. Maybe I'm not thinking clearly." I thought of Job and of David and others. God did allow tests, but God wasn't the tempter Himself.

I still wasn't absolutely sure what it was intended to test—my faith or my pride. My Father knew I had faith. I definitely had my answer. God did not tempt me and I would not tempt Him. There was no manipulation, no coercion in our relationship. He was God Almighty and I was His beloved son. I could still hear those words. Whatever He gave me, *He* gave me. I didn't take it. I waited on His gifts. I answered the man-angel,

"Thou shall not tempt the Lord thy God."[9]

What happened then?

After I had refused him a second time, he acted again as if nothing bothered him. I sensed something unusual about him then, because if he had really been an angel of God, I don't think he would have been able to be so indifferent if it were a true test of faith.

His third temptation came quickly and was exceptionally blatant. In the blink of an eye, he once again transported me to a distant place. This time it was to a tremendously high mountain, actually to several high mountains over a short period of time. There were all the kingdoms of the world below us. What a magnificent sight it was! That kind of power display could take your breath away. The little man was god-like. Then he showed me his kingdom—all the kingdoms of the world below us. As he saw me looking around almost in a state of shock at what I was seeing, he said to me, with all his cleverness, "I know you won't do this," and he paused ever so slightly, "but if you will bow down to me, all of these are yours." For a brief moment it was so appealing. All that power and no pain was offered, and I was meant to rule. As always, if you wait, evil becomes obvious. It was clear that this one last effort was utterly evil.

Just a good old bribe.

When all else had failed, his true colors showed. He used the oldest trick in the book: offering riches, power, and fame for my soul. Now I knew who this angel was. I had an eerie feeling. I was indeed in the presence of Satan himself. For a minute, I saw how great he could have been. He was powerful, persuasive, charming. But then I thought how unlike my Father he really is. My Father doesn't offer you riches. He offers you Himself. I detested Satan. He had wanted to take my Father's place. In fact, he still does! And I shouted at him,

> "Away from me, Satan! For it is written: 'worship the Lord your God and serve Him only.' "[10]

It was really my Father's world, not Satan's. A mean and most hateful look came over Satan's face. I had never seen anyone's face change so drastically. He was gone in a flash! Suddenly I found myself back at the boulder in the wilderness. Immediately, the loyal angels came and brought me food, and we talked about why my Father had let me go through these temptations. This, too, was similar to what had happened to Elijah. An angel had brought him food and water in the middle of a wilderness after his great spiritual battle. Manna.

All three of your answers to Satan came from Moses' sermon at the end of his life which was recorded in Deuteronomy.

It wasn't a coincidence that I had just been dwelling on Moses' words for forty days. The Scriptures were telling me that this was what I should think about before I went into public ministry. Those were the same words that my Teacher, the Spirit, used to lead me into the wilderness.

Moments After

How did you feel after the temptation?

I had vindicated my Father's methods. He had taught me to know Him through His Word. And when the test came, His plan worked. I showed Him that I understood Him very well. I thought of all those times I had questioned Him. "Was He going to lead me to be the Messiah of the world without ever directly communicating with me?" I had wondered. Well, He did it!

He had taught me to put His words above everything. If He said an event was going to occur, no matter what the odds seemed against it happening, it would happen exactly as He said it would. If He said I could do something, no matter how strong my feelings to the contrary, I could do it. If He said I was the Savior of the world, I was the Savior of the world. If He told me He was guiding me, He was guiding me even when I didn't know it. Many times I could see His guidance only "after-the-fact," just as He had guided me into exactly how to answer Satan. When I read back over the Scriptures I could see that He had even told me ahead of time what I was going to say. I had learned that reality was what He said it was, not what I or anyone else thought. Reality was His Word. I learned to live on those words and I never forgot how.

Suppose you had gone ahead and performed either of those two miracles. If it were an honest mistake, what would have been wrong with that?

That kind of thinking—"It doesn't matter"—is the most subtle of Satan's voices. It would still have been a sin, no matter how small. You can see how deceitful his appeal is at first. But remember, leprosy starts from the smallest sore. All Satan wanted me to do was to sin one time. Then I would have the disease, too. Another reason I waited was that as much as I wanted to see God work with my own eyes, I knew it was this same idea that led to idol worship. The people couldn't wait for God. They had to see Him with their eyes and not with their faith. They got so tired of waiting that they made their own gods out of wood and stone and gold. I would see God when He wanted me to, not when I wanted.

What do you see as the idols of today?

Whatever your eyes can see. What is it today in the world that attracts your eye? Is it houses, or jewelry, or cars, or bodies? Do clothes control you? Does art, a football team, or a boat entice you? Watch out. For whatever attracts you strongly can become your idol. It can also be your servant. Sometimes there's a fine line, but the greater your God, the clearer the line becomes.

It's a strange feeling to be living in what the world calls "reality," and to know that there's another, greater world all around you. The deepest reality is actually not in what your eyes tell you, but in what His words tell you it is. Human beings must never forget that they are limited. We don't get all our understanding in a day, in a month, or even in a year or ten years. We have to wait for it.

It was only later that I could fully understand that Satan was trying to separate us, to get me to precede my Father, to act independently of Him and to take that first step toward pride just as Satan himself had done. Presumption was the essence of the first two temptations.

Satan was particularly clever in the second temptation when he tried to make you think that you had already tested God by fasting for forty days without food and water. What was the difference between the fast and the temptation?

The difference was that God led me to fast for forty days without food and water. He didn't lead me to jump off a building. When I went into the wilderness to fast I had never felt more led to do something in my life. The writers of the New Testament report that I was driven into the wilderness by the Holy Spirit and that's exactly what happened. I had just been baptized and filled with the Holy Spirit in a special and new way. Certainly a man has to be careful when he says God leads him to do something because his feelings can mislead him.

But remember, I was God—and I lacked something you have—impure motivation. In addition, I had a special sensitivity to my Father, enhanced further by my unique anointing. Furthermore, there was an impulsive quality to Satan's urgings. He gave me no time really to think it over, and that's usually not God's way. For example, when I was led to fast in the wilderness, I had the whole way out there to think it over. In fact, it was on the walk out there that I decided He was leading me not to eat nor to drink. That decision, obviously, did not have the same irrevocable quality that jumping off that building would have had. I could have found something to eat or drink if I had really felt I was tempting God.

Some people say that only your divine nature was tested at the temptation, and not your human nature.

If that were true, then there would have been no temptation. Because of my omniscience I would have known ahead of time how utterly foolish Satan's urgings were. But if I deny myself that awareness—put myself under the same conditions as a human—then things aren't always so clear. And the Scriptures do say that it was a temptation and my Father does have a way with words.

If you study the Scriptures, you will see a picture of my temptation in the life of Job. Satan told God that Job, who was a faithful man, wouldn't be faithful if God took away all his blessings and power. God said that Job would be faithful. He allowed Satan to test Job by taking away Job's material power, his influence, and his physical comforts including his health and family. Despite some complaints, Job remained faithful nonetheless.

The same story was repeated in the life of Joseph. As a young boy Joseph was very wealthy and the most favored of all of Jacob's sons. Suddenly Joseph lost his wealth, his place of honor, and his earthly father. He found himself a slave in a foreign country without any of the usual resources to support him in his time of testing. Nevertheless, Joseph's faith grew and he became great because, when he was without his earthly power, he still trusted his "real Father." I was tempted when I was weak, not strong. I was "without" my power and my knowledge and the comforts of heaven. That's why my Father was so pleased. It was much more difficult when I was fully human to withstand temptation.

Some theologians think that one of the central elements of your temptation was that you would have been tempted to think God wasn't there and that He had forgotten about your hunger.

No. He had led me there and I knew He could send me food any time He wished just as He had sent Elijah food in the wilderness. For me, the times I was most strongly tempted to think God wasn't there were when my father, Joseph, died, and during those years afterwards when we struggled as a family in poverty. Watching my brothers and sisters grow up without a father was sad for me. Then, of course, later, when I was hanging on the cross, God seemed as if he had forsaken me.

Some people still have difficulty with the idea that you did not use your omniscience at all times. They would see that as denying your deity.

If you understand the Incarnation, you can see why it was not necessary for me to use my omniscience instantaneously in my humanity to be fully God. I could have used my omniscience at any moment that I wanted, just like I could have used all my power any moment I wanted, as I told Peter when they came to take me prisoner. On the cross I could have come down, but I chose not to. Long before I came to Earth, I obviously had had a plan, and was determined to carry it out. In a real way I submitted to myself, just as all believers must do.

Once I knew I was God, I realized everything was mine. I could do anything I wanted. But at the same moment I discovered who I was, I came into an awareness of my self-denial, of how much I had laid aside to come to earth, and I chose to continue with what my Father and I had started. After all, that was His will. His will was mine.

Is it possible that there are those who don't really want to allow me to become a human being, because they don't want to be human themselves? The minute they allow that, they "cease to be God." They secretly hate that vulnerability that comes with being human. Equally as secretly, they want to tell me what I can do. They say that I can't veil myself like that. That I can't make an infinite sacrifice based on infinite love.

You might say that the only ultimate way We could express Our love, would be for One of us to become a human being. The minute We created man, love demanded We become one of him, to become one with him. As Lu-

ther put it, "God has always longed for humanity as His own form of existence."

Coming back to the temptation, Satan must have made a strong impression on you.

I knew then firsthand why he was called the "Angel of Light." How subtly
deceitful he was, and how appealing and harmless he made evil seem. The only
way to counteract him was to know God's mind and to wait for God. I had
waited all those years, and even after I had heard my Father's voice, I still
had to wait.

*(The more I thought about Christ's three temptations, the more human
and divine He became at the same time. His first two temptations touched
on probably our two most basic fears. One is that of not having enough
food; the other is of being physically damaged. The first temptation had
to do with sustenance, both physical and emotional. It highlighted our
ever-present vulnerability. "Will we have enough—enough food, enough
love?" The second temptation had to do with our ever-present fears of
annihilation—anxiety over our children's health, fear of war, fear of disease or of an accident's occurring.*

*The third temptation is also ours, but not His. Forever do we crave
recognition. And yet, ironically, the most famous man in the history of the
world could have cared less about fame in the sense that we think about
it. He cared only about loving just as his Father Who gives us the freedom
to choose him. Who waits patiently on millions of His people for thousands
of years. I wondered if we were God, how long we would wait for "our
human beings." Three weeks, maybe?*

*I was comforted by the thought that while Christ didn't crave fame,
he did want recognition. As the New Testament says,*

"Who for the joy set before him endured the cross, despising the shame."[11]

*The third temptation revealed even further how unlike us He was. We
would have been tempted just to bow down to Satan and "not mean it,"
and would have missed the fact that at the exact moment we deceived
anyone to the slightest degree, we would have become deceitful ourselves.
But Jesus was too pure. The thought of just a tacit bow never occurred
to him, as evidenced by his vehement response. There was only one person
to bow before—The Lord God Almighty.*

*I reflected, too, on Jesus' comments about his self-imposed veiling of
his omniscience. He was right. He depended on the Scriptures as we do.
At the same time he revealed his innate difference to us, he was also one
with us. There in the second temptation, Satan had tried to tempt Jesus
with the Scriptures. If Jesus had immediately used his omniscience, it
could not possibly have been a temptation. The verse in Hebrews again
came to mind,*

"For in that he (Jesus) himself hath suffered being tempted, he is able to
succour them that are tempted."[12]

And now with overwhelming clarity, the Scriptures were revealing how much like us he became. Once again, I saw how much restraint was to characterize his life. By not acting, as Adam and Eve did, but by controlling himself, first at his temptation and later at his crucifixion, it was as if he were putting back in their place all those terrible forces which had been unleashed at the Fall.)

The Rewards of Waiting

All through this interview you have mentioned waiting a lot. Waiting seems to have been a constant theme which permeated all your teaching. For example, you said,

> "Blessed are you when people insult you, persecute you, because of me. Great is your reward in heaven."[13]

The so-called Beatitudes in the Sermon on the Mount all had to do with waiting:

> "Blessed are the meek: for they shall inherit the earth."[14]

One of the great tests of faith is waiting. That's why I emphasized it so. We all have to wait. The question is how to wait. Should we be complaining or waiting in expectation? Freud's thinking is not far removed from mine when he talks about delayed gratification as a sign of maturity. There are rich rewards for waiting. Some of those rewards we even get here on earth just when we need them.

After the temptation, I remembered distinctly my prayer before I journeyed into wilderness on my forty-day fast. As I meditated on my mission, I said, "Father, show me the way. Help me to make sure my way. This has to be for You, Father, for Your glory." Look what He had done! It was so like Him to work all things out for good. He had used the devil himself to show me how important my life was. I was worth all the kings and kingdoms of the world. I could do miracles now if I wished. Finally, through Satan, my Father showed me the tremendous protection that surrounded me because I knew I could have jumped from the Temple at that moment if God had said so. My Father had trained me and I had won the first battle. It encouraged me and prepared me for the next battle I knew was to come eventually. Then, as is so characteristic of Him, He gave me rewards beyond anything I had imagined for winning my battle with Satan. He sent a group of angels to minister to me.

What did you and the angels talk about? I'm assuming you had a conversation.

There was immediate intimacy. The first thing we discussed was my victory over Satan. We talked about how clever he was up to a point. I was awed by how impressed the angels were with him. They spoke of how great he had been in heaven before he fell. At one point, I remarked, "If he was so great, it makes you wonder how he could have done what he did." One of the angels answered, "I suppose it had to happen. He had so much intimacy with all of you and that freedom made him think he was as great as God himself. It was much the same with Adam. God would even forgive Satan if he asked, but, of course, he'll never repent. He's too proud."

I had many questions for those angels about my role, about heaven and about my previous life. But first I asked them if they had permission to answer my questions, "Your Father said you could ask anything you wanted," they said. "He said to tell you all that He has is yours."

So I inquired about my Father and His glory and what I'd been like before. They answered me, "You were just like your Father, and that words can't describe. You were both awesome and comforting—all at the same time. You've never seen anything like it." I asked them if they meant something like the way the prophets Daniel and Ezekiel had described God's glory in their visions. "Exactly," the angels said, "but those are only words, and words don't even come close to describing your Father or you. Heaven is the same way. You can't imagine the joy or the freedom there. All you're working for is worth it. You will bring happiness beyond belief to your followers—to those you and your Father have chosen. There's so much love there, and absolutely no fear." Another angel spoke up, "We constantly see your place at your Father's right hand. It's waiting for you to return. The reception that is planned for you will surpass the party we gave you when your Father sent you to the earth."

I wanted to know if my understanding of the Scriptures was correct. They had already alluded to the Trinity, and I went over my understanding of it with them. I began in the First Chapter of Genesis,

"Let us make man in our image."[15]

Then, in the Psalms, David had prayed to his Lord the Messiah who was already at God's right hand. In Isaiah, God the Father, Himself, called His only begotten son not only

"Wonderful, Counselor, The Prince of Peace,"

but also,

"The Mighty God, The Everlasting Father."[16]

The Father and the Son were so close that the Son was to be called Father also. We are distinct identities and yet have such an incomprehensible oneness that we both have the same name. I didn't understand all of that then, but I went on. Throughout the Scriptures there were continual references to God pouring out His Spirit upon certain people, and promises to do so even more in the future for all believers. The Spirit of the Lord was often referred to in such a way that He began to take an identity of His own.

Then it occurred to me that perhaps the Godhead had another partner —a "silent partner." How like God that would be—to be as great as God the

Father and yet so humble that You would never draw attention to Yourself, even to the point of keeping Your identity almost secret. That meant my Teacher had been not only my Father but also His Holy Spirit, another member of the Godhead, which now one could call the Trinity.

The more I looked at the Scriptures, the more signs there were pointing toward a triune headship. God was the God of "Abraham, Isaac, and Jacob." Joseph, Moses, and David all had three distinct periods in their lives. Joseph was the favored one, the prisoner/slave and finally the prime minister. Moses was the favored one, the rejected farmer and then the elderly statesman. David was the annointed one, the hunted criminal, the great king.

The Scriptures also proclaim, "the heavens declare his handiwork," and when I looked at nature there were "threes" all around me too. Most of the time there were three central parts of my environment—the earth, the sky, and the sun. When I looked at the earth in particular, there were three parts —land, sea, and air. When I looked at the sky, there were only three bodies in the heavens—the sun, moon and stars. I knew that water itself could take three forms. Parenthetically, had I "known" as much about nature then as I do now, I would have seen even more pictures of the Trinity. There are three parts to an atom (proton, neutron, and electron), the basic building block of the universe. I'd worked with trees all my life and I'd thought of the seed, the seedling, and the full grown tree. As I thought of that seed that one couldn't see in the ground, it made me realize how much of nature one can't see at first glance. In the daytime, the moon and stars are usually hidden and in the nighttime, the sun is hidden.

This idea of not being able to see everything struck me again and again. When they were young, Joseph, Moses, and David couldn't see how they would one day be used of God. I thought of Jacob again, of how often he was overlooked. Abraham and Isaac, as the Father and long-awaited son, dominated the historical scene initially. In many ways, they were more likeable and important characters than Jacob. Yet Jacob was the one who fathered the twelve tribes of Israel, the one who ended up with the Holy Name when God changed his name to Israel. Perhaps there was much more in the name that God had chosen for himself than I first realized. God insisted that he was the God of "Abraham, Isaac, and Jacob." There were three main characters and then the rest of the family.

There were three letters in Our name, G-o-d. Embedded deep in the unconscious was a universal rhythm of "threes." When people counted it was "1-2-3" or "A-B-C." The signature appeared everywhere. It seemed to me that the Scriptures and all of nature were telling me that there was an important third person of the Godhead whose work was vital and who was at first glance overlooked. That, I told the angels, was the conclusion I had come to, and I wanted to know if I had it right. "Is the Spirit that is leading me a separate part of the Godhead?" I asked. "You have learned well," they replied. "Nature shouts at you about who God is."

Then I told them, "I still can't believe I actually created the world along with my Father." They nodded and said simply. "You did, Lord." One of them said, "Lord, you used more of your power then than you do now. But you are about to use some of it."

So the son of God had to wait to see all his glory?

Just like you.

What else did you and the angels discuss?

Next we talked about my public ministry which was imminent. I went over what I thought the Scriptures were telling me. Besides performing miracles, particularly healings, I would teach in parables. The Scriptures seemed to teach that one of my intimate disciples would betray me for thirty pieces of silver. I wondered aloud who it was. One of the angels said, "You will know. There are clues." It was later that I realized that he used the word "are" instead of there "will be" clues. It was his way of hinting that the Scriptures were already telling me who would betray me. I asked if it were not true that after I was killed, my disciples would abandon me for a while. The angels agreed. I went over in detail with them my understanding of the crucifixion and they nodded in agreement. I asked them, "Will my Father completely turn His back on me?" They said, "Yes and no. You must work that out."

For forty days in the wilderness, I had gone over my Father's words and what I would teach the people. I told the angels my plan. I was going to make the relationship very personal between me and every man I met. Each person would accept or reject my Father depending upon how he reacted to me. I was His son and I was to be His spokesman. He wanted a personal relationship with them. I was going to make it clear to the people that my Father was paying an enormous price to have a relationship with them, and if they wanted one with Him, they would have to obey His commands as I did. I wasn't going to tone the message down. If they were to live, they would have to do what the Father and I were doing. They would have to give their lives for others. I planned not just to get people to say, "yes," but also to get them involved in a process. I was going to give them my life. Then my people would give their lives to others.

What kind of beings were these angels?

The angels were incredibly genuine and joyful people. After I finished going over my plans, they spontaneously applauded me saying, "We all continue to be amazed at the way the Scriptures have worked in your life."

The angels kept coming back to their awe of the Scriptures. I told them how real the Scriptures were to me, and that I had come to know my Father so well from them that my words were now His words. That's what I intended to tell the people. They approved. One said, "Lord, only you have truly seen the Father in the Scriptures. Think of how you will be able to share that vision with others. People will then be able to see more of your Father. You will be a great teacher. The Spirit has prepared you well. Indeed, you are so much one with Him that your words will be His words, too. And like your Father, one day your words will be written down in the Scriptures and will last forever. After all, you are God Almighty too."

Then I asked them about the end times.

What did you ask them about the end times?

I wondered when the end of time might occur and how long it would be before my Second Coming. They quickly informed me that only the Father knows exactly when. We talked about the specific signs to look for. The angels knew every word of the Scriptures backwards and forwards. We talked for some time about that Last Day, the Day of Judgment. One of the angels said, "Lord, the day is coming when you will lead us back here in judgment and in glory. We will await your command. One day it will all be over. The people who have attempted to destroy you, the people who don't listen to you will never be around you again. But the people, Lord, who love you, oh, will they love you! They will have an unbelievable Savior, and they will know it."

Finally, just before they left, the angels told me they had all been part of the choir that sang to the shepherds on the night I was born. They knew I hadn't heard it, and they wanted me to hear it now. They sang the chorus,

"Glory to God in the highest, and on earth peace, good will toward men."[17]

They sang a cappella, but it sounded like a two hundred-piece orchestra was accompanying them. It was the best music I'd ever heard on earth. I knew then that heaven was going to be beyond our wildest dreams. I'll never forget their last words. In unison they said with deep affection, "We love you, Lord." Then they began ascending into heaven, and as I watched them drift away, I knew what the prophet Elisha must have felt when he watched Elijah ascend into heaven with the angels. One day, I would do the same thing.

After the Angels

After that talk with the angels, I was a different man. Before, I was in the passive role—being baptized, waiting in the wilderness, being challenged and tested by Satan, being fed and ministered to by the angels. Now I was taking over. I was going to let my light shine. Until I assumed the passive role for one last time at the end of my life, I would be the active one.

(After listening to his interpretation of the Scriptures, it occurred to me that as human beings our present knowledge of God is limited by the boundary of Scripture. Having voluntarily become a man, Jesus limited himself, with few exceptions, by that same boundary—and yet look how much more he discovered within the same boundaries. Among his many accomplishments, he was also the most brilliant student who ever lived. I wonder if one day "after it's all over" if he won't pick up these Scriptures

just as he did with his disciples after his resurrection, and say to us, "Let's go through them again; I want to show you some things that you didn't see the first time.")

When did you begin to use this power you were now aware you had?

Not right away. But I knew He would show me when. And He did.

How did He show you?

Of all places, I was at a wedding party where they had run out of wine and my mother asked me to use my power to provide more.

I remember that story of your changing water into wine. Did you believe your Mother's encouragement was a message from God? Or did you feel that perhaps your mother was asking you to use your power apart from God as Satan had?

This wasn't the first time God had used my mother to get a message to me. Mother knew about the recent events, such as my baptism and the temptation. She was well aware that the Scripture had promised me power, and she knew I was waiting to use it. God encouraged her to give me a "motherly" push. When they ran out of wine at the party, the hostess was understandably upset. My mother was sympathetic with her friend's embarrassment. Because of the anxiety associated with her own wedding, Mother always had a particular fondness for and sensitivity to weddings. She especially wished for them to go well. It was almost as though she was making up for what she had missed. When she saw her friend's distress, she said, "I might be able to help you."

She immediately came to me with the story and with some servants. Incredulously, I looked at her and said,

"My time has not yet come."[18]

She didn't reply to me, but simply spoke these words to the servants:

"Do whatever he tells you."[19]

At first, I was caught completely off guard. It was so out of character for my mother, but then I wondered, "Is my Father trying to tell me something?" Immediately, I recalled Moses' first miracle. He had turned the water in the Nile River blood-red in order to get Pharaoh to set the Jewish people free. My first miracle would be to turn water into red wine as proof that I came to set all people free.

I also saw the beauty in what God was doing. Here was the woman who had given me life, who had sacrificed her life and her reputation for me. This beautiful lady who had taught me all my life about God, who had confirmed who I was, and who had encouraged me all along the way in accepting my role, was now being given the honor by God of launching me into the world as the Messiah. Her request was quite different from Satan's. She left it entirely up to me. "Do as he says." Satan had wanted to tell me what to do. He had wanted to control me.

Water into wine is an amazing miracle. But it seems so insignificant in comparison to other miracles such as healing the sick and raising people from the dead. What significance did you see in this first miracle?

My Father had set the scene. His message to me confirmed my mother's. The symbols around me were straight from the Scriptures. Water was the element used in Moses' miracle and John's baptism. When my mother asked me to turn that water into wine, it was just as though my Father were saying to me, "I know what I am asking you to do. The River of Living Water is a river of blood. Look at Moses. The Deliverer has to lead his people across the Red Sea. I even had them name that sea for you, for your blood. I've had it waiting for you all these years. Also, hear what your cousin John is saying. He told them that his baptism with water was not enough. It had to be your baptism with blood. I want the world to know the cost of the baptism, the cost of the new covenant you are negotiating on their behalf.* Go ahead, turn the water to wine. 'The seers' need to see it."

It was both a sermon and a picture of the great party to come. This impression of God's disliking pleasure is far from the truth. C. S. Lewis talked about my Father at heart being almost a hedonist. The writers of the Westminster Catechism understood that fact well when they wrote, "What is the chief end of man? To glorify God and to enjoy Him forever." Enjoy Him! Pleasure will permeate all of heaven. Heaven will be so continually full of surprises, it will be beyond belief.

By that miracle, my Father also was saying that I would make a drastic change in every believer's life. No longer were people to be burdened down by the cumbersome ceremonies of the Law. After my death and resurrection, those who believed in me would be instantaneously changed—as quickly as the water was changed to wine—into righteous priests before the Lord. He would indwell them and they would be His people.

That first miracle must have had quite an effect on you. Now you knew and had experienced that power.

It made me feel as though I were God. Perhaps that's what He intended. Before I told them to fill the containers with water, I remember asking myself again, "All I'm going to do is speak and the water will change to wine?" Then it went through my mind, "But that's the way the Scriptures tell me We created the world. God spoke and out of nothing the world came into existence." If I had done it before, I could do it again. I had known all along that one day I would perform miracles. It's like whenever you do something for the first time, it feels strange, unfamiliar. As usual, however, my Father had prepared me by letting me know in advance what I would do.

I told the servants, "Fill those containers with water and bring them to

---

*Through the sacrifice of His own life, Jesus negotiated a new covenant with God for man. Prior to this, the old covenant between God and man, which the Jews lived under for 1200 years, was basically a contract in which God had said to man, "If you are good and keep my commands, I will bless you." The new covenant takes into account man's basic nature as a rebel and says, "If you will repent and accept Christ's punishment as your own, I will forgive you and then, furthermore, I will give you the ability to walk in my way."

me." While they were gone, I thought about the Temptation and my encounter with Satan. I thought of all the power Satan had. If the "Rebellious One" had that much power, then the True Son would have all the more. When the servants returned with six huge vats, I looked at all that water, and I thought to myself, "It's never going to be the same after this. Crowds will come. And, in the end, my blood will be spilled in vast quantities like this water." I looked at that water again and prayed, "It's my blood to do with what I want, but Father, I give it to you. Accept it as my sacrifice for them. May many come and drink of it. World, I give unto you my blood. Here it is. Now."

Immediately, the water turned to the bright red wine. The partygoers said it was the best wine they had ever had. This kind of dramatic change was what our whole plan was about. The most bitter persecution and oppression the world had ever known would also be the sweetest event in history. Death would bring life. It seems paradoxical to say it, but that miracle increased my faith in what I was doing. It also humbled me.

Miracles

You are aware that today some theologians who claim to be Christians say that your miracles didn't actually happen. They say that people in your day were so primitive that they explained things in magical ways that really weren't accurate.

You must realize that these writers of two thousand years ago were basically educated men who could read and write, and who worked for a living. They were men who, like you, had difficulty believing in miracles. Could these men have consistently misinterpreted these miracles?

Another matter to consider is that God in his sovereignty has arranged trust at the heart of the universe. Can you take the word of these writers, which is really His word, or is His word no good? If you can't begin to try to trust an essentially honest person, then you can't begin to trust God. If that is the case, then you wouldn't be very comfortable in heaven, for heaven will be filled with people trusting one another.

I'll tell you something else. What many modern professors are really saying is that they are better observers than people of Biblical times. They mistake so-called knowledge for wisdom. But really they don't want to trust because they want to exalt themselves over their neighbors as well as over Moses, David, Paul, and you. It always comes back to pride, doesn't it?

My miracles were my calling cards, my personal trademark. That was the way I backed up my word. I was God before I came. I was God when I came here. And I will be God for all the tomorrows.

My Father worked in the same way. Almost every major character or event in the Old Testament is associated with a miracle: Adam and Eve's creation; Isaac's supernatural birth; Joseph's and Daniel's becoming national heroes in a foreign country because God gave them the interpretation of a king's dream; Moses leading two million Jews across the Red Sea that had parted with fifteen hundred-foot walls of water on the right and left. Elijah overwhelmed the false prophets of Baal by setting on fire wood soaked with water, David defeated Goliath by a miracle, and Solomon was given so much more wisdom than any human being ever before that people came from all over the world to see him. If you'll look in the mirror, or look at your child, you'll see another miracle. Any perceptive anatomist or microbiologist will marvel at the complexity of the human body—a modern miracle, and an ancient one, too. My Father's calling cards have always been miracles. That's how He convinced the people that He was their God.

One wonders how such brilliant people who deny your miracles can be so mistaken.

Look at Lucifer. He was more brilliant than any of the angels. Brilliance doesn't rule out pride. Usually the two go hand in hand. Many modern day teachers don't want me to have power. They don't want me to have something that they don't have. They don't want me to be God because they're not. It's an old story.

I know there have been scattered miracles performed in recent years and Christians continue to report spectacular answers to prayers. But it has been many years since five thousand people have been fed with a few loaves and one fish and it has been even longer since something so spectacular as the parting of the Red Sea. Why don't your people perform "major miracles" and record them in new Scriptures?

The greatest miracle of all is the fact that you have been blessed with God Himself in you and that you have His very words to you anytime you want them. That's more than many other people in history have had. Once someone learns how to use the Bible, he or she will find out that it's a true miracle. You will never exhaust the potential to be amazed with the power of the Scriptures. Believe me, my Father, the Holy Spirit, and I are still performing miracles. Look around!

Cleaning Out the Temple

Shortly after that miracle at the wedding in Cana, you went to Jerusalem for Passover. You began to testify to your Messianic identity not only with your miracles, but also with other actions. You surprised everyone with your grand entrance at the Temple when you introduced yourself to the money-changers, the first of two such introductions you made to them.

For eighteen years I had gone to Jerusalem for Passover and I had watched the corruption in the Temple get progressively worse, particularly as the money-changers became more prominent. Jews came from all over the known world to celebrate Passover. Among the Jews were Gentile proselytes—converts to Judaism as a result of the dispersion of the Jews to many nations. They came from their pagan lands and were joined by their fellow Jews from all over Israel to meet their Holy God in Jerusalem in His house as He had commanded.

What did they find in the Temple? Money-changers and merchants allegedly there to serve the people, but in reality, they were in business to sell the pilgrims animals, which the people couldn't bring long distances with them for sacrifice, and to exchange foreign money for Jewish coins which alone were required for Temple dues. They were victimizing the travelers. Here in my Father's holy Temple, people who had come hundreds of miles to worship were being forced to haggle over goods and were being cheated out of money. They were manipulated into buying merchandise in God's name by these merchants and money-changers who, you can be sure, had the blessing of the Pharisees who received a "kick-back" and derived a goodly portion of their income from these men. Worst of all, the money-changers discriminated against the Gentile converts to keep them out of the Temple. The moneychangers, with the help of the Pharisees, had desecrated this holy week as they slowly took over. This was in my Father's own house!

Each time I visited the Temple prior to my public announcement, my anger at the money changers and merchants grew. "Somebody ought to throw them out, animals and all," I thought.

The year before my baptism the moneychangers had been particularly corrupt and repulsed me even more than usual. For weeks afterward, I kept having the recurring fantasy of walking in and cleaning out the Temple. Then, one day as I was reading the Scriptures, I saw something else from that familiar Messianic psalm, the 69th, which had often comforted me as a young boy facing ridicule,

"Zeal for thy house has consumed me."[20]

Was my Father telling me that one day I would be the one to clean out the Temple? How like Him it would be to confirm my intuition and put my "instructions" in that particular psalm—the one that described the degradation of my mother and earthly father by some people I had wanted to throw out of town when I was ten years old. Then, all I could do was take the abuse. Now, as I watched my heavenly Father being degraded, I wondered if He were telling me I could defend His honor just as I had wanted to defend that of my parents before?

I knew that if I took action against the moneychangers, many people, particularly the Pharisees, weren't going to like it. More and more I was coming to understand why the Scriptures said what they did about my death —why the authorities were going to be the ones ultimately to kill me. They were not doing their jobs; I would do it for them, and they would hate me for it.

I had also often wondered how I would make my announcement to the world as to exactly who I was. I searched the Scriptures for clues. The 24th Psalm said that Jerusalem was to open her gates for the King. That was where my Father's house was, and where the Messiah's throne was. I had already made two journeys there from Nazareth with great revelations occurring each time. The first was when, at eight days of age, I was circumcised in the Temple at Jerusalem and proclaimed to be the Messiah by the two prophets, Anna and Simeon. The second was at age twelve when I discovered who I was at Jerusalem during Passover. I was the Passover Lamb. Would it be proper for Israel's long-awaited Messiah to make his announcement at any place other than Jerusalem or at any time other than Passover?

Finally, I saw the plan. I was coming in my Father's name to His house in judgment. That was how I was going to make my announcement. Just as Samson had cleared out a temple of pagans, I, too, would do so. After all, I was paying the same price that Samson had paid to do it.*

When I came to my first Passover after publicly being declared the Messiah by John, I once again saw this beautiful majestic Temple built for the glory of my Father being turned into a marketplace. I could not go into the Temple without being furious, and now I knew what my Father was saying to me: "Your feelings are My feelings. It is My house. Go, throw them out —in My name." So I did.

When I got to the Temple I saw the same corruption. I saw merchants selling cattle, sheep, and doves for sacrifices. I saw the moneychangers, and I went to work. First, I made a whip out of rope and then I struck quickly. I lashed at the moneychanger to drive him from behind his table, scattering his precious money everywhere and sending it clanging across the courtyard. I had no favorites. One by one I went to every table as rapidly as I could. A few of the men, whose initial impression was that a mad man was loose in the Temple courtyard, thought they could stop me. When they saw me using a whip with one hand and turning over an eighteen-foot long, three hundred pound table with another, they suddenly realized they couldn't. Samson was loose in the Temple!

Next the merchants selling animals for sacrifices felt the sting of my whip as I overturned their benches and began cutting loose their sheep and oxen, separating the merchants as I drove them out, "Get these things out of here. Don't you turn my Father's house into a market." The sheep and oxen I had freed noisily made their escape as the doves madly flapped their wings amidst the chaos. Now all of these animals were loose in the great courtyard of the Temple. Some moneychangers scurried out. Others wanted to stay and protect their property. Some merchants who were trying to get out, bumping and pushing, with their cages of doves converged and caused a chaotic roadblock. There I was, coming down the great courtyard of the Gentiles from one table to another right behind them, lashing away. Fear was in their eyes. This was Judgment Day!

---

*To rid a pagan temple of the enemies of God, Samson gave his life and pulled down the pillars of the temple destroying himself and all within the crowded temple.

All was confusion when I had finished. I was so angry! I had run five hundred or more moneychangers and merchants along with all the animals out of the Temple.

Gentle Jesus, meek and mild. That's not all there is to you.

Then the Pharisees arrived. Some of them had been inside the Temple. But most had been in the hallways of the porches just outside the courtyard when they heard the commotion and looked around to see people and animals flying out of the courtyard. The Pharisees came running to me, demanding to know on whose authority I had just done this, and demanding that I show them a miracle at that moment to back up my deed. I told them "All right, I will perform a miracle for you. Destroy this temple and in three days I will raise it up."

You totally confused them, almost intentionally, it seems.

He who wanted to hear could hear what I was saying. I was telling them, "Stay around, for you will see a great miracle—the greatest—which gives me this authority. When you kill me, I will come back to life after I'm in the grave three days." The Pharisees missed the announcement I made to them. I had walked in the Temple, changed things around, told them it was my Father's house, and they, as T. S. Eliot once said, had the experience and missed the meaning.

All they could do was to demand a miracle immediately. If they had just given me a chance they would have seen miracles. I understood that if a man was claiming to be the Messiah, he had better be able to back it up. Already I had given them a hint as to who I was when I performed my first miracle at the wedding in Cana. News spread quickly in the small country, particularly around Passover, but these Pharisees were not going to hear of it.

During that time in Jerusalem, I also performed several more miracles, but I saw that the Pharisees were not going to respond. I also understood that people needed much more preparation if any of them were going to hear me; so I picked up the message of John the Baptist, and, with several disciples, began baptizing people in the Jordan River. For almost the entire first year after my announcement, all I did was baptize people. As I had told my mother, the fullness of time for my ministry had not yet come. I had to do all I could to prepare the people's hearts to hear my real message. The work of repentance, of humility, still had to be done to open their minds.

And crowds came, bigger than John's. The Pharisees became more and more agitated, to the point that they tried to incite envy in John, telling him my crowds were larger than his. Unflinchingly, John told them he must decrease and that I must increase. The viciousness of the Pharisees was more and more apparent. I got the message. I had done my work in Jerusalem as completely as I could, and now I had to take my announcement to the rest of the people. If I stayed around Jerusalem, the handwriting was on the wall as the Scriptures made clear.

I would return to Jerusalem on my last tour and make one final major offer on Palm Sunday. Before I did that, however, I would spend the next year and a half in northern Israel, in Galilee, with only a few brief trips to Jerusalem for religious holidays. I went to Galilee to gather a following who would stand by me on what you know as Palm Sunday. And I succeeded.

On the Road Again

You had an interesting encounter on your trip back to Galilee from Jerusalem.

About midway on my journey I became fatigued and stopped at Jacob's Well which was near the land Jacob had given to his son, Joseph. In my day the area was part of Samaria. To put it mildly, Samaritans and Jews were enemies. Jews would have nothing to do with their "unclean" neighbors. The well was famous for its great depth, which brought forth wonderfully cool water. As I sat there resting, a Samaritan woman came to draw water. She had come alone in the hot part of the day—obviously at a different time from the other women who came in the morning or evening when it was cooler. She was most likely an outcast.

I asked her for a drink. Indignantly, she informed me that I was a Jew and she wanted to know how I could dare ask her for water. When she made that comment, I was sure she was an outcast because she had tried to make me feel like one. I told her,

> "If you knew the gift of God, and who it is that asks you for a drink, you would have asked him and he would have given you living water."[21]

My Father led me to this metaphor. I was thirsty, at Jacob's great well, and water had been at the center of my life for the last eight months, as daily I had watched hundreds be baptized.

The woman then asked me where she could get this living water and, in the same breath, asked me if I thought I was greater than their father, Jacob, who gave them this very well and drank out of it himself.

I told her,

> "Everyone who drinks this water will be thirsty again, but whoever drinks the water I give him will never thirst."[22]

I even added that a person who drinks this water will live forever. Very sarcastically, this feisty woman retorted once again,

> "Sir, give me this water so that I won't get thirsty and have to keep coming here to draw water."[23]

I told her that if she really wanted this water, to go get her husband and come back. Abruptly, she told me she had no husband. I told her I knew that was true. My Father had given me the information I needed. I knew that she had had five husbands and that she was not married to the man with whom she presently lived.

With that, she realized there was something different about me and the expression on her face changed dramatically. But this revelation didn't slow her down entirely. She said,

> "I can see you are a prophet. Our fathers worshiped on this mountain, but you Jews claim that the place where we must worship is in Jerusalem."[24]

She felt discriminated against. I told her the Jews had understood things correctly in the past, but a time was coming and indeed was here, when the true believers would worship God wherever they wanted. Only they would worship Him in spirit and in truth, for God was a spirit.

At this point, she looked completely puzzled, but fell back on the comfort of her limited knowledge and informed me that one day the Messiah was coming and he would explain everything. I looked straight into her eyes, and slowly said to her,

> "I who speak to you am he."[25]

For once, she had absolutely nothing to say.

My disciples arrived at just that moment. They all had that "What's he up to now?" look on their faces. During our years together, that became a look I saw many times. Once again, my disciples were puzzled by my behavior. All wanted to rebuke me or at least to ask why I was talking to this outcast, but they didn't dare. By now they were beginning to learn not always to trust their natural responses, which pleased me no end.

The Samaritan woman, leaving behind her water jar, immediately hurried to tell her friends who I was, and very soon there was a crowd of people from the nearby town approaching us. My disciples urged me to eat something since they knew it had been a while since my last meal. I told them I had food to eat that they knew nothing about. My food was to do the will of Him who sent me to finish His work. By now I wasn't hungry, because I was so thrilled at this lost woman's response and the response of her friends.

Whenever someone made a heartfelt commitment, I could see into the future and knew better than anyone else what it would mean to him, and I knew the pain and suffering from which he had just been delivered. At that moment, another person had been freed to be one day the most glorious creature imaginable. He became a person who would experience eternally a love, my Father's love, the depth of which he had no conception. He had been in a life or death struggle and I—Life—had won another soul. Death—Satan—had lost another battle. Those moments of victory we will talk about forever.

Isn't that when you made the great statement about evangelizing?

> "Open your eyes, and look at the fields! They are ripe for harvest.[26]

I harvested that day and the next, too. That determined woman brought everyone she knew, and many of them became my followers. The Samaritans were starved for the truth. Their response came on the heels of a planned attack by the Pharisees—the people above all who should have received me. Yet here were these people whom the Pharisees would have considered "spiritually ignorant," pleading with me to stay longer. They proclaimed for all their neighbors to hear that I was the Savior of the world. I was so moved by their warmth that one day when the opportunity arose, I made them the central characters in a parable and honored them forever. My disciples and I learned an important lesson during that unexpected two-day stop: because of me, many who are apparent enemies will become friends.

What happened next on your journey?

After I left Samaria, one of the first towns I visited in Galilee was the town where I'd performed my first miracle, Cana. A Roman government official from the nearby town of Capernaum heard I was there, sought me out, and pleaded with me to come home with him immediately to heal his son whom he had left near death. This man was so desperate he didn't even acknowledge me. He just begged me to come home with him. I looked at this desperate Roman and, although my heart went out to him, I wanted to teach him that there was more to my Father and myself than just our power. So I asked him,

"Won't any of you believe in me unless I do more and more miracles?"[27]

He was so distraught that he could hardly comprehend what I was saying. He pleaded with me again,

"Sir, please come home with me before my child dies."

I told him, "Go back home. Your son is healed!"[28] Suddenly, the man had a startled look on his face. He started to ask me to come home with him again, but thought better of that and eventually said only to me, "Thank you, sir". He walked off believing me. One thing the Romans had learned was to respect authority.

When he was about halfway home, his servants met him and said that his son was healed. The official asked them what time the boy had begun to improve and they told him at one o'clock the afternoon before—the exact moment I had commanded the healing. The Roman official had received the message, and he and his entire household came to understand that I was the Messiah. Then they gave me the acknowledgement I had wanted: they trusted me.

The heart of salvation is saying to you, "I trust you."

Trust is the ultimate compliment. Everyone who has ever lived or will ever live must say to me and my Father one way or another, "I trust you" or, "I don't trust you." There's no room in our family for distrust. That's why heaven is going to be so unbelievable. Just as every moment of life on this earth is filled with anxiety or potential anxiety—death is only a heartbeat away—every moment in heaven will be one of absolute, unwavering trust. Trust will replace all fear.

Trust is the one attribute you must have to get into heaven. It's a particular kind of trust; a test, if you will. One must say to God either, "I trust You, God," or "I trust myself, my own character, my own judgment." There's not room ultimately for completely trusting both.

All of life is designed to show us our need to trust. Trust or faith is woven into every moment of our beings. We are surrounded by organizations, business, governments, and leaders who constantly ask us to trust them. Every map you ever read asks for trust. Every time you go to bed, you trust the sun will be there in the morning. The very nature of history demands trust. You can't see a hundred years back or even back to your own birth. You have to depend upon someone else or someone else's book to tell you. God put history at the heart of the universe to testify to His Book. The intellectual who is always saying, "None of this faith business for me, I only believe what I can see," doesn't live in the real world. He or she is just like the Pharisees who didn't trust me and didn't live in reality either. How hard it is for one to give up his old faith in himself. How hard it is to trust that Someone else's mind is better than yours. That's the danger of power; it freezes your mind. Be careful about mind sets.

Another one of your bold moves shortly after you began your public ministry in Galilee was to go to your hometown on a Sabbath and proclaim the fulfillment of the Messianic prophecy recorded in Isaiah.

On the Sabbath, someone in the synagogue was to read from the Scriptures. As I was visiting my old synagogue on this particular day, they passed to me the scrolls to read, which "coincidentally" happened to be the Book of Isaiah where more is written about the Messiah than in any other Old Testament book. I marveled at the way my Father would lay these things in my lap.

Before I read the Scriptures, the rabbi introduced me and the people spontaneously applauded—something they were allowed to do in the synagogue in my day. They had heard of me—my preaching and some of my miracles. Although many were skeptical because they had known me and my family all my life and I had "been just a carpenter," still I was one of theirs and a celebrity. After the applause died down, I read the Messianic prophecy in Isaiah.

> "The spirit of the Lord is on me, because he has anointed me to preach good news to the poor. He has sent me to proclaim freedom for the prisoners and recovery of sight for the blind, to release the oppressed, to proclaim the year of the Lord's favor."[29]

When I finished, I rolled up the scroll, paused for a minute as I looked at everyone in the room, and then I said,

> "Today this Scripture is fulfilled in your hearing."[30]

The people were stunned. Their silence was broken as they reacted violently. "But we know you—you are just a carpenter—you are Joseph's son. You're a heretic!" I informed them that I knew they would react that way. Both Elijah and Elisha had been rejected by their own people but believed in by foreigners. This only made the congregation more angry.

Suddenly they shoved me out of the synagogue and immediately a mob formed. They began to push me farther down the road leading out of town, shouting at me, until we came to the cliff outside the city and I saw that they intended to cast me to my death. I was just a few steps away from the edge, but up to this point, I had not resisted. For a moment, I wondered if this would be where I would jump and the angels would protect me. When I got one step away from disaster, I simply walked right through them as though they were not there. Their strength was nothing compared to mine. When I got to the other side of the crowd, I walked away from them.

It was at that moment I realized what I had done. God had rescued me again in a surprising way. He had not planned a rescue for me after I would have been pushed over the cliff. That would have put me in a completely passive role. Instead He had done something so typical of my Father. He had let me—forced me—to use His power again, which was now my power. He wanted me to know that I had power over everyone on this earth, including an unruly mob, so that when that mob came for me at the end of my earthly life, it would be apparent to everyone that I was giving my life away. Nobody would take it from me.

(I thought about Jesus' entrance into the world as its Messiah. He had done it in such a subtle way that at first glance one could miss the boldness that surrounded his claim. Even the Scriptures told the story in parts. One has to read all four gospels to get the whole story, as if God were trying to say, "If you want to get the full impact My son made, you're going to have to work."

Here is how Jesus made his entry. First, he came on the wings of an introduction by a dynamic, frightening prophet, to this point the greatest and most awaited prophet in Israel's history. Then he began performing extraordinary miracles in Jerusalem at Passover. This was only after, however, he had had his "coming-out party" at a most fitting location— a wedding where he performed the first of thousands of miracles. It was as if Jesus were saying to his people, "I am wed to my followers for life." Then, like a ruler taking charge, he immediately cleansed his Father's Temple—the only territory, the only thing close to a material possession he ever identified himself with, and even then it was his Father's house, not his.

A short time later, Jesus fearlessly made his startling proclamation in his hometown of Nazareth. He was saying to the people he grew up with, "Whether you love me or not, I am a loyal son, and you who knew me first will have one of the first chances to see who I really am." Surely Jesus came in like a king. But it was as his kind of king and not the world's kind. He remained humble, full of grace and truth.)

A New Base and a New Team

After that experience in Nazareth, it's obvious you wouldn't want to spend much time there.

I had to find another place to establish my base. I headed for Capernaum. It was not far away, a beautiful town on the edge of the Sea of Galilee. It was an ideal location for travel to other towns either by land or by water, and I planned to travel. Besides, there was a certain Roman official in Capernaum who had a boat there, and I felt sure it would be at my disposal any time I wanted it.

The more logical reason for choosing Capernaum, for me, was that Isaiah had prophesied that I would live in that area. I had my instructions even as to where my base was to be.* After making that decision, I began to determine more definitely who the men were who would be charged with carrying on the message after I would be gone.

I'm glad you mentioned your disciples. I was interested in the way you selected them.

Andrew and John had originally been disciples of John the Baptist. They had heard John, himself, proclaim one day as I walked by, "There is the Lamb of God." Immediately, these two future disciples followed me to the place where I was staying. Later that day, Andrew introduced me to his brother Peter, and told him that I was the Messiah. We talked late into the night. Some time later when I was in Galilee, I was walking by the seashore early one morning when I saw Peter and Andrew out on a boat not far from the shore where they had been fishing all night. Until that time, Peter's catch had been very poor; so I shouted at him to cast his nets on the other side of the boat. He did so, and immediately his nets nearly broke from the huge catch he made. He was overwhelmed. There in the boat, he fell to his knees and loudly proclaimed to everyone around that I was the Messiah. Then I told Peter and Andrew to come with me and I would make them fishers of men. They did so.

And you did!

Peter was a leader. He responded quickly and wholeheartedly. He was a large red-headed fisherman who was afraid of nothing except for the time on the last day of my life when he denied even knowing me. Even then, when I was taken prisoner he followed me all the way to the Roman headquarters.

Two of my other disciples, James and John, were very responsive, also. These two brothers, like Andrew and Peter, were fishermen. They were also my first cousins, sons of my mother's sister Salome. I had known them for a

---

*The land of Zebelun and the land of Naphtali (on either side of Capernaum). . . . he will honor Galilee of the Gentiles, along the Jordan River—"The people walking in darkness have seen a great light."[31]

number of years as we would see each other on holidays or on an occasional visit. We had the same grandparents who had reared our mothers, and I knew what kinds of hearts they had.

Shortly after Peter's big catch he came to shore and told James and John what had happened. That's when I walked up to them and said, "Come follow me," and they did. These three—Peter, James and John—were natural leaders of the group. They were very aggressive. Because they were such effective leaders, I spent more time with them than with the others.*

I nicknamed James and John the "Sons of Thunder" because of their temperaments. One day John "caught" a man casting out demons in my name and rebuked him because the man wasn't a part of our group. I had to tell John that

"he who is not against you is for you."[32]

Later toward the end of my public ministry when I was making my final trip to Jerusalem, we needed a place to stay in a nearby Samaritan village. I sent several disciples ahead to make arrangements. Before we got to the village, these same disciples came back and told us that the Samaritans refused to give us any accommodations because we were from Judea. Immediately James and John asked me to call down fire on that village and I had to rebuke them.

Another time, the mother of these two, my Aunt Salome, asked me if her two sons could sit on my right and left when I attained my kingdom. James and John were nearby, with the other disciples not very far away, and their eyes indicated that they, too, would like those seating arrangements. I told them that they didn't know what they were asking, that the honor was up to my Father. I also asked them if they thought that they could drink from the same bitter cup as I. Did they want the same type of baptism that I was going to have?

You were implying suffering and death.

That's the cost of being close to me. They said they did indeed want the same baptism I would have. They still didn't know what they were asking, but I gave them what they wanted. As it turned out, they both suffered tremendous persecution. James was beheaded for being a follower of mine. John was persecuted throughout his life and eventually exiled to the Isle of Patmos where he ended up writing the book of Revelation. How John learned to channel all his assertiveness into an aggressive love! He was the one leaning on my shoulder at the Last Supper. He was the disciple who made sure my mother was comforted at my crucifixion. He stood by her side throughout the entire ordeal. He and Peter were the ones who, as soon as they were allowed, arose early in the morning to be the first disciples to visit my grave.

Later John wrote four great books on love included in the New Testament. For sixty-five years after my death, he was known to the early church

---

*Often Jesus took just these three disciples with him at special times. They went with him to observe his Transfiguration. And on the night before his death, these were the three he asked to stay with him and comfort him while he prayed in the Garden of Gethsemene.

as the Apostle of Love. The story has been told often that even at age ninety he was a revered old saint. When asked to speak, John would still be telling them to put their differences aside and would say, "Little children, love one another." He never quit talking about love.

After John came Nathaniel and Philip. Actually, they were chosen before James. They were from the same town as the two pairs of brothers—Peter and Andrew, James and John—and Nathaniel was a lot like Peter. He had been standing beneath a fig tree when Philip, who had just found out about me, came up to him and said excitedly,

> "We have found the Messiah!—the very person Moses and the prophets told about! His name is Jesus, the son of Joseph from Nazareth."[33]

Nathaniel's immediate response was,

> "Nazareth! Can anything good come from there?"[*][34]

Philip finally talked Nathaniel into meeting me and they walked several miles to find me. As they approached, I said to Nathaniel, "Here comes an honest man, a true son of Israel." At least Nathaniel had been direct about what he really thought about people from Nazareth. Immediately he asked me how I knew what he was like. I told him I even knew where he had been standing two hours ago—by a fig tree—when Philip had found him. Nathaniel blurted out,

> "You are the Son of God,"[35]

just as quickly as he had doubted me initially.

Then you told him that he would see greater things than just a little prophecy— that he would see angels visiting you back and forth from heaven. How did you know all these things? You've told me you didn't constantly use supernatural vision.

Usually when these incidents occurred, one of two or three things happened. Sometimes it just came to my mind the way most of our thoughts come to us. That's what happened with Nathaniel. Read the Old Testament and you'll see that's not so strange. Many times a prophet just "knew" something. God uses dreams, angels, and thoughts. They're all outside our control to some degree.

Other times, as when Peter was fishing, I would privately ask God to do something for me, such as put fish in that particular place. Then I would just tell others it had been done. "There are fish over there."

Another disciple that comes to mind was "Doubting Thomas". Was he as much of an "unbeliever" as tradition has it?

Every group needs a man like Thomas who, in many ways, was the opposite of Peter. Thomas was a thinker who usually asked questions before he acted. He

---

*Jesus' hometown was considered to be both rural and pagan as it was just off the great caravan-route to the East.

had to know why he was doing something. However, when enough of his questions were answered, he was a man of incredible devotion and courage. On one occasion toward the end of our three and a half years together, I had received a message that our friend, Lazarus, was very ill. He was the brother of two of our other good friends, Mary and Martha, at whose house we had stayed several times. When I received the news I said that we would go to see Lazarus. Lazarus and his sisters lived near Jerusalem, but the last time we had been in Jerusalem the Pharisees had threatened to kill me. All the disciples except Thomas warned me about that and didn't want us to go. I had constantly tried to tell my men I was put here to die, but they couldn't hear me. Thomas had heard my talking about my death and all he said, when I wanted to visit Lazarus, was

"Let's go too (to Jerusalem) and die with him.[36]

Of all my disciples, Thomas came the closest to understanding my mission. He was a thinker but his mind just wasn't comprehensive enough to conceive of the resurrection. If he didn't understand something he would speak up. At the Last Supper when he heard me say I was going away to prepare a mansion for them and that they would know where I was going and how to get there, Thomas was confused. He asked me how they could know the way because they had no idea where I was going.

And that's when you made the great statement,

"I am the way, the truth, and the life. No man cometh unto the Father, but by me."[37]

Yes. After my death, Thomas was confused. Being devoted to me, he was crushed and simply withdrew from everyone. He was much unlike Peter who had to be around others. After my death, I appeared to a few of my disciples individually. The first time I appeared to them as a group, Thomas was off by himself grieving, and missed me. Later the other disciples told him what had happened, but Thomas said that unless he saw the wounds on my hands and touched them, he wouldn't believe it.

Eight days later they were barricaded in another locked room, still afraid of the Jews, and at this time Thomas was with them when suddenly I appeared. I had seen all the others previously except for Thomas; so the first thing I did was look at Thomas and hold out my hands to him.

"Put your fingers on my hands, and touch my side; now believe."

Thomas fell to his knees and in utter amazement cried out,

"My Lord and my God!"[38]

That's as great a confession of faith as you'll find in all the New Testament.

Thomas had a capacity for unbelievable devotion, but he was very careful with it. He wasn't going to give his loyalty cheaply. That was one of the reasons I chose him. For years to come I wanted the world to look at my disciples and realize that these men were not blind followers. They weren't a group of people who had no identities like the followers of a cult. They were rugged men, who had difficulty bowing to any man or to God. They asked piercing questions. My claim to Messiahship was strong enough to withstand the scrutiny of a "doubting Thomas."

Another one of your men, Matthew, responded to your simple, bold offer, "Come with me." That was a very daring invitation, "Drop what your doing. Risk everything. Follow me."

Matthew was a tax collector. He was a sneak and a thief, a part of the most hated group of the Jewish society that I grew up in. A tax collector bought his office, and since Judea was a Roman province, he was responsible to Rome for a certain amount of money each year. Anything over that amount was his. You can imagine how corrupt and manipulative and what thieves the tax collectors were. Every one of them was wealthy. Furthermore, as traitors, as Jews working for Rome, they were even more hated by their fellow Jews.

One day I was walking by the booth of a tax collector named Levi, a name I later changed to Matthew. He was sitting in his booth with his fancy robes and all his rings, looking smug and in control. But I knew he was miserable —he had to be. He was created to give and receive love and respect from others and himself, and he had neither. I wanted as one of my disciples somebody who would qualify as "the last person you would expect" so that he would give everyone else hope. No one is ever so far away from me that he can't reach my hand. I was looking for a man like this, and as I passed by Matthew with the usual crowd of people following me, I suddenly turned and walked toward him. I stopped directly in front of him and with the crowd behind me, I said, "Levi, follow me."

"Risk it all."

Initially, to show me he was not intimidated, Matthew had remained seated. After my offer, his smugness evaporated. He couldn't believe that I would even talk to him, much less know his name and offer a personal invitation. There was a look of shock on his face but it was a shock of hope, and I saw him weighing the offer. He was getting one chance at a new life. He had to give up so much; at first, far more than any of the other disciples.

For Matthew to come with me, it meant no turning back. Peter, Andrew, James, John, and most of the others had a trade to go back to. They could always return to fishing. Once Matthew gave up his office, that was it. He would have no career, no security. If he were mistaken about me, he would be unable to return to his friends because he would no longer be able to keep up with them socially, and by then they would all think that he was crazy. To find a place in society when you were a former tax collector was extremely difficult. The decision which I was asking him to make quickly meant giving up everything, all his wealth, all his comforts. I was asking him to turn his back completely on a glamorous life-style to follow "a religious fanatic" roaming around the countryside with people he didn't know, and, at first glance, didn't care to know. They were "unattractive" people who had no gold rings, no fine robes, and no beautiful homes.

Was Matthew going to risk all of this because of me—an unknown man, physically rather plain, and yet who knew him and who asked him personally to be his follower? Should he give up everything because of this man whom he had heard was the Messiah, whom he had heard did the things a Messiah would do, and who, before Matthew's own eyes, appealed to him now with his boldness? This was a tactic that Matthew admired. He himself had often deliberately shocked people in order to get what he wanted. Frequently, Matthew would quote an astronomical figure as a shock tactic to a person who owed taxes. Then when he lowered the amount to a price he knew that person could, with great sacrifice at least, pay, the person in a way would be relieved and almost glad to pay.

As I looked in Matthew's eyes, I could see that he wanted to go but couldn't quite make the move. I began to walk away. After I'd gone perhaps twenty feet, suddenly there was a loud screech as he pushed his chair back from the table. Then I heard the sound of feet running after me. He had done it! Matthew became a beautiful man—a choice disciple. He was a man who once would have cheated a widow out of her last coin. But now, he repaid doubly all the people he had wronged and, over time, became a generous, loving man. That's what conversion is all about. Everytime I looked at him, he was grateful. He never got over my choosing him. And I didn't want him to. He was a constant reminder to me of why I was dying.

Matthew obviously was very special to you. Would that be any reason his book is the first book in the New Testament? Would you and your Father honor someone in that way?

My Father never forgot what Matthew gave up for me. And He looks for ways to honor His people. You cannot imagine all the honors He has in store for His people. Most of our time in heaven will be spent in honoring one another and enjoying it.

Why did you change Matthew's name?

Levi was a despicable name to everyone who knew him. I changed his name to Matthew, which means "the gift of God." And, believe me, Matthew became a gift to the whole world. What esteem Matthew has been held in for centuries. His name has been repeated billions of times. Thousands of people have been named for him and he has been quoted by millions of people for years. Whenever the gospel writers are referred to, it's always Matthew first. "Matthew, Mark, Luke, and John." He's a perfect picture of "the last shall be first." He's the first picture in the New Testament of me. The hated man who was nothing is now "everything." And not coincidentally, of the four gospels, Matthew is the one book that emphasizes most my royalty, my claim to the throne of Israel, and my claim to being the Messiah.*

---

*The Gospel of Matthew primarily emphasizes Christ the King. In it, his genealogy is traced from David. Originally this gospel was written primarily to the Jews. Mark emphasizes Christ the Servant; it is a very straightforward book written primarily to the Roman world. Luke emphasizes Christ the Man, and John emphasizes the deity of Christ.

There's another message in why Matthew's book is first. He's the kind of person I'm after and the only kind, really. He was so far away from me and yet he ended up so close. The whole world is full of Levis. And if one Levi can be saved, so can many more. To this day he offers hope to all mankind.

Matthew knew that himself. He never forgot where he came from and he insisted that we don't, either. In the tenth chapter of Matthew when he lists all my disciples, he refers to himself as Matthew, the tax collector or publican. Like all my followers, the more Matthew realized what my Father and I did for him, the more humble he became.

Matthew was an example to the rest of my disciples of the radical change that could take place in a man—a change I wanted to make in every one of them. When I picked my men, I constantly tried to create a sense of daring in them. Sometimes faith is a better word than daring. But I wanted to create enough faith and daring within them to make them the kind of men I needed. They were going to need that faith when I wasn't around.

Finally, Matthew did another thing for the rest of the disciples. He exposed them to an entirely different segment of society, one I wanted them to see. If they were going to take my message to the whole world, they had to get their feet dirty. It was to be only their feet, as I made plain later.

Matthew hadn't arrived at his station in life without being slightly on the aggressive side. Soon after coming with me, he turned his ambition to my use. He gave a party for all of his fellow tax collectors. You should have been there. There were well-dressed, cultured, but corrupt people, who crowded in with a group of mostly blue-collar fishermen along with some radicals like Judas and Simon who were advocating the overthrow of Rome. I was invited. The tax collectors had heard about me, and were skeptical, to say the least! You should have heard some of the conversations at the party. Of course, the Pharisees couldn't believe that I would go into such homes, even taking my disciples with me. Those religious leaders were quite vocal in their disapproval.

That's when you told them, "It's the sick who need a doctor."

As I looked around the room that night and talked with the people there, I saw on the faces of several of them the same look that I had seen on Matthew's face when I first spoke to him. There was gratitude, humility, and a hidden desperation crying out silently for love. Matthew was our first great evangelist. Several of his friends became my followers.

Heaven is going to be very interesting. You won't believe the circumstances a lot of people will have come from. We'll probably spend the first million years just listening to their stories.

I made sure my disciples experienced the challenge of faith just as Matthew had. When we began traveling as a group in my second public year of ministry I wanted to teach them to trust God for everything. We set out with no money, no food, no water, no roof over our heads—and, of course, in the beginning, with very little faith on the part of the disciples. They had the desire to trust, but not the ability. That's why I spent all the night before I chose the final twelve disciples praying that God would give me the right men and that He would supply the courage they lacked so that they could truly follow me. And He did. But it took some time.

The Final Twelve

You picked twelve men to be your disciples and by the world's standards they were just average, every-day folk, mostly blue-collar types; not particularly intellectual, and seemingly not overly religious.

That is the exception of Judas Iscariot who was a "religious" zealot.

Why did you pick that type of man?

They are the best ones—the humble. They were the same kind of men my Father always picked, the same kind of man He picked to be the Messiah. As I told you, Abraham, Moses, and David were just ordinary people. But don't confuse humility with lack of wealth and intelligence. Remember, the man who after my death became my leading apostle was Paul, who was both wealthy and brilliant. Once I broke through to him, what a heart he had!

For my disciples, I wanted men who were basically humble and who, despite their faults, would be teachable men, or at least want to be. Instead of religious professionals who would be so competitive with me that they couldn't learn, I wanted teachable men. In the end, that was Judas' problem. I also wanted followers who could understand what normal people have to go through such as worrying about money and struggling for self-esteem. I wanted men with no particular prestigious position. Most of them were laborers like me. And I wanted men around me who would respond, who would be grateful.

Another reason I picked these twelve is that they were real. Most of them were fishermen. They were rugged men who worked with their hands as I did. Before I learned that I was God, I appreciated plain people; false, overly-pious, folk never appealed to me. Such falsely pious people give God a bad name because they hide so much of the rest of themselves. They misused God's name often.

One thing that I didn't like at first about Judas was that he was a little too pious. That's why I picked the unpretentious men I did. They were the best examples around of who my Father was and eventually of the way He wanted people to be.

You picked two pairs of brothers—Simon and Andrew, James and John—and two other men, Philip and Nathaniel, from the same town as the four brothers. You must have had a reason.

I wanted the group to learn loyalty. Loyalty is at the heart of my teaching and there's no better example than to see two brothers stick together. I know you're wondering, "Don't brothers fight a lot?" They do. But remember, I was looking for a model and there were no perfect ones around. I had to take the best picture of unity and loyalty that I could find.

After picking twelve men from apparently a large number to be your primary disciples, you selected three of those to train even more intensely. Did the other disciples envy them?

You mean how much did they envy them? I was close to all of them but closer to some. That created envy, unfortunately. But Matthew was so grateful that he helped hold down the envy. Judas, by the way, hid his envy best of all. It showed up only in little ways. In his super righteousness, for example.

Tell me more about Judas.

His ideas were always slightly better than those of the others. His problem was that often his ideas were better and it went to his head. He was also very responsible; that's why he was our treasurer. When he had money, he always wanted to be the one to decide what to do with it. Of course, he rationalized his actions by appearing to be responsible, pointing out that we didn't have much money and we had to be good stewards.

Judas was the only disciple from Judea; the rest were from Galilee. The zealots were the radicals of my day who believed God had given Israel to the Jews and not to Rome or to anyone else. They were committed to bringing about the return of Israel to the Jews. Secretly, they wanted to overthrow the Roman government in Jerusalem and were prepared to make any sacrifice, even that of their own lives. There was something noble and bold, and seemingly righteous about them. Judas was a very appealing man—intelligent, articulate, unafraid. The other disciples were so impressed they made him treasurer.

I recall that Judas didn't like it when, just before your death, one of your closest followers, a lady named Mary, sister of Martha and Lazarus whom you raised from the dead, took a bottle of expensive perfume and poured it over you—annointing you, as it turned out, for your death. Judas became upset, saying that the perfume could have been sold for a year's wages and given to the poor.

You see, Judas' problem was that he was so smart he thought he knew everything. He believed he was righteous and became overly impressed with himself, just as Satan did. And, as often happens, his greatest strength—his brilliance and righteous determination—became his greatest weakness. He reached the point where he thought he knew more than I did, and when I didn't do things as he wanted me to, he took things in his own hands. Judas wanted to be God, just as Satan had.

The real problem with Judas and Satan was that neither of them were satisfied with the gifts God had given him. They received by far more gifts than most, but they both became just as the 109th Psalm describes them— wicked. Dissatisfaction is at the heart of sin, just as learning to be satisfied is at the heart of faith. There were two men named Judas with whom I had a special relationship, and, in a way, they stood for all men. My disciple, Judas Iscariot, started out allegedly as my follower but grew more and more dissatisfied, and eventually became my betrayer. The second Judas, my half-brother, started out disliking me and being dissatisfied with my reputation and with the fact I wasn't as good a father as Joseph, whose place I had taken. Later, my brother learned I was not only his loving big brother, but also his Savior. Eventually my brother Jude learned to be satisfied with who I was. Learning who I am is the essence of life. But it takes time to see who I am.

Before you chose your disciples, you knew from the Old Testament prophecies that one of them would betray you, but you didn't know who it would be.[39] *You must have done a great deal of wondering about each one.*

I wondered about every one of them. I began to look at all their strengths and weaknesses. Nathaniel was critical; Thomas tended to have doubts. Matthew had been corrupt all his life, and he continued to fight being a manipulator. All of them had major flaws. Remember the time I had just finished teaching them that I would sacrifice my life for them? The next minute James and John were talking about which of them would be the greatest in heaven. They all wanted power, and any one of them could have betrayed me.

In the New Testament in John's Gospel, it says you knew who would betray you from the beginning, implying you knew before you selected him who the traitor was.

It wasn't that pain-free. My friend couldn't betray me until he was my friend. I had to invest in twelve men, and find out which one I would feel a particular kinship with because of his brilliance. Then I would know. In essence, I had to find out which disciple I enjoyed the most. When a man is betrayed, it means he first trusted someone a great deal. The greater your trust, the greater your pain. I was a man, and I know how it feels to be betrayed even if I did know eventually before the actual event who the betrayer was. That's what the Scriptures are trying to say.

The Scriptures record that you were betrayed by an "old, familiar friend."

Judas had a heart for what I was doing. He was a man of extreme devotion to what he believed in—strong-willed like myself. In many ways, he was the brightest of the lot. We used to have long, enjoyable theological discussions that the others sometimes couldn't understand. I was aware that I would be betrayed by a close friend, as the prophecies in Isaiah and the Psalms had made abundantly clear, but Judas was the last one I suspected initially. I remember thinking when we would have our talks and I felt so close to him, "I know it will be a friend; surely this is not the one." But then it had happened to my Father, too. His best and brightest angel, Lucifer, had done the same thing.

But the Old Testament had all these coded messages for me. There were *direct* messages: one of my disciples would betray me, the one with whom I loved to have discussions—in conjunction with the *indirect* messages: the leader would be betrayed by his most gifted follower (Satan betraying God).

All of these communications pointed toward only one man, Judas. This is exactly what the angels I talked with had hinted at, after my temptation, when they told me the clues as to who would betray me were in the Scriptures. At first I could see Peter, because he was so impulsive, betraying me more quickly than Judas. It took some time for the depth of Judas' flaws to surface—the extreme piousness which eventually caused him to see himself as above the Law, to steal from the treasury and, ultimately to betray me. Three years later, even after I had watched Judas subtly slip away, it was still hard to believe.

Times Alone ... Times Away

What were the times like when you were alone with your disciples?

Most of the time we were surrounded by tremendous crowds. The demands on us were so great that when we did have time alone, all of us were ready for intimate discussions as well as merriment. They would ask me what I meant by a certain parable. Sometimes they would just ask me to repeat a parable they had particularly liked. Many times they would ask me the same questions that you have. How does it feel to have all that power? When did you know you were the Messiah? How did you feel when you found out? What was the temptation like? Did you really see Satan face to face? How did you decide to tell the world? Why did God place you in a poor family?

What else did you talk about?

With six fishermen in the group, we shared a lot of "fish stories." Peter would argue with James and John over who had made the biggest catch. He didn't count the time I had helped him. Or they'd argue over who had been in the roughest storm. Neither one of these three strong-willed men would give an inch, and the rest of the group took great delight in their ongoing battle.

Then I'd tell them about another fisherman, a man by the name of Jonah, who hooked the biggest fish in the world. For three days he battled the fish to a standstill, all without using a pole. Who else had battled a fish a hundredth that size for anywhere near three days? And to top it off, this was Jonah's first experience with fishing. I told them, "Imagine what he would have done if he had stayed at it." We had a laugh. We would often just sit around and enjoy each other.

Another frequent topic of conversation was my power. The aftermath of a miracle was one of their favorite topics, and mine too. No one could believe it at first, and that is exactly what I wanted them to experience—especially the scholarly, intellectual types.

The Pharisees provided us with many laughs. I don't know how many times we sat around the fire talking at night and someone, often Peter, would provide the evening's entertainment by mimicking a Pharisee. In a deep "religious" voice Peter, mocking one of these men, would say, " 'Jesus, is it really lawful to heal on the Sabbath?' and the Lord said, turning to the man with the withered hand, 'Let me answer that brilliant, penetrating question in this way—you're healed.' " Then Peter would say, "Did you see the look on the Pharisee's face?" And he would open his eyes mockingly very wide and everybody would be rolling in laughter by this time.

At other times I told them what my power had done for my faith. I constantly had to make sure they didn't see my power as a self-centered thing. The power was for teaching and for staking a claim. I never used it for selfish gain. I wanted them to be able to handle power because after I was gone they would have the same power.

But we were quite a group. There was a lot of action in three and a half years. We experienced big crowds, tremendous excitement, and great controversy. We were frequently on the road, and slept outside many nights. Those were some of the best memories, just sitting around the fire at night under an open sky, talking. There wasn't much we didn't talk about, and there weren't many experiences we didn't share—loneliness, uncertainty, tension between each other, and moral dilemmas.

Did you ever talk about sex?

Of course. What do you expect a group of young men alone at night to talk about? And with several of them away from their wives for weeks at a time, the subject did come up.

In the New Testament, it says you were tempted in all ways as we are. It makes me want to ask you something but I'm hesitant to do so.

I'll tell you if I don't like the question.

Were you ever tempted sexually?

The Scriptures say "tempted in all ways." Do you think that wouldn't include one of the greatest temptations? As a man, have you ever seen anything more striking in all of creation than a beautiful woman? Do you think I wasn't attracted to women, particularly knowing my Father had invented the whole idea of sex? I was a normal man with normal human instincts. But although I was close to many women, I abstained.

The sexual relationship has been created for the most permanent, deep relationship—marriage. That's the mystery about sex. Sexual fulfillment and committment are inseparably linked in ways beyond comprehension. Sexual fulfillment without committment is an illusion. Even more, a sexual relationship outside of marriage is an abuse of oneself and of one's partner. At the moment one participates in such a relationship one repeatedly says, "I don't love you enough to form an unbreakable bond."

That's not a very popular opinion in today's world.

I'm not talking about an opinion. I'm talking about truth. That's a word that modern man has forgotten.

Did you ever think about marriage?

I was in love once. Unfortunately, I had to give her up, and I was a man of passion. She eventually married someone else. It would sadden me at times to see her with him, having his children when she could have been having mine. I loved children, and I had to deny myself that privelege, too. But I loved her and the children I would have had enough not to leave them widowed and fatherless. I knew what that felt like first hand, and I wouldn't inflict that on anyone if I could prevent it. That was another one of the sacrifices that I made. Losing her was nearly as painful as losing my father, Joseph. To add to the pain, the second loss brought back all the grief of my father's death. I really learned the meaning of the word, "No." She was the most beautiful woman I ever saw. My life was fulfilled, however, as I went about my Father's business.

A few moments ago, we talked about miracles. Was there one miracle that seemed to stand out more than others to your disciples?

The one they talked about the most was "The Storm." We were out in a boat on the Sea of Galilee. I was exhausted and had gone to sleep in the tent-like cabin toward the back of the boat. A short time later a huge storm hit us and the winds brought waves higher than the boat. The waves were unrelenting and powerful. Even the experienced fishermen on the boat who had grown up on the water were afraid. They had reason to be afraid, because Satan was trying to destroy me while I was asleep. My disciples kept thinking I would wake up. But I didn't.

They waited and waited and waited until finally their panic became so great they awakened me. The first thing I was aware of in that half-dazed state when you're first awakened was the tremendously uncomfortable feeling of being screamed at—"Don't you care about us?"—and being slung roughly back and forth because of the momentum of the waves. Keep in mind that for some time before I had been working diligently with them, teaching them not to get anxious in difficult situations. I wanted them to understand that God would take care of them. When I stood up and got my balance, I looked at the raging storm and thought of the 89th Psalm, which unquestionably referred to the Messiah who will sit on David's throne.

> "You rule the oceans when their waves arise in fearful storms; you speak, and they lie still."[40]

Images of Elijah stopping the rain and of Jonah stopping a storm at sea with the sacrifice of his life also flashed through my mind. I knew what to do. My Father was showing me. I walked to the side of the boat, looked at the storm and then commanded at the top of my lungs,

> "Peace, be still."[41]

The storm was over instantaneously.

The disciples would always talk about the strange sensation of the boat's rocking to a halt on a perfectly calm sea.

How uncomfortable did these displays of power make your disciples feel?

I made them uneasy a time or two. One other time when they were out on the Sea of Galilee, in the middle of the night, I walked out to their boat and got in it. That shook them up a bit. When I had first come near the boat and before they could recognize me, they thought I was a ghost. Another time, I raised Lazarus from the dead after he had been in the grave for three days. Here came a man out of his tomb with his head and body wrapped in white funeral clothes. That got their attention.

Often after a miracle they were a little frightened of me. But most of the time they were comfortable enough with me often to tell me what to do. They told me when to get rid of the crowds. The people were hungry, they said, as if I didn't know it. They told me with their eyes that I shouldn't be talking to the Samaritan—the woman at the well. And Peter assured me that I didn't have to die after I told him I did. I had to rebuke him for that.

My disciples were secure enough with me to ask me to call down fire on some people who didn't believe. I had to teach them again what I was about and why, of course, I couldn't do what they wanted me to do with that fire.

Did you and your men laugh much on these journeys?

One of the great things about our group, about any good group, was the camaraderie. We'd be in the middle of a serious conversation about power and how to use it, and Thomas, or somebody else, would jokingly say, "If I had all that power I would make myself a big farm with a lot of cattle and a big house on it and retire." Frequently they joked about my power. One of them would say, "Lord, it is so late and I have to cook breakfast in the morning and all I have are some old beans. Could you muster up some fresh, broiled fish and wheat cakes?" I remember comments at night, before going to sleep, such as Philip's saying, "Lord, when your Father made this earth, He missed this spot of ground I'm sleeping on; it's a little hard. It's probably His only other mistake besides Peter." Those were the times I'll always treasure.

You loved your men.

I would look at my disciples and think, "This is who I'm dying for. Is it worth it?" The answer would always be, "Yes." There was the indescribable feeling I had about each one of them. Real brotherhood would probably be the best way to define it. With all their faults, I loved them. I could see the worth in my men despite the stain of their sins. That's when I best understood how my Father could look at a man like David—an adulterer and murderer—look past his sins and say, "There's a man after my own heart."

My disciples were one big reason I could go to the cross. Those men, whose fellowship I shared, were doomed to death. They were desperately trying to believe, but they didn't know how to trust. They wanted to be courageous, but they were cowards. They wanted to love, but they were filled with envy. They wanted to be honest, but they were all secret manipulators. All of them wanted to be devoted, but couldn't do it. Every one of them was terribly flawed, and I knew it. In short, they were sinful. Sin is not a popular word but that's what it was. Those self-destructive flaws were literally killing the disciples. I saw there was only one way to get rid of those flaws, and that was to judge them as they deserved and then get rid of them. I was to take the judgment my friends deserved. That's why I had to die. They could then be all they were capable of being.

Why death? It's so severe.

I must have asked myself that question a thousand times. The answer is both simple and tremendously complex. I was the only person who could satisfy God's conscience and everybody else's conscience too. Do you think people don't punish themselves terribly for their sins, even the non-believers— especially the non-believers? Everyone knows he or she is evil enough to deserve death. Think about that phrase, "I am so mad at what I did I could kill myself."

Are you saying that there is a universal death wish, a wish for punishment?

It is for justice. Deep down everybody knows they deserve death. I was the only man who ended up in a grave who had the right to come out. If I didn't overcome death, everybody was doomed.

Is this punishment wish a conscious or an unconscious thing?

Consciously, very few people think they deserve death because of their sins. Unconsciously, they know it.

With all they witnessed and with all you talked about, it seems your disciples never really understood what you were about and, in a way, lacked faith in you.

They never understood I had to die until after it was all over. But they weren't and aren't alone. Many people who attend Christian churches today don't understand what I was about either. One reason is that the price I paid is so high—death is so frightening.

In fact, I remember as I was coming to terms with my own death, it was constantly on my mind. I knew what was going to happen, and even though I dreaded it, I always tried to face it. One time, during this process, there was the day two of my disciples came up to me and wanted me to destroy some uncooperative Samaritans who had refused us accommodations when we were traveling about. Here I was thinking of how I would control my aggression when I was attacked, and my own men were encouraging me to be destructive —all in the name of God.

Shortly after that, with my death still weighing heavily on my mind, was the time when the mother of James and John wanted to know if, when I reigned, I would let her boys sit on my right. How absurd it all was. Here I was thinking about sacrifice and obedience and all around me were envious, selfish people. Even my own men—particularly my own men. But that was why I was dying. I can tell you they surely forced me to seek out my Father. He was the only complete source of love.

The way you answered James and John's mother was interesting. You never put her or them down for wanting to be important.

They were created to be important. The whole question was how to do it. You should have heard the other disciples when they found out what James and John tried to do. The way the other disciples reacted revealed very quickly that secretly they all wanted those places; so I told them that among the heathen, the leaders lorded it over those beneath them. That's the world's greatness, I said. Among my followers, if you want to be a great leader, then be a great servant. You want to be recognized, then sacrifice your own interests. That's what I was doing. As I told them,

> "I, the Messiah, did not come to be served, but to serve, and to give my life as a ransom for many."[42]

That was in truth living and why I always emphasized that if you want to find your life, lose it, for my sake and the gospel's.

Essentially you told them to give themselves up for the good of the team. I was interested that the Scriptures report that even you wanted recognition and that you sacrificed to get it. In the Book of Hebrews, it says that for the joy awaiting you, you endured the shame of the cross. [43]

My Father's the same way. He is pleased to be honored and He made His creatures like that, too. And for anyone who will recognize His glory and appreciate Him, He will pour out every blessing upon him. Heaven will be a place where everyone is recognizing his brothers' and sisters' glory. If you've ever been part of a crowd and cheered for somebody—for a team, a performance—you'll know what I mean.

Miracles Enjoyed

What were some other miracles you especially enjoyed?

One day I was walking down the road to Nain, a city in Galilee, with my disciples and hundreds of other people. Just as we got to the city gate, we had to stop and wait for a funeral procession. From the mourners, I learned that the only son of a widow had died. And as I saw this procession and the mother who was overcome with grief, it moved me to tears.

I thought of my mother, a widow, who in just a short while would lose her oldest son. I went to the dead boy's mother and said,

> "Don't cry."[44]

I walked over to the coffin and put my hand on it, looked up to my Father and said,

> "Young man, I say to you, get up!"[45]

The boy immediately pushed the top of the coffin off, sat up, looked around as if he had just awakened from a nap, and asked what was going on. First there was silence and then the crowd went wild. That miracle had great meaning for me, because one day I would be dead and my Father would bring me back. The joy that I saw on that woman's face would be my mother's joy.

There was one other time which I probably enjoyed as much as bringing back to life that widow's son. I was standing in the middle of a crowd and Jairus, a Jewish rabbi, came up to me, fell down at my feet, and begged me to come home with him. His only child, a twelve-year old daughter, was dying. Here was a proud rabbi with his heart breaking who was turning to me in utter desperation. He had put aside his pride, humbled himself, fallen on his knees and pleaded for mercy. I couldn't refuse.

We fought the crowds, pushing them back, all the way to his house. About half way there, I felt someone touch me, then felt the healing power go out of me for just a second. I stopped, turned around, and asked my disciples who had touched me. They looked at me as if I were crazy, "Lord, we're surrounded by crowds; everybody's touching you." Then suddenly the woman who had done it, fell to her knees in front of me, telling me she had touched me because she wanted to be healed and now she was. Then I said to her,

"Your faith has healed you. Go in peace."[46]

Jairus continued to stand beside me, watching all this.

Immediately after this incident, a messenger from his house arrived telling him there was no use to trouble "the teacher" any more because his little girl was dead. The effect on Jairus was devastating. The look on his face changed from great hope to total dejection. Before he could say anything, I told him to trust me, that everything would be all right. We walked the rest of the way and I could see it was almost too much for him. He wanted to believe, but he was fighting back the tears.

When we got to the house, it was packed with mourners. Remember, he was the preacher, the rabbi, with a large following. I remember telling everyone in the room to "quit crying, the little girl isn't dead, she's only asleep." Some of the people became furious with me, and others began jeering aloud. They tried to throw me out the door, but I took Peter, James and John, along with Jairus and his wife, to the little girl's room.

There lay a pretty girl with long, beautiful curls and the sweetest look on her pale face. Her eyes were closed. She was not breathing. This helpless young person was dead. Then I took her cold, limp hand in mine, looked at her, and thought of the day when my hand would be cold. I said, "Get up, little girl." Suddenly, her hand was warm and alive. She sat up in the bed. I looked at her big brown eyes and said, "I'll bet you're thirsty. Get this wonderful little girl something to drink".

The people in the room heard Jairus' wife screaming ecstatically and watched her run to get the water, smiling and shouting: "She's alive! He's healed her!" When I walked out of the girl's room, I looked at the people who had been so angry and hateful just a few minutes before. They hated death like I did. But now they had the most incredible look of joy and gratitude on their faces, and I thought, "This is the kind of change that I will bring about in people. Those who hate me will one day love me."

How did you feel after a miracle like this, after seeing you had a tremendous power that no one else had?

Both the moments before a miracle and those after a miracle had an equally powerful effect on me. I would look out at those crowds coming to see me. No matter where I was, there came the crowd. People came leading blind relatives by the hand. Others were carrying the paralyzed on stretchers. There were crippled of all types. Some were on makeshift crutches, some were deformed, and, of course, the lepers came if they could get anywhere near me. The sheer impact of those crowds was overwhelming. Never was I any happier than when I was the Messiah, the world's doctor, at those moments.

I also took particular pleasure in being able to perform miracles, because it enabled me to defend my Father's honor. There were people then, just as there are today, who said that God doesn't care about suffering. By so doing, they made Him the author of evil and pain. Every miracle was a message from my Father. It thrilled me to be able to say, and I always did:

"Be healed in the name of God,"
"God blesses you, be healed,"
"Your Father in heaven heals—you are well,"
"You are healed in the name of the God of Abraham, Isaac, and Jacob."

And today, nineteen hundred and fifty years later, many theologians allegedly from your own church deny your miracles.

All the arguing, particularly from modern liberal theologians, about whether I actually performed miracles or not amazes me. Why shouldn't I have done miracles? I myself was the greatest miracle the world has ever known. I was The Prophet. Moses, Joshua, Elijah, Elisha and Daniel all had done miracles or participated in them. Can't those theologians see I was bringing in a new day? I was a living testimony of what man was meant to be. With all of their dislike of conservatives, the liberals who disdain miracles should at least wish with all their hearts that the conservatives are right. It would make all of mankind so much greater.

Tell me about the messages behind the miracles.

My miracles always had two messages. One was physical, and one was spiritual. It takes the spiritual side of a person to make him or her truly great. I came not only to heal the blind but also to give people the vision of faith. I healed "untouchable" leprosy and I was there to heal everyone's untouchable sins. I healed the deaf because I had come to help people who had been deaf to God's voice. Every miracle I did was a triumph over the misery of the world. All of my miracles mattered to me. It was an incredible experience to watch someone hear who never had heard before, or to watch a grown man walk or talk for the first time. It was particularly special to watch a blind man see. But probably of all my healing miracles, I appreciated healing lepers the most.

Constantly, I was surrounded by incredible faces of gratitude after a miracle. There were thankful relatives, and the wonder in the "patient's" eyes is like a child when he sees something exciting he has never seen before. There was a look I can hardly describe in a person's eyes when he or she was not only healed from disfiguring leprosy but also touched for the first time in years. Lepers were not only untouchables; they were unreachables. They couldn't even be touched emotionally.

Because lepers were banned from the rest of the populace, they would see me after the crowds had gone late in the evening. Or they would catch me before I entered a town.

Once toward the end of my life, as I was heading toward Jerusalem, I came near the border of Galilee and Samaria. I was far outside any town but there were ten lepers waiting for me. I healed them instantly and told them to go to the Jewish priests and show them they were healed. All ran for town except for one of them. And he was the "foreigner" among them at that, from "despicable" Samaria. But this man shouted and fell face downward in the dust at my feet in true joy and humility. Finally I picked him up and told him, "Stand up," and he did. Now, with his face covered with dust which only accentuated his marvelous eyes filled with indescribable gratitude, he looked at me and I told him,

"Go; your faith has made you well."[47]

I knew a day was coming when I would lie face down in the dust underneath the load of the cross and, at that moment, I would think about that leper and his eyes. Many times during the crucifixion, I would think about the faces of all those people I had healed and their relatives who had watched. They would be part of the crowd inside me, urging me on when I had to climb that impossible mountain known as Calvary.

Your miracles are so different from those of fabled ancient wonder-workers in pagan literature. Your miracles were first and foremost for the purpose of helping your fellow humans. They were miracles steeped in love, gifts reserved for those who trusted you to the slightest degree. You did not do them just for popularity. Nowhere was this more obvious than at your temptation and also you refused to do miracles for a sign when the Pharisees or your hometown skeptics demanded one.

The miracles were for helping others and also for demonstrating who I was. It may seem strange, but when I was on the cross and I'd given up the privilege of using my power, for just a moment there came a time when I didn't feel like I was God. I had to look back on those miracles of faith to believe that I was God. It's strange—the thoughts and feelings that different circumstances produced. Even though I knew I could call on my power any moment I wanted to, as long as I didn't use it and as long as I was hanging there engulfed by pain, I didn't feel particularly like God.

Often before you performed a miracle, you told the people you were doing one "so that they might believe." Building faith seems to be the constant goal of your teaching.

That was the same goal as my Father's. The Jews, the Chosen Ones, would forget about Him; so He wouldn't do anything for them. He would let things get worse and worse—persecution, fear, famine. Midway through this process, God would bring in a prophet to warn His people. If they still wouldn't listen, He would finally tell them, "So that you will know that I am the Lord, your God, this is what is going to happen to you." The Israelites would then be told that they would become slaves of Babylon or that Jerusalem would be destroyed or some other prophecy would be given to them. Whatever it was, the event would happen exactly as the Lord said it would. Things would go from bad to worse until Israel was finally humbled. Then some of the people would return to God and there would be a great deliverance.

Take courage when you see things getting worse and worse in your world —pornography, murder, crime, infidelity, materialism. My Father's deliverance always comes when things couldn't be any worse. When it comes, you will know Who did it.

Many of your followers today feel as if they can't relate to miracles.

If you're a follower of mine and have the slightest spiritual awareness, or if you know anything about prayer, you have seen miracles; the supernatural participation of God working in a situation. Always, after the brief period of ecstasy that accompanies a definite experience with my Father, a person must return to the darkness of his everyday world. It is a world where, in their flesh, people can't see the other world, the real world. Unless you've really worked on developing your "nighttime" other worldly vision, you'll never see that real world very clearly.

Even at best, there are great challenges in the seen world to divert and to block our spiritual vision: glitter, and glamour, and most of all—clamor. There always comes a time after an experience with God when people find themselves beginning to doubt again, and beginning to fear, and beginning to live strictly in their humanity—or being tempted to do so. An individual then has to start all over with the skills of faith.

In a way it was the same for me. Every time I performed a miracle, I always had to return to my humanity and, once again, overcome the limited vision of my retinae. Miracles didn't stop my need for faith, just as they don't stop yours. In a way, miracles increased my need for faith. It was the miracle of the Scriptures, the fact that there existed an absolutely accurate communication from my Father about what was happening now, and what was going to happen to me in the future, that caused me to have a terrible burden. Because of my faith in my Father's omniscience, I knew death was staring me in the face every day. Omniscience doesn't always remove pain. My Father had known all along how things would work out and even He had to wait on it to happen.

You say you always had your humanity waiting for you after a miracle, but several times, particularly in John's gospel, you said you did only what you saw the Father doing. That implies you saw things we couldn't. It hints that you used your omniscience.

I could have been talking about what I saw Him doing in the Old Testament. I was completely human, but I could still see my Father at work, and everything I saw Him do, I was allowed to do. Every miracle I performed had been done in the Old Testament or was alluded to, except for casting out demons. That was my idea, but then my Father had already led me to conquer Satan himself. Then I knew I had authority over all the Evil One's followers.

The Pleasure of Faith

Anytime you saw faith, it pleased you tremendously. Why?

Because it shows so much respect for my Father. My Father's honor was at stake, and anybody who had faith took my Father at His word. Anyone who lacks faith at that moment does not believe my Father. It's a rare thing to find a person of faith. It's the most precious commodity in God's economy.

I remember the Roman captain whose faith was unshakable. His servant was ill; so he sent several Jewish elders to ask me to heal him. Even though he was a Roman, the Jews loved and admired him for his kindness to them. And because of this, these elders came to ask me a favor. As I went with them and approached the Roman Centurion's house, he sent one of his servants to tell me not to come into his home. He said he knew he wasn't worthy of that, but if I would just say the word, he knew his servant would be healed. After all, he was a man who gave orders, who understood the chain of command, and he knew of my power.

Here was an untaught Roman who had more faith than a Jewish rabbi. He didn't have to see me. He didn't have to touch me or to have me touch the sick. He didn't even have to hear my voice. All he needed was to know that if I was willing to do something for him, it was as good as done.

As I recall, you healed that servant.

I believe I did. That Roman was like the millions of people I ask to believe in me who have never seen me or touched me or heard my voice. Another reason I love faith is that it is the vehicle through which people know God. You can't see God with your eyes or hear him with your ears. You have to look for signs that He's there, and that always involves faith. If you miss those signs, you miss His magnificence. If you don't believe He answers prayers, that

He really affects circumstances, then you will miss Him. If you don't believe He has written down His words to you, you won't hear Him. You will miss all His guidance for you. You will miss His attempts to comfort you and love you through friends, His blessings, and His Scriptures. You won't see His work in the circumstances of your life. You have to have the eyes of faith.

As the Apostle Paul told the believers later, "We are those who walk not by sight, but by faith."

There is nothing like the victories faith brings, the last-second relief when all seems lost. It is joy indescribable. And faith is the key to that joy.

My Father is a master dramatist. Drama is tension. And the resolution of that tension is where He works. Without conflict you'll never see God. Next to healing lepers, I always got my greatest thrill out of healing blind people, watching them see for the first time. That was the essence of what I was doing —helping my followers to see.

The Roman soldier obviously inspired you with his faith. Who else did?

Many times someone would inspire me. And often the inspiration would come from the least-expected source. Once in Capernaum, I was staying at a friend's house, and news spread excitely that I was in town. Before we knew it, the house was packed so tightly that there was not room for even one more person. Even outside, the crowd was so great that no one could get near the house.

As I began teaching the people, all of a sudden in the middle of my talk, clay started falling from the ceiling. I looked up to see what was going on, and I saw someone digging a hole in the roof from the outside. At first the hole was small, and I could barely make out a face peering down through it. Then I heard the man who was doing the digging yell, "We hit it. He's directly below us." He and his friends began digging some more, until there was a large hole with three faces looking down at me through the roof. The diggers paused for a moment, and, with smiles on their faces began lowering a stretcher with ropes. On the stretcher was a paralyzed man. The ingenuity and determination of his friends moved me. They had incredible perseverance! You don't think I would disappoint them, do you?

There were some scribes, "learned scholars," standing around, and it was obvious they disapproved of the sick man's friends. It's bad manners not to knock at the front door, and some of the clay had fallen on their precious robes. I was moved by the moment; the hunger of my Father's people, my people. I looked around at the clay that was still in our hair and on our robes. Everyone around me was a little dusty, and I thought, "I want all of you to see that what I am doing is more than just healing someone so that he can live a few more years. It's a lot bigger than that. I'm here to remove your dirt —your sins—and I want you to know it." So I looked at this pale, thin man who had no strength even to hold up his head and who just lay there staring at me with these pleading eyes. And I said,

"Your sins are forgiven."[48]

That made the scribes furious. I could see it in their eyes, and I knew what they were thinking: "Only God can forgive sins." Several of these scribes had been in the synagogue and had tried to kill me that day I had made "my announcement." I looked at them and told them,

> "Which is easier to say, 'Your sins are forgiven,' or to say 'Get up and Walk?' But so that you may know that the Son of Man has authority on earth to forgive sins,"

I turned to the paralyzed man and said,

> "Get up, take your mat and go home."[49]

Before you could blink an eye, this man jumped to his feet and was staring me in the face with a big grin. He was so excited that he picked up his bed and pushed his way through the crowd. He hadn't walked in years, and now he wanted to get outside and *run* as soon as he could.

As I watched him part that crowd, that man made me think of my Father when He parted the Red Sea. The scene was that compelling!

As they witnessed this miracle, the shock that went through the crowd turned into the most joyous shouting and singing to my Father you have ever heard. I was especially pleased that they were thanking my Father, for they understood for the moment whose power it really was. The people kept saying, "We've never seen anything like it!" What a special time! We were so tightly packed together in that house that you could really feel the crowd in a unique way. We were one. I remember thinking, with that electricity flowing through the crowd, "Heaven is going to be like this."

Finally, I looked up at the ceiling and there were these same three faces, now with incredible smiles, and they were laughing and singing with me. Then before they left, they fixed the roof.

That particular miracle had a special impact on me. People were surrounding me in that tightly-packed room desperate for good news and new life. More and more, I began to see the hunger that was there in every person. If I could just satisfy that deep spiritual need. My heart was moved for mankind. So many people wanted God so much, but many couldn't admit it.

All of this was going through my mind as I walked down the road after leaving that house with the crowd still following me. Suddenly, I felt the strongest urge to ask my Father to lead me to the most despicable person around, who I knew deep inside was yearning to know God. My Father answered that request and there I saw Levi, the tax collector, sitting smugly in his booth. He was about to have his life and his name changed.

You are unpredictable. You've done everything possible to urge the worst sinner into heaven, thereby bringing tremendous comfort to the people— "If Matthew can make it, I can, too." And yet, at other times, you often intentionally increased the people's tension just as you did with the scribes in the house with the hole in the roof. You warned them frequently that if they didn't listen you would disown them. You told them that if they didn't stand up for you now, you wouldn't stand up for them in the future when you returned. You backed in a corner a potential follower, a wealthy young man, when you told him that if he really wanted to follow you he had to give all his money away. You often asked your disciples to do things they couldn't do. This seems largely to contradict the image the press and the media today have created for you.

As I made plain, I came to bring a sword. Truth is never comfortable in this world.

There was tension in my life and I was the Son of God. Do you think anyone will escape from it? But tension helped to make me into the Son of God. Pain made me cry out. It taught me to wait, to pray, to trust, to look for answers, to be humble, and eventually, best of all, to be rescued.

Your life was a drama. It has often been called "the greatest story ever told." What do you think of those today who are creating drama, the entertainment industry?

The great danger is that your talent can become your idol, and then you become your own god, the same temptation Satan faced. Throughout history, people are so quick to forget where they got their talent. It always comes back to pride. I would remind the people in the entertainment world never to forget what my Father said to ministers, that He holds teachers more accountable than others.

Don't think for one minute if you're in media or entertainment you're not a teacher. You're one of the most important teachers in today's society. Every movie, every television show, every performance is a sermon, whether you like it or not. You'd better make sure that your gospel is "The Gospel," for The Gospel will prevail, and by it all other gospels will be judged. That I promise.

When the Statler Hotel was opened in Los Angeles several years ago, a number of actors and actresses were invited to write their deepest wishes on a "wishing wall." Ginger Rogers wrote, "I wish that all men knew that God is impartial." That would be another thing that I would say to the entertainment industry.

Did it bother you that many people didn't believe in you?

My Father had told me in the Scriptures to expect unbelief. I saw everything coming true just as He said it would. The people really were lost, and the Pharisees really hated the truth. Miracle after miracle had no effect on them except to make them determined to destroy me. That increased both my confidence and my dread.

At the same time, my followers were confused, the Pharisees were planning to dispose of me and all the time I was wondering, "What do I have to do to convince them? I've healed the sick, raised the dead, walked on water, turned water into wine and fed twelve thousand people with five loaves of bread." I knew they were blind, but I couldn't stop trying to convince them.

Still, it hurt when they didn't accept me, I was sensitive just as my Father.

He's not so far "above you" that you can't hurt Him. This is what makes you so important and what makes Him such a great God. He made Himself vulnerable to you. He takes it very personally when He's rejected. But His promises comforted me, I knew that one day truth would reign.

The response of many people was more than I had expected even with all the prophecies telling me that I would someday be famous. My popularity took off like a rocket, almost overnight. It became so great that I couldn't enter a city without a tremendous crowd. That's why I spent so many nights in the wilderness with my men. But I could see how hungry the people were and my heart was moved. They were crying out for a shepherd.

Everything was coming to pass just as it was supposed to happen. The Pharisees saw very clearly that they either had to kill me or make me their king.

THREE

*Opposition
and
Confirmation*

The Pharisees

You didn't care for the Pharisees very much, did you?

All those years I visited the Temple at Passover, I listened to their "wisdom." Their hypocrisy was ever before me. They had created a religion of externals and had forgotten about the soul. They ate the right food, they had the right hygiene, they washed before eating. They spoke the right language in the sense that they didn't swear, and they went to the right places—the Temple or synagogue—on the right day—the Sabbath, but their hearts were all wrong.

The Pharisees had started out with a good idea—trying to separate themselves from evil and to follow the God of Israel. But they confused their heritage with their own spirituality and thought they were automatically God's special chosen people. They failed to learn the same lesson most of their ancestors had failed to learn—that they were proud and spiritually blind and that only those who recognize their blindness and cry out to God for help are special. The Pharisees forgot that they belonged more on their knees than on their feet. The externals in which the Phariseess put so much stock were only to be representative symbols of what was inside. But inside, the Pharisees were corrupt.

They didn't love God or their neighbors as much as they loved themselves. Their way of life, with all their rules, was for one basic purpose—to gain control and to glorify themselves.

Secretly the Pharisees loved material things more than they did God—their long robes, their rings, their gold. And oh, how they loved power: the place of honor, the public recognition, the catering of others to them. They were good at keeping minor rules like fasting and tithing by which they could measure their performances, but they had no heart for the people.

To the Ten Commandments they regularly added laws of their own which they considered, "divinely inspired" and which regulated every aspect of Jewish life. They wanted control. They wanted to be God.

In response to this legalism came a reactionary Jewish religious group, the Sadducees, who rebelled against all the imposed restrictions and called for a return to the Scriptures as the only standard for life. Theirs was not truly a scripturally-based reformation. Instead, it was based on their secret liberalism and their own materialism. The Sadducees had carefully maneuvered their way into the upper echelon of Jewish-Roman life, with a lifestyle more Roman than Jewish. This they wished to preserve at all costs. Of course, the Sadducees didn't believe in the life hereafter, a fact consistent with their lifestyle of getting all they could while they were on earth.

So these were the two groups of leaders responsible for teaching God's people The Truth. The Pharisees, the most powerful of the two, had a tremendous opportunity to teach the people the Word of God, The Truth. Instead, they devoted themselves—and make no mistake, they were devoted—to keeping their rules and reading their words instead of God's Word. Many of the

Pharisees had written commentaries and religious treatises on the Law which eventually became the focus of their teaching, discussion, and authority. They became experts on the words of their fellow Pharisees until they reached a point where the words of God were pushed backstage. That same thing has happened with some religious leaders today.

The Pharisees were charged with the responsibility of teaching the people the Truth: that repentence was needed, that they were far from God, that they didn't really love their neighbors, that they were selfish and self-centered. They needed to humble themselves before God as the writer of Chronicles said,

> "If my people, which are called by my name, shall humble themselves, and pray, and seek my face, and turn from their wicked ways; then will I hear from heaven, and will forgive their sins, and will heal their land,"[1]

If the Pharisees had done that, they would have given the people victory over their biggest opponent—themselves—and would have made everyone a true neighbor. But the Pharisees didn't believe their own religion and weren't true to their own faith. Worse than that, they exalted themselves and their performances at the expense of their neighbors—the students they were supposed to teach. They made their neighbors constantly feel inferior to them and made their neighbors carry their guilt. The Pharisees were charged with lightening the people's burdens and presenting them a God who would lift their spirits as He lifted their guilt. Instead of humility and freedom, however, they gave their charges slavery and oppression. The greatest oppression in my country at that time in history was not from the Romans, it was from the Pharisees. The more I saw it, the more I understood the truth of spiritual blindness. At first I tried to reason with the Pharisees about what they didn't see but as I found out, they were not men of reason despite their continued attempts to convey the opposite impression. Every time I saw what they were doing to people, I was greatly annoyed. Here were men taking God's name in vain in the worst possible way.

It seems that every time you turned around, the Pharisees were harrassing you.

They complained because my disciples didn't fast. They called me a "drunkard" because I drank some wine. While at the same time they accused John the Baptist of being puritanical for not drinking wine. When I allowed a prostitute in my presence, or when I associated with a tax collector, that really brought out their self-righteousness. You're right. They never stopped harassing me.

Consistently the Pharisees devised traps to get you arrested, but you were always one step ahead of them.

If you give people like that enough time, they'll always hang themselves. I remember the day a Pharisee named Simon invited me to his home for dinner. During the meal a prostitute brought me a gift, some perfume. People always surrounded me, and it wasn't so strange for some of them to be sitting around while I ate. This prostitute didn't interrupt the conversation or say anything at all. She just knelt before me and began to cry. She washed my feet with her tears and dried them with her hair. Then she anointed me with perfume and kissed my feet reverently. While this was going on I observed my host. It was obvious he didn't like what was happening. I knew he was thinking, how could I be a prophet if I would even speak to a prostitute, much less let her touch me.

Here was a condescending man who hadn't even offered me water to wash my own feet, as was the custom. He couldn't treat me quite like a normal guest. He had little need for me, particularly for the forgiveness that I had the authority to give. At the same time, here was a woman cleaning my dirty feet with her own hands, literally begging for forgiveness. So I told the Pharisee a story.

"Simon," I said, "A man loaned money to two men. One he loaned $5000, the other $500. But neither could pay him back. Being a kind man, he forgave both debts. Which of these two men do you suppose loved him most?"[2] Simon, not knowing I was talking about him—it was always amazing to watch a perfect picture of someone in a parable go right over their heads —answered correctly, "The one who is forgiven the most must love the most."

Then I interpreted the parable for him. "You didn't even offer me water for my feet, but she washed them with her tears. You denied me the customary kiss of greeting, but she has not stopped kissing my feet. You neglected the usual courtesy of oil to annoint my head, but she has covered my feet with rare perfume. Therefore, her sins which are many are forgiven. The one who is forgiven little has little love."

It was in moments like this that the spiritual world was manifested. It was clear whether the spirit of humility or the spirit of pride dominated a person.

When you forgave sins, you did that in a way on credit. You were banking on the fact that you would complete your task. With all your troubles, you were a very confident man.

I can never say it too much: "Man shall live on every word that proceeds out of the mouth of God." I had His word that I would complete my task and that I could forgive others. There's nothing that makes you more confident than that.

(As he talked about his confidence, I realized how closely confidence and faith are related to each other. True confidence looks not only to the past, but largely to the future. And of all the men in history, Jesus was the most confident, the most certain that events would take place.)

You were constantly outsmarting the Pharisees—always a step ahead of them. You knew the Scriptures better than they did and you turned their questions which were meant to trap you back on themselves.

Once when I was teaching the people, a group of Pharisees and political leaders approached me trying to trap me into an offense against Rome. They wanted the Romans to have a reason to arrest me, so they asked me a question they were sure would entrap me:

> "Sir, we know that you are very honest and teach the truth regardless of consequences, . . . Now tell us, is it right to pay taxes to the Roman government or not?"[3]

I told them they were hypocrites. Then I asked one of my disciples to give me a coin and he borrowed a penny from someone in the crowd. I held up the coin and asked the Pharisees,

> "Whose picture and whose name is on it?"

They replied,

> "Caesar's."

So I said to them,

> "Render therefore unto Caesar the things which are Caesar's; and unto God the things that are God's."[4]

Another time you adopted their tact of asking a question from Scripture, and the Pharisees couldn't answer it. The question had to do with your divinity.

They would harass me any time I would even hint I was the Messiah so I continued to say it indirectly. I assumed if they didn't get the message when I raised somebody from the dead, telling them in words what I'd just done would probably have less effect.

This one particular day they'd been trying to trap me with one question after another so finally I turned to them and said, "You've asked me a lot of questions, now let me ask you one: If the Messiah is to come after David, and is to be a descendant of David, how could David write in the book of Psalms,

> " 'God said to my Lord, the Messiah, 'Sit at my right hand until I place your enemies beneath your feet.' ' "[5]

In essence I was asking them how David could call the Messiah his Lord at that time if the Messiah hadn't even been born yet. The Pharisees stared at each other with puzzled looks, each hoping their fellow scholars had the answer, and of course, they didn't. There were no more questions from that faction that day. The Pharisees walked away, muttering to themselves. Justice had been served.

More on the Pharisees

As I read the gospels, I never cease to be amazed at the number of times you provoked the Pharisees. You said or did things you seemingly didn't have to say or do.

Remember, I was the Truth. Several times I told them that purity was best demonstrated in generosity and that they were fools. They washed the outside, but inside they were full of greed and wickedness. They wouldn't accept the truth—they hid it from others and prevented them from having a chance to believe it.

Once, a Pharisee informed me,

"Sir, you have insulted my profession,"[6]

and I replied, "Not only are you Pharisees hypocrites, you are murderers, too. You killed all the prophets." Never forget, "preachers" killed me. And I hope preachers today don't forget that.

John Calvin declared that those with the most power are always the most dangerous. They have the greatest temptations. There have been plenty of great preachers—John the Baptist, Samuel, Isaiah, John Wesley, Charles Spurgeon, to name a few. But there have been some terrible ones, too. People shouldn't be surprised, however. Satan always tries to infiltrate his enemies' quarters. That's the first place he attacks.

Be wary of those hypocrites, those ministers who change my words and my Father's words and say, "God didn't really say that, this is what He said. . . ." That voice goes all the way back to the Garden of Eden. Many a famous man by the world's standards has made the same disastrous mistake. They have taken that fatal step from which there is no return and have changed the holy words of Scripture into "what they really mean." This is where more than one scholar has been converted into a fool by his pride. This is exactly the place where man wants to become God, speak for Him, even correct Him. And it is here that C.S. Lewis reminds them—it is impossible for man to be right and God to be wrong. Frightening, isn't it, to be so certain, and yet so potentially deceived by one's own perception? Everyone likes to forget that Hitler was really a human being.

I remember another incident with the Pharisees when, on the Sabbath, you were in the home of a Pharisee. A number of them were watching you closely to see if you would heal a man who had suffered chronically from fainting spells. You asked them if it was lawful to heal on the Sabbath day or not.

I took the sick man by the hand and gave them my answer. I healed him. Then I turned to them and said,

"Which one of you doesn't work on the Sabbath? If your cow falls into a pit, don't you proceed at once to get it out? And how much more valuable is a person than a cow?"[7]

The Pharisees as usual became enraged.

They were such religious zealots. Another time on the Sabbath I was teaching in the synagogue and a handicapped woman who was bent over and unable to straighten herself was there. Later I learned that she had been this way for eighteen years. I called over to her,

"Woman, you are healed of your sickness!"[8]

Then I went over and touched her and she immediately stood up straight and began thanking me profusely. The local rabbi at that synagogue became very angry because I had healed her on the Sabbath. He shouted to the crowd,

"There are six days of the week to work, . . . those are the days to come for healing, not on the Sabbath!"9

The Scriptures say that you had a quick answer for him.

I told him just what he was—a hypocrite. Their hypocrisy was beyond belief. Imagine standing there with a woman who was dying and who now is tremendously excited to be free of the pain that has enslaved her for eighteen years. Imagine having the capacity to totally ignore that, and at the same time the audacity to tell the person who helped free her of her pain that you are better than he is.

The utter insensitivity of human beings at moments amazed me, and I wasn't about to let any of the Pharisees continue teaching this false religion of "look how good I am."

I wanted the people to know exactly where I stood and where the Pharisees stood. I was going to be murdered and I wanted it well-known who did it. I didn't want the Pharisees coming back and saying, "We were really on your side."

Remember, I was a prophet, and it was my job to warn the people about the Pharisees and about the potential Pharisee inside each of them. I wanted to let the light shine on who the Pharisees really were. If you wish, you can call that provoking.

You called the Pharisees on different occasions "egotistical," "corrupt," "fools," and "murderers." Somebody might get the idea you called them names.

Once I told a story about the typical Pharisee. "Two men went to the temple to pray. One was a proud Pharisee, and the other a cheating tax collector. The Pharisee prayed, 'Thank God I am not a sinner like everyone else, especially that tax collector. I never cheat, I don't commit adultery, I go without food twice a week, and I give to God a tenth of everything I earn.'"10 "At the same time the corrupt tax collector was praying with his head bowed almost to the ground, feeling totally unworthy even to look at heaven, as he prayed with great sorrow, 'God, have mercy on this poor sinner.' And the tax collector, not the Pharisee, returned home forgiven."

You never let up on the Pharisees.

The Pharisees were everything my Father wasn't. I told my followers: "Of all the people to be aware of most, watch out for the Pharisees." The men who claimed to be the best were the most evil. I thought the people ought to know.

I also tried to teach the people that living is not in what you have. It's not what you store up, as the Pharisees were teaching, but living is in spending —in giving. Big spenders are a lot closer in some ways to my Father than people think they are. Spend your time, your money, your beliefs, your heart, your soul, your life. Spend it. Spend all you have on me and my Father, and on your neighbor, and you shall see the Kingdom of God.

(As I reflected on Jesus' persistent attitude toward the Pharisees, I became more aware of his extremely subtle but powerful intensity. Fire burned deep within him, and it became clear how much of a radical he really was in his day—ruthless in his confrontations with the authorities, the false shepherds. But after all, they were in charge of guiding his flock. Indeed, He had come to bring a sword, too. Yet even when His sword was out of its sheath, his winsomeness must have shown through, for several Pharisees did invite him home for a meal, even after getting "an earful." Even at his most confrontive, Jesus was always open to reconciliation with whoever would accept the truth, just as His Father was.)

Some people think there are plenty of Pharisees still around in the churches today.

Every person who enters a church, whether he or she stays there fifty years or not, has a blacker heart than one can ever imagine. Many people in the church have admitted to that in part and have some understanding of why I went to the cross, but very few really see themselves deserving of capital punishment. And that was my message to every person from the cross. There's more envy, anger, slander, and materialism in any church than you can believe, and plenty of lust—however mental. That's why I had to die.

Someone ought to stand outside the church door on Sunday morning greeting each worshipper kindly with, "Good morning, murderer; Good morning, lustful one; Good morning, envy; Good morning, greed; Good morning, evil one."[11] Then right inside the door should be another minister greeting them again, saying, "Welcome; come and receive forgiveness. Come and receive Christ's gift. Welcome to the house of peace. Good morning, saint by His righteousness. Good morning; receive his righteousness."

There are many people sitting in church every week who deep down don't really feel like they need to be forgiven. I'll tell you what makes great Christians and a great church—humble hearts. Of course, the price for humility is the same as the price for compassion—pain. This means death to the myth of the good self, the good person, the "sweet lady," the "gentleman." And myths die hard.

Nicodemus

There were a few Pharisees who listened to you, weren't there?

There's always a remnant of truth-seekers, but even they didn't come out boldly and declare themselves at first. I remember one night a Pharisee named Nicodemus came to see me long after dark, dressed plainly and not in his usual tailored, bright robe. He didn't want to be recognized, but had the courage to be honest and consider new truth, truth from outside himself. He came directly to the point. He told me that everyone could see by my miracles alone that God had sent me to teach. But I didn't want Nicodemus to see me as just another great teacher or prophet, I wanted him to know I was The Teacher. So just as forthrightly, I told him, "You must be born again."

"But how can an old man go back to his mother's womb?" he asked. I told him that he didn't understand that I was talking about a spiritual life. I was talking about "Life from heaven," which could only be gotten from God, Who gave the Spirit of Life when He wanted to do so. I explained that anyone who believed in me, in fact, had this spiritual life, which was also eternal life, now. I explained that one was born again, and had a new spirit when he linked himself to my spirit, and not until then.

Nicodemus looked at me incredulously. He had come for a discussion. He hadn't come to meet the only Begotten Son of God. He never expected me to tell him that he wasn't born again, nor did he expect me to make the claims that I did.

I told him that I would be lifted up on a pole just as Moses had lifted up a brass serpent on a pole, saving from death all the people of Israel who looked at the serpent.*[12] I told him that God had sent me, His only Begotten Son, into the world to save the world, and I implied how I would do it by my death. I told Nicodemus that I was God's only son, the Light from heaven. I said that many people loved darkness more than me, more than Light, because they were evil and the Light would expose them. But I told him that there were some who came gladly to the Light to see who I was and who they were, I was encouraging Nicodemus to continue to search for who I was.

During that talk you told Nicodemus that you were giving him special knowledge as to what was going on in heaven. You said you had seen things others hadn't. Were you manifesting your omniscience at that time?

I was talking about how the Spirit moves and causes men and women to come alive in a new way. I was thinking of my own baptism when unexpectedly the Spirit of the Lord came upon me in a new way, the time when "I saw the heavens open" and a dove come down and I heard my Father's voice. Remember, too, I had talked with some angels shortly after my temptation and they had told me some of the events that were taking place in heaven. I was only telling Nicodemus about my experiences as a man.

Nicodemus left that night with much to think about. But he was a remarkable man because he had the humble strength to be open to new truth. So few people can do that. Many don't want to admit that someone might know something more than he or she does.

You were an enigma to the Pharisees. Every time they asked for a miracle, you wouldn't perform one. Yet you did miracles freely for others. The time immediately

---

*After the people of Israel had been delivered miraculously time after time from all kinds of enemies, they continued to complain because circumstances were not as they wanted them. God sent punishment on one occasion through numerous poisonous snakes. In a panic, the Israelites repented and cried out for the deliverance which Jesus refers to here.

after you cleared the Temple, throwing the money changers out for the first time, the Pharisees asked you to prove that you had authority to do it by performing a miracle and you gave them a seemingly bizarre answer. You said, Here's your miracle,

"Destroy this temple, and in three days I will raise it up."[13]

You were an ornery fellow.

They just wanted to destroy me. I wasn't going to cast my pearls before swine. I was just going to warn them. They were throwing down the challenge, "You're not God." And I was answering them, "Stay around, you'll see."

You had them all figured out.

Jealousy is easy to spot.

(Many times Jesus gave brief but to-the-point answers to my questions just as he had done centuries ago,

"He who is without sin among you, let him be the first to throw a stone at her."[14]
"Get thee behind me, Satan."[15]
"Love thy neighbor as thyself."[16]

That fact impressed upon me how perfectly his use of parables fit him. The parables were meant to reveal in a brief moment everything or nothing. They were never gushy, rarely overwhelming. And they combined beautifully his desire to teach and, like his Father, his need not to intrude. He was the same way with his miracles, often letting them speak for themselves, and certainly never pushing them at the people.

Restraint and brevity characterized his whole life, not just his words or deeds. They pointed to a remarkable self-containment, particularly evident after a miracle. Jesus never flaunted his power, but used it only to draw attention to his role,

"I am the bread of life."[17]

As I further reflected, Jesus was like his Father, Who in the thousands of years of human history available to Him, chose just three years to make a public statement with His son. The Father and the Son both thought there was something powerful about brevity; after all, they just spoke and the world came into being, and later "They put all of Themselves into the size of a man.")

There were other times you responded to the Pharisees in surprising ways. On one occasion, you refused to answer a Pharisee's question.

The closer I got to my destiny, the more aware I was of the tremendous price I was about to pay, and the more aware I was of the Pharisees' attitude toward me. They had no use for me or for what I was doing.

They came up to me the day after I had cleaned out the Temple and said, "Tell us, by whose authority do you remove the merchants from the Temple?"

But they didn't care about the answer. So I judged them. I told them I would answer them if they would answer me. "Was John the Baptist a prophet sent from God, or was he deluded?" I asked. John was very popular with the people and the Pharisees wouldn't answer me. So I refused to answer their question.

The Pharisees' rage toward you finally became intolerable for them. They had to get rid of you.

From the beginning of my ministry, it was obvious that they couldn't live with the differences between myself and them. Finally, the Pharisees became terrified that the people were about to make me king.

Closed Minds, Closed Eyes

Here were these men—ambitious, educated, intelligent by the world's standards. With their own eyes, they had watched you heal hundreds of people, turn five loaves of bread into fifteen thousand, raise the dead; and still they didn't believe in you. You even fit many of the Messianic prophecies which they understood from the Old Testament. How did they miss you?

Oh, they were intelligent, capable, determined. You didn't get to be a Pharisee without hard work. They were from elite families. They were the chosen people of the chosen nation. They were oppressed and they resented their oppressors, the Romans. They also resented their forefathers. They were certain they were better than their ancestors; for if they had lived years before, they thought, this Roman oppression would never have happened because they would have listened to God just as they thought they were doing now. They wanted a Messiah, a deliverer, who would usurp the power of Rome. They deserved that kind of Messiah, they believed, and that was the kind of Messiah their forefathers had said would come.

They knew the Messiah had to come from Judea, almost certainly from the Holy City Jerusalem. That was God's city. That's where He put His Temple. Surely His son would come from there. It had to be. It was the only place that made any sense. Surely the Scriptures said the Messiah would be born in Bethlehem, which was fitting. It was David's city, but was just down the road from Jerusalem. The Scriptures did mention something about Galilee and Egypt, but who could understand all of Scripture? One must go with the obvious, and it was clear—the Messiah had to come from Jerusalem. It couldn't be any other way.

Pride closed the Pharisees' minds, as it always does, even to the point that they couldn't see their own Scriptures. They invented their own Messiah and insisted that he be their kind of Messiah even when that distinctly contradicted much of Scripture.

They could not believe that I could be in any way the Messiah. Here I was, a man from contemptible Galilee. I was from Nazareth, of all places—right on the road to the corrupt pagan world. I was a man who was not rabbi trained, a man who was just a carpenter and who didn't measure up to their standards of greatness. They were certain that this man—that I—was a megalomaniac troublemaker, a man whom Almighty Holy Jehovah God surely hated worse than they did because of his presumptuousness. There had never been a rebel like this in all of Israel's history; not even Jezebel, they thought.

But the Pharisees of my day had to explain my miracles. They couldn't use the explanation that Pharisees used a century later and the one that 20th century Pharisees use today, "The miracles never really happened." The Pharisees of my day were too close to the situation to use that explanation. They could come to only one conclusion: I was straight from Satan himself. There was no other explanation in their minds. They were so sure of themselves.

The Pharisees had one other marvelous trait that obstructed their view—envy. It's one of the worst four-letter words imaginable. Not only could they not duplicate my miracles, but it was becoming more obvious, to anyone who wanted to see, that their characters were flawed and mine was not. They were jealous. I was God and they wanted to be.

Look at all of history. It's the same story. Satan wanted what God had and tried to take it. Cain envied his brother Abel and murdered him. Ishmael, Abraham's illegitimate child, envied Isaac. Isaac's son, Jacob, envied his brother Esau, and stole his birthright. Jacob's older sons envied his younger son, Joseph, and sold their brother into slavery. Saul, the first king of Israel, envied David, who was to be the second king, and repeatedly tried to kill him. Somewhere in their hearts, everybody wants more than his brother has.

So with envy in their hearts, they had to kill you on the pretext that you and Satan were in collusion.

They did. But, as Solomon said. "There's nothing new under the sun." Many of today's religious authorities are still "killing" me, not only for my miracles but also in other ways. These modern Pharisees water down my words. "I am the Light of the world," becomes "I am a nice man and on occasion a nice symbol." "I am the Way, the Truth and the Life" becomes "I am only one among several important men in history." These teachers do not know of the truth about me or about themselves.

Defenders and Deniers

You have indicated your strong feelings about those who water down your words. You must also have strong feelings about those who haven't toned down you or "the pure gospel."

They are the defenders of the faith.

> "Eye hath not seen, nor ear heard. . . the things which God hath prepared for them that love him."[18]

What about the independent humanists? They exalt humanity to the highest place and claim to have values such as compassion, sensitivity, and justice. But they also deny a belief in God in practice if not in actuality. And, if they recognize you at all, it's only as a "good man" or "another prophet."

You're either going to say to my Father, "Thy will be done," or "My will be done." The independent humanists, people who deny any real significance to the spiritual world and feel that man is on his own, obviously say and think the latter. They have no use for my Father or for me. Secretly, they want to take His place. It's an old story that's still being repeated wherever you look. Pantheism, which includes Hinduism and Buddhism, tries to take my Father's place by claiming equality as the core of its teaching. It says we're all the same. The tree, the dog and the human are all the same. What's more, we're all God. We're all just a drop in an ocean called God. Equal parts.

The western version of that is egalitarianism, one of the greatest counterfeits in history. In the name of justice, fairness and equality, truth is forsaken. Heresy is only a footstep away. "All men are created equal," becomes, "All men's ideas are equal, all men's values are equal, all men's religions are equal, all men's religious leaders are equal." Finally, all men's ideas are equal with God's, and thus man has become God. Once again, man has assumed his "rightful place" at the center of the universe. But God answers him back, "you are not a member of the Trinity; you are a creature."

That's an uncomfortable thing for almost anyone—to be just a creature when you can be God. That's primarily where the theory of evolution came from. Humans were looking for a theory to get rid of God. Do you think Darwin wouldn't have interpreted his evidence much differently if he hadn't come along after the Enlightenment when humans had declared themselves free from God? Darwin and his followers should have been doing the same thing the great, early scientists who happened to be Christians did—standing there with their hats in their hands in awe of the wonder of creation. Their attitude was, "We don't have all the pieces; we just know a very little bit."

(At this point, I couldn't help but think how differently Jesus did things, not by grasping for equality with his Father, though it was his, but by

humbling himself and becoming human. In so doing, he reversed all of human history, as do his true followers even to this day. Humility is the mark of the Christian.)

How can you justify Christianity's claim to be the only way to God, a claim that offends many people?

Because it's the truth. Because I am the only God. In an egalitarian society, those are very hard words. But as I said, egalitarianism is a Christian heresy. There's another side to life besides "justice." It's called "truth."

I am God's only son. I am the only one who paid the price and could pay the price for the justification everyone so desperately seeks. No other important person in history has ever made the claims that I've made. I have been here once as the King in all of history and was refused. I'm the only one who came from heaven. That's either true or false.

The heart of the egalitarian gospel says, "there are absolutely no absolutes," thus revealing the intrinsic illogical nature of their faith. Gospels become heresies when they get out of the balance of truth. If you want pictures in nature of absolutes, they're all around you. You can begin with the law of gravity. The sun is absolutely the center of our solar system. You are either dead or alive. Maybe in a dark and dead universe stretching billions of miles, We intended for there to be life on only one planet as a sign that there is only one way to Life. Maybe the earth is a picture of me, a picture of the Incarnation. One man unique among billions. Just so you would get the message, it's no coincidence that the earth is the third planet from the sun, the planet the third member of the Trinity lived on when He left His glory with the other two members. We could have done it that way. One thing is sure, absolutes do exist.

Even though you live in a day and age when humans have become so bigoted that they have tried to kill truth, that will never happen. That's why I make the same offer today I made twenty centuries ago. If anyone will do my will, he will know who I am; he will know the truth.[19] You must choose your will or my Father's will. The problem is that nobody really wants anyone's will done but his own.

Everywhere we look today humans are proclaiming from all corners of the globe, "We don't need you God." They think God is just an idea, just a word. This is where the independent humanists are foolish. If you could get rid of my Father tomorrow, it would not be long before all the humanists would destroy themselves in the name of humanism. In the last days, God will give men that chance as the book of Revelation makes plain.

You see, independent humanists are self-destructive because they destroy the truth: the truth that God exists. Once they do that, they'll destroy the next truth they don't like and the next one after that until they're the most self-destructive people in the world. All the while they'll be denying their destructiveness. Humans are capable of that, you know. Do you think the self-proclaimed humanist Adolph Hitler got up every morning and looked in the mirror and said, "You're a ruthless mass murderer?"

There are two perspectives. The first is a worldly perspective, a secular view limited to this world. The other perspective has a clear view of the unseen, the transcendent spiritual world. You have either one or the other. All those who share only the worldly perspective position have an unconscious alliance. They are a living testimony to the spirit of this world.

These people think they are going to give others purpose and meaning. The problem is that in the depths of his soul, everyone lives his or her truth and it will prevail. If your truth says, "Man's not eternal and I really don't believe in anything eternal. It's not really an important question," then you're going to begin somewhere to live out your truth that nothing is eternal. Logically that "truth" ultimately says nothing matters and eventually reaps a society that doesn't care, because there is nothing worth caring about.

The people of this world today are being fed one of the greatest propaganda lines in history, and they don't see it. They're being told, "You make up your own mind. Do your own thing; it doesn't matter." That's an age-old lie. "It doesn't matter, Satan. Overthrow the Father." "It doesn't matter Eve. Eat that apple." "It doesn't matter, Judas. Betray Jesus; someone else can be a better leader."

I want to say that it does matter. Everything matters. You matter. Your choices matter. Your words matter. Your children matter. Isn't that a wonderful message that I was privileged to bring to the world two thousand years ago? And through my people and my Word I still get to speak to the whole world every day; to a world that's indifferent, and careless, and self-destructive, because nobody has given them a reason not to be. And to that world I get to say, "I am Life, come."

You were anything but dull and stupid and yet there is a mentality that says that Christians are rather stupid, weak people. Many Christians themselves seem to have agreed with this idea and even refer to the Scriptures to justify this self-concept, using verses such as,

"God has chosen the foolish things of the world to confound the wise."[20]

Humility is the queen of the virtues, but my people forget about their heritage that was full of brilliant people whom my Father used mightily. Moses was tremendously learned, educated in an Egyptian culture that was centuries ahead of its time. Daniel, as a foreigner, like Moses, was recognized as the genius in one of the most powerful empires in the history of the world, the Babylonian empire.

Another one of my followers was David, who was not only a warrior and a king, but a brilliant poet. David's son, Solomon, had wisdom far beyond anything this world has seen before or since with one exception, and people came from all over the world to observe his wisdom. They found it to be far greater than they had imagined it would be.

Then, after my death came a brilliant Jewish lawyer and scholar who became the greatest missionary the world has ever seen, a man named Paul. Few people know that Paul in his time was known as the genius of the Middle East. His teacher, Gamaliel, who is mentioned in the Scriptures, was the foremost teacher in the most respected school in the Middle East and Paul was his outstanding pupil.

That's why Paul's fellow Jews and scholars were so stunned when this man with the great mind bowed to God and became a missionary, a "despicable Christian convert." Yet Paul stood on Mar's Hill in Athens and brilliantly debated "the best thinkers" in the world and came out the winner. To this day Paul's great mind, sanctified by the Spirit, is still blessing people all over the world through his epistles. As is so typical of Him, my Father had responded to Paul's offer to use his mind and his brilliance in my Father's service by blessing Paul's work beyond belief. Just as He did with the others I mentioned. All these men of God and many more had superior minds and, better yet, loving hearts.

I'll tell you how much my Father loves wisdom and knowledge. He made His only son the most-quoted man in history just to show how much brilliance comes from walking in His light. Part of being almighty is being brilliant. I never felt handicapped intellectually. My Father made sure of that. That is another proof of the Scriptures—what they can do for you intellectually. God gives His people great insight. As David said in the 119th Psalm,

> "I have more insight than all of my teachers, For Thy testimonies are my meditation. I understand more than the aged, Because I have observed Thy precepts."[21]

Your teaching and your brilliance, just like your Father's, penetrate all areas of life. You predated by about 1900 years Freud's discovery of the unconscious and the particular unconscious mental mechanism or "trick" of projection, both cornerstones of modern psychiatry. Freud said that unconsciously people see in others what really is a part of themselves. You said it better so that everyone could understand it—the speck you see in your neighbor's eye is the log in your own eye.

You weren't particularly bashful, either, about saying how gifted your Father had made you. On one occasion when the Pharisees were ignoring you, you told them that "one greater than Solomon is here."[22]

One of the reasons my followers sometimes are much more timid and retiring than they have to be is because they are afraid of being like Satan and, in a way, rightfully so. Satan had so much talent that he became proud and forgot that he wasn't God. To protect themselves from their pride and their universal secret wish to be God, my people at times debase themselves.

Do you think that secretly everybody really wants to be God?

Everybody wants things exactly his own way—wants to be the Father—except me.

Even the little godly old lady who bakes cookies for the church bake sale and raised two sons who became missionaries?

Within every sweet person lurks an Alexander the Great. It may take the form of just wanting your son to be "the great one" or making sure everybody knows your minister is the best one in town. This wanting to conquer the world, and the fear of expressing that wish, and becoming like Satan cause us to forget we're like God. And there is nothing stupid about God. The Gospel does say that there is something desperately wrong with you, but the Gospel does not minimize the intellect. It's not that Christianity is stupid; it's offensive to one's pride.

Christians are not to accept the role of the village idiot. God never asks us to believe that for one minute. When I went out to do battle with the Pharisees, I had confidence in the wisdom God gave me. Because of that I knew I could see farther than they could.

I get the feeling you enjoyed out-maneuvering the Pharisees.

I didn't mind winning encounters with that kind of people.

That sounds very un-Christian.

I got it from my Father. Truth should always win out when it can. You haven't seen anything yet until you've seen the victory party He's got planned in heaven. People have stereotyped images of my Father, but as I read the Scriptures I got a very different picture. I paid particular attention because this was my Father talking. His character was stamped on every page. His personality exuded from this book, and I remember being constantly surprised. He was so much like I was.

Suppose I described my Father as someone who loves beautiful things. He ought to like them. He made them. Read Ezekiel where my Father talks about what He had given to His people, Israel,

> "I gave you beautiful clothes of linens and silks . . . I gave you . . . bracelets and beautiful necklaces . . . And so you were made beautiful with gold and silver . . . You ate the finest foods and you became more beautiful than ever. You looked like a queen and so you were! Your reputation was great among the nations for your beauty; it was perfect because of all the gifts I gave you, says the Lord God."[23]

Look how He dressed His priests and look at the splendor with which He surrounded His kings. People forget that the most splendid king in the history of the world was Solomon. As the Scriptures record, he was

> "richer and wiser than all the kings of the earth."[24]

The Queen of Sheba, who had heard of Solomon's fabled wealth and wisdom, made a six-month's journey of 1500 miles by caravan to see Solomon firsthand. She saw his great palace with the great room 150 feet long and 45 feet high. There were 500 huge solid gold shields on the walls. Then she saw his unbelievably immense ivory throne, the most famous in the world, overlaid with gold. It had a gold footstool, and was surrounded by six gold steps with two enormous gold lions on each step. The Queen of Sheba saw nothing but solid gold cups used at Solomon's tables which were immaculately set, surrounded by hundreds of beautifully dressed servants. She saw his 4,000 stables and 1,200 chariots and all the gold in his treasury.

But all of this was as nothing compared to how Solomon impressed her with his wisdom. He was an architect, a musician, a composer, a poet, a philosopher, and a statesman, in addition to being a king. Before she left, the Queen of Sheba told him,

> "Everything I heard in my own country about your wisdom . . . is all true . . . The half had not been told me! . . . How the Lord must love Israel—for he gave you to them as their king!"[25]

Everything Solomon has or had, my Father gave to him. He was a picture of my Father. When you think of someone that great, do you think of God? And even though I was poor, I always loved beauty. I had appreciation, even if I was a "blue-collar" worker.

Piety

You never seemed very pious.

In many ways, I never wanted to be. That's why I did some of the things I did. I ate meals without the ceremony of washing. I allowed my disciples to gather grain on the Sabbath for a meal. I healed on the Sabbath and visited the homes of "pagans." I wanted to break through this phony pious image of what it meant to be spiritual. I wanted people to live out the exciting task of being believers, of having vital relationships with my Father.

I hate hypocrisy and false piety. There's something about religious hypocrisy that's particularly offensive, maybe because believers are supposed to represent the ultimate in authenticity. But remember, too, there are hypocrites at the country club or at the "most honest business in town" or wherever people look in mirrors. Hypocrites in part mean well, in the sense that they are trying to be better than they really are, and, in their own perverted way, testify to the Truth.

There's no perfection in this world. And if I asked that of my followers, I wouldn't have any and my people wouldn't really need a saviour. Nobody sees all of his or her phoniness, but I want my people to admit their imperfections and their need for me.

You don't expect your followers to be perfect?

How can you expect someone who has a heart so deceitfully wicked ever to be perfect? The flesh is ever-present—that part of you that wants to sin. You may control it most of the time, but you can still feel its presence. It is the part of you that lusts for materialism, that secretly delights in gossip, that privately enjoys your neighbor's failures. It is the part of you that wants to look at that pornographic magazine or wants to go to that erotic movie. That's the curse, and one day it will be gone.

One day all of my followers will experience complete purity. There will be nothing about themselves they won't like. Until then, I've made adequate provision for them to walk free from guilt. It cost me my earthly life.

Their Christian lives now are much like a football team with a game plan going for a victory. There may be some fumbles, some mistakes, but when the mistakes come, they have to keep going; never giving up, always striving. When they fall, they are to come boldly to the throne of grace to obtain mercy in their time of need as Paul said. That's one of the big victories they are to have down here—the victory of forgiveness. One day their total victory will come, but for now, as C.S. Lewis said, one of the first things a Christian learns is to get back up after he falls.

Many people think the church today is insignificant.

The church is not perfect and it won't be until my return, but it's not insignificant. In the first century, the church had its beginnings in a small, out of the way, "peculiar" country, and to all outward appearances was insignificant. Rome ruled the world.

Within three centuries, Rome was gone, the church had mushroomed, and up to the present day has dominated the scene for two thousand years. Whatever else you may think of the church, with all its factions and hypocrisy, it has remained on center stage all these years and will continue to do so until my return. I meant it when I said,

"The gates of hell will not prevail against my church."[26]

Preview of Pain

Luke quotes you as saying,

"Oh, that my task were completed! There is a terrible baptism ahead of me, and how I am pent up until it is accomplished!"[27]

Obviously you dreaded what was ahead of you. In your own parables and the lessons you taught your disciples, death and bodily damage were recurrent images. We see it in the parable of the Good Samaritan who was beaten, and the parable where you talk about the crippled coming to a banquet. The death parable shows it; you talk about a rich fool who is going to store up his wealth and enjoy it, but he dies that night.

On other occasions, you told your disciples not to be afraid of death. Once as you came into the City of Jerusalem, you proclaimed,

"O Jerusalem, Jerusalem! The city that murders the prophets."[28]

Another time you called the Pharisees murderers. These images suggest that death was very much on your mind.

The closer I got, the more sharply it came into focus. Every day it became more real. It was one of those things you know is going to happen, but you don't think it really will and you half hope it won't. But I felt the pressure. I thought about my crucifixion day often; that day which I waited for forever. Just one day of extreme suffering was all I had to take—one day out of my whole life. At first I would tell myself, "Anybody can do that." But nobody ever had. No one had ever come close to the way the Scriptures described.

The pain was horrible. Pain can break anybody. It's what dictators over the years have used to conquer. When all else failed to break a prisoner, they would send in the torturers. And I was going to face The Torturer himself.

I was the world's prisoner; voluntarily maybe, but still their prisoner. And they were going to try to break me. Their hope was that I would have so much pain I couldn't stand it and would give up, so much pain that maybe I would lash out at them and become like they were. Or perhaps I would even lash out at my Father like they did, blaming Him for their woes.

I was determined to go through with the crucifixion. My Father had said I would make it. But just how would I stand the pain? I had to wait until that day arrived to find out. I would have lost my mind had I thought about it all the time.

As you said,

"Sufficient unto the day is the evil thereof."[29]

That's why I could teach the people, "Don't worry about tomorrow." I learned to go to my Father and live in Him, each day. But I thought about that last day a lot. The anticipated pain of that short period of less than twenty-four hours extended over the whole day of my life. I fought to keep it from ruling my life for the twenty-one years I knew about it. After that day was over, I would then ask everybody to make one decision upon which their whole life would hang. Did I or didn't I accomplish salvation? I, too, had to make one decision upon which my whole life hinged. I had to choose my way or God's way. I knew a lot about choice and I couldn't escape having to make the hardest choice myself.

The consistent theme in many of your parables is now or never—choose God now or the door is shut. When you think of "being saved" in those terms, then salvation takes on a deeper meaning.

The spirit of this world has helped make salvation a trite word. The world has scoffed at the idea of being saved and, in their blindness, many human beings have bought that idea. But you're in a terrific struggle for life and death even if you don't know it.

When a doctor enters a patient's room and says "You've got cancer," what's the first reaction universally, the first stage psychologically? It's denial: "Not me!" That's the psychological mindset of the whole world—denial. Everyone around you has a terminal disease, and so do you. The Scriptures tell you that you are utterly defeated, in turmoil, hopelessness, nothingness, and dust. Your deepest fear is realized—death. When the patient realizes he or she has the disease, cancer research takes on new meaning.

In the same way, when a person really gets to that same edge of reality in his or her life, salvation is no longer just a word. You can hear the "Doctor's voice" in Scripture. That voice, for some, is hard to hear. Ask any doctor who has to bring painful messages. He or she is hard to hear. If you can hear those words, if you can hear how sick you are, how black with sin you are, then hope, cure, life itself is yours. Victory at the last minute is snapped from the jaws of defeat. One can look death in the face:

"O death, where is thy sting? O grave, where is thy victory?"[30]

But you can say that only with confidence if the word, "salvation," means anything to you.

You must have prepared yourself mentally for the crucifixion.

I can't tell you how many times my mind played out that scene, particularly the closer I got to it. I knew so well what was going to happen. I could see them beating my face, spitting on me, pulling my beard.

After my face then came my back. Thirty-nine times they would lash my back, ripping it open. If I was able, I planned to meditate on the Scriptures as the punishment continued, particularly the passage in Isaiah,

"He was wounded for our transgressions . . . and with his stripes we are healed . . . he opened not his mouth."[31]

I also planned to think of everyone I loved whose punishment I was taking, present followers and past as well as future believers. I was going to keep reminding myself I was their shepherd. Without me they were all lost. Moses would be lost. David, Elijah, and Daniel as well; I had to do it. I would remember that.

Each time I envisioned in detail them beating my face and lashing my back, it always amazed me that I would have to take more after that part of the persecution. I knew I would be very tired by then, and I knew what would come next—the crucifixion. There would be nails in my hands and feet. I couldn't imagine the pain. I anticipated correctly that I would have to carry my cross outside the city as criminals always did, and I would have to do this at a moment of tremendous physical weakness.

So from the start I understood I was in for a real battle. The question kept coming to me, "How am I going to do it and not say a word?" It just didn't seem possible. But I knew that if my Father filled me with enough love, I could do it. I would think back over how my Father had done impossible things before, and I knew if He wanted this deed carried out, He would help me.

By the time I was actually crucified, I had died a thousand deaths. But I also knew what I was going to do when I got there. My Father always prepares you. I didn't go into that battle untrained or undisciplined.

Signs of the End

Often persons dying of a terminal disease describe how the awareness of their death significantly affects how they look at the world. What effect did your being a "marked man" who was going to die have on your perceptions of the world?

Aside from the pain, it had its positive effects. It caused me to see the world for the way it really is. It was obvious to me that nothing on this earth was going to last forever. The only eternal things besides the Scriptures surrounding me were my fellow humans, and even they wouldn't be in the same form or place forever.

The more I pored over the Scriptures, the more I understood my role and at the same time how transient everything was. That's why, at times, when my disciples and I would be walking down the street they would see a beautiful temple, but I would be thinking about how one day soon everything around us would be destroyed.

You took the opportunity to point that out one day when they were commenting on how magnificent the Temple in Jerusalem was. You warned them about the end times when the whole Temple would be leveled. As you said, there would be "not one stone here left upon another."[32]

I did point that out to them. That same day we left Jerusalem and stopped on the Mount of Olives. At one point in the afternoon, I was sitting with four of my disciples. As we looked out across the Kidron Valley to Jerusalem on the opposite hill, we could still see the Temple behind the walls. My disciples had been thinking about what I had said earlier and asked me when the destruction of the Temple was coming to pass. They wondered if there would be a warning; so I told them the signs of the end time.

How did you know what the signs would be?

It was all there in the Old Testament, every one of the signs. I told them that, just as in Jeremiah's day, it would be a time of false prophets and false Messiahs. The prophets Daniel and Joel had prophesied that the end time would be a period of the worst and most horrible devastation in history, almost incomprehensible. It would be far beyond the suffering Hitler and Stalin brought about. The Great Tribulation would live up to its name. There would be wars everywhere, in nearly every nation.

Never before would my Father have allowed humans on a worldwide basis such free reign of their basic instincts. This time they would be turned loose and would prove for all to see what humanity really was like. As if to match mankind's destructiveness, nature would have its own upheaval. There would be famines everywhere. Earthquakes would be commonplace. Untreatable diseases would abound. Even the oceans would be turbulent. Nature's chaos would also be an answer of judgment from my Father on the destructiveness of humans.

Christians would be persecuted everywhere, frequently being made prisoners or slaves. In the middle of this chaos, with seemingly perfect timing, a "Great Leader" would emerge offering worldwide peace. He would become the most powerful leader to this point in human history. So desperate would people everywhere be that, unbelievably, they will make this ruler the dictator of the world. This dictator who secretly would love war and power would masquerade as a man of peace. He would be "so beloved" that he would almost deceive God's own people, even though they knew this deceiver was coming. He would demonstrate supernatural power at moments. After ruling for three and a half years, this man, the Antichrist, would march into Jerusalem. And in the Abomination the prophet Daniel predicted hundreds of years before, the Antichrist would sit on the throne there and declare that he is God.

Tremendous persecution of my followers would take place, much worse than the horrible abuse they were already enduring. Then the citizens of the world, who would feel that they were just coming out of the worst time in history would be plunged back into depths of destruction they had never believed possible. Newspapers, where they continued to exist, would describe a fresh worldwide catastrophe almost daily. People would cry out, wishing they were dead. Wars and destruction would be everywhere. Nonetheless, some of my followers would shine, as they fearlessly declared the Gospel—the Good News amidst a world that would be destroying itself.

Unless my Father intervenes, the world will literally destroy itself. But humans will not wipe themselves off the earth with nuclear destruction. My Father controls even the buttons that set off the bombs. At precisely the preordained moment, I will return to take over the world.

You gave them a very specific description of that moment.

The Scriptures gave me a very specific description of that moment. The whole earth will get dark. The sun, moon and stars will no longer shine. The moon will turn blood red and the heavens will literally tremble. The whole world and everyone who has ever lived will see me arriving on clouds in all my glory. They will hear a mighty trumpet blast like they've never heard before as I send out my angels to bring in all my followers from around the earth and from heaven to make my entry with me. Just as I predicted, I will descend to the

Mount of Olives. As I do so, it will divide in half, forming a great valley. I will come once again to divide.

And you learned all of that from the Old Testament?

My Father arranged the Scriptures so I would understand my role. I reached a point where I realized what He had done and began looking for myself. For example, when my Father "came to this earth" on a special occasion in the past, he had Moses gather all the people together at Mount Sinai with a mighty trumpet blast. I felt that told me indirectly about my second coming. Zechariah also mentioned the trumpet, and the prophets Joel and Daniel were storehouses of predictions as they specifically talked about the Messiah's final return.

Of course, my Father also arranged all of history so that I would understand what was going to happen. When I was a young man it was hard to miss the fact that Daniel had been correct in his prediction that there would be four great kings and world rulers before the Messiah. These four had already come —Babylon, Medea-Persia, the Greeks, and the Romans. Less than two hundred years before I was born, a cruel ruler named Antiochus Epiphanes* conquered Israel and he was still talked about in my day. On a smaller scale, he was a precise picture of the future Antichrist. Besides having the Scriptures and history to teach me about the future, I had one other advantage. I was able to talk with some angels and to go over the events of the end times with them.

The Man and the Mission

Seemingly, you alone understood thoroughly your mission. The Pharisees weren't the only ones who misunderstood you. The records seem to indicate that even your own mother, who had participated in the miracle of miracles, your birth, didn't understand what you were doing. She once came with your half-brothers to ask you to restrain yourself.

Once I set out on my journey, my family quickly heard about my following and they heard the criticism, too, particularly that from the rabbis and scribes. Everyone in Nazareth was saying, "He was just a carpenter," and my family heard what a radical I had become. Not only was I talking to untouchables such as the tax collectors, but I was also eating dinner in their homes and going to their parties. People said my followers were nothing but tax collectors, radicals, and fishermen. For the most part, they were right. My religious critics

---

*Antiochus Epiphanes (175–164B.C.) was very charismatic and deceitful, and came to power suddenly. He had conquered Israel and in 168 B.C. tried to destroy Jewish worship and Judaism altogether. He stopped the daily burnt offerings that had been going on for centuries. He desecrated the Temple by erecting a statue of Zeus there and storming into the "Holy of Holies."

complained that my men were not particularly learned, and certainly not men of God, true men of the Scriptures. Of course, that wasn't true. My men knew the Scriptures.

My family also heard that I was deviating from the Law. I was not observing the sabbath, not washing before meals. They were told I was making incredible claims: "I am the Light of the World; I am the Bread of Life," and that I was, on my own authority, forgiving sins. People were saying then that I was insane just as some do today. Worst of all, my family heard that I was attracting my following by using demonic powers to heal, to drive out demons, and even to raise the dead.

The pressure on them became so great that they came to see what I was doing. My mother brought only my brothers. She thought they could best confront me without my sisters. They asked me not to stir up trouble and not be so provoking to the Pharisees. They felt so strongly about this that when they came to where I was one midday when I was surrounded by a crowd, my brothers couldn't wait until I was through teaching to talk to me. They sent a message that they needed to speak to me immediately.

You sent them an interesting answer.

The messenger couldn't get to me because of the crowd. So he yelled loud enough for everyone to hear, "Master, your mother and brothers are here and want to speak to you." Because they so obviously had to interrupt my teaching, I immediately surmised the reason. So I looked at the crowd and asked them, "Who among you is my mother and my brothers?" Then I pointed to the people around me and said,

> "These are my mother and brothers! Anyone who does God's will is my brother, and my sister, and my mother."[33]

Did you make your relatives wait?

They had to wait all afternoon. They needed to be reminded of who I was, and they obviously needed to learn more patience. My family had had all sorts of advantages to know who I was, one of which was seeing me perform my first miracle at the wedding in Cana. Afterwards, my disciples and I spent several days in Capernaum with my mother and these same brothers. In spite of the fact that mother had witnessed various supernatural events which she told them about, they all had trouble believing I was someone other than their brother or son. In fact, they were so sure I needed their help that they made a long journey to find me. They were sincere, but sincerely wrong. However, it worked out well eventually because my brother James, whom they had elected as spokesman for the group, later wrote in his Epistle about not letting first impressions or rumors sway you.

I am surprised that your mother reacted the way she did.

She was human. Just because she was the savior's mother, she wasn't perfect. If you were told by your rabbi and all the people you had respected all your life that your son had lost his mind and was attacking religion, you would probably go to see him. I was not around to defend myself, and my mother temporarily lost perspective. Like John the Baptist, she thought that maybe I didn't understand my role. And since she had been my advisor all my life, she still thought she had some say-so with me. She wasn't prepared for all my teaching, either, and she didn't realize how evil the Pharisees were. She was my mother. She couldn't bear to see me die, and she knew that I wouldn't live long teaching what I did.

Your mother wasn't the only one who began to wonder about you. As you mentioned, even your own prophet, John the Baptist, later questioned whether you were really the Messiah.

John was making bold efforts to proclaim me the Messiah, and when he saw me "just walking around from town to town teaching," he began to wonder why I wasn't consistently denouncing the Pharisees publicly for their hypocrisy. Why wasn't I making bold efforts to become the king? He himself would have done so had he seen the Messiah.

John and I had very different personalities. That's why my Father chose him to be my prophet. John got concerned, but true to himself, he handled things very straightforwardly. He sent one of his disciples down to ask me if I really was the Messiah or if someone else were coming after me.

What did you tell him?

I told him that the blind see, the lame walk, the lepers are healed, the deaf hear, the dead are raised, and the good news is preached to the poor. I reminded him: "Blessed is the man who doesn't lose faith in me."

John's death must have had an impact on you.

It shocked me. I wasn't prepared for it even though I should have been. Most of the Old Testament prophets were killed by their own people, you know. There's nothing like death to open the door to reality, and John's death brought home the largest reality of all—my own death was imminent. John was murdered by Herod for telling the truth just as I would be. He had been a good man, and they took his life. I remember thinking again, "It's all coming true, just as the prophets said."

In a strange but real way, John comforted me in his death just as he had during his life, for I was not to be the only one who died for truth. My Father had known that in coming to terms with my mission I needed confirmation that He was at work. And as only He can do—working all things out for good—He used John's death to encourage me. Just as John was similar to me in his birth, John was like me in his death. Later when I was being crucified, my tormentors tried very hard to make me feel that I was evil and dirty. Even then John helped keep me from being overwhelmed by feelings of shame, because I could recall that sometimes a good man is killed.

Nothing affects you like the death of someone you're close to. When I heard about John's murder, I wanted to be alone and spend time with my Father.

You left town for the country, but many people followed you. Why didn't you turn them away at a time like this?

I meant what I said: to live is to deny yourself for the sake of others. You don't simply deny yourself. That's the world's distortion of what I said. You deny yourself for others.

I saw people crying out for a reason to live, for a purpose, for real life. I began to teach them there in the wilderness. I stood in a little valley and looked around me at several thousand people scattered about on the sides of the hills, miles away from home, listening to every word I spoke.

And was that one of the times when you fed a great crowd?

Yes. Late in the day, my disciples came up to me and said the people were very hungry. It was late, and I should send them back to town to find food. Then I remembered the scriptures. I had an idea. I told my disciples, "You feed them." They looked at me with one of those, "Are you crazy?" looks that I was getting used to by now. They informed me it would take a fortune to feed several thousand people and, besides, there were no markets anywhere around.

I asked how much food we had. Andrew was trying so hard to believe. He said meekly in a half-hearted way, "There's one little boy with five loaves of bread and two fish." I told them to bring that food to me.

That was one of my favorite miracles. I held the food up to my Father and asked Him to bless what I was about to do. Going through my mind was my imminent death at the hands of the priests, and I thought to myself: "You can kill John. You can kill me. But you can never stop me, and you can never stop my people from following me. My sheep know my voice, and I will feed them. I am the Bread of Life. That's who my Father made me to be."

Then I took the five loaves and two fish and fed five thousand men and their families all they could eat. As I divided the food, I looked out at that crowd and kept thinking, "This is my body broken for you." And at the same time, to comfort myself, I thought, "The Kingdom of God will multiply just as this food is multiplied." After it was over, I had my disciples gather the leftovers. There were twelve large baskets. They said it was the most delicious fish those people ever had. You can confirm that in heaven.

Was that when the people tried to make you king?

They had never seen power like that, and they were immediately ready to challenge Rome. If I could make food, I could do anything. I must be the Messiah, and in their minds that meant only one thing—power! A group of men tried to overtake me, throw me on their shoulders, and force me to be king. They were willing to participate in riots, rebellions, or whatever it took. Rome was coming down in their eyes and their dreams.

They hadn't learned at all what I was trying to teach. They had ignored my "Sermon on the Mount."

"Blessed are the meek, for they will inherit the earth . . .

Blessed are the peacemakers, for they will be called sons of God.

Blessed are you when people persecute you, . . . for great is your reward in heaven."[34]

Blessed are those who mourn, not blessed are those who overcome others." They were going to do it the world's way—with muscle, with power, with rebellion. I came the first time to win men's hearts, not to overpower them. I would use my muscle one day, but that would be when I came in judgment. Now I was coming in peace. That was to be Our way on this earth. These men hadn't comprehended that. Galilee was no more ready to receive me than was Jerusalem.

I felt that my teaching had failed. These men were coming to make me King. They didn't even ask me what I thought about their idea. They didn't have the slightest idea of how heavy my heart was because of John's death. I was so disturbed, I didn't even wait for them to reach me. There would be no reasoning with that crowd any more than there was with the crowd in my home town or the crowd waiting for me in Jerusalem.

Before they got to me, I slipped away and climbed high up the mountain where crowds couldn't come and no one could find me.

I knew something had to change. Now I had the time with my Father that I needed. I spent six hours with Him. It was one of those times when I needed Him, desperately—His confidence, His calmness, His vision. I couldn't get John's death off my mind. The shock. The grief now. The grief to come.

As usual, and you can say this only if you've experienced it, I had His peace, His. I was surrounded by people who didn't understand, who were trying to force my hand before I wanted it played. I needed to know where to go from there. At the rate I was going, there would be a riot the next day and I could forget about Palm Sunday and Passover.

The Mountain and the Miracle

What did you and your Father talk about on the mountain?

That night I asked the Lord: "Where now? What now?" And over the next few hours it became clear to me. Many who followed me weren't my true followers. They were power-mongers. And I could see the cost. Many, probably most, would desert me, and I counted that cost.

Despite the tension that persisted, I had the most incredible peace from my Father. For the next few hours before I left the mountain, I spent time praising Him, meditating on His words, and singing some songs.

I remember that night how grateful I was that I had learned how to get that degree of oneness with Him. How grateful I was that I had learned the skills of faith. I couldn't have been that comforted when I was fourteen, but now I knew how to abide, how to live in Him.

What a thrill it is when you eventually come to know that your Father in heaven is so omnipotent that He is your friend who constantly goes before you every, every step of the way. He looks for ways to reassure you and delights when you turn to Him. He holds every situation in the palm of His hand. The verses,

> "There is a friend who sticks closer than a brother."[35]

and

> "many are thy thoughts toward us."[36]

kept coming back to me. If you can know those words, you will have Him and you will have life.

Before I left the mountains that night I asked my Father one last thing, something very special. I knew this was to be a major turning point in my ministry and I wanted to send the people, and particularly my disciples, one more important message about why I was here. My disciples could easily get caught up in this frenzy. They still didn't really understand who I was and what I was about. I was also still grieving over John's death and my own death which was becoming more imminent, and I thought of the verse,

> "Cast thy bread upon the waters: for thou shalt find it after many days."[37]

Suddenly it occurred to me to ask my Father for something special. "May I walk on my grave, on my death?"*

Just as I accepted my grave when I went to be baptized, might I now have the privilege of walking on top of it, a foretaste of the day that I would walk out of it? Immediately I knew I could—the Scriptures told me I would do awe-inspiring deeds for myself as well as for others. It was clear to me that all things that the Father had were mine, and He held the oceans in the palm of His hand.

Moses had walked through the ocean, Noah had walked on it—on my grave—and Jonah had spent three days in it, and all three had come out alive. They were all pictures of my ruling the ocean, ruling nature as King. Later I would further declare my lordship over nature by cursing a tree and causing it to wither. At this time I began to realize my Father was commanding me to go ahead.

It was another one of those moments when I bowed before the awesome Scriptures. I'll tell you this—many people will end in hell, but they'll do so shaking their fists at reason. They'll never be able to say they weren't told what was happening.

Where were your disciples all this time?

---

*The sea, the water, was the symbol of death and the grave. It's where baptism comes from, which also contains the picture of resurrection.

I had already sent my disciples across the Sea of Galilee in the only boat we had. Somehow, in the back of my mind I knew what I would ask my Father for, and I knew that He would grant it. He did! And I walked on the water to my disciples. All the way out there, part of me couldn't believe it. I was actually walking on water. It was the first time I'd ever done it.

I had some fun with it, too. I thought of strolling up to my men and saying, "Nothing to it, fellows." I was impressed. I said to my Father, "You did show me Your power, didn't you?" I kept thinking of my Father, how great He really was. He never laid on us more than we could bear, and He always gave us a taste of our future glory to keep us going.

When I got to the boat, my disciples were, you might say, slightly alarmed. *(He laughed again loudly.)* They thought I was a ghost. They thought the crowd that wanted to make me king had somehow lost control and I had been killed. Now here they were, huddled together on the far side of the boat afraid of a ghost. It was a very comical sight. Even after I told them who I was as I neared the boat, they were too frightened to do anything. That included, of course, everybody but guess who?

Peter.

Peter was his usual self. He was leaning over the side of the boat toward me, looking at me, and saying, "Lord, let me do it, too." So I let him. He walked for a little way, but when he realized what he was actually doing he became frightened and sank. Peter's like a lot of folks. He lacked some of the faith he needed. But at that moment he didn't lack courage.

So if Peter had believed in you completely, he would have made it?

Absolutely.

Did you have some of the same feelings Peter did when you were out for your evening stroll on the water?

I almost always had the same feelings others had. I had the sense that, "This is strange." I wondered, "Is this a dream? What if I start to sink? I'm a long way from the shore." But I'd just come from six intense hours alone with my Father and I knew He could do anything. In the face of doubt, I knew how to trust completely. Peter didn't. So I had to hold him by the arm as we walked back to the boat together. Peter was much more humble on the way back, but that wasn't too bad a lesson for him to learn. Without me and my Father, neither he nor the rest of them could ever accomplish anything.

By the time you and Peter got to the boat, the New Testament indicates that the disciples had finally caught on or thought they had and said, "Now we know that you really are the Son of God." What brilliance! Whenever I read that, I always chuckle and think of the people who say that God has no sense of humor.

My Father's sense of humor is seen all through the Scriptures and in nature. Remember the time God wanted to stop a prophet of sorts by the name of Balaam from taking a particular action? He had Balaam's donkey stop, turn around, and talk to Balaam. That's funny. Don't you think my Father was amused by changing an old man's name from Abram to Abraham which meant "the Father of many nations" when the man at age seventy-five had no children and his wife was post-menopausal? Abraham's friends would come up to him and ask him his name, and he would say, "Abraham" meaning Father of Many Nations." They asked him when he was eighty-five, with an old wife, how many children he had, and he had to tell them, "None, so far." Then years later here there was an expectant new mother, Sarah, walking around eight months pregnant at age ninety-one while Abraham, the proud father, was one hundred years old. That's humor for you. Don't you think God had a good time dressing up my cousin, John the Baptist, "to begin his public ministry"? And anybody who created Peter had to have a sense of humor.

Surprised by the Spirit

How surprised were you with some of the things you did?

That was one of the surest signs to me that I was God, that my Father lived through me. I would often ask myself after a miracle, "Where did that come from?" I would amaze myself because "I was not just I." At times I could actually feel His power in me.

That impressed you.

Many times I would sit and think, "So you're God." It was amazing to me. The 45th Psalm described what I would do, and it was beyond my wildest imagination at first. The Scriptures even told me I would be impressed. Of course, it was all because of Him. The 45th Psalm says,

> "Thy right hand [shall] teach Thee (meaning myself), awesome things."[38]

In other words, my own deeds would teach me. Being one with the Spirit was magnificent. The things He did through me inspired me. Isn't that the way He works with you, with all believers? Aren't you honored when He uses you to do good things?

Yes. Of course I am.

It was the same for me. I never completely ceased to wonder who I was. Frequently I felt like just another man, but the more closely I stuck to my Father and His words to me, the more I realized that I was the Messiah and the more I thought like the Messiah. It's the same thing that happens to a man when he becomes a world leader. It's hard to believe at first, but then one grows into the role.

In my day, the condition of the world helped to clarify my identity. One day before I went public with my announcement, I perceived that the world really had no leader. They were all sheep without a shepherd, and the more I saw that somebody needed to be the shepherd, the more I realized that I was the logical choice.

Still, from time to time, the awesomeness of who I was would overwhelm me. To think I was God was amazing. That's why I never quit having empathy for people who have trouble believing me to be God. I had trouble also. That's why I told them to look at my miracles if they were having trouble with that overwhelming perception. I did. I never stopped having a sense of wonder at my true identity and at my power. That's why my so-called "progressive followers" who say they worship me but don't believe I did miracles end up with such a weak faith, if they have any faith at all. They have such a low opinion of me, and hence of themselves.

If a man was to be the Messiah in the way my Father intended it, the role itself demanded that the Messiah have some supernatural powers. He had to stand not only beside his fellow men and women but also above them, not just in character, but in power, too. My Father obviously knew that in order for people to believe "a man was going to be God," that man must do some extraordinarily powerful things.

God did the same thing early in the church history in the first century. when He asked people to believe that my disciples were telling the truth. He gave the disciples unusual power. My Father doesn't ask people to take a wild leap, although sometimes, I must say, He gives you a Fatherly push. No one can really believe who I am without believing that I did miracles. Otherwise I'm just another man.

Also, the Scriptures told me how great I was and promised me that I would do things such as ride forth with splendor and majesty on behalf of truth and righteousness. This whole idea was unbelievable; but, of course, that's the way He works. The whole human race was going in one direction, the way of death and destruction, and I—I was going to turn it completely around. That was my mission. Afterwards, He was going to let me bring my people with me to live with us forever. His plans were so magnificent.

To get back to my story, the next morning after their great push to make me king, all the crowds were down by the shore at the base of the hills waiting for me to come down. They knew I had already sent my disciples across the Sea of Galilee to Capernaum. After waiting some time, the people got into their boats and came on over to Capernaum where, much to their surprise, they found me already at the synagogue.

They asked me how I had gotten there and I told them that they just wanted to be with me because I had fed them, not because they really believed in me. The people confirmed that impression, telling me if I wanted them to believe in me as the Messiah, I would give them free bread every day, just as their forefathers had been given nourishment in the wilderness. To add stature to their unrealistic desire, they quoted the Scripture,

"Moses gave them bread from heaven."[39]

In so doing they misused the Scripture as non-believers as well as believers will do at times until I return. I hadn't come to remove the pressures of life from them, but rather to give them strength and character to face life's trials. My miracles were primarily for the purpose of drawing attention to where their source of strength was to lie. So I replied that Moses hadn't given them bread, but God had. They should seek the True Bread sent from heaven.

"I am the Bread of Life. No one coming to me will ever be hungry again."[40]

The same day that I actually claimed to be the Messiah, many of the people were disturbed; particularly the ones who said they knew my parents. The crowd was confused. Some wanted to declare me as the Messiah on their terms. Some didn't want to declare me the Messiah under any terms. I kept going. I told them that no one could believe in me unless the Father drew him to me, and at the Last Day I would raise those believers from the dead. The look of unbelief continued to grow on all their faces, but I was not deterred.

"How earnestly I tell you this—anyone who believes in me already has eternal life . . . I am the Bread of Life. When your fathers in the wilderness ate bread from the skies, they all died. But the Bread from heaven gives eternal life to everyone who eats it. I am that Living Bread that came down out of heaven . . . This Bread is my flesh given to redeem humanity."[41]

It was too much truth. They couldn't handle it. But I went even further.

"Unless you eat the flesh of the Messiah and drink his blood, you cannot have eternal life within you. But anyone who does eat my flesh and drink my blood has eternal life."[42]

That did it. They thought I was crazy. How could I say, eat my flesh, drink my blood"? It was too much. I could sense a large number of people pulling away from me. But it had to be. Even those who wanted to believe I was the Messiah couldn't, now. They didn't want a Messiah talking about his death, making his followers cannibals, and speaking of waiting for the Last Day and redemption for all mankind. They wanted a Messiah who talked about conquering Rome—now. A Messiah who hated the Romans.

My Bread of Life talk got me into trouble. The people were never quite the same after that. And Jerusalem was waiting.

On one occasion there were other teachings you gave that confused your listeners. You said that no one could come to you unless the Father attracted him to you. The debate in the church for years has been, "Can a person choose you, or does your Father choose your followers?" It's the old free will versus predestination question. Your speech on that day seems to favor predestination.

Remember that in the same talk I urged people to eat my flesh and to drink my blood, to believe in me as though they had a choice. I also said at another time, "Whosoever will may come." You don't think you will understand everything about salvation, the Incarnation, or my Atonement, do you? That confusion is meant to lead to humility. It's a boundary between God's intelligence and yours, to highlight the difference in you. All God's roads lead to humility.

Alone with the Father

During this time did you ever feel alone or abandoned?. . .

The fact that everyone had his or her mind made up resulted in a tremendous sense of being alone for me. Sin always extracts a high price. All of God's people have to spend time alone. I was like Job. None of Job's friends understood him, and the need to be understood is so great. I was carrying a heavy burden every day. I wanted others, particularly my disciples, to see what I saw, to encourage me and to share the battle with me. But they could see only with their eyes, no further. I knew great pain awaited them and me not much farther down the road.

I kept thinking that if they didn't "see" what they were up against, they would never make it after I was gone. They were going to have the challenge of taking my message—taking me—to the whole world. It was obvious I was going to have the challenge of taking my message—taking me—to the whole world. And it was obvious I was going to die soon.

According to the Scriptures, I would come in my full glory and in judgment at my Second Coming. If the world was to be evangelized before that day—and my Father had promised that it would be—I would have to do it through my disciples.

Because I had no one else to turn to, times alone with my Father were especially rich. He kept me going. Again, through His word, He told me exactly what to expect,

"Strike down the Shepherd and the sheep will scatter."[43]

My disciples would run from me. I knew that. I also knew from the Scriptures, the Book of Psalms and from Isaiah that my good friend would lift up his hand against me. That was Judas. God left me with no illusions. He was saying to me, "Your disciples are blind right now, but take courage; I will establish them in time. I know one of them will betray you; be prepared. Only you can have faith and overcome the world's lack of faith in me. That's why I sent you."

Times with my Father provided the oneness I couldn't find in this world. Then I would once again understand my role. I was going to have to overcome everything, even betrayal and abandonment by my best friends. I also knew that there was never going to be a time in my first lifetime when I stopped reacting like a human being, when I didn't need faith. One day all of my teaching would bear fruit.

In the process I learned how little to trust my feelings at times. I fought the eternal battle between faith and feelings just like you do. And, as you know, it's our faith that pays such high dividends.

I thought of how all of life is designed to teach us faith. A good example is being a parent. For years you think your children will never catch on, and then one day you see that your discipline of them has worked.

You and your Father repeatedly brought stress to your disciples to teach them. You constantly chided them about their lack of faith. I remember the time they couldn't cast the demon out of the boy and you easily did it. Or the time your Father put them through the frightening storm at sea.

One of the best ways, and for many people the only way, to discover Him is in the middle of impossible situations. That's how He's worked for centuries. I always tried to create those kinds of circumstances for my men. They had to learn to pray and to wait, particularly to wait. First there would be my death, and then the resurrection. The joy would come after the wait. To have joy, one had to have an element of the unexpected, the unknown. In fact, the greater the fear, the greater the uncertainty, the greater would be the joy. There's nothing like having God to rescue you. There's nothing more secure than that.

Did anything else happen during those times when you went to be alone with your Father early in the morning?

Several times I asked God to keep me in bounds. I asked Him to give me the words to tell the people how important I was without being a braggart.

It's would probably not be a bad idea if those Christians with the most talent would pray the most.

It would have saved Satan. Remember that at one time he was my Father's fairest angel. You have no idea how great he was.

But let me tell you something else about my quiet times with my Father. You know how you feel the electricity when an "alive" person comes into a room? That's how you should come to feel about your devotional times—You are meeting with the most charismatic Personality who ever lived. My "sessions" with Him taught me that. Of course, that's everyone's experience, the story behind every conversion.

Think of it. How many people have seriously considered that God is the most exciting personality they've ever met? And the central question of life is, "Can you really trust this Personality?" You have to find that out. Quiet time alone with Him is the place to do it.

Teachings on Prayer

Tell me about prayer.

Prayer was a great experience for me. I went to my times alone with God to be treated as I would treat others. Daily it became an experience in which I would know by faith that I was in the presence of Someone who personally cared about me beyond belief.

Because I constantly let God teach me through the Scriptures, I could respond to Him in prayer. Often I would come to a point in my prayers where I knew I was surrounded by His great protective love. Faith eventually enables you to sense God's presence, that He's always there with you. When you have that, you can go through anything.

He had a special love for me, so evident in those portions of Scripture that were meant just for me.

"I will appoint you a Light to the Nations."[44]
"Kings and queens shall serve you. They shall bow down to the earth before you and lick the dust off your feet."[45] I will fight those who fight you."[46]

It sounds like your prayer life was different from that of most people. They describe it more as a ritual and less as a passion.

That's why I prayed for so long many times. You have to work at prayer. You have to work to get the sense that He's there, that point of knowing. To do it takes time and often, initially, some rituals to help focus your mind. Some prayer times are better than others just as some times with friends are better than others. I reached the point where all of the times with my Father were good. Of course, when your needs are strong, your spiritual sense is much more acute.

Your disciples were impressed by the way you prayed and asked you to show them how. That was then when you taught them what we call "The Lord's Prayer." What can you say about that?

I can say a great deal. I tried to teach them to pray from the heart and to pray for what was most immediate, such as daily bread, daily failures, and daily temptations. I tried to teach them to pray wherever they were and at whatever they were occupied.

I wanted them to talk to God as they would talk to a friend who was really interested in them. Most of all, I tried to get them to accept who they were —human beings—and to let God be God.

And so you opened "The Lord's Prayer" with "Our Father, Who art in heaven . . . Thy will be done . . ."

That was to be the heart of every prayer and to be the means to set them free. Once you learn that you're not God but that He is, you're halfway there.

But you were God.

I was. But I was not God the Father; I was also a man at that time.

You were so consistent in prayer. And yet so many believers describe having trouble with their prayer lives. As a friend of mine said, "We're all foxhole Christians." We're on our knees in crises, but at other times we take prayer lightly.

There are two diametrically opposed elements in prayer. One couldn't be easier. It's asking someone to do something for you. That's almost totally a passive role, and eventually there is tremendous relief to get to that point. The other element involves work. It's asking frequently for what you want Him to do along with continually praising Him for the power He has. My prayer was focusing on my need until I realized Who He was and who I was. Merging with praise became a part of me.

I also viewed prayer in part as joining a giant tug-of-war. I was pulling on my end of the rope, cheering for my side with my whole heart until I couldn't cheer anymore. Even in prayer, God built in by design a way of losing your life for others, of sacrifice. That's one main reason why people don't pray enough. They hold on too tightly to their time.

The opposite view of time can also present a problem. People think that to really pray they have to be alone for long periods of time. They don't realize that God is their friend who is always with them and Someone they can tell things to at any time, just as to a husband or a wife or a dear friend.

Another major reason people don't pray enough is that they're afraid of the power they've been given. Imagine this: you can move the hand of God. Listen to what He says,

> "Call to me and I will answer you and tell you great and unsearchable things you do not know."[47]

He's waiting to answer you. That's why I told my disciples so many times to ask. Six times in my last message to them before my crucifixion, I told them to ask. Power makes people uncomfortable. They back off from the influence they have, and then their God becomes too small. I hope my people never forget how great they are and why. It's because they're made in the image of God.

Often people are unaware or how hard God is working to communicate with them daily. Remember, He is the one who said,

> "I will guide thee with mine eye,"[48]

and who said,

> "The Lord is your Shepherd."[49]

Take God up on it. Look for His message daily. Look for His guidance.

Reaching Back

You always seemed to be able to reach back for something extra and to demand that of your men. I'm not just talking about the cross. For instance, when you wanted to be alone after John the Baptist was killed you headed for the wilderness only to find five thousand people following you. But you stopped and taught them. Another time you gave of yourself totally to a large crowd, teaching and healing the sick, and yet you were the first one up in the morning to pray. The night before your death, you were more concerned about your men than about yourself.

And you asked that of your men. After they'd been out healing for three weeks, performing miracles in your name, the first thing you did when they returned was to challenge them even further. You said you were human. As a human being, how did you learn to reach back for that something extra?

I gradually learned. My Father trained me through experience. I faced a great deal of natural opposition in the form of people and circumstances. I was taunted as a child. I saw my earthly father die. I wrestled with Satan. I faced the scornful. I learned in the face of all doubt how to be strong, because I learned the way to my Father, the way to find Him. Whenever I reached back for something extra, He was there.

Nowhere was it more real than when I had to wait. His words were the reason I could. He encouraged me with His words in a thousand fresh ways by constantly telling me things like, "You'll make it, you will do it, I will deliver you." He continually instructed me to wait.

"Wait on the Lord: be of good courage, and He will strengthen thine heart. Wait, I say, on the Lord."[50]

By waiting on my Father, I discovered just how strong one's will can become. Faith and determination are so closely related. I had this strength because He developed it.

You talked a lot about perseverance in your teachings.

It is the most overlooked of the virtues. I would not have attained my goal without it. All the experiences that I had demanded it, even including being misunderstood by my own family, my special prophet, and my chosen disciples. Above all else I needed perseverance while having death my constant companion.

That's why I said, "Count the cost," before you agree to do something. Counting the cost is half of persevering.

The Book of Hebrews says, "For the glory set before you, you endured the shame of the cross." In your teaching you frequently mention that great day, Judgment Day, when you return in your full glory. Did you think a lot about the future?

That's the other part of persevering—knowing your goal. I knew my reward, and I constantly thought about it. I would experience heaven, glory. But most of all, I would be with my Father. To have a Father like mine who had communicated with me intimately and finally to be able to see Him again face to face and talk with Him—what anticipation!

Walking with God on this earth is difficult. That's why the Apostle Paul later said,

"I have fought a good fight, I have finished my course, I have kept the faith."[51]

That's why I said,

"Seek, and ye shall find."[52]

Persist, lose your life and you shall find it.
Paul said,

"Work out your own salvation with fear and trembling, for it's God which worketh in you."[53]

Fasting and praying are not easy. Once you have learned to ride a bicycle, it is easy. But bicycle marathons are a different story.

My own marathon was difficult. A short time after John's death, the pressure of my death was on me again, like a constant pain that returns after some relief from an analgesic. It had not been totally relieved by feeding thousands or by walking on the water or by times alone with my Father. And the daily burdens themselves were enormous. People wanted to see me at all hours for healings. I couldn't escape the crowds wherever I went except late at night or early in the morning.

And I always had to be aware of my actions lest Satan deceive me. The people of the world never failed to push me to act like they did. Frequently I was surrounded by Pharisees who attacked me, and all of this weighed heavily on me.

I was so alone. I had been rejected in Judea and rejected in Galilee when I wanted to be accepted. I was misunderstood by my mother and my family, by the people, by my own prophet, and continually by my disciples. It was as if my teaching were in vain. And then there was Jerusalem and the final Passover staring me in the face.

I was now in the middle of the grief the Scriptures had told me I would feel,

"a man of sorrows acquainted with grief."[54]

only I hadn't expected it this early. And the fact that this grief was unexpected gave it even more power. When I was a child and a teenager, I knew the end of my life would be full of grief. But I hadn't completely anticipated the grief of alienation. I had forgotten that I was to have Job's role as well as David's. How easy a role it was to forget.

It became harder to experience relief during those times with my Father, and attempts mentally to focus on the future were increasingly difficult. One morning after this had endured for several days, I felt discouraged. As I was praying and meditating in the quiet of the early morning, I repeated the Scripture I had memorized, the part in Exodus where Moses, in a moment of discouragement, asked God to show him His Glory.

That request came at a very discouraging time for Moses. His people were learning little and were so possessed with evil that when Moses was on Mount Sinai getting the Ten Commandments from God, in God's own hand-writing, they were down below building an idol, having feasts and orgies. In his distress, Moses reached the point in which he had to know for sure that God was still with them. So he asked God to make clear that that was the case, "to show me Your ways." Jehovah then personally guaranteed Israel's eventual greatness and, at the same time in a very intimate way, reassured Moses by telling him that He had found favor with Him. As He said to Moses,

"You are my friend."[55]

Moses was so moved that he asked to see God's glory.

God told him that His glory would be too much for Moses to take, that His full glory would kill him, but that He would show him part of it. Moses was instructed to go to Mount Sinai where the Lord passed in front of him while convering Moses' eyes. But God allowed Moses to see His back, and then He proclaimed the meaning of His name.

"The Lord, the Lord, the compassionate and gracious God, slow to anger, abounding in love and faithfulness, maintaining love to thousands, and forgiving wickedness, rebellion and sin. Yet he does not leave the guilty unpunished; he punishes the children and their children for the sin of the fathers to the third and fourth generation."[56]

God then gave Moses the second copy of the Ten Commandments because Moses, as you probably remember, had broken the first when he came down the mountain to find his people wallowing in the vilest of sin. When Moses came down the mountain for the second time with the tablets of the law, his face glowed so brightly from having been in the presence of God that the people were afraid even to come near him.

As my mind went back to that story, I wondered if I could ask God to show me His glory, which was also my own. I was greater than Moses. God had told me that. And Moses was a picture of me. I knew that. I was the man who would lead this nation out of bondage. Moses, because of all the stress he had been through, needed reassurance when he asked God for that favor, and God had seemed glad to give it. Now was a time when I needed the same assurance.

I also thought of Elijah who was distraught to the point of wanting to die because of the constant persecution of Queen Jezebel who wanted him dead. At the time, Elijah thought he was the only man still standing for God. God sent an angel to comfort him and to lead him to travel for forty days and nights to the same Mount Sinai on which Moses had stood. Elijah hoped that God would speak to him and encourage him on that mountain just as he had Moses, and God did.

Both Elijah and Moses had felt particularly alone, and God let them have a brief look at the unseen spiritual world. It seemed evident that I could ask Him for the same privilege. At that point in my life, He had already taught me that there was nothing He wouldn't give me. I had already asked Him to put hundreds of fish in Peter's net, multiply one meal to feed thousands, heal multitudes of people, cast out demons, and to give me the power to walk on water and even to raise the dead. At this point I still needed more confidence and more encouragement to see why I was going through all that suffering.

By that time I also knew that I wasn't motivated by fame or lust for power. I simply needed encouragement, and I wanted my men to be encouraged so that one day after I was gone, when they finally understood who I was, they would have an unforgettable event to look back on. My Father had done the same thing before when He, with His great power, parted the Red Sea and forever gave Israel an event on which they could build their lives. He understands that there are moments when we need to see His power.

The more I thought about it, the more strongly I felt led to ask Him for The Transfiguration. There was a beautiful picture of it already laid out in the Old Testament, even down to the timing of it—during a period of discouragement. At the time this idea was going through my mind, my disciples and I were near Mount Hermon, the highest mountain in Palestine. Moses and Elijah had met with God in the mountains during their days "in the valley."

Through all these circumstances in the Scriptures—always the Scriptures —I felt my Father was leading me to ask Him for the same privilege Moses and Elijah had received. So I did. I asked Him to show me my glory on Mount Hermon, and let some of my disciples see it.

Apparently you were so confident in your Father's answer that you took three disciples; Peter, James, and John, with you to see God's answer.

If God says He will do something, it is done.

We know that Moses and Elijah suddenly appeared to you there on Mount Hermon at one point. Did you know they would be there?

That was a complete surprise, but afterwards it seemed so fitting. My Father always had such a perfect sense of history. Before the Transfiguration I didn't know exactly what I would see, but I went in great expectation. I expected to get a new look at myself. But Moses' and Elijah's appearance was a special gift.

I felt that perhaps there would be some angels similar to the time after my temptation. I'd always wondered about the prophecy that Elijah would come before the Messiah. I knew John the Baptist was the symbolic Elijah, but in the back of my mind was the thought, "Will Elijah himself one day make an appearance?" But I never expected it at that moment.

What happened?

We were on top of the mountain praying. I'd been asking my Father to "let me see my glory." I thought that if Moses could see part of my Father's glory, my men should be able to see mine. Suddenly a bright light appeared. When I opened my eyes I saw that it was coming from me. My robe was the most brilliant white you could imagine, and my disciples said my that face shone like the sun. Then Moses and Elijah were standing there and we began talking.

How did you know who they were?

I just knew. It was just like it will be in heaven. You will intuitively recognize others.

Why were these two men sent?

They represented the two pillars that always sustained my nation Israel, the Law and the Prophets. I was the fulfillment of being both a priest and a prophet. By Moses' and Elijah's appearance, it was as if my Father were saying again, "See who you are—Moses and Elijah. See your greatness."

I was the fulfillment of the Law. I was the Law. And I was the priest. Also, I was the fulfillment of the prophets. All had talked about me and looked forward to my coming. Now here was Elijah standing in their place. It was as if all of them were saying to me, "You are the One we have been waiting for." I knew who I was. But I was a man and I needed to hear from my Father again that I was The Prophet, the last in the line.

Have there been none since?

None.

Moses and Elijah

You obviously have a special attachment to Moses to and Elijah. Why?

Both Moses and Elijah were surrounded by Jews who never quite understood them, both were persecuted unfairly, and both endured that persecution alone except for God a great deal of the time. With God's power, both eventually performed great miracles to deliver their people. Moses parted the Red Sea. Elijah defeated the prophets of Baal. In essence, we were a great deal alike in what we faced in life.

Elijah in many ways was the most like me. He also once fasted for forty days without food or water before he heard God's voice. He too was fed miraculously in the wilderness. He spent a period of time living with and caring for a widow and her offspring. He performed some of the same miracles I had—raising the dead, supernaturally providing food, controlling the rain. Also, as to me, the authorities of the day—Jezebel, the queen, and her husband, King Ahab—tried to kill him because he was loyal to the true God, but they couldn't, because he was constantly protected by my Father.

Elijah was an outspoken, forthright man who confronted the false prophets of his day head-on. The day he challenged the prophets of the god Baal to a contest to see whose god could start a fire, he let Baal's two hundred priests go first. They marched around and around their altar chanting and beseeching their god to start the fire. Nothing happened. They marched all day, and the whole time Elijah stood there taunting them, "Is your god asleep? Perhaps he's gone on a vacation.

The last thing Elijah did in his life was to ride on a chariot up to heaven in a whirlwind. One day I would ascend to heaven in a similar way. Also, Elijah never died. He was a picture of both my resurrection and of my ascension.

What did you talk about with Moses and Elijah?

Through my study of Scriptures, they'd both been teachers of mine. The first thing Moses said to me was, "Lord, look how glorious you are. You shared it with me once on this very mountain, and my face shone too, like yours is shining now." Then he said, "Lord, all of us in paradise know what you're going through and what is about to happen." It may seem strange, but I was struck by Moses calling me Lord. Then Elijah said to me, "Lord, we all have waited for this for centuries." I told them, "I dread what is about to happen." Elijah said, "We know, Lord. Everybody there knows. Abraham, Joseph, David, Job and the rest are talking about you and watching you and encouraging you."

Very sensitively, Moses and Elijah begin to talk about their hardships when they were here. Elijah told me how he had battled almost a whole culture. He told me about the most evil person he had personally ever known, the queen Jezebel, and the religion of the state with all the false priests of Baal. Elijah was the leader of the remnant who represented God.

He told me that at the time his task seemed impossible. As he said, "Israel had become so pagan, you can't believe how bad things had become." "Temples to Baal, like the one standing over there," and he pointed to another peak of Mount Hermon, "were everywhere." Then he smiled and said, "But you know how your Father works. He is the God of Impossible Situations. He allows these situations to develop so He can reveal His Glory.

"The hardest part was the waiting. I thought it would never end. Being alone was not easy either. That may even have been more difficult. However, your Father is so sensitive. Just at the moment when I couldn't take any more, He showed me His power. He encouraged me just as He's doing with you now."

Moses told me about having to put up with forty years of constant rebellion from the people God chose him to lead. As he put it, "God's people, if you can believe such people would ever rebel, were incredible. They saw one miracle after another, and I do mean miracles!

"They saw the Red Sea parting, and then walked across the bottom of it with ten miles of fifteen hundred-foot walls of water on either side. Suddenly they saw the mountain of water cave in upon and swallow up the enemy army right behind them just before they would have destroyed us. After that, every day for forty years, they saw a cloud with their own eyes. It was the same beautiful white cloud thirty feet above us where clouds never are which God put there to guide us. They saw a pillar of fire in the same place every night, and still they didn't believe.

"On top of that, every morning there would be bread on the ground. There would be sweet fresh manna which spoiled after twenty-four hours except every Friday, the day before the Sabbath. The Friday batch was good for about forty-eight hours, so the people didn't have to work on the Sabbath.*

"But that wasn't enough for their faith. After that, in the middle of a dry desert, God brought forth water for three million people out of a rock. It was a rock, mind you. And still their faith was good for only about three days. Then they would all start worrying again. Their faith was 'manna faith.' After twenty-four hours it spoiled except on occasion."

I'll never forget what Moses said after that. "Faith seemed impossible to teach."

Elijah and Moses both talked about how much people hated to hear the truth and how the people would do anything to stop it. Then Moses said to me, "But look at you, You're the Lord, and you're going to change all of that. All of us before you, all the prophets, have failed; but Lord, you won't. Nothing can stop you. You are the true law, the law of love, and you will show the world what that word really means.

"I walked down a mountain to failure.** But you know your Father's promise. You will stand here in absolute victory one day. With your Father's power, I parted the sea, but Lord, you will open the Holy of Holies."

Elijah, who was as forthright as the Scriptures had described him, told me, "Lord, Jonah lived when I did, and he told me his story. Just as he rose from the deep after three days, you will rise from your grave. Then one day, Lord, you will do what only two of us—Enoch and myself—have done. And that's leave this earth alive.

"Before that day, you will honor us by giving your life for us. You as the Lord of the universe will pick the time and the place.

"They can't touch you until you allow it, just as they couldn't kill me because God wouldn't allow it. But it won't be easy, Lord. At the moment you are in the middle of your suffering, you will feel all alone and powerless. You will probably have thoughts that will surprise you—even after all God has shown you." Then we went on. "Moses and I were two of the very few men who ever talked to God directly, and, still, moments came when our faith wavered. It was as if we'd never heard God's voice." Moses added, "Lord, I went into a rage over my people's disobedience and I did something that God had told me not to do. I exploded at them and dishonored God, and because

---

*The Sabbath was originally on Saturday, but Jesus rose from the grave on the first day of the week, Sunday. Because of that fact, most Christians have come to celebrate the Sabbath on Sunday.
**When Moses came down from Mt. Sinai with the Law from God, written in God's own handwriting on tablets of granite, he found God's people worshipping idols.

of that I was never allowed to go into the Promised Land, to this land, even after leading them there for forty years. In fact, this is the first time that I've ever set foot on it."* But when you're on that cross, you won't lose your temper as I did. You won't retaliate. You're the Lamb of God, chosen by your Father before the foundation of the world. Look at you. You know what you have to do, Lord. You have to do what none of us could do.

"This world thinks it is so mighty to retaliate but one day the people will know that the greatest deed, the greatest strength in history was shown not by retaliating but by an act of self-control beyond belief." "It will be 'The great submission,' " Elijah said. Moses said one more time, "Lord, look at your glory. You can do what we could not."

Almost in unison, they reminded me, "You will do it. Your Father has promised. He is so confident that He has already let us into heaven because of your deed." The last thing Elijah said to me before they left was, "Jesus, whatever you go through, your Father who is great and almighty will find some way to comfort you. You know His words. You will do it."

Then suddenly my Father spoke aloud to me again for the *third* time in my life,

"This is My chosen one; listen to Him."[57]

The last thing Moses said was, "Cherish those words."

I thought about everything that had been said on that mountain. I thought about it all the way to the cross.

What were your thoughts after the Transfiguration?

As I told you before, when one of these things happened, it impressed me as much as it did anyone else.

When Moses and Elijah appear to you, tell you how important you are, call you Lord, and your garments and your entire countenance turn a dazzling supernatural white, you might think God is trying to tell you something.

Once again it was clear that one day my suffering would be over, and then I would have my glory back. I thought about what was waiting for me. I'd also heard my Father's voice again. This time when He spoke to me, He had added even more. He told my disciples to listen to me. I got the message that He was pleased with the way that I was fulfilling my Messianic role and He was telling me to emphasize my authority even more. Also, He was telling me, "See how much power I have given you. All that I have is yours."

I thought about the transfiguration over and over again, just as I had my baptism. I'd asked Him to show me my glory and, as usual, He had done more than I expected. Looking back, I should have realized that He might speak

---

*Once when he was leading his rebellious followers, Moses had instructions to speak to a rock and water would come forth. That miracle was intended to help Moses quiet his people. Instead of just speaking, Moses was furious with his people and hit the rock twice with his staff as hard as he could. The rock was a symbol of Christ, the Immovable Savior, and was not meant for man to strike, but only for God to strike—and He would strike it only once. Because Moses had disobeyed God, he was never allowed to enter the Promised Land, although God permitted him to lead the Jews to the entrance.

to me, because when He showed Moses His glory, he also spoke to him. Once again, my Father had really lifted my spirits.

Elijah had been right. My Father always finds a way to comfort me. And I want to tell you again how good His timing is. I had seen living proof of the resurrection—Moses and Elijah—just when I needed it most. Another thing I'll always remember about them was the powerful sense of peace on their faces. You don't see that often in this world.

Before Bethlehem

Were there other moments when you wondered about what you were really like before you became a man; when you were God unveiled?

Constantly. I thought about what it would be like to know everything about the universe and every thought everybody has. To have all that power, to be able to hold the ocean in the palm of my hand, or to be able to create oceans and mountains. No, that seemed incredible. Yet I'd used just a fraction of that power when I healed the sick or turned water to wine. And I had first-hand proof of the existence of that kind of power.

I thought about being omniscient, and yet at the same time being so personal that I would really care about each individual. That for me was almost incomprehensible. Still, I had experienced his guidance and personal love firsthand. I knew how passionately I cared about every person I really knew, and it struck me that my Father feels the same way. He just knows *everybody*. And I did, too, before—and I would again soon.

Some people will be puzzled as to how you could have been an all-powerful God and yet couldn't remember it.

My memory of "those billions of years" of eternity past with my Father was one of those privileges I veiled. Remember, my Father said:

> "So are My ways higher than your ways."[58]

You won't totally understand everything until you see God yourself, but I'll show you a picture in nature of what I'm talking about. Can you remember the day you were born, or most of what happened to you at one or two years of age?

Could you and your Father have created us with that built-in memory gap to give use a clear picture of the Incarnation?

We could have.

I can think of two groups of people who won't like what you said about your omniscience. The non-believers will say you are just dreaming again, and some believers will say you weren't that limited when you were on earth, that you always used your omniscience.

The unbeliever doesn't know how gifted he or she is. But my Father always leaves clues in nature to communicate with you, just as the Book of Romans says. Here a person won't have to look any further than himself. The average person knows about five percent of himself. If he's been properly analyzed he may know a bit more, but by far the largest part of a person is buried in that vast reservoir called the unconscious.

It shows you how deceptive feelings are, because we experience subjectively knowing all of ourselves, or think we can find out about our hidden selves just by asking questions and being honest with our answers. Of course, the unconscious is a lot more sophisticated than that, requiring great understanding of its secret code to gain access. But the unconscious is a picture of our greatness. One day every person will get his complete identity, and find out he was more deeply complex, much bigger than he imagined. That's the picture in nature of what I'm talking about.

Consciously, our lives don't seem so big unless you're a faith healer.

They can be. I promised you that if you believed in me, greater things than I've done you would do. That doesn't mean you'll do the same things. Look at the power you have. You are in God's inner circle and have influence with Him. If you will ask Him and wait for Him to act in His timing, you can ask for a lot. You—"an average citizen"—wherever you are have more power and influence than you can imagine. How few times we pray, and how many fewer times we look for His answers. They are there. "You see not because you look not."

Not every man wants to change directions and follow you.

I will let people go in whatever direction they choose, but my sheep know my voice. One day this world will be run the way my Father and I want it to be. My followers will be taking over completely.

I know your Father uses the term "sheep" in an affectionate way, but some people don't like to think of themselves as sheep.

Tell them to try the word "creatures." But they probably won't like that name either; they want to be called God.

I understand humility is a virtue. Yet your Father is generous beyond belief— He gave us His only son. If you were so loved, why did your Father make you so poor financially?

He wanted me to have adventure. Usually, if you have this world's certainty, you will miss out on "the other world's" certainty. Then you really miss out on living. Above all He wanted to teach me how to get life.

Living is trusting?

That is what I said in the 12th Chapter of Luke. Living is not in the abundance of things you have, but is in giving and trusting that He will provide for you. Every day I went to the spiritual world to get what I couldn't get here. All this world offers is false certainty and fear. I needed peace and confidence and true certainty. The only place to get it was from Him. I would go to my Father to get His life, His certainty, so that I could give that to my people. I would give them God. We're always giving each other something good or bad in our interactions. We should be prepared every day to give someone the Kingdom of God. To give others my life.

The God Who is Love

You talk about how innately loving your Father is, but some people criticize Him for being self-centered. They say all He wants is to have others praise Him all the time.

That sounds like projection. You can read the Scriptures that way if you ignore everything about God's giving, but that would mean ignoring a great deal of Scripture. In any case, when God says you were made to serve Him, substitute the word "give" for "serve" and you will be all right. You're made to give to God just as He wants to give to you. C. S. Lewis called Him "The Great Giver." As I said, all of heaven will be people giving to one another.

There are people who say you were a kind man, as the New Testament reveals, but that the God of the Old Testament is different. He is angry and cruel. How do you react to that?

I was the Old Testament fulfilled. I came straight out of those pages. Everything He told me to do, I did. Whose idea was it not to retaliate on the cross? His. Read the Old Testament. He was the one who said for me to keep my tongue silent. He was the One Who was giving up His only son. If you want to see what the God of the Old Testament was like, look at me. I'm no different in the New Testament, and neither is my Father.

The people who say He is harsh have never read about His patience. Imagine someone Who is the King, the Lord of the Universe. He takes abuse and rebellion—not just for an hour or a day but for years, centuries; from people who do nothing but bring grief to Him and to others, people to whom He gave everything, including the breath in their lungs. He watches them destroy themselves and others until they are a shell of who He made them to be.

People can worship pieces of metal that race through space such as automobiles. Or they can worship one part of a person's life, such as sex, until it destroys the rest of their personality. But God won't stand for it. After demonstrating incredible patience, He finally says, "Because you continually reject me year after year and spit in my face, I do the same to you. I will watch while your enemies kill your children, torture you and rape your wives just as you have done to others, and I will do nothing."

Imagine someone that angry. At first I thought, "How could someone that angry be holy?" But I didn't understand how great He was, how great His plans for His creatures were, how holy He intended them to be, how holy He was. That took me years. Once I did understand, I saw that only a God with that much feeling could send His only son to die. At the same time, it made me fear His wrath. I had to bear it, and that was incomprehensible.

On the other hand, this is how passionate He is when He is on your side.

"He brought you out of Egypt by his Presence and his great strength, to drive out before you nations greater and stronger than you."[59]
"Call to Me, and I will answer you, and I will tell you great and mighty things, which you do not know."[60]

Look how powerful He is!

"The earth trembles at his glance."[61]
"He counts the stars and calls them all by name."[62]
"Who else holds the wind in his fists, and wraps up the oceans in his cloak."[63]

Look how He makes you promises, how He guarantees them.

"Never will I leave you; never will I forsake you."[64]
"I will multiply your posterity as the stars of heaven."[65]

Isn't that the kind of God we want? Does that sound like someone who is weak or unconcerned? His anger was never wrong, and never will be. People just get what they deserve. Don't you see? God had to judge. His honor was at stake. Would He let injustice win out? Would He ultimately allow an unjust universe? Do you think He will not demand absolute fairness?

People are right when they see injustice. Do they think my Father doesn't see it? Do they think they see more than God does? Or are they better than He is? Don't worry, God will take care of all of the injustice in the world. He's just trying to allow as much mercy as the world will permit.

When that Great Judgment Day comes, people will truly understand how unjust everyone was, particularly themselves. Those who are Christians will then see the extent of God's great mercy. Those who are not will see how much they needed it and what they refused. There will be no complaints about injustice on that day.

Can you really love a Spirit, "someone" you can't see, like God?

You can love Him enough to die for Him. We have all loved people we haven't seen through their books, and, in essence, we loved their spirits. Everything I did was because I loved Him, and others have had similar experiences. That's why the Psalmist could write,

"As the deer pants for streams of water, so my soul pants for you, O God."[66]

For a long time, part of the Scriptures may seem just like words until repeatedly you experience that breakthrough phenomenon. One day you gradually come to see that you were made for these words, that they are you.

God is good. That's why you can love Him. He strengthens our faith at just the right time with events and circumstances which carry the message, "See, I hear you." Over the years, my faith in Him had become so strong that I began to have a sense of expectancy as I waited before my Father. I came to the point that I knew His personality so well that I could predict what He would do. He would comfort me with specific words at just the right time, and then eventually arrange a circumstance to comfort me even more. I never knew what the exact event would be. I left that up to Him, but I always expected Him to relate to me.

I always expected Him to do something tangible. Perhaps to provide a tangible material need or a tangible specific word of comfort. In a way, I loved it when I reached one of those points of really needing something from Him. A small part of me would tell myself, "He's going to help you in a unique way." And I would cry out to Him, search His words and wait. Sometimes His answers came quickly. Sometimes His answers were slow. But I could always count on an answer.

I remember one particular time when I had been pressured by crowds for days. I had been healing late into the evening, and it was wearing on me. I was fatigued. As I was walking with my men in the crowds to another town, John came up beside me and said, "There's an old man walking with us who has something he wants to tell you that I think you'd be interested in." I nodded in consent and John motioned the man toward me and the other disciples let him through.

As we were walking, this man, who was quite tall and much older than I, began to tell me that over thirty years ago, thirty-two to be exact, he had been tending his sheep one night with two friends outside Bethlehem. At the time, they were all young shepherds. All of a sudden, one star became so bright that it was almost like daylight. An angel appeared to them telling them that the Messiah had been born and was lying in Bethlehem in a manger. They remembered how odd that had seemed. The Messiah was in a manger, a feeding trough from which animals eat! And yet here was an angel telling them it was true.

At the same time, the shepherd felt strangely comforted by the idea because he was very familiar with mangers and it made the Messiah closer to him in a way, more personal, as though they had something in common. Then the old man told me how hundreds of angels had appeared in the heavens and began to sing. After the angels had left, he recalled the three of them running into Bethlehem to find the Messiah, and how awestruck they were when they did. He even mentioned that they had been so overcome at first when they found me that they forgot to ask if I were a boy.

Then he said, "I know you were that baby because I asked your mother and father your name, and they told me. I asked them their names, too, and they told me Mary and Joseph. I've never forgotten your name, Jesus. I've never forgotten that night or your mother and father. It was such an incredibly beautiful and clear night and your mother, who was such a pretty young woman, had the most radiant glow I'd ever seen. And this was after delivering a baby, and her first one too! I don't know the whole story but both of them had a look I'll never forget. The look on their faces would almost have been proof enough of who you are. They had a glow but also a look of disbelief, almost of shock, like they had just witnessed a miracle.

"We left right after that. Your mother and father were such gentle people, and they thanked us for coming. I'll never forget that night with you in that stable. The whole world seemed to be at peace."

You can imagine how God used that old man to lift my spirits.

FOUR

Instruction and Celebration

The Teacher

Let's talk more about your teaching.

Everyone remembers my miracles, my birth, my death and my resurrection —all of which were statements. But people often forget that the primary thing I did was teach. The people were getting such poor teaching at the time.

How did you decide exactly what to teach the people about who you were?

I learned the Old Testament until I understood my Father and myself and my mission. Then I knew what to teach. I did a great deal of thinking about how to describe myself. At first I wondered if He wanted me to use the names He did in Isaiah where He prophesied the Messiah's coming:

> "For unto us a child is born, unto us a son is given: and the government shall be upon his shoulder: and his name shall be called Wonderful, Counselor, The mighty God, The everlasting Father, The Prince of Peace."[1]

But I didn't have all my glory yet, and the government wasn't going to be on my shoulders on my first visit. Personally, I wasn't comfortable with all those names yet. I let Him describe me in that way. I asked Him to guide me as to what to teach in my own way. He did. For example, after I had fed the multitude I told them I was the Bread of Life.

Another time when I met a woman at a well, I told her I was the Living Water and any person who drank of it would never thirst. That image also came from the Old Testament. On one occasion the people of Israel found themselves in the midst of a barren wilderness with no water, and were complaining to Moses again that God was going to let them down. Then Moses in a moment of extreme frustration, hit a rock with his staff after God had told him just to speak to it. Out of the rock poured enough water for two million people. That rock was a picture of me. Out of nowhere I would come to give life to millions.

I always wanted people to get an idea of a relationship that was vital and alive. That's why I tried to use images that were basic to life, such as bread and water. That's why communion is so primitive—it is the same sort of idea.

My Father emphasized further the kind of relationship I would have with my people. I told them the same thing that He did; I was their shepherd.

You referred to yourself as "The Good Shepherd."

God used that image not only in the 23rd Psalm but all through the Old Testament. It was particularly in the 40th chapter of Isaiah, one of the great chapters in the Word of God.

> "He shall feed his flock like a shepherd: he shall gather the lambs with his arm, and carry them in his bosom."[2]

Remember, too, who David was before he became Israel's great warrior king. He was a shepherd who risked his life protecting his sheep. David, as I've said many times, was a picture of me. First, he was a protective shepherd. Then, in the second part of his life, he was a great king. The first time I came I was the shepherd. When I return I shall be the King.

Privately, before my death, the most common way I thought about myself was as the people's shepherd, the shepherd who lays down his life for his sheep. Self-sacrifice was at the center of my teaching, and that was at the heart of the Scriptures which informed the Messiah he was to suffer—Isaiah, the 53rd chapter. It was that part of the Scriptures that Jewish scholars totally ignored.

Read it. It couldn't have been more precise. It shows you, as T. S. Eliot said years later, how little truth human beings can tolerate. But when I thought of my mission, the one verse that always stood out to me directly referred to my people as sheep.

> "All we like sheep have gone astray; we have turned every one to his own way; and the Lord hath laid on him the iniquity of us all."[3]

In one of your greatest sermons, you forever stamped your identity on their minds as their shepherd,

> "I am the good shepherd. The good shepherd lays down his life for the sheep. I know my sheep, and my sheep know me."[4]

Then, with incredible authority you promised them that there would be worldwide unity, one government with you at the head,

> "I have other sheep that are not of this sheep pen. I must bring them also. They too will listen to my voice, and there shall be one flock and one shepherd."[5]

I had to teach my people who I was. Whatever I told the people, my Father had definitely led me. The idea of one world government with one ruler was distinctly there in Isaiah,

> "And the government shall be upon his shoulder."

I had two identities which I had to communicate to people, and my Father taught me how to do both. The most common way I referred to myself and often thought of myself was as "the Son of Man." It was a name with two identities. In the book of Daniel the title referred to the future divine Messiah. It was also the way my Father repeatedly addressed his very human prophet Ezekiel. Literally, son of man means "son of dust." He is vulnerable, perishable, finite—not eternal. The body that I had was going to die. I felt like a man; I thought like a man, completely. And I never wanted the people to forget that. At the same time, I was more than a man. I was God.

There were other titles the Scriptures led you to call yourself.

In Isaiah, my Father talks about the farmer planting his vineyard. It is a beautiful parable and I often use His image of planting and growing in my parables, particularly at the Last Supper,

> "I am the vine, you are the branches."[6]

Another time, my Father called me the Light,

"The people walking in darkness have seen great light."[7]

That's where I got the idea to tell them,

"I am the Light of the world."[8]

That is why I told my followers not to hide their light under a bushel. That's the plan.

Develop the lights and let the world see them. They point the way toward the Light. Almost everybody has to overcome his reluctance to let his light shine.

Except Peter, you have noted.

Peter's personality sparkled from the first day he was born.

You understood so much. But did it take you a long time to comprehend just how fully you were the Light of the world?

As I said, that's what I had to be about for thirty years, to work out my own theology—the theology of the church. When I finally understood I was the Light—the Pure Light, the Only Light, then everything fell into place. I was the one who was to reveal the Father. I was the one who would speak for Him. I was the one who was to confront as He was to confront, as He had sent all the prophets before me to do. I, however, had more light and more power because I was the Light.

You know you can speak with frightening authority when you are God. I saw the people react to me, even the Pharisees. My power frightened them. But my Father was not passive. Look at the ones He sent before me—and not just my unruly cousin, John. Listen to the booming voices of Isaiah and Jeremiah, their declarations that unnerved people with their authority, with their prophecies that were alarmingly accurate. And was I, the only Son of God, to be any less?

When I saw who my Father was, felt His heartbeat in the pages of the Old Testament, it resonated deep within me with the passion I had for the oneness of mankind. I could see that I was pure and I could see my brothers' blindness. I was prepared to put everything on the line for them when I came to see that my Father had put out everything He had for them, too. He had sent His only Son, and you don't think His only Son was going to let Him down.

And I wasn't going to ask anything less of my brothers. There will be no room in heaven for the timid, the ultimately timid. Many there, if not all, will have overcome their timidity.

Even Peter at times?

Even Peter.

For centuries, there's been a prevalent mentality among Christians that we're not to use our talents. Instead, we are to "lose our lives for Christ's sake," and deny ourselves completely. How does that fit with "letting your light shine"?

To give balance to the true meaning of "losing your life" I said,

"Let your light so shine."[9]

What kind of God would He be Who gave us light and told us not to use it? Our light shines brightest when we use our talents to the fullest. When we do that, we're always serving, and we are also in the process of denying ourselves. Serve and self-denial will take care of itself.

Never forget that the second great commandment is,

"Love thy neighbor as thyself."[10]

You're never to quit loving yourself. How could you? You're made in the image of God. To quit loving yourself would be in a way to quit loving God. But you've got to keep it in perspective.

As I told you, there is a feeling that comes with asserting ourselves that makes us cautious. I knew I was at the center of the human race and the central part of my message was at my atonement. "I have given myself up for you." Imagine having to say to every man alive, "You need me; without me you will perish. I am the Light of the World." That was one of the most difficult parts initially. It took years before I could say that. Eventually, when I realized fully who I'd been chosen to be and particularly what it was costing me, I could state the facts. The more I realized who I was, the less my concern became about sinning; for example, losing control and bragging. My Father was not a braggart, and I was like Him. He asked me only to do what I could, and I could do everything because "I was He." He was so good, I wanted the world to see who He was.

That's why I could say that I would make it through the cross. My Father was sensitive. All the gifts He had given me were perfect. Through the Scriptures and through the events in my life, He revealed Himself to me so clearly that my knowledge of Him made me tremendously confident. I knew what He was thinking. I knew what He was going to do for me. He gave me the ability to teach, to think, and to speak about what I had learned. From knowing Him, there comes natural courage and peace at the same time. That's how He sent me into the world. That's why I love Him so much.

Clarification

Let's talk specifically about some of the statements you made. In the 12th chapter of Luke, you said not to worry about what we had no control over, such as to-morrow. But that almost seems like hopeless counsel because it's so natural to worry.

Living in reality is difficult. What I was saying when I told people not to worry was that they should accept reality at every moment. If you're poor, you're poor. Don't fret about it. God knows it. If you have cancer, you have cancer. Accept it at first. You can fight whatever you don't like and try to change any situation, but not to the degree that it disrupts your entity as a creature, as a Christian.

Carl Jung, one of the early psychiatrists, talked about not fighting life. He said to give in to what you can't change. I said the same thing, only I added "give in to a situation in light of the fact that God has given into nothing, and He will ultimately prevail." He allows the situation in which you find yourself.

All of life is to teach us to submit. As Thomas Merton said, "The will of God confronts us every minute."

Let's discuss swearing. Why is God so opposed to what seems at times to be such a natural expression of feeling?

Isaiah had the same problem controlling his tongue. The problem with swearing is that it's a lie. Think of every profane word you can think of and how it is used. He's a son of a ———, or a ———, or a ———. That's a lie. Your neighbor may be a terrible neighbor, but he's made in the image of God. There's no person too far gone to become the most holy being you can imagine. And you never curse holy beings. Even a profane expression at a moment of frustration, like "Oh, ———, or Oh, ———" is a lie. There is no situation too hopeless for my Father, and no situation He doesn't permit. In a way, every moment of life is holy if you see Him as Lord over it. That is why the biggest lie as concerns profanity is taking my Father's name in vain.

When you speak for God, you become the word of God. When you swear you condemn. And there is no one, no nation, no situation, that He condemns until He condemns it. He has patience and mercy and kindness beyond belief. If you were holy, would you want someone speaking for you and saying things you wouldn't say, using your name over and over in a careless degrading way? Would you want people telling someone you hate him when You gave Your son for his life? Would you want someone swearing at you over a situation when it's that very situation you're using to save his life—to get his eyes off the seductive hell of this world that attracts him like a magnet? Do you swear at the surgeon who operates on you to save your life? Swearing is always a lie.

You made statements like,

"I and the Father are one."[11]
"These words you hear are not my own; they belong to the Father."[12]

Did you feel God inside you?

Can you feel your red blood cells or your liver inside you? Of course not! But if they're missing, then you'll know it. I didn't usually feel God inside of me although at times when I was healing, I literally felt a tingling throughout my whole body. It was my Father's power and I could feel it going out of me to the other person. But most of the time I just felt like me.

For being a servant, you really said some very tough things to your followers. They were statements like, "If you don't stand up for me on earth, I won't stand up for you in heaven," or, "If you don't listen to me now, it will be too late later." You also said, "Unless you give me everything, you will have nothing," and another time, "Unless you use your talents now, I will take them away later and give them to someone else. Even if you have only a little bit of talent and don't use it, I will take that talent away and give it to someone who has much more and who has used his or her talent."

What I did for them cost me everything. I expect a great deal in return. Besides, I'm not only your servant, I'm also your sovereign.

You really love to teach.

I was born to teach.

Parables

Why did you teach in parables?

It's how my Father told me to do it. It was prophesied in the 78th Psalm that the Messiah would teach in parables. When God asks you to do something, He always prepares you. Both my fathers had taught me through parables.

As I told you, my earthly father, Joseph, was a master story teller. Looking back after his death, I was amazed to learn how many of his parables had stuck with me. And my heavenly Father communicated with me through stories. In a way, the whole of the Old Testament is a parable about me. But the primary reason He wanted me to teach in parables is because they are most effective. He knew I had some powerful truths to communicate, and the only way I could do it without overwhelming the people was indirectly through parables.

If I had told them directly everything I knew, it would have caused so much chaos that my teaching would have been hindered. Think how many people would have reacted initially had I come right out and said, "Look, I'm God." As Emily Dickinson was to say centuries later, "The truth must dazzle gradually, or every man be blind." If I had immediately declared my identity, you could predict that the Pharisees would have immediately tried to destroy me. That naturally would have led to some riots. All of that would come soon enough. I was wise to the ways of the world, and I knew how to avoid as much trouble as possible. That's why I later told my men to be as wise as serpents and as meek as doves.

Another advantage of parables is that there are intrinsic values in using an indirect method. Often you see yourself in another person through a parable. At that moment, your innate self-protectiveness is off guard.

Is that why you said, a person could see a speck in his brother's eye and miss the log in his own?

Often the speck you see in your brother's eye is the log in your own.

Another reason I taught in parables was to demand humility. The meaning of a parable is hidden and will forever be hidden to those who refuse to see. Parables are a test, and a prophetic one at that. It's how I was instructed to test the people.

You knew how you would teach. Did you practice making up parables?

In my own family I had continued Joseph's tradition of telling stories; so that situation molded my thinking. My brothers and sisters were the first ones to hear certain parables. Also, for years I had thought about what stories I would use to tell people who I was and who my Father was. Later in my public ministry when I saw crowds gathering, I knew I would be speaking to thousands. I planned what I would say. But more often than not, I would just answer a question with a story on the spot. It was a talent my Father had given me just as He said He would. It was another personal confirmation of who I was.

Had you anticipated many of the questions?

Remember, I said to be as meek as doves and as streetwise as serpents.

(He smiled slyly here and it was obvious to me how much he enjoyed the give and take of human interaction, being the teacher who had anticipated his student's questions and being an adversary who outfoxed his opponents.)

Not many questions came up that I hadn't thought about. And, again, it's so interesting how God prepares you, because in my search for my identity I had asked myself most of the questions that came up.

Did you have a favorite parable?

The parable of the Prodigal Son was one I deeply felt. Interestingly enough, it was the story that my disciples asked me to repeat frequently when we had our "fireside chats." You know the story. A young adult son of a wealthy man insists on getting his inheritance early. His father grants it. The man squanders it rather rapidly and then returns home expecting judgment, begging for mercy, and hoping to be able to obtain a job as a common laborer for his father. He's walking over the last hill before home when his father sees him, and in joy and gratitude begins to prepare a feast in his honor. The son is met with a reception beyond his wildest dreams. His father forgives him, kills the fatted calf, and has a tremendous celebration. But the older son is jealous.

One of the reasons I appreciate that parable so much is that I'll never forget the experience in my early years when I felt as condemned and worthless as the prodigal son and my Father surprised me with greater blessings than I had ever dreamed of. To go from feeling that you are a stumbling block to people wanting to be close to God because they think you are "illegitimate," and later to find out that you are not a stumbling block, but an Only-Begotten Son, "the redeemer," does wonders for your self esteem. It felt much better to be a stumbling stone* than to be a stumbling block, although both roles hurt.

What other parables did you especially like?

I liked the growth parables. One such parable is about the seed planted in a garden. Soon it grows into a large tree and the birds live among its branches, but it all began from one seed.

I started out hardly believing that I was the Messiah, and I came to the point of knowing that I was God Incarnate who could perform miracles. I started out trusting God to provide for my family when my father Joseph died, and I ended up trusting Him to let me walk on water and to raise me from the dead. My life was like the single seed.

One of my favorite parables occurred when an attorney approached you to test you with the "great question" and you eventually answered him with the parable about the Good Samaritan.

A scholar who had been listening to me teach for several hours approached me with a question. "How does a person inherit eternal life?" He had expected to find flaws with my answer, but instead I told him that he knew the Law, and therefore the answer to his question. He replied that the whole of the Law could be summed up in two Commandments, "Love thy God with all thy heart, and soul, and mind. And love thy neighbor as thyself."

This attorney had come to the heart of the matter brilliantly, and I told him so. To further prove my assessment of his perceptiveness, he asked another penetrating question: "Who is my neighbor?" That's when I told him the parable of the injured man who was ignored by the people who should have helped, but was rescued by his alleged enemy, the Good Samaritan. I told him our neighbor is anyone who needs help, and I said, "Now you go and do likewise." Everyone should have the chance to be a Good Samaritan. I did.

You seem to have a special heart for the downtrodden.

Life is so difficult. God made that plain from the first book in the Bible on. Since Adam fell, there has been a curse on man. But there is relief. One thing I tried to get people to do was to turn to God for everything, particularly when they were in trouble.

---

*Here Jesus was referring to the prophecy in Isaiah that many people would overlook the identity of the Messiah—"and He shall be . . . a stone of stumbling and a rock of offense to both of the houses of Israel." Isaiah 8:14

I tried to teach them, "When you're in trouble and you don't feel you have faith even to go to God, go to Him for the faith. Go to the Scriptures." Our usual mentality is the opposite. We avoid God because we're embarrassed about our character flaws and about our lack of faith. If you need faith, read the Bible. It will provide the faith. It's the most creative communication in the world.

Did you know that you would be written about later?

When He told me that I was to be the Light of the World, those weren't just nice, theological words. There were things I knew that no one else knew, and the people had to learn them from me. I was the only person who ever really knew God. I was going to teach them how to love, maybe for centuries.

The Spirit had worked that way before. He was used to working through one man at a time; taking a man's words, those of Moses or David for example, which really were God's words, and giving them to generations beyond in the written word. I knew the Spirit was going to do it again. If my coming was so important that it had been written about for centuries, I presumed my deeds would be worth writing about, too.

The Scriptures said that one day the Messiah would come and teach all. Since I knew there would be a significant period between my first and second coming, just as the angel said and just as the Scriptures confirmed, I knew that I would be written about. The words would be the same and yet fresh generation after generation. From then on, every person who lived would have the same opportunity to hear me.

It's interesting how your disciple, John, described you in his gospel after spending three-and-one-half years with you day and night.

"In the beginning was the Word, and the Word was with God, and the Word was God. And the Word was made flesh and dwelt among us."[13]

That's why I could say,

"Heaven and earth shall pass away, but my words shall not pass away."[14]

The Scriptures were explicit. My Father's words endured forever, the Father and I were one, and all that He had was mine. If that was true, why shouldn't my words therefore endure like His? That's why I could call myself the Truth.

If you knew your words were that important, you must have felt a fair amount of responsibility for every word you said.

That's why I always studied the Scriptures. If you were going to teach people for the next twenty or more centuries and on into eternity, and if they were going to write down the words from your mouth as The Gospel, you might think a few days or maybe years about what you were going to say. I was teaching people how to live, and that was important. Yes, I chose my words carefully.

Besides teaching, did you ever think about doing some writing yourself?

I didn't have enough time. I was a doctor, a teacher, and, besides that, a Savior. That was one reason I could say to my disciples, "Greater things will you do than I have done." They would write the books which would have their names on them.

Did you know in advance who would write the books?

I thought Peter, James, and John would do some writing. Peter and John did, but James was killed before he had an opportunity to write. I thought that Thomas might, because he was a thinker. But he didn't. At first, Judas seemed by far the most capable. And I knew there would be some surprises. Matthew was one, and my half brothers James and Jude were also surprises.

The Unexpected

You often did things that people didn't expect. Not only did you walk on water and frighten your disciples, you even let one of them walk on water. You also did other things that were unusual for a religion teacher. You had meals in the home of men who were essentially criminals, tax collectors. You went to parties and performed a miracle at one of them, changing water into the finest wine the guests had ever tasted. One day you bodily threw people out of the Temple. In a word, why? Why did you act this way?

I found that doing the unexpected often brought people out of their enslavement to their preconceptions. I learned that from my Father, who planned to have me say to every human being who ever lived: "You think you are a bad person? You are. Even worse than you think!" Or to the good men, "You are nothing like you think you are; you are worse than evil." And to say to both of them, "You deserve death and I sentence you to it."

 Can you imagine telling every person in all of history that he deserves capital punishment? Equally as shocking, He comes and says, "But My son, My only son, is paying the price for you." Who is prepared for those kinds of messages. For that degree of truth? I had an important message to deliver to the world, and I tried to do it in as many creative ways as I could.

A characteristic of your teaching that stood out to the people then, and still does, was the authority with which you taught.

It took me thirty years to understand my Father completely. The price for true authority is always high.

You're saying that even though the Spirit of God indwells a believer, the believer still has to work to know the Spirit?

You have to work on any relationship. Nowhere is that more true than with God. You always reap what you sow. That's why people need to pray and to read the Bible to get to know my Father and me.

How would you define faith?

First of all, it's a belief, an awareness of your own limitations. Faith is also an awareness of what's really there. The Book of Hebrews where the most clear-cut definition of faith in the Scriptures is found, defines faith as being "certain of what we do not see." Faith and truth are inseparable.

Faith brings patience and hope. It enables you to see beyond today or tomorrow, to get a glimpse of "the day relief will be here, to see past the darkness of the moment." Faith is the only thing that sees that far, that can give you hope.

Faith really is a part of knowledge. It is knowledge of the unseen world. That knowledge, that perspective comes only from God. The awareness that faith brings is very helpful as an antidote against the pain the world offers. But just like an analgesic, it doesn't take away the pain; it only helps you to live with it.

When you've lived with faith long enough to know how well it enables you to see, you have confidence about every moment you live. It makes you certain about things in the past "you didn't know."

A Word About the Teacher

(I realized what a gift for word pictures, for images, Jesus had. Besides the Good Samaritan, there is the Prodigal Son, the seed and the sower, the Light of the World, the Bread of Life, and the Good Shepherd, as well as the vine and the branch. His ideas have penetrated our culture to the core, like it or not. Besides being the Savior of the world, Jesus was a remarkable teacher whose brilliance is sometimes taken for granted because his words are so familiar. Most famous people in history have only one or two quotes, or maybe one speech that people remember. But through the centuries, Jesus' words have been pregnant with meaning and quoted, or even misquoted, a million different ways. As John the Apostle said in the last verse of the gospel that bears his name, if all the words and deeds of Jesus were recorded, "the whole world would not have room for the books that would be written." Listen to some of his familiar sayings which are with us daily:

"Do unto others, as you would have them do unto you."[15]
"Get thee behind me, Satan."[16]
"Why do you look at the speck that is in your brother's eye but do not notice the log in your own."[17]

"Man shall not live by bread alone."[18]

"Love thy neighbor as thyself."[19]

"He that is without sin . . . let him first cast a stone."[20]

"Oh you of little faith."[21]

"Seek, and ye shall find."[22]

Furthermore, in today's world, people are measured by him one way or the other. Great individuals "walk on water." Traitors are "Judases." Followers are "disciples." Befrienders are "Good Samaritans." Events in his life are indirectly referred to thousands of times a day every time such common words as savior, salvation, conversion, scapegoat, redemption, and crucified are spoken. In word and in deed he was the greatest teacher the world has ever known.

As if to add an exclamation point as to who The Teacher was, who the true King of this world was, his Father even gave the calendar to His son. Every day of our lives as we look at our calendar, we acknowledge Christ one way or the other. All rulers, great and small, even those who went before him, now bow to him in the history books. For all of them are recorded in his framework—B.C. or A.D. He is the cornerstone of history.

Reflecting even further on The Teacher's personality, it was apparent how much Jesus loved to interact with his fellow human beings whoever they were and wherever they were. Constantly, he was teaching someone: from a "foreign" lady at a well to a Jewish scholar late into the night, from a group of children to a hated tax collector. He spoke to individuals and to crowds. Everywhere he went, Jesus looked for the opportunity to teach, to give himself to the world.

He had such great compassion for the lost. Day after day, late into the night, he healed people because he loved them. But he also healed to draw a crowd so that he could teach them about the things of his Father's world. He traveled from town to town going to synagogues, accepting invitations to the homes of Pharisees or tax collectors, attending funerals, and speaking to large crowds in outdoor gatherings.

He never quit pushing his disciples to become the best teachers they could be, so that they could carry on his work after he was gone. He was always asking questions. "Peter, whom do men say that I am?" He was always challenging their lack of faith. Up until his last hour on earth, he remained The Teacher, speaking nowhere more eloquently than he did with his life as he hung from the cross. He was the only Teacher in history whose deeds completely matched his words.

His life was also an indication of the kind of student he had been himself. From an early age, he loved to learn, to ask questions, to engage in the delights of the intellect. His life testified to the fact that he had first been the good student. Beginning with the brilliant discussions he held with the scribes in the Temple when he was twelve, he handled all the intellectual challenges that came his way. In his first major battle, Jesus outwitted the most deceptive personality in the world, the "Angel of Light," Satan himself, in a face-to-face meeting. Consistently, Jesus turned the tables on opponents who tried to trick him with questions like, "Do you worship Caesar or God?" or "What do you say to this adultress we've thrown at your feet?"

He was equally adept at meeting force with force when the occasion arose. A Pharisee approached Jesus, complaining because Jesus had called the Pharisees fools. Jesus replied by telling the man not only were they fools, but also murderers. At moments he was so bold he personally threw people out of the Temple. He was always a step ahead of the brightest minds of his day, constantly out-thinking the thinkers, always with the goal in mind of teaching, of reaching the lost.

As I listened to him teach, I also thought of how the people in his day had reacted to him. They recognized him as one who had tremendous authority, unlike all the other teachers of his day except for John the Baptist. Jesus was making the same impression upon me. He was so sure of who he was. He had taken the Scriptures and made them his, day after day incorporating them until he was the Scripture. He had reached a point as a man where he was certain that every word he spoke was true.

Long before he told us he was The Truth, he had discovered that Truth himself. His certainty was elegant and overpowering in itself, and within the bounds of humanity, it was a testimony that he was God. Through this "man," God was saying to all of mankind, "You want to know how great I am? Except for being sinless, I will limit myself just as you are limited. I will subject myself to those same conditions, face the same stresses, and even then I will shine so brightly you will know that I am God.")

Back to the Narrative

After the Transfiguration, you remained almost entirely in Galilee, going from village to village, teaching in synagogues, and, as the Apostle John reported, staying away from Judea and Jerusalem where the Jewish leaders were plotting your death.

Before the last week of my life and my grand entry, I made only two brief trips to Jerusalem, both for ceremonies on religious holidays. The first was in the early fall of my last year on earth for the Feast of Tabernacles, one of the three yearly ceremonies all adult male Israelites were required to attend.

My own brothers, including James and Jude, had urged me to attend this feast, knowing well that the Pharisees in Jerusalem felt even more strongly than they did that I was a phony. Secretly, my brothers wished the Pharisees would judge me, stone me, and provide the end of my embarrassment to the family. My brothers made no effort to hide their contempt, very sarcastically telling me,

> "Go where more people can see your miracles. You can't be famous when you hide like this! If you're so great, prove it to the world!"[23]

I told them their visit to Jerusalem made no difference, because they weren't being attacked for telling the world the truth. I was the hated one, not they.

They went on ahead of me to the feast, and I made a secret trip to Jerusalem. The Pharisees were desperately searching for me, and I was having some fun frustrating them. The people were being increasingly stirred up by the Pharisees' constant questioning of anyone who might have seen me. Typically, some of the people thought I was wonderful and others thought I was deceptive. Does it sound familiar? Even those who agreed with me kept quiet, because they feared the Pharisees.

In mid-week, halfway through the festival, I went to the Temple and began preaching. The Jewish leaders wondered how I could know so much, not having been to their school. I told them I was not presenting my ideas, but God's. I asked them what law I had broken. If I had done so, this would explain why they were trying to kill me.

I told them I healed a man on the Sabbath and was condemned, and yet they circumcised infants on the Sabbath. Wasn't it just as right to heal a person on the Sabbath as to circumcise him? Many of the people there, mostly those from out of Jerusalem who had seen and heard about my miracles and heard me teach, believed I was the Messiah. Most natives of Jerusalem didn't believe in me because they looked to their leaders to tell them what to believe. As a result of their dependence upon the Pharisees, the people didn't know the Scriptures at all and knew little about the facts of the Messiah.

You were getting more and more outspoken at this point in your career. Did the Feast of Tabernacles have anything to do with it?

The Feast of Tabernacles was one of my favorite times of the year. This feast was the third and last required holiday of the Jewish year. It was the most joyous. The crops were harvested. The work was done. It was a time for giving thanks unto the Lord, not only for the present blessings but also for the deliverance of our nation out of Egypt. We thanked Him for giving us the land we now lived on. Also, as emphasized at crucial times in the feast, the Jews looked forward to the future when God's goal would be accomplished and He would reign over all the world.

Besides Passover, this feast contained the ceremonies richest in symbols. At the end of the first day after the evening service, there was a special time of rejoicing. People filled the Temple, and the central element of this first night was light, symbolic of God's Light that one day would penetrate the surrounding pagan darkness and light the whole world. On this night, light was everywhere in the Temple. There was so much so light that every court in the city of Jerusalem was lighted. Men and women danced in the Temple before the people and before the Lord with torches in their hands. Music also joyously prevailed. Harps, lutes, cymbals and trumpets were played by the Levites as they stood overlooking the people on the fifteen steps which led to the court of the altars. The people sang with jubilation. Israel's choir at the Temple in Jerusalem was famous all over the world.

The seventh and last day of that feast was called "the Great Day." On that day, the priests and a large number of the people went down to the nearby Pool of Siloam outside the Temple to fill a golden pitcher with water and return to the Temple to pour it out over the altar at the height of the feast. The water being poured out was symbolic of God's blessing and provision of water for Israel's crop. More importantly, it was a symbol of the future outporing of the Holy Spirit, and, most importantly, a symbol of the day God would pour out His salvation on the people of Israel, the day He would send the Messiah, the Son of David, to reign.

At that point in the ceremony, after the priest poured out the water, he would hold the empty golden vessel upside down for everyone to see that it was empty. Then the people would respond with their 'Hallels.' There would be three trumpet blasts and all the people would wave palm branches symbolic of God's deliverance from their wilderness journey and His promised future deliverance. I waited for this moment.

With the interest of the crowd at a peak and with the priest holding out the pitcher at the altar above them as the people chanted the last words of the 118th Psalm, I stood up and shouted for all to hear,

"If any man is thirsty, let him come to me and drink."[24]

The Temple guards were supposed to arrest anyone out of order, but they were too shocked. They had never heard anyone speak with such authority, and they didn't lay a hand on me.

The people argued, "He is the Messiah." "No, he isn't. The Messiah will come from Bethlehem, not from Galilee." Now some of the people, mostly non-Jerusalemites, began speaking up for me. The Pharisees answered them characteristically with mocking. "Is there anyone among your leaders who believes in him?" Suddenly, for the first time Nicodemus spoke up. He wanted to know if a man could be convicted without a trial. This was the first crack in the Pharisees' armor. Many of them began to believe in me, though they kept it silent.

Caught in the Act

What happened then?

The Pharisees openly rebuked me and were determined to arrest me, but the crowd's reaction alarmed them and they held off. I spent that night on the

Mount of Olives. By the time I returned to the Temple the next day, the Pharisees had a trap planned to turn the crowd against me. That's when they brought me the woman "caught in adultery." They had set up the whole scene by arranging for a man to pay a visit to this promiscuous woman, and then they piously caught her in the act. Then they rushed her to me, threw her at my feet, and tried to trap me into judging her, thereby hoping to deflate my popularity. They were vicious, judgmental men who had never heard of mercy. They knew I was quite aware of the law. Adultery was a capital offense in Jewish Law.

Somehow they must have sensed that you really didn't want to judge her at that time.

See how controlling they were? They wanted to tell me and everyone else how to act and when. Secretly, they wanted to be God. I looked at those self-righteous men in their long robes, men who had just thrown this woman on the ground. The crowd had moved back, and you could see the tension in their eyes. Again I asked my Father for special knowledge, and He answered. I reached over and borrowed Phillip's staff.

In the dirt, next to the girl, I began writing the names of each of the Pharisees and a particular sin of which he was ashamed. For example, I wrote, "Jacob bar Shanda—stealing, age fifteen. Joshua bar Samuel—lying, age thirteen." Some of them had sinned sexually earlier in their lives, and next to their names I would write the name of the person with whom they had sinned. I hadn't said anything to the Pharisees until I had finished the first six names. I pointed out each name and looked at each man directly. I said, "The law regarding adultery says that if this woman is found guilty, she is to be stoned to death. He who is without sin, let him cast the first stone."

No one moved, and I continued writing names. Each time I finished one, I would look up for just a moment and stare at that man. You should have seen the looks on their faces, a mixture of shock and embarrassment. "How did you know?" And I'd put down another name. Very quietly, the crowd began to thin out. Finally, I looked around and they were all gone. Some of them didn't even wait for their names to be called. It's strange, isn't it? People usually like to see their names in public.

Then I looked down at the shamed woman who was just beginning to come out of her fetal-like crouch. She had been expecting a hailstorm of stones and, to her amazement, not one stone had been thrown. As she raised her head and glanced around there was surprise and relief on her face, for none of her accusers were there. I said to her, "Well, they're all gone.

'Neither do I condemn thee. Go and sin no more.' "25

I will never forget her face when she heard those words. She was so grateful. It was another reminder that I took with me to the cross. She was the other person I thought about when I lay in the dirt at the feet of the Roman soldiers, beneath the Roman cross. She was one of the reasons I was going through all of this.

Some people look at that adulteress and say you condoned adultery and sexual sins in the way you handled the situation.

I didn't condone them. I justified them. I meant what I said, that I came to fulfill every jot and tittle of the Law. I judged that woman, too, and I paid the price for her sins.

Justification means you took the stones in her place. So on the cross, in a way, you agreed with your own death.

Absolutely. I preached a sermon on the cross just by hanging there. And, if taken in the right way, every cross you see is a sermon. I'm saying to every man, "See who you are. See what you deserve." As much as I dreaded it and as much as I hated it when I was going through it, I definitely had a great sense of justice being done.

We all know the feeling when justice wins out. In heaven, that's what will bond me to every man. I will know each one's sins have been paid for by me personally, and we will share that tremendous feeling that justice has finally prevailed. Never think for one minute that justice won't prevail in heaven.

Maybe that will keep us humble and grateful throughout eternity.

It just might. It's going to feel so incredibly new for everyone to feel totally justified. By faith, many people today know they are justified but they often don't feel it because they still have their evil nature with them that's constantly letting them down. What they have to take on faith is that they will one day experience first-hand what it means to be totally pure. I ought to know. I've felt this way for years.

Did your encounter with the Pharisees over the woman relieve you of harassment for a time?

It didn't really. The Pharisees left that confrontation with their hats in their hands, unable to utter a word. But a few hours later I was still teaching in the Temple when another group of Pharisees gathered in the background in time to hear me teach. I repeated the statement

"I am the light of the World."[26]

The Pharisees were furious, called me a liar, and then made a sarcastic comment questioning my ancestry. "Do you know where your father is?" I replied, "You don't know me and you don't know my Father." I warned them that unless they believed in me they would die in their sins. I was from the Father above; they were from below. I was going where they could not come. I also gave them another chance at the truth. "If you believe in me,

'You will know the truth and the truth will set you free.' "[27]

But they informed me they were Abraham's descendants and nobody's slaves.

"Our father is Abraham."[28]

"No,", I told them, "Your father is Satan. Abraham wouldn't try to kill me."

"We were not the ones born out of wedlock. Our father is God himself. You Samaritan devil—you are demon-possessed."

"I have no demon in me. It's the Father Who wants me to be great, not me. In all honesty I tell you, anyone who obeys me shall never die. Abraham and the other prophets never even claimed they could do anything like that. You think you're greater than Abraham and the other prophets? If I am just boasting, what I am saying is nothing. But I know the Father and you don't, and I always obey him. 'Your father' Abraham rejoiced to see my day."

"You couldn't have seen Abraham. You're not fifty years of age."

"The truth is, I existed before Abraham was born." That was the final straw. They tried to stone me, but miraculously they couldn't see me, and I walked past them and left the Temple. Not far away, I came across a blind man who had been that way since birth. My Father prepared the way again. He set the stage and I carried out the plan.

To prove my words to the Pharisees, I healed this man, so that they would know who had the light. Once again I was telling them, "If you can't believe my words, believe my deeds." I was also saying to them "You're blind and need healing in order to see."

The man who had formerly been blind really gave the Pharisees a hard time. His friends who had known him all his life were so frightened at what had happened they immediately took him to the Pharisees who, in turn, attacked me. Of course, the Pharisees' first accusation was again that I was working on the Sabbath. They started pressuring the man. "Who do you say this man is who healed you?" The former blind man said he thought I was a prophet. The Pharisees wouldn't even believe the man had really been blind until they sent for his parents, who came and established the fact that their son had been blind from birth. The Pharisees then pressured them. "Why can your son now see?" The parents wanted nothing to do with the situation. The Pharisees had threatened to excommunicate anyone claiming I was the Messiah, so the parents told the Pharisees they had no idea what had happened,

"Ask him," they said, referring to their son. "He's old enough to speak for himself."[29]

So the Pharisees turned back to the little man who was busy seeing for the first time, putting pictures with the mental images he had formed all his life. They began pressuring him to give the glory to God and not to Jesus, because Jesus was evil.

The man told them he wasn't sure if I was good or bad, but he knew one thing

"I was blind and now I see."[30]

The Pharisees, not knowing when to leave well enough alone, kept asking him exactly how I had healed him. This man was no theologian, but he was having no trouble seeing through the Pharisees' "theology." He was beginning to make up his mind as to who was good and who was bad. He said to them, "I've already told you once. Didn't you hear me, or do you want to hear it again and become one of Jesus' disciples, too?"

The Pharisees cursed him, accusing him of being my disciple and proudly stating they were disciples of Moses. They shouldn't have pressed the issue with a grateful man, because now he wasn't backing off an inch. "You know, it's strange that he can do such good deeds, heal blind people, and you don't know anything about him. There's never been anyone like him, and if he weren't from God, he couldn't do it."

" 'You illegitimate bastard, you!' they shouted. 'Are you trying to teach us?' "[31]

Then they threw him out of the Temple.

I heard about this and immediately found the man and asked him one question. "Do you believe in the Messiah?" The man said, "Who is he, sir? For I want to." I said to him, "You have seen him and he is speaking to you." All he said was,

"Yes, Lord, I believe!"[32]

and fell to his knees. As he would later tell his friends about this event, "My eyes worked for the first time in forty years, and the first person I saw was the Messiah. It was not a bad day!"

As I left, I told the crowds,

"I am the Good Shepherd. The Good Shepherd lays down his life for the sheep, I know my own sheep and they know me. The Father loves me because I lay down my life. No one can kill me without my consent—I lay down my life voluntarily. I have the power to take it again."[33]

Some said I was crazy. Demon possessed. Others believed.

Final Months . . . Great Faith

When did you next return to Jerusalem?

Three months later, in December of that year, I was back in Jerusalem. As I was walking through the Temple, in the part known as Solomon's Hall, the Pharisees again gathered around and said to me,

"If you are the Messiah, tell us plainly."[34]

So I obliged them and told them I had already said who I was, and that the miracles I performed in the name of my Father were my proof. I knew, of course, that they couldn't believe in me, because they weren't part of my flock. But I knew exactly who was, and, in case they wanted to know, no one would be able to take my followers away from me because my Father had given them to me. No one was stronger than He was. Finally, so they could hear it straight from the source—a fact I will remind them of one day—I told them,

> "I and the Father are one."[35]

While they were still confused, I tried to reason with them. One last time I reminded them,

> "Don't believe Me unless I do miracles of God. But if I do, believe them, even if you don't believe Me. Then you will become convinced that the Father is in Me, and I in the Father."[36]

The Pharisees again had received an earful, more than they expected. And, at the same time, they didn't hear a word of it. Immediately they tried to arrest me, but I just walked through the middle of them just as I had done with another crowd in my home town. When your time is not yet come, you can be as bold as you want to be. My Father was the timekeeper, and it was His clock we were going by.

Previously, I had also gone back to Nazareth just to send them that message, too. I taught in the synagogue there and could only perform a few miracles because of their unbelief. Finally, I told them that a prophet is honored anywhere but in his own country, and I left. I wasn't afraid of anything except that last day.

There were now about four months left before the crucifixion. How did you spend your time?

Often I was alone with my Father. I also visited a number of small towns in Galilee. I wanted to visit as many towns as I could. I came to all the people, and I wanted to spend a lot of time with my disciples, something the traveling enabled me to do.

Frequently I tried to teach them that my death was near, but they would have none of that. They "knew" the Scriptures. They knew the Messiah was to sit on David's throne. Death was an impossibility. Of course, John the Baptist had died, but they pushed that out of their minds. The Baptist wasn't talked about much after he was gone.

Every time I mentioned my death, my disciples always thought I was talking in parables. Surely, they thought, I meant my movement was to die in the way it presently was, an obscurity of sorts, and "rise again" into a grand and glorious kingdom. Even when I pressed them with the details of my death, my men couldn't take it. They just argued endlessly as to which one would be first in the kingdom which they were sure was imminent. As I said, James and John even put their mother up to making certain suggestions about who should help me rule the kingdom.

Toward the end, I sent out seventy disciples in pairs for two weeks by themselves to do miracles in my name and to prepare the way. I continued to heal the sick. The response was great at times, but I knew the end result. I had already been to Jerusalem and had seen my Father's words coming true.

Still, wherever I went there were crowds, however fickle and uncertain they might be. I knew all of them were going to be at Passover and, if Jerusalem wouldn't accept me, I would bring my own crowd. Word was out that anyone who believed I was the Messiah would be excommunicated. Word was out that I would be arrested when I came to Jerusalem. Oppression, however, never ultimately stops people. Besides, I had already been to Jerusalem twice and nothing had happened, or would happen, until I allowed it.

My burden became increasingly heavy. Don't think for one minute I didn't feel it every step of the way. My Father knew that, too, and always arranged circumstances to lift my spirits as He had done with the blind man at the Feast of Tabernacles.

Take Zacchaeus. One day I was walking through Jericho with great crowds surrounding me, following me everywhere I went, lining the roads I walked. As I was coming down a hill, I saw ahead of me one little man in a sycamore tree. Obviously he was there because he couldn't see me from the side of the road. He was very small, but more of a handicap than his size was his beautiful robe, more expensive than that of almost anyone in the crowd. He was a tax collector.

I knew the crowd wouldn't have dared let a tax collector through to the front to see me, and I felt for this helpless, rich outcast who cared enough to climb up in a tree, robe and all. That told me something about him. He wasn't too proud to get up where everybody could see him and certainly mock him. I knew he was determined. As I walked towards him, I asked my Father to tell me his name.

When that answer came, I thought of how many times He had answered me. That was why at the Last Supper I could tell my men to ask my Father for things if they wanted to have my joy. My Father constantly thrilled me with His answers to my prayers, often after He had created the very situation which prompted the prayer. Joy is one the gifts He creatively built into prayer. I was a man like all men and women who didn't always know what was going to happen. I had to wait for His answers as you did. That's why prayer gave me so much joy. That is how I heard my Father. Many times I had to wait for His answers, but thousands of times He answered me immediately. Because He heard me, joy was mine in abundance. C. S. Lewis was right. My Father wants to give.

I reflected on these thoughts until I was almost under the tree where this brave little man was. With the crowd surrounding me, I stopped and looked up at the man. There was first surprise and shock on his face, and then fear. He wondered what I was going to say to him. He thought that perhaps I would judge him. As he later told me, he had already heard about my physically throwing some greedy people out of the Temple. Then I called him by name, "Zacchaeus, come down here with me. Do you have anything to eat at your house?"

You've never seen a man come down a tree any more quickly. He walked beside me for about another mile with a crowd following, frequently making sarcastic comments about my daring to associate with a tax collector, particularly the renowned Zacchaeus. I had to ask him where he lived, because he was obviously excited and couldn't say a word for a while. Tears filled his eyes.

All the poor man really wanted was for someone to love him, to recognize him. And I had.

By the time we got to his house, he was a new man. Gentle. Repentant. Sensitive. I didn't have to say anything to him about his sins. He knew. By the time the meal was over, he had more than confirmed my initial impression. He had responded to my compassion with enormous repentance and a generosity I rarely had seen. After the meal he announced publicly that he would give half his wealth to the poor, and promised to repay four times over those whom he had cheated on their taxes.

Some people don't respond like Zacchaeus. Why do you think that is?

As I was to say later to a Pharisee in his home, "He who has been forgiven much, loves much." People who have been the most overtly evil and then have a fresh chance at a new life often are the most ready to take advantage of it. Sometimes it's because of their situations. These are the people who deep down see themselves most clearly. Other people have to be convinced over the years that their "little" sins are really just as bad.

We all are in great need of forgiveness. But it seems to me that the central truth in the story of Zacchaeus is the same as it was for Matthew. No matter how evil people are, potentially they are not far from the Kingdom of God.

Many people are much closer than you think. No matter who they were, I saw everyone as potentially one of my followers. Remember, whenever you talk to a man about God, his conscience is on your side. Everyone you will ever meet is made in the image of God, and we must encourage people to believe that, to have faith in who they really are.

Faith is such a delicate thing. We have to be careful with it, nourish it. It's at the same time both the easiest and the hardest thing to have.

Even if we've had a clear look at another reality, God's reality, we forget so quickly. My disciples saw me feed about twelve thousand people* with two fish and five loaves of bread, but a few weeks later when we were surrounded by four thousand men and their families who didn't have any food, my disciples asked, "What do we do now?" They saw me raise the dead. They themselves performed many miracles. They healed the lame, made the blind to see—and still they tended to panic even after all they had seen and done. Later when I was crucified, they all abandoned ship and ran.

The day I was resurrected, I appeared in a disguised form to two of the disciples and walked with them for miles on the way to Emmaus. I asked them all about this Jesus they had followed and they said, "We thought He was the Messiah." They weren't sure, but they thought, mind you, thought I was the Messiah. What faith! This was after I had told them exactly what would happen. That I would be killed but I would return. It's not easy to have faith. That's why there will be great rewards for those who do.

---

*Only the men were counted in the crowds the Scriptures record. Estimates vary, but actual crowd size was significantly higher.

Life That Springs Eternal

What did you do after leaving Zacchaeus?

I left his house before sunrise the next morning and began walking toward my goal—Jerusalem. The sun began to shine on the countryside lined with flowers. Spring was in all its beauty in Israel. What a sight it was!

Suddenly, I realized that my Father had done something else for me. He had given me spring as an eternal picture of my resurrection. Not only that, but He had set the stage for my death to occur in the early spring. Would it do for the Savior of the world who was coming back from the dead to die at any other time? When God had initiated the Exodus and the Passover centuries before, was it any accident that He planned it in the spring so that Passover would be celebrated then? He was telling me, "Even the seasons of the year are yours." I was moved to tears as I looked up at the beautiful sun coming over the horizon. It was yet another present for me. It was the Rising Sun. Not just the sun, which I had noticed before had my name, but the Rising Sun.

The Rising Son.

All of nature was mine, too. My Father was saying to me at just the moment I needed to hear it, "Look around. See the flowers, the light, the sun. You, too, will be back in unbelievable glory." And He has been reminding people every spring and every day since of the same thing.

Martin Luther got part of the message. He once said that every spring is a testimony to the resurrection.

The same thing is true every time someone awakens from sleep. My Father and I left many pictures to remind humanity of our great gift.

You were headed toward your death at Jerusalem. You knew it, yet the Pharisees didn't. What finally made the Pharisees decide to murder you?

I'd saved the best for the last. The Pharisees couldn't stand the power that I was demonstrating for the glory of my father. When I came to the aid of my friend, Lazarus, it was more than they could tolerate.

A few weeks before the third Passover in my public ministry, I got a message from two good friends and sisters, Mary and Martha. They had sent word that their brother, Lazarus, who lived with them in Bethany was very ill. Immediately, a vision of Lazarus lying dead came into my mind. I knew it was "a special vision" from my Father. I wondered for a minute why He would be showing me that now. Then I understood and saw what I was going to do.

I waited in Bethabara on the other side of the Jordan River for two days, just as they would wait for me in that grave two days. The third day was the day for action, and that morning I told my men, "Let's go to Bethany." Only two miles down the road from Bethany was Jerusalem, where the Jewish leaders had just tried to stone me. My men became anxious about going there, and I told them not to worry. Nothing would happen in the daytime. I always thought that when the authorities came to get me, it would be at night and, as it turned out, I was right. Thomas was the only one who wanted to go with me to Bethany, however.

I had waited until Lazarus had died. On the way to Bethany, I told my men what had happened to Lazarus, but said for them not to worry, that I would go and awaken him and give them another chance to believe in me. I told them this was happening for my glory. I saw what my Father was doing. He was getting me ready, encouraging me every step of the way.

Apparently your disciples still did not understand. Didn't they think you'd somehow been telling them another parable and using the word "death" symbolically?

Death is a blinding word. When we got to Bethany, Martha heard I was coming and ran to greet me. She told them that if I'd been there her brother wouldn't have died. I promised her that her brother would come back to life. I said, "I am the one who raises the dead and gives them life again. Anyone who believes in me shall live again."

Then I asked her if she believed, and Martha amazingly replied,

"I believe you are the Messiah, the Son of God."*37

She was the only one besides Peter and Thomas who had ever called me that, and, ironically like Peter and Thomas, many have ridiculed Martha, too. But how she had learned. Before it would have been her sister, Mary, who ran to greet me. But after I had rebuked Martha, she was a different person. What faith she had!

Immediately Martha ran to get Mary. She came at once. Her house was filled with people who had come to comfort her. Thinking she was going to the grave to mourn, they followed her. When Mary finally saw me, she said, "Sir, if you had been here my brother wouldn't have died."38 She fell at my feet, clutched me around my legs, and started sobbing. Following close behind her were friends who began to weep with her.

Again, I felt the sting of death. I was reminded of my father Joseph's death. I still missed him. Then the utter finality of death swept over me. There's nothing like it to convince you that sin costs everything, that evil is not to be taken lightly. In a moment, all my hatred of death came storming back. Then a strange thought went through my mind. I understood more clearly why hell would exist. My Father hated death so much that He would let everyone live forever, only in different places.

---

*Once when visiting their house, Jesus was teaching people in the "living room," when Martha began complaining about her sister, Mary, who was listening to Jesus instead of helping her in the kitchen. Jesus said, "Martha, why do you worry and get upset about many things, but only one thing is needed? Mary has chosen what is better."

I looked down at Mary and Martha. I was indignant, and said, "Show me where he is buried." I started walking to Lazarus' tomb with one arm around Mary and one arm around Martha as they each cried on my shoulder. It reminded me of another funeral I had walked to, listening to the sobs of another Mary crying on my shoulder, my mother Mary crying at the loss of Joseph. That moment with Mary and Martha was so powerful I couldn't contain my emotions any longer. As we walked down that road, I wept for my friend Lazarus, for my father, and for my own impending death. And everyone surrounding me would go through that shattering experience.

Some people are kind, some aren't. As we came to the tomb I was still crying, and I heard one person say, "They were close friends. See how much he loved him." I heard some other people say, "He healed a blind man; why couldn't he have healed his friend?"[39] The whole situation made me mad. Death was so senseless. Their faith was so weak.

I walked up to the tomb. A large stone was in front of the entrance. I told them to roll it away, but Martha's faith wavered. She was worried about the odor, because Lazarus had been dead for four days. I reminded her that I told her she would see a tremendous miracle if only she would believe. I looked at the heavens and thanked my Father for hearing. This was for the people's benefit, not for mine, because I knew my Father always heard me. With much uncertainty, several men rolled the stone back. I could see a look of fear on all their faces, with just a tinge of hope trying to break through. My last thought before I said anything was, "Three weeks from now I will be in a tomb and the third day after that I will walk out of it." Then I commanded in a loud voice "Lazarus, come forth!"[40]

Out of the tomb walked Lazarus, looking like a mummy, wrapped from head to foot in the white grave cloths. The wrappings were so tight he couldn't talk, but you could hear him mumbling as we unwrapped him. His mumblings scared everybody until they could unwrap him.

Imagine waking up from an illness to find yourself dressed in a shroud surrounded by dozens of people.

Two weeks later, six days before Passover, I had dinner at his house and we laughed about that.

But the miracle with Lazarus was more truth than the Pharisees could stand. That's when they set about destroying me.

Palm Sunday

Tell me about Palm Sunday.

I was staying at Lazarus' house, a thirty-minute walk from Jerusalem, just on the other side of the Mount of Olives. I knew the time has come, and early

Sunday morning we began walking toward Jerusalem. I sent my disciples on ahead to Bethphage where I told them they would find a donkey they were to bring to me.

How did you know where the donkey would be?

I knew this was the day for my announcement. The Scriptures had told me, as the 118th Psalm said,

"This is the day the Lord has made."[41]

This was the day promised to me for over four hundred years by the prophet Zechariah, the day the Messiah would ride into Jerusalem,

"Righteous and having salvation, gentle and riding on a donkey."[42]

This was the day for which the Jews had waited for centuries, and since my Father had set the stage, I knew he would have a donkey waiting for me. I just asked Him to leave it in a certain place.

Why did you want a donkey?

All of God's kings ride donkeys, at least at first. The world's kings, men of war and fame, ride great white stallions to denote power. God's kings rode donkeys of humility and peace. It was the same way I came into the world. My first bed was a donkey's trough, and I never quit identifying with the common person. That was who I came to save. But my disciples had at the time no understanding of why I was riding a donkey. It was only later they understood that it also had been prophesied.

My Father had done His part. There were great crowds, and they were ready. There were two to three million people from all over the world, from wherever Abraham's seed had gone, now in the "Holy City" for Passover. And they were at a fever pitch. My fame, on the wings of my greatest miracle— raising Lazarus from the dead—had reached its peak, and the crowd, hearing that I was coming into Jerusalem, couldn't contain itself.

They had been promised a Messiah by Jehovah, and surely I was the One with the power to overthrow the Romans. It was only a matter of time, they thought, until I would bring my angels with me to overthrow Rome and the rest of the world. They knew I could do it. And they were right. There was no question about that. Anyone who could raise the dead and heal the sick and feed thousands could take on the Romans. So the crowd rushed to get their hosannahs. A hosannah was a palm branch signifying not only peace, but peace following a great conquest. Traditionally, leaders would ride through the towns they had conquered surrounded by palm branches. Now the thousands of people, in anticipation of my conquering the Romans, began waving their hosannahs and shouting hosannah at the same time.

Although they had my method backwards—I would conquer through peace, not war—it was tremendously moving to be in the midst of this huge throng of people, hearing them shout over and over that verse in the

118th Psalm which I had anticipated hearing for years, "Hosannah, Hosannah,

'blessed is he who comes in the name of the Lord.' "[43]

Suddenly, my usual thorn in the flesh, the Pharisees, came running up and said, "Tell your disciples and followers to stop shouting." They wanted me to refrain from giving the impression I was the Messiah. What a perceptive lot they were! I told the Pharisees that if the people stopped shouting the very stones around me would cry out. Scripture had proclaimed that my Father had planned this specific day for centuries, and the Pharisees were not going to be able to stop it. Is it any wonder that I accused them of being related to Satan?

This day in one sense was the centerpiece of our history, before and since. I'm the only Prince of Peace who's ever come to this world. I had thought about this moment for years, but this was my official announcement. I knew in a way it would be in vain. But for now, the king was here. The Prince of Peace was here bringing peace himself, peace itself, to Jerusalem and to the world. This was my Coronation Day, even though I had to wait five days to get my official "crown."

As I rode on and on into the growing multitude, with everyone crying out ecstatically as my disciples parted the throng like the Red Sea, I realized they didn't understand at all who I really was. They were lost. I looked up at the beautiful city Jerusalem standing majestically on that hill, a view that was always awe inspiring every time I came into the city, but particularly at Passover.

Instantly, I was reminded of what really lay ahead for me and for this elated crowd. I knew the prophecy awaiting them. Soon they would be utterly destroyed, along with their children, within their own walls. Holy Jerusalem would be leveled again. Not one brick would be left upon another. And whoever was left would be dispersed. Forty years after my death that came true. Before I returned and they had another chance to proclaim me King, the worst suffering in human history—The Great Tribulation—would take place in this very city.

With all the shouting going on around me, I remember thinking, "O Jerusalem, isn't eight hundred years of suffering enough? Since the days of David and Solomon, you have been constantly persecuted. Rulers have made war on you time and time again, destroying your families and taking your children captive. What's it going to take? Can't you hear the prophets? Even though you've ignored them before, listen to them now. You have another golden opportunity. This time it is a once-in-a-lifetime chance. Listen to who the prophets say I am—the Prince of Peace. Listen, the Prince of Peace is here. This is the day set aside for you to receive your Messiah. I am your king. My Father is your God. You are my people. Do you know what I'm offering you, what peace I bring to every one of you? Do you understand what kind of a nation we could build?"

"But you are lost. You can't receive me, because you can't really see me.

Some of you may wave at me from a crowd today, but next week many of you will be in another crowd that condemns me. Look at what your blindness is costing you. After you kill me, they will kill you."

And I wept for them and for all mankind at that moment, for the curse they were all under was obvious. The Fall had made them foolishly blind, like one of those old misers who starves to death in his apartment and has two hundred thousand dollars stuffed away in a mattress. I knew it couldn't be any different until I died and they were no longer lost. I couldn't help wishing it weren't so. Jerusalem, named the "City of Peace," would continue to be the "city of war" until I returned.

Were you so consumed by your sadness that you couldn't respond to the crowd?

Hope is a marvelous thing. After I wept, I thought, "Now I know again why I'm going to the cross. I'm going to take away your blindness so that one day you will be able to see, and then we will have a reception that will surpass all others.

I had waited for this moment at Passover for twenty years. As I rode into Jerusalem on the back of that donkey, the crowd became larger and larger, and louder and louder. They began to chant until they reached a tremendous roar, singing at the same time, "Hooosannnahh, Hoosannnahh." And people were crying out,

> "Blessed is He who comes in the name of the Lord! Blessed is the King of Israel!"[44]

Many were waving palm branches as a sign of peace. Others began throwing the branches on the road in front of me. With each branch came the message, "You are the Prince of Peace." Finally palms covered the ground until the road in front of me, which was usually a dusty brown, became a sea of green. From brown to green, dust to life, my Father had thought of everything. As I came up the final hill to the magnificent city gates surrounded by the tremendous walls seven stories high, thousands of people were lining the walls above, leaning over to see me.

During all of Jerusalem's years, the Jews had seen many a king and ruler ride through those gates in triumph. I thought particularly of Alexander the Great, by whom all conquerers were measured then and now, who three hundred years earlier had ridden down this same road on his great stallion as he conquered the world for Greece. I thought to myself, "Move over, Alexander. A carpenter from the little town of Nazareth riding on a donkey is the true king of this world. This is the kind of kingdom he and his Father are bringing in. See what his Father calls him. Prince of Peace, Prince of Life."

I also thought about all those times people from Nazareth had been laughed at and ridiculed. In front of me, busily parting the crowds, were several of my disciples, one of whom was Nathaniel. As I looked at him I remembered the first words I had ever heard from his mouth.

"What good can come out of Nazareth?"[45]

"Well, here's your answer, Nathaniel. Look around. Nazareth produces kings. Take heart, Nathaniel, and the rest of you who are my followers, for one day you will be as royal as a king's brother."

It's strange the thoughts that occur to you at those moments which stand still in your mind forever.

The nearer I got to the walls, the greater the crowd. The people began to sing in unison the 24th Psalm, which David had written, announcing the Messiah's entrance into Jerusalem. The people on the wall started it off, asking,

"Who shall ascend into the hill of the Lord? Who shall stand in His holy place?"

Down below, the crowd surrounding me answered, singing,

"He who has clean hands and a pure heart."

Then above and below, the whole crowd, as they had done for hundreds of years at Passover, sang,

"Lift up your heads, O ye gates, be ye lifted up, ye everlasting doors, and the King of Glory shall come in."

Then all of the women sang,

"Who is the King of Glory?"

And the men answered in unison,

"The Lord, strong and mighty, the Lord mighty in battle."

Then together they again sang the chorus,

"Lift up your heads, O ye gates; even lift them up ye everlasting doors; and the King of Glory shall come in."[46]

Over a hundred thousand people were singing that psalm. Remember, it was Passover, and Jerusalem was packed. And everybody knew the words to the song.

Now I knew firsthand what David felt when he danced alone before his people along this same road and stood symbolically in my place as he came into Jerusalem as their king, returning the ark to the City after recapturing it from the Philistines. The whole scene that particular Passover day was for me just as the Scriptures said it would be. It was one of the most moving experiences of my life. From studying the Scriptures, I had always thought my Father was telling me they would sing that psalm to me. I had always believed that Palm Sunday would occur just before my crucifixion, and I knew that it would be an incredible experience if my Father had anything to do with it. It was beyond anything I had imagined. But that's the way He is. That's the kind of gift He gives.

Using that great 24th Psalm, the composer Handel, wrote his most famous work, "The Messiah," still sung by choirs all over the world. It must have been a tremendous thrill to hear that psalm sung to you.

As Hebrew poetry often does, verses are repeated in a slightly different way for emphasis. The last verse of that Psalm goes,

"Who is this King of glory? The Lord of hosts, he is the King of glory."[47]

A more modern interpretation for the Lord of Hosts would be Commander of All of Heaven's Armies. As I was riding into Jerusalem that day, my Father had literally taken a scene from the Scriptures, cast it, directed it, and made it come alive in the theater of reality. The scene had never been played before except by David in a "dress rehearsal," and my Father was telling me over and over as I was going to my death: "You are the Prince of Peace. You are the Prince of Peace." I kept thinking, "Now I know what a king feels like." It was a taste of the future, and I was overwhelmed.

It went through my mind, "This is what I am working for. One day I will be back. I will have all my glory, all my heavenly hosts, and they will see me mighty in battle. But for now I am come to give my life on a cross." I savoured every minute of that experience, and thought about it the whole week before my death. It was an experience that would enable me to get through the tremendous shame just ahead.

The reception my Father planned for me brought all the leaders in Jerusalem to their knees. The Pharisees and the Sadducees knew Jerusalem was mine that day if I wanted it. The people had revolted before. They had killed numerous oppressors and had fought for years, making life miserable for the Romans. If the people rioted, the Pharisees and Sadducees would lose their power. The Romans would strip them of their authority if they thought they were losing control of the people. The authorities were relieved when I made no effort to take over. They didn't realize I had much greater plans in Jerusalem, much larger than those of Alexander the Great. I had the whole world in mind. My plan wasn't to oppress the world, but to free it.

The Jewish leaders, however, missed my final offer to accept their king. That reception made the Pharisees move more quickly than they had wanted to with their plan. The usually uninvolved Sadducees became so frightened that they formed an immediate alliance with the Pharisees to get rid of me. The Pharisees didn't want to kill me at Passover, but once again I was forcing their hand. We were still going by my Father's calendar, not theirs.

How could this great crowd, so totally enthralled with you, cry out five days later for your execution?

First of all, they were manipulated by the Pharisees into betraying me. But they got themselves into that position because they were all naturally traitors. Like Judas, they wanted me to be the kind of Messiah they were looking for, to rule in the way they wanted. They wanted me to conquer the Romans immediately. When they saw I wasn't going to do that, they were extremely disappointed and became bitter, so bitter that they didn't want me any more. I died for many Judases. He wasn't the only traitor.

Choosing to Die

How did you know when you were going to die?

I knew it would be when I chose to die. I decided. But the timing was perfect. I was more and more a threat to the Pharisees. They were becoming more and more vicious in their attacks on me. My disciples were as ready as they would ever be. I always knew that I must die during Passover, because I was the Passover Lamb. My Father was too good a communicator for me not to die then. You know the story.

Years before, when the Jews were in captivity in Egypt, God acted to free His people. He judged the Egyptians with an angel of death who took the lives of all the their first-born sons. However, the angel passed over the Israelites' homes because they had put the blood of a lamb on the door according to God's instructions. Symbolically, the Israelites' sins had been covered. Interestingly, the blood was placed over the top of the door and in the middle of each side so that if two lines were drawn from top to bottom and side to side, they would form the sign of a cross.

My Father showed me in many different ways at which Passover I should die. Moses, Elijah, and I had said at the Transfiguration that the end wasn't far off. The Scriptures led me to see precisely at which Passover I would ride into Jerusalem as the Messiah on Palm Sunday. That would be when I was thirty-three.* I knew if I made my historic entrance on that specific Palm Sunday, the Pharisees would at least try to kill me because they wouldn't be able to tolerate my popularity.

But no one could take my life. I chose the Passover at which to die. I gave my life. I was the King. I had power over all of nature—the wind, the water, the land, and the body. I had power even over life and death. I had always given life, and never once used my power to take a life. But now I would allow a death. When Palm Sunday came, I sent for the donkey. I dropped the gauntlet.

Did your Father give you any other signs that it was to be this specific Palm Sunday?

Every interaction with my Father had also confirmed His will that this was *the* Passover. Six days before my final Passover, my Father sent me a sign that the time was very near. It was one of the nicest things anyone ever did for me. It was on the Friday night before Palm Sunday.

---

*Detailed studies of the Book of Daniel and the Jewish calendar reveal that Palm Sunday had been prophesied to the day for over 490 years.

My death was very much on my mind. It was a very hot day. All of us were tired and needed a bath. We all smelled a little back then. *(He roared with laughter.)* Lazarus, his sisters, the disciples, and I were having supper nearby in the home of a man I had healed known as Simon the leper. At the end of the meal, Lazarus' sister Mary got up and walked over to me carrying a large bottle of perfume. She began to pour it over my head. It was tremendously refreshing, like a cool sponge bath. I knew that it was an enormous sacrifice for her financially. It was worth a year's wages. It was also an encouraging message from my Father. Through Mary and her deed, He was saying, "I know the cost, and I honor you." It was a symbolic anointing for my impending burial.

At the same time the cool oil was covering me, I looked at Lazarus, the man I'd raised from the dead. My Father was also saying to me, "You will be back from the grave. Look in the mirror. See Lazarus." I looked at the other end of the table and there was Simon, one of the most deformed lepers I had ever seen. Simon's face had at one time been so offensive most people couldn't look at him. From Isaiah, I knew my face would be so distorted by my persecutors that no one would be able to look at me.[48] Once again my Father was telling me, "Look in the mirror. See Simon's face now. Your face will soon be healed. The damage won't last long." My Father was telling me I could handle my two biggest obstacles—bodily damage and death. He always found the most touching ways of reaching me.

When Mary was anointing me with the perfume, Judas began to scorn her for wasting money. I stopped him immediately and told him that the poor would always be with them, but this anointing was for my burial. You should have seen the shock on Judas' face. Every time I revealed that I knew my death was imminent, he became frightened. I told them that wherever the gospel went, wherever my story went, people would know what Mary had done because her deed would be included in the story.

And it has been, all these years.

She had given everything she had. When you do that, don't worry—honor will follow you. God will make sure of that.

The incident also reminded me of the time when I was eating dinner at a Pharisee's home and a prostitute washed my dirty feet with her tears and dried them with her hair. I was moved by the love of both those women. Three days later when I was alone with my disciples preparing to leave them and wanting to do something comforting for them which would also leave a lasting impression, I thought of those three women. And I washed my disciples' feet.

How did you cope with your impending death?

I handled it the same way I coped with everything. I looked to my Father. The Lord is my shepherd, He always knew what I needed.

I envy you. If I could truly know that those words, "The Lord is my shepherd" are not just words, but that He is my shepherd at all moments, then I would have truly lived. But listening to you has helped me understand and trust the Lord more.

You are not far from the Kingdom of God.

What other events about that last week stand out to you?

I thought I should clean out the Temple one last time. It had been two years since I'd straightened out the matter of whose house the Temple was. Although the money changers still had a sharp recollection of what had happened then, they continued to ply their trade in the Temple. But at each of the three annual feasts they became a little uneasy as they continued to hear of my deeds. Nevertheless, they had rapidly become just as corrupt and as raucous as before.

The day after Palm Sunday, I walked into the Temple . As the money changer at the table closest to the eastern wall saw me and the familiar look in my eye, he called out, "He's here again!" I didn't want to disappoint him. So his table was the first to go. After I turned it over he reached down to try to save some of his money. I kicked it away and literally threw him out with my hands. The rest of the money changers had a few bodyguards. But they didn't stay around after I turned over a few of the heavy tables on them. Once again, there were greedy money changers running in sheer panic, their pockets jingling as they tried to hold on to as much money as possible.

I thought of Judgment Day, when they were going to wish they had never seen that money which continually weighed them down in more ways than one. There were merchants selling their animals, and I overturned their benches and drove them out, too. When I got to the entrance, there was another group of merchants about to bring in fresh merchandise, but I forbade them from entering the Temple courtyard. As usual, they had to be convinced, because they hadn't seen what I had done inside. One person tried to test me. He thought he would overpower me, but suddenly his friends were picking him up off the ground. Then I looked at the crowd which by now had become quiet and told them,

> "Is it not written: 'My house will be called a house of prayer for all nations. But you have made it a den of robbers.' "[49]

Word quickly spread to the crowd about what had happened. Many of them were at first hesitant to enter the Temple, having heard the courtyard was in chaos. But those with needs did not hesitate, nor did the children. First the blind and the lame heard I was there. They came in droves and I healed them. Then groups of children came. Some of them I'd met. Many were children who had seen me on Palm Sunday. When they saw me standing there teaching, they began to shout again, "Hosannah, Hosannah, to the son of David."

Some of the scribes and the priests who were watching all this once again became vocally upset with my supporters. They asked me if I heard what the children were saying. I reminded the Pharisees of another prophecy to let them know that nothing they could do would stop me or my Father. "Have you never read,

'from the lips of children and infants you have ordained praise'?"[50]

I left the Temple and returned to Bethany.

Four Days

What do you most vividly recall about those four days between Palm Sunday and the Last Supper?

In spite of the Pharisees' threats to arrest me, I continued to go to the Temple daily to teach. They were afraid of the people now. My parables were intentionally directed at the Pharisees. I repeated stories about ungrateful servants who didn't listen, who killed their masters' favorite son. Like a good prophet, I proclaimed the judgment awaiting those teachers. The other focus of my parables was the Last Days at the end of the world. I tried to heighten the people's awareness of the fact that the end was coming.

Every time the Pharisees saw me teaching the people, they became incensed and tried to discredit me. This time they brought me a coin and tried to trick me into taking a stand against Rome for which I could be arrested. "Sir"—it was the most respect I had received in three years from them—"You are an honest man and tell us the truth. Is it right to pay taxes to the Roman government or not?" That was when I told them that I certainly thought Caesar should have his due.

"Render therefore unto Caesar the things which are Caesar's; and unto God the things that are God's."[51]

Once again the Pharisees failed in their mission. Not only did I embarrass them in front of the people, but shortly thereafter I confronted them with the question about how the Messiah could be David's son and yet exist before David had. But I told you about that before. As usual, a big crowd surrounded us and awaited their answer. But again not one of the Pharisees could answer the question, and they had to walk away. The Pharisees didn't understand that I had already been challenged by their best, their leader, and had won.

Not only did I embarrass them in front of the people at every encounter, but on several occasions I directly and rather loudly told the people what the Pharisees were—hypocrites. "You hypocrites. You pray long prayers in public and kick widows out of their homes. Hypocrites! You tithed to your last nickel and ignored justice. Hypocrites! Everything you do is for show. You load the people down with rules you don't even try to keep. Hypocrites! You are so concerned with appearances, with the outside, while inside you exploit your neighbor and are filled with greed. You say you wouldn't dare kill a prophet like your fathers did, and yet you are following in the same steps. You snakes, sons of vipers, hypocrites, do you think you will escape the judgment of hell? You won't ever enter heaven."[52]

Now they had to get rid of me. I had humiliated them in every way. But I was also giving them a chance to see their true colors and their real need to repent.

On Wednesday of that week, some Greeks who had traveled a long way for Passover asked your disciples if they could speak to you privately. You refused to see them. Instead, you made your last public speech. In the past you had been more than receptive to foreigners, to people Jews disdained, like the Samaritan woman at the well and the Roman soldier. You had even spent time with tax collectors. Why didn't you talk with these Greeks?

I was comforted by their request, by Alexander's people coming to me. But I left the work with the Greeks for my men to do, Paul in particular. I was signing off, in a way. But I did speak to those Greeks and the rest of the world in my talk. I told them that I had to be like the kernel of wheat that dies and falls into its grave in the earth. For if I didn't, I would produce no harvest. It was my last public talk, and one last time I wanted to say, "If you love your life down here foremost, you will lose it."

I told the Greeks and everyone else listening that if they wanted to follow me, they should come and be where I am. And if they did, my Father would honor them. Was I to back off from my death even though it was a terrible burden? "No," I answered them, "this was the reason I came." At that point, I stopped and prayed,

"Father, bring glory and honor to your name."

Immediately a voice from heaven declared,

"I have already done this, and I will do it again."[53]

I heard that beautiful voice again. My Father knew the cost of living. I had to tell the world again that living is losing your life. It is Sacrifice and Love. That was the best thing I could do for the Greeks at that time.

I wanted to see those Greeks, but I had to put aside my wishes. My time was up. Do you think I didn't have dreams of taking my message to the whole world, of doing what Paul later did? But I had to give up my dreams and die.

Years later, Paul would have to do the same thing. He spent the last years of his life in a jail in Rome. But then, when you lose your life you multiply it. Paul spent his final years in a cell writing books that have blessed people for centuries. He was a living laboratory, testifying to people forever that there is a Way for men and women to rise above their circumstances. The death of my own dreams had its reward, too. My last days were not in vain.

(Jesus came in and he went out like a king. In the two weeks before his death, he performed his most famous miracle. He raised a man from death to life, a deed which had caused the crowds in Jerusalem to swell to enormous proportions in the week before Passover as they anticipated Jesus' presence there. Not to disappoint them, he had made an unforgettable entry into Jerusalem on the Sunday before his last Passover. He made that entry in daylight; humble, unarmed, cheered by the masses, and knowing full well he was headed toward his death.

He was keeping his promise to the Pharisees who once had tried to intimidate him into leaving Jerusalem by telling Jesus that Herod would kill him for causing trouble. And Jesus had replied, calling Herod a name. "You tell that fox, Herod, I will keep on healing and casting out demons until I reach my destination."

Now he had reached his destination. Shortly before he had been anointed by his friend Mary.

In a way so radical it was almost beyond comprehension, in the last week of his life Jesus confronted the authorities of his day. He made them the villains of his parables. He publicly denounced them. He out-taught them, outwitted them and continually demonstrated greater authority even to the point of taking control of "their" Temple again. At the end of his life, Jesus was at the height of his popularity and his authority and the Pharisees were afraid of him. They were sure the people were going to make Jesus king and then they would lose their "positions of honor." As they put it,

"The whole world has gone after him."[54]

He would have been king had he allowed it. But he knew that wasn't his Father's plan, so he permitted them to manipulate the scene to bring about his death. Jesus was so popular, however, that the Pharisees didn't dare try to challenge him in daylight in front of the people. In order to apprehend him, they had to contrive a devious plan to capture and try him at night. Away from the people. Every step of the way his power testified that he was the king from Nazareth and from above.)

The Last Supper

Four days after Palm Sunday, on Thursday night, you had your last meal before your death. Tell us about the Last Supper.

After three years of constant companionship, the disciples and I gathered together in a room on the evening before my death for our last meal together. This was also the famous Passover meal of the bitter herbs, the unleavened bread, and the paschal lamb, along with the ceremony of the Great Deliverance.* Over the years my disciples and I had usually been surrounded by hundreds, sometimes thousands, of people. But we tried to keep mealtimes private, just for ourselves.

As I was preparing for the meal, knowing this was the last meal I would eat before I died, memories of my men came flooding back. I thought of the first time we had met, of their courage in dropping what they were doing and following me. There were the talks, the laughs, the good-natured kidding that goes around the dinner table. I thought about their struggle to believe, about their unique personalities. I remembered Peter's exuberance, John's devotion, Matthew's gratitude, James' determination, Thomas' intellect, and Phillip's humor. I remembered all the different places we had stayed, each with its own special set of memories.

I saw how much I was going to miss them. I thought about what I was asking them—things they didn't even know yet. They would have to carry on. Most of them would be killed for being my followers. All would be martyrs. I had to prepare them for what was to follow one more time.

It was the last time I would teach them "in person," and most of all I wanted them to know how much I loved them. And I wanted to say goodbye. Because I wanted it to be a special time we would always remember, I saved the best secrets for them until last.

Earlier in the evening I'd been thinking of what I could do that night that would stay with them, that would remind them of the kind of persons to be. When we came to the banquet room prepared for us in the upper room of a friend's house, everything was so elaborate that one of the disciples, in jest, said, "Everything's here but the servant to wash our feet." I knew for sure then what I would do. What a picture it was of my task and of theirs. I thought of those women who had comforted me, who had anointed me.

Traditionally, the cup was passed around three times. After the first cup, a blessing of praise was given and everyone washed his hands again to signify the need for repentance and purity before the Lord. At this point in the meal, I got up, took off my robe, wrapped a towel around my waist, and one by one washed my disciples' feet. They were shocked. But if they were to enter my Father's house, I wanted them to know I was the one who had to make them clean.

Judas was there?

He was. When I washed the disciples' feet, I looked at each one of them directly while I was doing it to let them know how much I cared. When I got to Judas, who was going to betray me within the hour, he wouldn't look directly at me. He was extremely uncomfortable, and as I was washing his feet said to me several times, "That's enough, Lord."

Did you try to convince him not to go?

---

*The bitter herbs signified the bitterness of the Jews' oppression by the Egyptians. The unleavened bread was the type of bread eaten on the road as the Jews scurried to leave Egypt. The paschal lamb signified the lamb which took away the sins of the Israelites, causing the angel of death to pass over their homes.

Before he left I quoted the Old Testament prophecy that the Messiah would be betrayed by one of His own to show Judas that he was Satan's puppet. I didn't want him to do it.

But at the same time, you knew your Father's prophecies were never wrong.

I was hoping against hope that he wouldn't go through with it, just as later that night in the Garden I wanted out of the terrible situation I knew I had to endure. In each instance, I knew from the Scriptures what was going to happen, but that didn't stop me from being human. I didn't want either event to happen, and I tried to change them to the degree that I could. Even after Judas had betrayed me, as we stood there in the Garden surrounded by the guards who had come to get me, I looked at him and said, "I know what you have done. Now return to me."

(Obviously, on the eve of his death, serving was very much on the mind of Jesus. How typical of this man it was to wash his disciples' feet with his own hands less than twelve hours before his crucifixion. And how fitting it was. For he was getting ready to wash the feet of the whole world. If one act apart from his crucifixion portrayed above all others the essence of his life, his central message, this was it. The Lord of the Universe, intrinsic to his regal nature, came to serve. He was a king unlike any other.)

What happened then?

After washing their feet, I sat down, said another blessing of praise, and passed around the second cup. Then, according to ceremony, we each prepared the unleavened bread with the herbs to give to our neighbors. This is when I told them I was not speaking to all of them, for one of them was about to betray me. I wanted Judas to know how bitter his betrayal was for me, and ultimately for him. I wanted the others to know I knew about the betrayal in advance, so that when I was on the cross they would know I had gone willingly. I wanted them to know I was still God, even when I appeared helpless.

When I told them about the betrayal, their anxiety immediately became apparent. You could see the self-doubt in their eyes. "Betrayal?"

As I recall, most of the disciples didn't know who would betray you until after the deed was done.

They were too frightened to ask, and most of them immediately blocked it from their minds. Later in the evening, Peter, who faced everything head-on, whispered to John who was sitting next to me, "Ask the Master which one will betray Him." So John leaned over toward me and said,

"Lord, who is it?"[55]

Just as the Scriptures had prophesied in the 41st Psalm,

"Even my close friend, whom I trusted, he who shared my bread, has lifted up his heel against me."[56]

I picked up a piece of bread and dipped it in the sauce on the table. There was a custom in my day that if you wanted to honor someone at a feast you would offer him the sop. As I did that I answered John by telling him it was the one to whom I gave this piece of bread.

Was what you were doing when you gave him the bread was fulfilling that prophecy you quoted?

I didn't give Judas the bread. I offered it to him. I offered him a chance to refuse me, after I had quoted the Old Testament to warn him. It was bitter bread and he knew it. In effect I was asking him, "Judas, do you really want this bitterness? Do you really want to be the bitter herb? Do you really want to be the one who punishes God's chosen?"

As I held that bread out to him, his eyes were like a kaleidoscope showing a hundred things all at the same time. There was fear, sadness, guilt, anger, and most of all, confusion. I'll never forget the uncertainty on his face. It was an uncertainty on which he was basing his whole life. Then there was a fleeting look of hope when he hesitated and, finally, for one second, his face was the saddest face I had ever seen. Then he grabbed the bread. I told him to go and do what he had to do quickly. He immediately left and I knew it had begun.

The Scriptures record that you were in great anguish as you talked about one of your disciples betraying you. Even though you knew it was going to happen, it hurt when Judas left.

Never forget that I was divine. And never forget that I always kept my humanity. Even at the Last Supper, when I was so confident about who I was and what was to come, I was still vulnerable. I couldn't escape the grief Judas caused me. Even though I knew it was coming, even though I had prepared myself, even though I was God, Judas could still hurt me because I was a human being. I never once in my entire life gave up that vulnerability.

Was your reaction similar to the way God reacts? Even though God knows some are going to reject Him, He's still offended and hurt by that rejection?

God never made us immune to pain, because He's not immune. The only kind of relationship worth having is one where you are sensitive to the other person. All of life has always been and always will be personal to the core.

At first Judas had such a tremendous view of my Father, and he understood things about God that the others didn't. He often answered their questions before I did. It was sad. He was so gifted. We could have had so much together.

(Jesus paused here for a few moments with a deep look of grief on his face. He still felt the pain from Judas' betrayal, so poignantly expressed in the way he said the one word, "sad." Yet, he was more concerned about someone other than himself. He grieved for what his friend, Judas, had

lost. It was also striking how freely he expressed his emotions and his vulnerability. And yet these powerful feelings did not detract in any way from his strength. Perhaps his Father has similar emotions. That's what Jesus told me.)

Judas

You seem to have been closer to Judas than many people think.

I shared everything with Judas—my trials, my blessings, even my power. The time I sent my men out with my power, Judas performed miracles in my name. He healed the sick, and made the blind see. Every day for two weeks from sun up to sun down he performed hundreds of miracles, and yet he still didn't believe in me. He used me, but he never worshipped me. He never deeply honored me. He saw me walk on water, calm the sea, and raise the dead, yet he still thought he was wiser than I.

There were three-and-a-half years of living together and often comforting him or being comforted by him. He was the only other disciple besides Thomas who at moments understood total sacrifice to the point of death. He was the one disciple who would make sure I had time to be alone because he knew the importance of it. Many times he would keep the others from interrupting my prayer time. And he would never bother me. Judas always waited for me to approach him.

Only once do I recall his interrupting me or challenging me directly and that was at the end of my life when, in Judas' eyes, Mary wasted the expensive perfume on me. He hated materialism and thought the money could be used for better purposes. He was the disciple who was the least concerned about "things of this world."

When I started my public ministry, he wasn't working like the rest of the disciples. He had already given up the security of a regular job to "do God's will." Even though toward the end of my ministry he began to take money from our treasury, it was because he thought he knew how to use the money better. He was giving it to the Zealots. Contrary to what he said, Judas cared more for power than for the poor. When he saw me allow Mary to pour costly perfume on me, he became incensed because the money could have been used for "the true cause."

Sadly, he was secretly proud of his brilliance. And as so often happens when one trusts his own vision completely, he took the next fatal step of deviousness.

My anointing was the final straw which made Judas decide to betray me. Not only was I "passive and lacking a vision" but I was simply "extravagant." When he took the thirty pieces of silver from the Pharisees to betray me, he did that only to have some friends continue "the movement" to restore Israel to the Jews, which he was certain was God's will. Judas could have cared less about gold or silver in and of itself.

It must have hurt deeply to have a person on the inner circle betray you.

I would not have hurt nearly so much had an enemy found out where we were and led the soldiers to me. But to have a friend do it hurt deeply. He was not just a friend, but the first close friend I had had after being alone for so long prior to disclosing my identity. Before I announced that I was the Messiah, you can imagine that I was keeping much hidden. I hadn't been able to tell anyone except my mother who I was. I could share with no one my visions, my struggles. When Judas came into my life, he was like a breath of fresh air. All the other disciples I had gone looking for, but Judas came looking for me. He was the one who looked forward to the Messiah the most, so naturally I could talk to him about things I had never talked about before. He was a true friend.

He was the one I could leave in charge if I went off by myself or with a few of the others such as the time I spent with Peter, James and John. I could count on Judas. That was who he was to me. After all I had shared with him, all of myself that I revealed to him, he was the one who betrayed me. Though I had known for some time before the actual betrayal itself that it would be by Judas, I could always see his good side.

Because I knew he would be the one, it made me try harder to keep him from doing it. I would take special pains to let Judas know I loved him. I'd praise him, acknowledge his wisdom, pray with him, share his burden, reveal myself to him, and give him authority. I tried to honor him in every way I could think of, even at the Last Supper when I gave him that piece of bread dipped in the sauce. That was done for the guest of honor at parties.

The moment Judas left to betray me, he did so on the wings of honor, in the midst of tremendous acclaim. He had just had his dirty feet washed by the Son of God's own hands. He had just been the honored member at the banquet given by the Son of God. It will be the same for anyone who chooses hell. Every step of the way will be on roads where I have laid out the royal carpet, stained red with my blood, just for him.

When Judas left to betray me, I had a tremendous personal investment in him. When I saw him leave that night, I understood more clearly what my Father felt when Satan betrayed Him. At one time Satan was so great, just as Judas was. But pride got to both of them, and it became so strong that it destroyed them. Satan was once the most gifted angel in heaven. He had been given the distinction of being the most brilliant creature in existence. Outside the Trinity, there was no one who could compare with him. He was so like Us. So close to Us in his ways because he had been given beauty, magnificence, intelligence, and power. He had so much power that he was God-like, so much power that he forgot he was a created being.

Judas forgot the same thing. He wanted to take over "our movement." He had plans to take my place. Upon my death, he would mobilize the movement we had begun in the direction it should go. He wanted more power and immediate social changes. Jerusalem was ours. Judas saw the weakness in the other men. He saw the strength in himself. But he underestimated one person—me. He never figured out that I was God. His envy colored his vision.

One wonders how he, one of the inner circle, could really miss the fact that you were the Messiah. What went through his mind?

He heard me say I was the Messiah, but in truth he never really believed it because I wasn't what he wanted me to be. He thought to himself: "Jesus is deluded. He says he is the Messiah, but look at him. All he is doing is healing people with some kind of mystical power. But he won't take over. He just sits back.

"Oh! He'll tell the Pharisees what he thinks of them, but he will never really do anything about them or about the Romans. Jesus has no plan. All I've ever heard him say is some high-sounding nebulous business about humility, 'a seed must die before it produces fruit'. Does he think I don't know about humility? I gave up all I had in a lucrative business to follow him, to follow someone whom I hoped would turn the country around. Someone has to lead if we're going to fulfill our destiny. And if that somebody has to be me, then so be it. At least they can't say I don't have a plan. They're just going to kill Jesus, and where is that going to leave the rest of us? I believe in being humble, but not stupid.

"I thought Jesus was on a mission. He understood so much. But he's making no effort to start a real movement. Most of the people just use him and forget about him, but that's his own fault because he hasn't given them a vision. As a man, he's kind. As a leader, he's failed. Look at the people. There are thousands of them, and he is doing nothing but giving them nice platitudes such as,

'Blessed are the peacemakers.'[57]

"Well, these bloodthirsty pagan Romans have God's country in a stronghold. Has he forgotten that? I will not rest until Jerusalem, Zion, God's Holy Hill, is once again His and not Rome's. Has Jesus forgotten whom his Father loves and who formed this nation? You can't tell me God did that just so some pagan Roman could take over. No, Jesus doesn't see far enough. He just thinks he's the Messiah. But the real Messiah would deliver us. At least the Pharisees see this. Give them that much credit, even though they're cowards. Die for God. For Zion. Don't be a doormat to Rome. It will be Jerusalem or death.

"There are not many brave ones around. Look at all these disciples trying to prove which one's the greatest. They'd all probably run if it came down to taking on the Romans. What about Peter and his big mouth. James and John with their great tempers? Even if Jesus does spend more time with them it won't do any good, because he's not teaching them anything.

"Just because they're fishermen they think they're so bold, those Galileans! They were just as scared as the rest of us in that storm. I have to give

Jesus credit. He doesn't panic, and he does have incredible power. But if he wants to die, if that's his goal, I'll help him do it. It's going to happen anyway. Even he knows that. He's always talking about how Scripture says this and Scripture says that all to justify this extremely passive position. He twists the Scriptures. Hasn't he read in there the parts about the Messiah reigning, putting his boot on the enemies' necks, treading them down?

"I'll tell you what I think. I think Jesus never got over the loss of his father, Joseph, at an early age, and he never had a father to teach him how to be truly assertive. He and his followers don't really have a heart for Zion because they're not from Judea. Jesus is a nice man. But somebody has to take advantage of the people in their present rebellious state. Jesus and John the Baptist got them fired up and we may never get another chance this good in my lifetime. I know what I have to do. Somebody has to see the light. And after all, I'm not going to do anything but lead them to him. They would have found him sooner or later, anyway. He'd just as well get it over with. I'll be doing every one of them, even Jesus, a favor."

Talent is a dangerous thing. It is a powerful tool for good or evil, because it tempts you to worship yourself. Judas was brilliant and perceptive, but he forgot he couldn't see far enough by himself. He thought he was the Light, didn't he? Just look at a man like Judas. He was so accomplished.

By far he was overall the most singularly gifted man I ever knew on this earth, except for one thing. He had a bad heart. He could have been a Paul. In fact, Paul in a way took Judas' place. Everything Paul did might have been planned for Judas to do. All the honor that Paul has could have come to Judas if he had trusted. Judas and Satan were whom I thought of when I said,

"But many that are first shall be last; and the last shall be first."[58]*

Judas tried to give the money back after he betrayed you. Why?

He felt the guilt. And when the Pharisees wouldn't take it, he threw the money away and went into a deep depression. God who loved Judas had prophesied the betrayal down to the specific amount of thirty pieces of silver, and to the actual dissatisfaction that Judas would have with himself.[59] But Judas' pride ruined him. Even after the betrayal my Father and I would have taken him back had he repented. But he wouldn't. He was his own savior, who provided his own cross and had no use for my atonement. He found those lacking and committed suicide shortly after betraying me. There's a real danger in being a "good person." It tends to make you forget your own evil and forget who made you. Obviously, in the end Judas was a very foolish man. He had let his pride turn him into an evil man—into a Son of Satan. One of the most talented men in history became one of the most evil, the greatest traitor in history by

---

*After Judas' suicide and following Jesus' resurrection, the remaining eleven disciples cast sticks to decide upon the man to take Judas' place as a disciple. They knew there had to be twelve disciples to fulfill the prophecy that each would rule one of the twelve tribes of Israel upon Christ's return. Matthias was the man the disciples selected, and little was known or heard about him after that. However, shortly thereafter Paul was selected by Jesus himself to be an apostle in the miraculous conversion on the road to Damascus.

whom all others pale in comparison, the biggest fool mankind has ever produced.

(Though Jesus here called Judas a fool, there was no vindictiveness in the way he said it; rather there was a regret. It made me think of the grief God must bear in watching children He has given life to choose hell over Him. God must understand well a mother who loses a child, and particularly one who loses a child by watching him turn into a drug addict or a monster like Hitler. He has lost millions of them forever, even after paying the ultimate price to save them.)

You didn't reach Judas. Was that a failure for you personally?

No, that was the price of freedom, the same price that my Father paid with Lucifer. Love can come only from freedom. I did all I could for Judas. I never quit holding out my hand to him even after I knew he had betrayed me. Four hours before he led the Roman soldiers to me, I washed his feet with my hands. Even when he brought the soldiers to capture me, I called him "friend."

It amazes me that you contained your feelings toward this man whom you knew was going to betray you, destroy you. When you told the disciples that one of them was going to be a traitor, none of them knew who it was. They obviously didn't pick up any bitterness you had toward Judas.

I could not stop loving him until he totally refused my love and walked away. It was his only hope. After Judas had made his choice and left, I remember looking at the still uneaten paschal lamb in front of us, the last part of the Passover meal. This lamb was roasted over a fire, not allowed to touch anything, undefiled. And then it was eaten without breaking any of its bones, meaning the sacrifice was complete and unbroken. It was a picture of me. How anyone could miss the fact that the Messiah, the Lamb, was to suffer, amazed me. Sacrifice was the heart of Passover, of worship. How appropriate it was that Judas had left before eating this sacrifice, because he didn't think he needed it. As I was mulling over the pain Judas had left me, I looked around the table and there were the faces of John, Peter, James, and the others. With all their faults, they had not betrayed me. I took great comfort in knowing that what I did, I did for the Johns, the Peters, the Jameses of the world; not the Judases. They didn't want it. They couldn't accept it.

Despite the pain, it was also a great time. That day was finally here. Now I was attaining my glory. As I told my disciples right after Judas left, "Now is the Son of Man glorified, and God is glorified in Him." I was getting ready to do the most courageous thing a man had ever done. The fate of the whole world hinged on what I was going to do the next day. My deed was to be the centerpiece of history. I had waited a long time for the world to see my glory win out over pain. And I was ready.

(What unbelievable personal strength Jesus had as Judas left to set up the betrayal. Jesus met the challenge, in effect saying, "I'm waiting for you;

bring me my glory." And for centuries to come, Christ's strength would enable his martyrs to demonstrate an uncommon courage in the face of persecution. Jesus's deed was so great that his courage would permeate his church for centuries until his return. Interestingly, at the same Last Supper he demonstrated the tremendous range of his emotions and his unusual sensitivity by comforting his disciples, lovingly preparing them for the separation anxiety they would soon experience—

"I will be with you only a little longer . . ."[60]
Let not your heart be troubled . . . In my Father's house are many mansions . . . I go to prepare a place for you."[61])

Peter

When you told the disciples that one of them would betray you, didn't Peter vow that he wouldn't?

When I had made that prediction, Peter immediately vowed that under no circumstances would he deny me. He would die for me at a moment's notice. That's when I looked at him and said, "Peter, you will deny me not once, but three times before the sun comes up." I had to tell him, "No, Peter, there's only one man who would die for his neighbor at all times in all circumstances, and it's not you." Peter was the bravest of the lot, but I had to show him and mankind for centuries to come.

"There is none good but one."[62]

I wanted Peter and the rest of the world to know I wasn't under any illusions. I had to be firm and honest with Peter despite his good intentions. But I made it up to him.

You obviously loved all your disciples. But you really liked Peter.

Peter was always Peter. Earlier that night when I washed the disciples' feet, he reacted to that, too. As usual, he had his own thoughts which he freely shared, He insisted that he would not let me do something so low as to wash his feet. I informed him that,

"Unless I wash you, you have no part with me."[63]

Peter, as quick to admit a mistake as to volunteer an opinion, a man of extremes, but so honest, immediately said: "Well, Lord, wash all of me." It was all I could do to just hold Peter down a little. I told him gently, "A person who is clean needs only his feet washed, and all of you are clean except one."

Down through the centuries, Peter has often been laughed at, yet he is the one disciple we know the most about. Why did you choose him to be in your inner circle of three?

Peter had an exuberance that was contagious. He was always expressing himself. Sometimes it was not with enough thought, but it was an honest boldness, a straightforwardness. There was no guile in Peter. What you saw was what you got.

Peter was not the one who asked behind everyone else's back to be favored like James and John did. When Peter wanted to be special, everybody knew it. If he wanted to walk on water, he asked to do it in front of everybody. If he thought you were wrong, he told you, "Lord, you shouldn't wash my feet." His boldness was his greatest weakness, but also his greatest strength.

There was something comforting about being around Peter. You always knew where you stood with him, and there's nothing like having someone such as Peter on your side. At one point, when the rest of the disciples were confused, Peter was the one who understood most clearly who I was. And he declared it. Peter said he knew who I was. I wasn't Elijah or John the Baptist come back to life as some people said. And I wasn't just another prophet, He said:

"You are the Christ, the Son of the living God."[64]

At that time, you gave God credit for showing him that.

God did reveal it to him, but he picked a man like Peter who could think big. It took that kind of man to see how big I was. Peter would do anything for you, or at least try. Although he knew my abilities to prophesy, he was so determined to please me that he insisted I was wrong when I told him, "Peter, you will deny me three times before the cock crows in the morning."

He took criticism well, however. After each failure, he came roaring back: "Teach me more, Lord." He never let his failures slow him down. "If I'm wrong, Lord, then wash my whole body." The time I was teaching the disciples that I had to die, Peter told me,

"Lord, you're not going to die."

I had to rebuke him with,

"Get thee behind me Satan."

Undaunted, a few days later at the Transfiguration Peter wanted to build me a temple. He always wanted to learn, and he was bold.

People have laughed at Peter for his impulsiveness.

Everybody always laughed at Peter. He had some obvious faults. But Peter's indomitable spirit reflected what my Father intended men and women to be when He created them. Remember, Peter was the only man other than myself to walk on water. What potential for faith he had, and ultimately he fulfilled it.

After Judas left the room, you taught your men some great truths that last night.

It was a bittersweet time. I had all the memories of my disciples and I knew I would miss them. At the same time, I was about to see my Father again. After all the years of waiting and wondering, now it was almost here. In less than three days, I was going home. That long-awaited reunion with my Father was just around the corner, and yet in front of me was the horrible battle I had dreaded for years. At the same time, I had just felt the pain of enormous rejection. I was having to leave these men into whom I had poured my life. Even the last time together couldn't be perfect, for it was obvious to me my men did not completely understand, and I knew from the Scriptures that each of them in his own way would deny me.

Still, you loved them.

There was no perfection on this earth. We all wait on heaven; even the Messiah, even the Father. All of my work, all of my hope, all of my life in a way had come down to these eleven men; and now, in just a few hours, I would be gone. I would never be with them again in the same way as a human being. I would never again teach them face to face in this way.

Another Teacher—my Spirit, the Holy Spirit, would be taking my place. And in a real way it would be better for them, as He would continually teach them my words and I would indwell them spiritually. But it would never be like this again. I knew that. I wanted it to be very clear in their minds what their calling was; so before I told them I was leaving, I reminded them of their duty to serve. I washed their feet and I was their Lord.

As soon as Judas left, I told the rest, my true disciples, that I would be leaving, that this would be our last meal together. As soon as I said it, the panic of abandonment was written all over their faces as I knew it would be. So I immediately told them I was going to prepare a place for them, and I promised them I would be back to get them so that "where I am you may be also."

> "Where I am going you cannot come."[65]
> "I am going to prepare a place for you, and if I go and prepare a place for you, I will come back and take you to be with me, that where I am you also may be."[66]

I had nothing materially to give them now, but I knew that at my return each of them would have a permanent mansion in my Father's kingdom.

> "In my Father's house are many mansions."[67]

As far as the world was concerned, there was going to be a poor man on that cross. But I tell you I was a rich man, and everything I had I gave to them.

(On the eve of his death, the greatest man the world has ever known had no material possessions except the clothes on his back. By the next day, even those would be taken from him. When he fed five thousand people, he had to borrow the bread to do it. When they asked him about his allegiance to Caesar, he had to borrow a coin to make his point. Even the Last Supper was held in a room that was loaned to him for the night. Jesus intentionally was saying to a world whose primary standard of worth was measured in material wealth, "There is more to being human than wealth. Living does not consist in the abundance of things that you possess." He was also making another statement: "My Father looked after me, and He will look after you.")

What did you tell them after that?

After I told them of their future inheritance, I gave them their earthly inheritance in the way they had longed for. For three and a half years, they had heard me refer to myself as the Light of the World, the Good Shepherd, the Bread of Life, the Son of Man—but rarely directly as the Messiah. They had watched me heal people and tell them to keep it a secret. During the time they had observed my restraint, my disciples had wanted me to come out boldly announcing who I was. John the Baptist urged me to do the same thing. My disciples had wanted to hear me say who I was. Now they got their wish. I was going to say it to them clearly.

"Anyone who has seen me, has seen the Father."[68]
"I am the way, the truth, and the life. No one comes to the Father except through me."[69]

I told them, "I have glorified God on this earth," "I have power over all flesh," and "I was with God in all my glory before the world was created." Later in that same talk, I would give them my glory. In fact, that was the essence of their inheritance.

"I have given them the glory that you gave me, that they may be one as we are one."[70]

But first among their gifts I gave them their duty to serve. Then I gave them my authority. If they were going out into a hostile world, they were going out armed. To make sure they were, I gave them my Teacher, my Guide, the Spirit of Truth to be with them forever.

"Because I have said these things, you are filled with grief. But I tell you the truth. It is for your good that I am going away. Unless I go away, the Counselor will not come to you; but if I go, I will send him to you. But when he comes he will guide you into all truth. All that belongs to the Father is mine. That is why I said the Spirit will take from what is mine and make it known to you.[71]

Even though my disciples were temporarily about to abandon me, I was very confident in them because their Teacher had been mine, too. And I knew what kind of results he got. He never failed.

As I continued to "arm them", I gave them my power. It was the influence I had with my Father, the influence that heals people, that raises people from the dead. I prayed that my followers could know how great their inheritance was. I told them that anyone who had faith in me could do the same things I had done, and even greater things because I was going to the Father.

"And I will do whatever you ask in my name, so that the Son may bring glory to the Father. You may ask me for anything in my name, and I will do it.[72] "The Father will give you whatever you ask in My name".[73]

Never before had they had this much power, this much influence with my Father. I told my disciples to use their power. Go ahead, ask. Ask for anything? Six times I told them, Ask. Ask. Ask. Ask. Ask. Ask. With their power, I gave them my confidence, my success. I gave them the exact guarantee my Father had given me. I personally guaranteed them that their mission would succeed just as my Father had promised me mine would.

"You did not choose me, but I chose you to go and bear fruit—fruit that will last."[74]

So that they would know for sure that my Father and I delighted in letting their lights shine, I pushed them to do great things. I told them that my Father got much joy when they did great things, and so did I. "Plan, think, ask us. —We will help you."

"I tell you the truth, anyone who has faith in me will do what I have been doing. He will do even greater things than these, because I am going to the Father."[75]

In addition to my power I gave them my peace. And mine was a different kind of peace then the world offers. It was immune to circumstances. It was peace over fear, over discouragement, and over death. Particularly it was over death.

"Peace I leave with you; my peace I give you. I do not give to you as the world gives. Do not let your hearts be troubled and do not be afraid."[76]

Then I gave them another priceless gift which is really the essence of all gifts. It was my joy, the greatest joy that any person on this earth has ever experienced.

"You love righteousness and hate wickedness; therefore God, your God, has set you above your companions by anointing you with the oil of joy."[77]

This joy would come from their influence with the Father and their importance to the Father.

"Ask and you will receive, and your joy will be complete."[78]

The one thing that had given me happiness beyond belief was that I knew how much I was loved. When I gave them my joy, I gave them my love. As I told them,

"Greater love has no one than this, that one lay down his life for his friends."[79]

and

> "As the Father has loved me, so have I loved you."[80]

They were the most loved people in history. To show them exactly how much they were loved, I gave them my glory so that I could give them above all my Father. They now had my righteousness so that they could have the one thing I treasured most—my oneness with my Father.

> "I have given them the glory that you gave me, that they may be one as we are one."[81]

They were now "a member of the family called Trinity." I had given them a new identity, unique in human history. As C. S. Lewis later said, I had made them little gods.

When the great Resurrection Day would come in the future, I would live inside them. Just as my Father had lived in me and I had spoken His words, they would speak my words. I had literally given them myself.

> "On that day you will realize that I am in my Father and you are in me, and I am in you."[82]

Not only had they seen God when they had seen me, a privilege very few men in history have had, but now they were going to be a part of Him, and He of them. The isolation that had existed for centuries was now broken. Now they had far more than Adam had possessed in Eden. They had been given my ability to love, and from that time on they were to love as they had been loved.

> "A new command I give you. Love one another. As I have loved you."[83]

This was their heritage. This was to be our power that would conquer the world. Not the power of might. Or of material wealth or political office. Not the power of fear. But the power of love. This was to be our calling card. A new day was dawning for all people everywhere, and my disciples were the first to know. Those who believed in me and my Father were to be my brothers and sisters, and there would be a oneness that the world had never known.

Warnings at the Table

You also gave them some warnings.

At this point I gave them a warning. I talked to them about obedience and discipline. I said the key to protecting the gifts they had been given, the key they would need to use all the other gifts, the same key I had had to use was obedience and discipline.

"If you obey my commands, you will remain in my love, just as I have obeyed my Father's commands and remain in his love."[84]

Now I had shared almost everything I had with them. They were being told my secrets. Things no one else in history knew. All my blessings, all the treasures of my heart, even my own inheritance I was about to receive. Everything. Then, and only then, could I give them the other part of their heritage—my cross. If they were to live out the truth, pain would come. Pain always follows truth. They would be martyred, just as I was to be.

"If the world hates you, keep in mind that it hated me first. If you belonged to the world, it would love you as it's own. As it is, you do not belong to the world, but I have chosen you out of the world. That is why the world hates you. Remember the words I spoke to you; 'No servant is greater than his master.' If they persecuted me, they will persecute you also."[85]

Again I told them so they would be sure to know my persecution was no surprise to me. The Scriptures had predicted this moment and it must be fulfilled.

"Those who hate me without reason outnumber the hairs of my head; many are my enemies without cause."*[86]

This was from the 69th Psalm, the psalm which had comforted me all the days of my life. Now I wanted it to comfort them. One of the tremendous things the Scripture did for me was to say, "See, this is happening just as it's supposed to." When you know what to expect, it certainly helps you to get prepared. That's what I wanted to do for my men. It was a difficult gift to give but that gift brought us closer together and made us even more one. At the same time I gave them my cross, I also gave them my courage.

I have told you these things, so that in me you may have peace. In this world you will have trouble. But take heart! I have overcome the world."[87]

Finally, I prayed with them. I asked God to protect them and to teach them so that the world could see this oneness and believe that He sent me. I asked God to give me glory for what I was about to do.

Right after this, didn't some of your disciples start arguing about who would betray you and which one of them would be the greatest in your kingdom? Wasn't that somewhat discouraging?

They did. And it was. At that point, they were still much of this world. Even the oneness of the Last Supper was tainted with envy. That is why I was having to go through the crucifixion for them. That is when I told them that the gentile kings lorded it over their servants but they were not to imitate them. The one who ruled should be a servant. I told them not to worry about their rank. All

---

*In the New Testament, the most quoted Old Testament book is Psalms, and among the Psalms, the 69th is the second most quoted next to the 22nd. The two great prophetic Psalms of Messianic suffering.

one day would eat at my table. Each of them would rule over the twelve tribes of Israel.

Why, at the moment they least deserved it, did you give them their blessing?

For the same reason that, after I washed their feet, I assured them they were clean. I was preparing them for their failure so that they could teach the rest of the world how to respond to failure by witnessing God's mercy and forgiveness. After I was gone, I wanted my disciples to treat the peole of this world in the same way. In the face of abuse, they were to respond with kindness. That's the type of love that overwhelms people, the kind they don't understand.

After my gifts to them, we completed the Passover ceremony. We finished by passing the traditional cup around seven times. When it came to me the last time I did not drink, but told them: "I will not drink this cup with you until we drink it together in heaven." I would drink the final cup later that evening and the next morning by myself. It was to be the most bitter cup of my life on earth. Finally, we sang one of the great Messianic Psalms, the 118th, the way we traditionally ended the Passover meal. Afterwards, we left the room and set out for the Mount of Olives where I would prepare myself to make my final entrance into Jerusalem, this time not as a prince, but as a prisoner. I had to resist one last temptation to turn away from my Father. It was a strong one. You can't imagine how strong it was.

(In what was the most moving and most important speech in history, and perhaps the most overlooked, Jesus the Messiah was ending his life on earth in a blaze of glory.

On the eve of his death, he was able to give those closest to him his joy and his peace. To have any joy or peace six hours before undergoing the most horrible persecution in the history of the world, you must have overcome the world. Only a great man could face his impending death with courage and at the same time be concerned with alleviating the fears of others. He made incredible promises to his disciples, concerned that they might overlook the tremendous power they now had if they would but ask. Jesus not only dominated life then but does even now. He made it plain that his involvement with his men was to be far from inactive, even though he was "stepping up" to a new role. He would be busy answering their many requests in which his Father would take great delight.

"And whatsoever ye ask in my name, that will I do, that the Father may be glorified in the Son."[88]

The Book of Hebrews records that Jesus will also serve as our high priest in heaven, never ceasing to make intercessions for his people before God.

It also struck me how Jesus went out as he came into the world, most humbly. While those in the world secretly, and sometimes not so secretly wish to do greater deeds than their neighbors, Jesus, the Lord of the Universe, left his men saying:

"Greater things will you do than I have done."

For centuries to come he gave his servants hope as he directly connected their service to him. Not only were they to serve as he did, but also they were to serve him. As Paul taught, "Whatever you do, do it as unto Christ and he will reward you accordingly."[89] Jesus brought dignity to every moment of life, whether it was the life of a king or a servant.

After my talk with him, I was utterly convinced that the key to life is in seeing God and His son for who they really are. Many times since my talk with Jesus, my thoughts have taken me back to the Last Supper, and I have gone over his words to his disciples more times than I can count. Each time, it's like viewing a masterpiece of art from another angle. I discover something I had never seen before.

Nowhere else in the Scriptures than at this last meal with his men, as John recorded it, is there a more intimate conversation. Of all the parts of Scriptures that inspire, this is my favorite. It's how I imagine He will talk to me in heaven, for it's how He talks to me now.

I have often been struck by how frequently he used the word, "I", and how plain, almost primitive his phrases were:

"I am going away."[90]
"I am going to prepare a place for you."[91]
"A new commandment I give you."[92]
"I am the way, the truth, and the life."[93]

They had a familiar, comforting quality to them. The universal "mother tongue," telling us "everything will be all right."
How much I loved those words,

"My peace I give you."[94]
"I am the vine, you are the branches."[95]

These particular words of the Last Supper make me realize how desperately I want to hear God talk to me, to hear Him say, "This is how I feel about you," and "This is what I will do for you." It's a personal universe to the core.

With each successive reviewing of his last talk before his death, I am more and more amazed at Jesus' authority and confidence. If indeed he had to grow in "wisdom and stature, and in favor with God and man," then certainly on this his last night as "just a man," he was in full bloom—

"Anyone who has seen me has seen the Father."[96]

He had become all of what man was meant to be—the perfect blend between a man of faith and a man of authority. He was the only true man.

At other moments of reflection, I am again impressed by Jesus' brilliance as a teacher. Imagine that you, the Son of God, have to tell the world who you are, who they are, who God is, and what the relationship between all of you can be, and to do this in a way that all will understand. These words have stood the test of time, and down through the ages have spoken with the same impact to both the scholar and the unlearned.

The focus of his brilliance was always the Father. All the gifts that Jesus gave to his disciples and to us at the Last Supper were because the Father had first given them to him. Only then would he say that the Spirit could take what was his and give it to us. Always it was what the Father wanted, "I only do what I see the Father doing. What I say are not my words but my Father's."

His was not a submission based on weakness and dependency, but on love.)

Random Reflections from the Master

Here you were—God with no flaws—even in you humanity. Here were your men with all their shortcomings. How did you really feel about your disciples?

I wanted to take them with me to spend eternity together. I could have had anybody in heaven with me and I chose them. I took care of their failings. They won't have them when they're with me.

The Book of Hebrews says about you,

"For the joy set before Him endured the cross, despising the shame."[97]

At the Last Supper, at the end when you prayed with your men what many people have called the true "Lord's Prayer," you asked your Father to restore the glory that was once yours before the world was created. Were you looking forward to heaven?

I really wanted to see my Father. I understood how people look forward to heaven, because I did. Heaven for me was receiving and being received by my Father in all His glory. All the memories of times past with my Father that I had laid aside along with my own glory would be clear to me again.

Why did you choose the symbols of bread and wine for communion?

My Father taught me to use those. The first priest mentioned in the Scriptures, Melchizedek, was a prototype of me. In the Scriptures he came from nowhere to be a priest to Abraham. He also was the king (of Salem). Abraham, after his first great military victory, offered his tithes to God through this priest,

Melchizedek, then sealed his pledge with bread and wine at Melchizedek's instructions.

In one way, communion is a picture of the basic sustenance we need for life—bread and water. Now, however, the water has been changed to wine, symbolic of the new covenant. You must depend upon and take into your very being my sacrifice. There is something morbid and desperate in communion. It says, "Now you eat what you killed if you want to live."

You told your men that after you were physically gone, your spirit would be in them, and your Teacher would be, too. How did you know that?

It's talked about all through the Old Testament. It says,

> "I will put my law in their minds and write it on their hearts. I will be their God and they will be my people."[98]

That's clearly saying, "I in Him and He in me." Never forget the old saying, "The new is in the old concealed. The old is in the new revealed." The New Testament is in the old and vice versa. There is a unity to Scripture. Once you look, it's obvious.

FIVE

*Crucifixion
and
Resurrection*

On the Way to the Garden

You were so confident that you would conquer the cross that you could promise your men everything ahead of time. A few days before your persecution, you made a bold proclamation that you had come to drive out the prince of this world. Yet privately, in the Garden, just before you were betrayed, there were some anxious moments. Were you frightened of the possibility of denying your mission?

I was ready. I knew my Father. I knew His ability to prepare me and I knew His strength. I was one with Him. Of that I was certain. I knew His word was never wrong and I had all my trust in it. When the end came, I was determined. There was never a better-prepared man on the eve of a battle. Nobody ever before had God's promise that they would win. That's how confident I was. That was one side of me.

As the Scriptures make clear, however, I had a real battle on my hands. There was always the other side of me. My humanity. My emotions. My senses. I had to overcome that side again the last day of my life, just as I had every day of my life. After the meal, the challenge I had waited for all my life was imminent, and I knew from experience that I needed to be alone to finish preparing myself. I was to play the role another Old Testament character had played—Job. And I was not looking forward to playing it.

If I remember the test correctly, Satan told God that Job, a righteous man, would deny God if he had to suffer. God said that he would not, and allowed Satan to bring all manner of suffering on Job to see if he would

"curse God, and die."[1]

Job's suffering led him to great doubts, but he never denied God.

He never did. But he was tempted. So, to answer your earlier question, "Was I tempted to deny my mission?" I was tempted in all ways as you are.

But God even prepared me for that. My temptation was no surprise intellectually. God had told me to expect it, particularly the doubt. I knew my instructions but I also knew how much was being asked of me, and I knew that Satan would do everything in his power to defeat me just as he had done with Job. I had an idea that, like Job, I would come to a moment when I would have to depend totally on my faith, not on my senses.

That challenge appealed to me. Could I obey and trust my Father when everyone and everything around me, including my own senses, was telling me to give up, that it wasn't worth it? In a strange way, I welcomed the battle. I knew the temptation would be great. I didn't know at the time how great it would be. Preparation helps tremendously, but there are certain things you never appreciate until you go through them. I knew there would be a moment when I would be on my own, and God would have to judge me. I figured Satan was hoping to break me at that precise moment.

I've always appreciated the Book of Job, but at the same time I've wondered why the suffering went on so long—forty chapters, and on and on about suffering— with Job's having to go through such strange tests. Now I understand why God put all that in the book. It was perhaps more for you than for anybody else.

One difference between Job and myself that made it more difficult on me was that Job had no choice. I did.

I never thought of it before, but I can't think of one sane man in history who chose to die willingly when he could have avoided it, and no one else in history who knew for years before the event happened exactly how he would die, down to the last detail.

My Father is an interesting director. The first major human event which affected all of history and which placed a curse on the human race involved a battle with Satan in the Garden when Adam and Eve were deceived. Now a second great event was taking place, also in a garden, which was to undo the damage of the first event. As it had begun, it was ending.

So you headed for the Garden of Gethsemane, a familiar place to you and to your men.

My time with my men was over, and I went to the Garden to wait alone with my Father. Immediately I had the wish to leave. I had taken Peter, James, and John with me, and left them in another part of the Garden. I had told them how sorrowful I was, and had asked them to stay awake and to pray for me and for themselves. Waiting for your torturers puts unbelieveable pressure on you.

My mind began to play out the next scene over and over again. I was to taste hell for all of them. It was to be hell in its subtle forms, such as regret, and hell in one of its more direct forms, such as physical pain. I knew I would have to suffer at the hands of others, and willing to be totally at their mercy. Not knowing exactly what torture would follow increased my anxiety.

It would be the most vicious abuse in history, for all the forces of evil would be despising me, trying to crush me. I would be judged for all their sins. And they would tell me that I was the evil one—not them—just as it will be in hell. I was literally to take on the sins of the world at the moment they were giving them to me, and it would be a heavy load. I was to feel the shame, the curse. I would be tempted to act as they did, particularly since I would be tired and in pain.

I had to hold it inside. I could sense that everything inside me would naturally want to escape from that situation. I had to be on constant guard lest at any minute I would choose the option of escape. Grief became pronounced when I thought of my own Father joining them in the abuse. He had to judge me.

(He said those words very slowly, and even in the retelling, the grief was palpable.)

I can't describe the utter darkness I experienced at that moment. My own Father, my great Father, would be cursing me. You would have to be as close to Him as I was completely to understand how it hurt.

It would be as if you were a child with the kindest, most loving mother in the world, who one day tied you up and then very slowly began to torture you to death. All the time you would be looking up at her with your trusting eyes but all you could see would be enormous fury that she would be taking out on you. Somehow you would know that she hated the pain too and that she was doing it because she was punishing you to save others who really deserved the punishment.

The moment I dreaded was when my Father would see me not as His precious son, but as the most evil sinner in the history of the world. He had to see me that way if I were really going to take their places.

I feared His judgment because I knew how great His power was. I'd used it, and I had felt just a minute fraction of His fury when I cleansed the Temple of those despicable men and destroyed their belongings. His wrath had been stored up for centuries. Read the Scriptures and see how angry He was. It was all righteous indignation—an inconceivable amount—and all of it was to be directed at me. This was not going to be an average sadistic crucifixion. God, Himself, would be laying on me all the sins of the world. All the evil imaginable would be condensed into that one experience that day, and it would be mine. I would feel a darkness such as no man had ever known before, and no one ever will until those who so chose take their first step into hell. This was Judgment Day, and I knew God was right. I saw people just as He did. Knowing that I would experience hell for them, not only its physical pain, but also in its worst form—complete, utter abandonment by God—was shattering. Having nothing good, nothing kind, nothing comforting around you, nothing but utter blackness where there is no God and where God lets the whole world turn its fury loose just as it will be in hell was a devastating reality.

"Cursed is everyone who hangs on a tree."[2]

I knew His plan and I was already feeling the shame. In feeling so despised, so hated, the emotional pain was almost worse than the physical would be. During that experience all I would have to tell me I was good would be my faith. I was to take on all of their shame, the identical shame that will permeate hell for eternity as everyone blames his neighbor for being there.

I knew how they were going to give me their shame. To convince me I was despised, they planned to beat me unmercifully. They would spit on me, laugh at me, ridicule me, beat me again, and starve me. They would put nails in my hands and feet, strip me naked, and abuse me continuously in front of everyone—not only my enemies, but also my friends and family, which in some way was even worse. Could you have someone do this to you for hours and not feel it?

The thing we all dread the most as human beings, at least initially, is physical pain. What was ahead of me was the most intense period of physical pain in history, plus the most enormous emotional pain ever experienced. I knew how pain humbles anyone. I knew how it can break you, how worthless it makes you feel, how you can doubt yourself. I was aware how much more vulnerable it makes you to verbal insult of any kind, how you will want to do anything to stop it. I had my instructions, however, "Take it, and say nothing; accept the pain, the shame."

Is that what hell will really be like?

Everyone will despise everyone else. Everyone will attempt to destroy his neighbor. Everyone will distrust his neighbor because no one can be trusted. Hell will be ruled by one commandment. Hate your neighbor as you hate yourself.

None of this, "I want to go to hell because that's where all my friends will be"?

There will be no friends in hell, not one. There will be no commaraderie, no laughter, no sunlight. There will be only ever-present darkness, condensed evil. There will be nothing likable about anyone. Hatred, suffering, and violence will abound. People there will understand as never before what it's like to be in an environment where no hope for justice exists. Every waking moment, and there will be no sleep for escaping, will be filled with fear and regret. They will regret that they never took God seriously, regret that they underestimated His presence in the previous world where there was some sense of or hope for justice. They will miss God in ways they never thought possible. Every person's pain will be accentuated because of the constant, inescapable reality that a different choice could have been made. But it will be too late. God will be gone forever.

Suffering and hell are unpopular subjects with everyone, including my Father and me. This is why we went to such great lengths to help the people who choose to avoid it.

Your Father's judgment still seems extremely harsh in a way. Your teaching is that all men deserve death, yet to take someone's life who has never killed another seems unfair.

Everyone has been killing for years, both others and themselves. Where do you think aging comes from? Do you think doctors know? The world is engulfed with hostility. Some is overt. Much is hidden. But it is ever-present.

Is hostility significantly present in nice neighborhoods?

It is even in ministers' homes, even in the homes of the nicest people in town. Do you think hostility, however subtle, doesn't take its toll? Just because it is a slow death doesn't mean it isn't murder. Where do you think the expression "that's killing me" came from. Pressures from the boss, from our neighbors, our spouses, and our children all affect us. Or take the expression, "I'm so mad I could kill myself." Listen to any talk show, any political race, almost any pastoral selection committee, and you'll see that someone's always degrading someone else, slowly "doing each other in."

Do you think everyone knows this?

Somewhere in their minds they do, in one of those big closets of the mind that most people aren't aware that they have.

Alone in the Garden

Let's get back to the Garden. What went through your mind there?

What kept going through my mind were these graphic images of a man dying on the cross. I had witnessed it before, and the Scriptures defined precisely what I would go through. The Scriptures were not fantasy. This was really about to happen and I had seen men before hung on a cross with their backs raw from the beatings. Every time they had to take a breath, their faces would show the tremendous pain of putting pressure on their feet and hands to draw up to breathe. I had seen the scraping of their raw backs on the wood of the cross, collecting splinters in the wounds each time they breathed. I'd seen them scream. I'd seen the crowds gawking.

My Father had made it very clear what He expected of me. I kept trying to think of who I was, "the Lamb of God which taketh away the sin of the world;" of verses that taught me what I was to do,

"He was oppressed and He was afflicted, yet He did not open His mouth."[3]

I would tell myself, "You are the sacrificial lamb; that is why you came into the world. It is your mission; you can do it." I had His word that I could. I was the Messiah. I knew my Father as no one else did, and as I was about to come face-to-face with His anger, it caused me to ask all over again every question I had ever asked about suffering. They were questions such as "How can a merciful God allow suffering?" They were questions I had answered years ago.

I suppose you would have a word to say to the intellectuals who have pondered the question for years. Why does evil exist? How could God allow it?

That's a tremendously important question. Everything they ever thought about asking, I asked with great emotion. There was nothing theoretical about it at that point. I had thoughts like, "Why can't He just forgive them? Couldn't it be done another way? Can't I just take a few men and improve the human race that way? I could take my men and slip away. Nothing could stop us. I have the power. If I were cornered I could walk walk right through them."

Every possibility occurred to me all over again that night, all of which I knew weren't real possibilities. But, for just a second, every alternative seemed much more possible. Thoughts about how unfair this was came to me. I had done nothing—nothing but cure the sick, make the blind see and the lame walk, feed the hungry, and teach people the truth. What I got in return was torture and death. Even among my own followers, one had betrayed me and the rest were insensitive men who, I knew, would run when they got scared.

The temptation for me to run was getting stronger. I could feel one of my greatest battles beginning. I wanted to retaliate, but I couldn't. I had to take the evil of the world—death itself in all of its forms including my Father's judgment—and not give it back. I had to take it to the grave. I knew horrible destruction was mine if I accepted it, and fear began to engulf me.

The next day was already so real to me that my sorrow and grief were too much. It was literally killing me. Once, when I opened my eyes I looked down at the ground where I was kneeling and saw a pool of blood. As I wiped the sweat which was pouring from my forehead, I realized I was in so much agony that I was sweating drops of blood. I pleaded with Him,

"Father! All things are possible for Thee, remove this cup from Me."[4]

I reminded myself that I had been chosen before the foundation of the world, before all of history for this moment. But the grief and the suffering wouldn't let up.

I arose to walk around for a minute, and went to where my men were just to be with someone, just to break that agitating, depressing anxiety for a minute. There they were, asleep—asleep after I'd asked them to stay awake with me. It was the only time I'd asked them to do something for me personally in three and a half years, and all I'd asked them to do was just to comfort me by praying for me and themselves. Peter, James and John—how much I had loved them. I had spent so much time with these three in particular, pouring my life into theirs. How boldly they had talked. How loyal their words were. But now there was this. I woke them up and asked them if they couldn't please stay awake for just an hour. I wondered aloud if that was asking too much.

You also told them,

"Pray that you may not enter into temptation."[5]

Were you also thinking of yourself when you said that?

That's what the whole evening was about. They needed to be prepared for what was about to happen just as I was trying to be. They were in the middle of a battle and they didn't even know the war was on.

When I went back where I'd been praying in the Garden alone, still nothing seemed right. I prayed more earnestly than I'd ever prayed in my life, but the pain only got worse. After about an hour I came back to my disciples the second time for comfort, and when I needed them most once more they were asleep. At that point I didn't think I could go on. Wherever I turned, I was surrounded by sin, pain, and, in the case of my men, apparent indifference.

The image of the cross overwhelmed me. My Father's enormous rage kept coming to mind. Death was everywhere. And death always brings its companions—fear, self-pity, retaliation, and cowardice. Death was trying to produce death in me, and it almost succeeded. There seemed to be no escape. I was trying the best as I could to say, "Thy will be done" and mean it. But it was almost too much hostility to contain.

The grief was literally killing me. I was sweating more blood. I remembered wondering what would happen if I died before I had a chance to atone. That scared me. It occurred to me that it might happen, but I remembered that He had promised that I would complete my mission. Yet I was having a difficult time hanging on to those words completely. It kept coming back to me that at the time when I needed Him most, He would be turning all His fury on me. That was the moment I thought I was really going to die.

The 6th Psalm came to my mind, and I fell on my face and in tears and began praying it.

> "Pity me, O Lord, for I am weak. Heal me, for my body is sick, and I am upset and disturbed. My mind is filled with apprehension and with gloom. Oh, restore me soon. Come, O Lord, and make me well. In your kindness save me. For if I die I cannot give you glory by praising you before my friends."[6]

My deed on the cross was to be a statement of praise for my Father. As I hung there, hour after hour I would, in effect, be saying: "He is righteous." I continued repeating the 6th and the 116th Psalms, which also told me He had been waiting to hear this particular prayer of mine for centuries.

> "Death stared me in the face—I was frightened and sad. Then I cried, 'Lord, save me!' "[7]

I cried out to my Father. "You said you would make me well. You said you would save me. You told me to ask you to visit me. Come, O Lord, and make me well. Lord, I'm asking you, deliver me from this hour of grief. I know you still want me to go through with the cross, Father, but deliver me from this hour. Come, O Lord."

Suddenly there was someone with me in a shining white robe standing very calmly before me. My Father had sent an angel! He just looked at me for a moment before he said, "Lord, all of heaven exalts you and is praying for you at this moment. Heaven anxiously awaits your return to your glory. The preparation that everyone is making for your return is all encompassing. The music alone that they have written for the celebration of your arrival would make what you're going through almost worth it. We all wait to praise you for your mighty deed, for we know you will do it. You are His only begotten son." I knew this was His angel. There was none of this, "If you are the son of God," I had heard from Satan.

I prayed to my Father again and rehearsed everything. The visit from the angel had brought to me some sense of perspective.

Yet nothing could make that image of the man on the cross go away.

He would be gasping for breath, with nails in his hands and feet with all his weight on them and finally death would come because he couldn't get enough oxygen when his muscles gave out. He would be dying, with a look of horror on his face and panic in his eyes. He would experience total helplessness, with everyone's eyes fixed on his torment. I was going to let them do that to me. That man would be in the hands of an angry God. It was my duty, and my duty to do it His way, without uttering a word.

"He was oppressed and he was afflicted, Yet He did not open His mouth."[8]

Except for those forlorn words of desperate abandonment,

"My God, my God, why hast thou forsaken me?"[9]

All my life I had feared those words. I couldn't imagine myself ever experiencing that, and yet I had known the 22nd Psalm all my life. With my Father's help, I could endure the cross. For Him to forsake me, however, and not only forsake me but to judge me, was a bitter pain. My Father would really judge the people of this world through my torment. There would come a time when He really hated me and what I stood for. He had to!

I could already feel the torture of crucifixion and hear Him saying to the people of this world as I stood in their place, "For all the physical pain that you have brought to others, first I bring you physical pain. For all the lives you have taken, I take yours, but not before I let them torture you just as you have tortured others. You have stripped them naked. I, also, will do so. You have made their families and friends watch them writhe in pain. I, also, will do so. It will be a slow death so you can experience it likewise.

"For all of you who think you have never hurt anyone, I will show you all the ways you murdered and tortured your fellow man. There are many ways to kill. For all the names you have called others at moments they least needed it, I call you names. For all the mocking you have done, I mock you. For all the times you have hated and provoked others to hate you, I hate you and cause the people to despise you. For all the people you have judged to be despicable, I judge you in the same way to be one of them. For all the times you took advantage of your brother when he was defeated, I trample you even when you are down.

"For the various ways you've made others your victims, manipulated them with your power, insulted them without thinking or caring, I do the same to you. All the helplessness you created I give back to you. For all the pride you demonstrated at others' expense, subtly lording over them and for all the times you secretly tried to take away your brother's self-esteem while pretending to be rightous, I surround you with "righteous" men openly to lord over you, men who will strip away your dignity while they deny their pride. For all the poor suffering people who surrounded you for whom you had no time, in their name I neglect you in passing. For all the times that your pride made you certain you were right, I surround you with proud people who are certain you are evil."

He was deliberately going to judge them through me. That was what I feared most.

The Scriptures say

"Our God is a consuming fire."[10]

You were going to feel the heat of His flame.

I knew that, and by my silence I would be saying that I agreed with the punishment. I did. I was not sure I had the strength to withstand it.

The helpless panic was beginning to overwhelm me, and there was no break in the tension. I was praying as earnestly as I could, "Lord, help me to do it, to accept it. Give me the strength. Everything is at stake here. I knew it would be hard, Father, but I never knew it would be this unbearable." The pressure didn't decrease, even after I prayed long and intensely, even after the angel had been there. I remember thinking, "Father, I don't know how you would do it, but please get me out of this if it is your will. All things are possible with you; please let this cup pass from me." Drops of blood were still pouring from my head.

I had spent three hours trying to overcome this, but I could not. I was tempted to doubt myself. I wondered, "Would the son of God really be this frightened? Despite the confirmation all along, the Scriptures and the miracles and the angel having been there, I began to ask myself: "Suppose all of this is phony? Suppose I am just some special kind of being and that a 'god' I don't even know about is running the universe, and He's playing a terrible trick on me." Even after all my preparation, I was beginning to worry about death. I wondered, "Are you being a hypocrite? Would the Son of God be this afraid?"

I was losing perspective and struggling not to do so. Then I remembered what Elijah had said on the Mount of Transfiguration. "You will have doubts that will surprise even you, but remember His promise. You will do it." Recalling Elijah's visit at the Transfiguration upheld me. It made me once again know my Father and his constant faithfulness in preparing me. He had sent Elijah to warn me of this trial of confusion, which is often Satan's greatest weapon.

Something else Elijah had said moved me: "He has already let us into His kingdom because of what you will do." I thought of His words again, and how powerful His promises were. In the face of all my emotions, He was telling me that He knew I would face them and that despite their power, I would overcome them: I would do it.

He was so utterly benevolent. In all circumstances, even this one, if I looked for Him and waited on Him, He was there teaching me, strengthening me, guiding me, comforting me, living in me.

I thought of Abraham who trusted God to raise up Isaac even if he had to kill him. I thought of Job;

"Though he slay me, yet will I trust in him."[11]

With that strength I was able to say against all my pain and confusion,

"Nevertheless not my will, but thine, be done."[12]

I gave Him my life in a new way at that moment because He had given me His life in a new way. With a great struggle, everything was once again all His. I then could finally take in death itself, contain it, and not be destroyed by it nor become destructive because of it. I had overcome the world. I had overcome every evil emotion that destroys souls.

(How easily we overlook the third most significant event in human history after the Incarnation and the resurrection. Suppose Jesus had put that cup down. How different history would have been. There would have been no salvation, no Christian church, no apostles, no martyrs, no New Testament, no Reformation, no Augustine, no Martin Luther, no John Calvin or John Wesley, no lasting democracy, no women's rights, no children's rights, no abolition of slavery, no civil rights, no hope, and no life. There would be only ultimate and final death for everyone.)

Final Resolution

So God had to struggle. No matter how many times I read about you in the Garden of Gethsemene, it's hard to believe. But a major resolution took place in that Garden.

In some ways the hardest battle had been fought. When I left the Garden I knew that I could do it.

I had done it in a real way. But, (he paused here and I could see the pain in his eyes) when I think about what happened in the next fourteen hours, the pain had really just begun. When I finally resolved my accepting my assignment, I stood up. Not too far away I could see the lynching party coming across the Kidron Valley towards me with torches and lanterns.

For a moment, there was the peace before the storm as I watched the lights across the valley briefly penetrating the darkness. There was something beautiful about a light in the darkness, even more so a moving light, and once again the words came to me: "You are the light of the world." I thought to myself, "But my light is so different. I leave no darkness behind."

As they got closer, I could hear the clanging of the soldiers' weapons. I went to find my men but they were asleep again. I told them to get up, the time had come. I went to meet the mob. I thought again of David's going to meet Goliath. Neither of us had been crowned king when we went into our biggest battles, but we both went in like kings—advancing.

The Temple guards brought many soldiers with lanterns thinking I would run or hide from them in a cave. They thought they would have to search for me. I surprised them.

When the soldiers came near I stepped out from behind some olive trees and said,

"Whom are you looking for?"

They told me,

"Jesus of Nazareth."

I said,

"I am he."

Suddenly, they fell backwards to the ground. While they were on the ground I asked them again,

"Whom are you searching for?"

As they stood up stunned at what they had experienced, the leader of the guard said,

"Jesus of Nazareth."

I said to them,

"I told you I am he—let these others go."[13]

They did. It had been prophisied that none of my men would be lost and that prophecy was fulfilled.

Then Judas, who had obviously brought the guards, walked over to me and with feigned affection said,

"Master."

He then embraced me and kissed me on the cheek. I looked at him and asked him,

"Judas, how can you do this—betray the Messiah with a kiss?[14] My friend."[15]

The kiss was to indicate to the soldiers my identity.

Judas had wanted to make his encounter with me as brief as possible, but he found himself unable to move. He stood in front of me unable to break his gaze. The word "friend" stunned him. I could see the hurt in his eyes from the guilt he was trying so desperately to hide. He had already gone this far, but now he was uncertain. Judas was in the same situation Herod had been in, when in front of a similar crowd he had a chance to either betray John the Baptist or stand up for him.

Judas had one last chance. He could have freed himself from this situation, but he didn't. Judas made the same choice Herod did. It was the same choice every man makes who chooses hell. The look in his eyes changed from one of hurt to one of determination. When I saw that, I told him,

"Go ahead and do what you have come for."[16]

The look I never saw on Judas' face was of repentance or true sorrow, and without that no one can attain heaven. Even though I knew what had been going to happen, I'll never forget the feeling I had looking into Judas' eyes for the last time. We had been such close friends.

When they started to take me away, Peter, who had just been awakened from a deep sleep, stormed in and pushed two guards aside and quickly seized me. He drew his sword swiftly and cut off the ear of one of the guards. That's like Peter, isn't it? Immediately I cried to him, and told him to stop and to sheath his sword. I said to him, "Don't you think that my Father would send 40,000 angels here this minute if I asked Him?"[17] I picked up the guard's ear, put it back in place and healed it.

The mob had quieted for a moment, and I looked at the host of guards with all their weapons, spears and swords. I asked them, "Am I some dangerous criminal that you had to come arrest me armed for battle? Why didn't you arrest me when I was in the Temple? I was there every day." I reminded them, "Nevertheless, this is happening just as the Scriptures said it would."

You never quit pointing towards the Scriptures.

I was trying to get their attention. If anyone will read the Scriptures they will understand the plan and purpose of my death and resurection.

Why was it judgment, if God is a God of love? Wasn't there another way?

At the very center of God's being is the desire to express love continually. That desire is the driving force behind His personality, and that by necessity includes the protection of love. Eternally, He will make sure that love prevails, and He will prevent anything which would hinder it. Justice, then, is the protection of love. Hell will therefore exist to protect love, and it will be an eternal testimony to how great God's love is. You cannot understand the need for hell entirely yet, but God's determination to establish it gives you just a hint of how passionate his love is.

When justice is served, the scales within us and within the world are once again balanced in order to allow love to operate. In this way, justice creates love. Listen to Proverbs:

> "Punishment that hurts chases evil from the heart."[18] "Foolishness is bound in the heart of the child; but the rod of correction shall drive it far from him."[19]

Justice received is meant to work inside you to create a different person. Actually, the desire for love inside each of us demands justice from ourselves because we are made in the image of God. That's why God couldn't "just forgive" us. Forgiveness has its limits. We would not yet be balanced inside. The lovely, impartial lady of justice inside each one of us would be unsatisfied. We would still continue to punish ourselves as well as our neighbors. There's an intrinsic need for fairness within us. Every person cries out "I can love only myself and others if I am a fair, just person." No one can balance that lady's scales except through me.

Why did God allow evil in the first place?

It was necessary. The question you are raising is why God didn't just place in our hearts from the beginning the new covenant. Why didn't He create us with the ability and strength to keep His laws? When We planned the whole creation, We realized the high cost of making people free to choose. The easiest way to have really free creatures worship Us included my Atonement. That was the only way. Certainly your evil testifies to your greatness. As C. S. Lewis pointed out, the higher up the scale of development one goes, the greater the capacity for evil one has. A cow can be only so bad, but a man can be really evil and an angel like Lucifer even more so.

We wanted to make men and women totally free to love Us or reject Us. The type of relationship We wanted demanded total freedom. You were made strong and free so that We knew you would eventually try to succeed without Us. The bonds that would forever hold us together to prevent that break from ever happening again and the bond that would cause such a love to exist on both parts would occur only when an inconceivable price was paid for you. Then forever we all would know the true value of our relationship.

That was one of the reasons We allowed evil to exist.

The Trials

I was impressed with your resilience. You had just been through an emotionally draining experience in the Garden and yet you were bantering with the mob, challenging them. All through your trials with the Pharisees, Herod, and Pilate, there was this same toughness.

I was still letting them know that I was doing this of my own free will. As I have told you, no one took my life from me; I gave it.

Later that night and early the next morning, you had many "legal" trials, if I can call them that.

There were seven in all.

The first one was with the Jewish High Priest.

It was the "religious court." The first thing the High Priest did was to ask me what I'd been teaching my followers. I told him,

> "What I teach is widely known, for I have preached regularly in the synagogue and Temple. I have been heard by all the Jewish leaders and I teach nothing in private that I haven't said in public."

Then I asked him,

> "Why are you asking me this question? Ask those who heard me. You have some of them here."

Just then one of the soldiers standing around caught me unexpectedly with a huge fist. The pain had started and the blow knocked me to my knees. He reprimanded me,

> "Is that the way to answer the High Priest?"

And I told him,

> "If I lied, prove it. Should you hit a man for telling the truth?"[20]

The authorities tried to determine some way legally to find me guilty of a capital offense. But they couldn't. Their phony witnesses would try to make up or distort what I had said. For example, when I had told them,

"Tear this Temple down and in three days I will build it back,"

referring to my resurrection, one of the witnesses claimed that I said I was going to tear the Temple building down. But they couldn't get their stories straight, and it was almost amusing how they contradicted each other.

Soon it became apparent that this court had no evidence. The High Priest who was also the judge turned to me and asked, "What do you have to say"? I remained silent. I was thinking, "I have nothing to defend, and you know it." I was also amused, saying to myself, "These people are even botching my crucifixion. Am I going to have to bail myself out so I can get myself killed?" Sure enough, after two and a half hours, their witnesses had proved nothing.

Out of desperation the High Priest decided to force me to answer the question and said, "Are you the Messiah, the Son of God?" To help him out of his dilemma, gladly I said, "I am." I added, "And one day you will see me at the right hand of God returning to earth."

I wanted to remind the High Priest and everyone else that I was giving up my life willingly, but that later I would return and they would have a chance to see me then, also.

Immediately this religious, pious man was offended: he stood up and tore his robe. I understood the message. If God's holiness was being debased, it was the only time the High Priest could tear his beautifully decorated robe, specifically designed by God. Later my Father would tear the great curtain that separated the Holy of Holies from the people to answer the High Priest, but at this time I said nothing.

What did they do with that answer?

The High Priest and his associates became vicious at that point, vehemently attacking me, screaming at me. Repeatedly they told me that I was the most evil person who had ever lived. "Liar! Liar! Liar!" They made verbal attacks against my mother again. "No wonder I had turned out to be evil; look how I had begun life."

My anger grew as I had expected it would, but I said nothing, just as I was instructed. All along I kept talking silently to myself. I had planned to recall certain Scriptures at different moments, and the Fifth and Seventh Psalms were two that had been reserved for this moment for centuries. As these men battled my soul with their rage, I battled their rage with the Word of God.

"O Lord, hear me praying; listen to my plea, O God my King."
"Lord, lead me as you promised me you would, otherwise my enemies will conquer me. Tell me clearly what to do, which way to turn."[21]

The Seventh Psalm in particular described me in the midst of my enemies' plot.

"I am depending on you, O Lord my God, to save me from my persecutors."
"It would be different, Lord, if I were doing evil things—if I were paying back evil for good."
"God is my shield; he will defend me."[22]

I was still a man whose feelings could be hurt. I handled the anger that they stirred in me in just one way. I turned it over to my Father. My task was to forgive the people of this world, and that I intended to do. But I was not stupid. I knew that some of these men who were taunting me incessantly would never, under any circumstances, accept my forgiveness. I took great comfort in knowing my Father's justice would prevail with those people who had no comprehension of my justice.

The Pharisees and the guards and the servants began spitting on me. They blindfolded me and everyone began to hit me in the face with their fists saying, "Tell us, Prophet, who hit you that time?" After the hearing even the three bailiffs on the way out of the courtroom hit me in the face.

Not having enough evidence, they rushed me to a Roman trial with Pilate, the Governor of the Roman Territory. This being the Jewish holy days, my people couldn't be responsible for sentencing a person to death during that time.

What happened with Pilate?

The trial actually started outside on the steps in front of Pilate's palace. You see, the Jews couldn't go into a Gentile house because it was their religious holiday. What they didn't know was that this was happening to fulfill the prophecy of my crucifixion because only the Romans used crucifixion as a death penalty. For capital offenses, the Jews stoned people to death, but again, not during the Jewish Holy Days. When they brought me as a prisoner before Pilate, he came out on the steps. They told him I had caused much trouble, that I'd been telling the people, on the authority that I was their Messiah not to pay taxes to the Roman government. Of course, I had not said that.

Pilate looked at me. I was dressed in an old robe, my face swollen from the beatings and stained with spittle. Surrounded by guards, to the onlookers I was a dangerous character. He asked me, "Are you the Messiah—their king?" I told him, "Yes, it is as you say." I wasn't there to plead my case.

The entire Jewish council and the crowd that came with them screamed at me, "Lucifer's child! You set yourself up as God and claim to be the special son! Vanity, vanity, all is vanity! Liar, Son of the Devil, you'll see God all right, looking up at Him as He judges you for blaspheming His holy name!" Some of them started quoting Scripture, "Cut off your enemies, Lord," and similar verses.

I just looked at them and said nothing. Pilate was impressed. I wasn't pleading with him as prisoners typically did. He tried to stop the screaming, but they continued, telling him I'd been causing riots from Galilee, some forty miles away. When Pilate learned that I was a Galilean, he seemed relieved and sent me to Herod, the governor of Galilee who happened to be in Jerusalem at the time.

As they shuttled me to my various places of trial, first to the Sanhedrin, then to Pilate, and now to Herod, I walked across the tremendous bridge high above the Tyropoen Valley separating the Temple from Herod's Palace. One last time I looked out over Jerusalem as its rejected king.

As we continued walking over the bridge from the Temple, we passed by the place where Satan had miraculously transported me and tempted me to jump down the four hundred fifty feet. When we reached that point, one of the Temple guards said, "If you want to get out of this, you had better jump." I knew that voice by now. Satan was urging me again to jump. One more time I thought to myself, "I could do it." I kept walking. I was headed toward Herod's palace, which was originally David's. On this last day of my life, I finally was able to visit the palace of my royal ancestor David, the palace which was to have been mine.

I met Herod. His father, Herod the Great, had murdered thousands of Jewish infants trying to kill me. He was the man who had had my cousin, John the Baptist, unmercifully beheaded. When I got to his palace, Herod told me he had heard about me for many months. I'm sure he was particularly interested because his business manager's wife, Cuza, was one of my followers. Herod said he wanted to see a miracle. I said nothing. He then asked me many questions, but I refused to answer. He had said nothing to prevent John's death when he could have and I had nothing to say to him. He and his soldiers then began to mock me. They put a kingly robe on me. Still I said nothing, but I thought: "You don't know what you're doing. One day I shall come into my kingdom in shining raiment indescribably greater than this." Even in persecution, in the mocking, I was reminded of who I was.

With all his bravado, Herod was frightened of me just as he was of John. Finally, finding nothing wrong with me, he sent me back to Pilate.

Round Two: The Flogging

What happened when you were returned to Pilate?

He had the guards bring me inside his palace to talk to me alone. The Jewish authorities had continued to tell him that I claimed I was king and that I was going to lead a riot. When we were in private, Pilate asked me again if I were the King of the Jews. I asked him if he meant "king" like the Jews meant it or like the Romans. He snapped at me, "Am I a Jew? Your own people brought you here. What have you done?"[23]

I told him, "My kingdom is not of this world. If it were, my men would be fighting for me. But my kingdom is in another place."

Pilate asked me again, "You are a king, then?" I said, "I was born to be a king, and for that reason I came to bring truth to the world. All who love the truth are my followers."

He became sarcastic and said,

"What is truth?"[24]

I didn't reply. He looked at me for a moment and returned outside.

Thinking of a way to escape the situation, he told my accusers that neither he nor Herod found me guilty of inciting riots against Rome and that I had done nothing warranting punishment. In an attempt to appease their wish to condemn me, he let them know that he considered me a prisoner. He suggested to the crowd of Jews that, since it was his custom to free one Jewish prisoner every year at Passover, he could free me, the "king of the Jews."

As Pilate was holding court and presenting this offer to the crowd, a messenger came with a message from Pilate's wife. Pilate became irritated and rumbled, "What does she want with me at a time like this?" The messenger said, "Sir, she is very worried."

He looked at me as soon as he read the message. His eyes told me that it had to do with me, and that whatever his wife said frightened him as well. Now, more than ever, it was obvious that he didn't want to go through with this. Later I learned that his wife had sent a message telling him to have nothing to do with me, that I was an innocent man and that the night before she had a vivid nightmare about me.

By now the Pharisees had the crowd in a frenzy, and, in response to Pilate's offer of releasing a prisoner, they screamed, "We want Barabbas—give us Barabbas." Barabbas was a convicted murderer who had led riots, and they were calling for him to be freed instead of me. I couldn't believe it when I heard it. They wanted Barabbas. How fickle they were!

Emotionally, I was caught off-guard and suddenly I was almost ill as I thought, "That sadistic mob: They want Barabbas." I really hadn't been expecting the viciousness of the crowd at that time. I knew the Jewish priests would involve the Romans, but it now seemed as if the entire city was against me.

It was about ten o'clock in the morning. I'd been up all night. I hadn't eaten or drunk anything since supper the night before, and my face was throbbing. My Father had prepared me for fickle crowds. Still, each rejection was fresh pain. The thought went through my mind, "Barabbas, the murderer, goes free and the free man becomes the murderer. Now, more than ever, I can see who I'm dying for, whose place I'm taking. I'm dying for all the Barabbases of the world." As I told you, my Father thought of everything.

When Pilate saw that he couldn't stand up to the crowd the first time, he had another idea. He ordered the soldiers to flog me. As the Roman soldiers were taking me down to the stake in front of the Praetorium, the governor's palace, to be flogged, my mind immediately went to the Scriptures and to my role in Isaiah.

"I gave my back to those who strike Me,"[25]
"He was wounded for our transgressions, He was bruised for our iniquities: the chastisement of our peace was upon him; and by his stripes we are healed."[26]

I kept telling myself, "The Lord is my strength; through him I shall triumph valiantly." I was preparing myself. I had won the first round when the Jews had beaten me at the first trial early that morning. But the infamous Roman flogging was another story. It was feared throughout the Empire.

They stripped off all my clothes, and tied my hands to a half pillar so that my back, my buttocks, and legs were fully exposed.

Then it started. The whip was a "cat-of-nine-tails" with nine lashes of thick leather and little iron balls on the end that dug into your flesh and then ripped it out with each blow.

The first lash came, and the pain was excruciating! By the third lash my entire back was on fire. I had never experienced pain like that. I never knew I had so many nerves. Before the pain could subside more than a second, the next blow came, worse than the one before. Every time he hit me—thirty-nine times in all—I didn't see how the pain could get any worse. But with each succeeding lash became more searing. Finally it reached a point that between lashes there was no subsiding of the pain whatsoever.

As I began to bleed, my blood stung the raw flesh. My back and legs were so sensitive by now that even the air current that came just before each blow of the whip hurt. Between blows I tried to think of my Father's words to me.

"Yea, though I walk through the valley of the shadow of death, I will fear no evil: for thou art with me."[27]

Then another blow would come, taking me to a new depth of pain. I would try to concentrate,

"Though he slay me, yet will I trust in Him."[28]
"Weeping may endure for a night, but joy cometh in the morning."[29]

Several times I almost cried out, but I was determined not to. My Father had promised me that I wouldn't:

"He was oppressed, and he was afflicted, yet he opened not his mouth: he is brought as a lamb to the slaughter and as a sheep before her shearers is dumb, so he openeth not his mouth."[30]

With every blow, I clung to the power of those words as the torturer ripped off more of my back. Most prisoners by this time would be screaming in agony, some reaching the point of hysteria, begging the man to stop. Although obviously I was in pain, I "opened not my mouth."

The man with the whip noticed my silence. You can imagine the type of soldier who would volunteer for the job. He began to mock me, "So we've got a tough one here." The contest was on. He was determined to make me beg for mercy. He was accustomed to having prisoners beg him for help, and I was determined that I would not. I begged my Father all the way, but not him. Between blows, I would try to talk to myself. I could think only for brief moments, and much of the time I just held onto the words, "He openeth not his mouth"—lash—"He openeth not his mouth." Other times I would think,

"By his wounds we are healed"—lash—"by his wounds we are healed"—lash—"by his wounds we are healed"—lash—"or maybe,"

"The chastisement of our peace was upon him."[31]

—lash. "This one is for Matthew's peace."—lash. "This one is for Thomas' peace."—lash. The soldier began to whip me more and more forcefully until he had lashed me with all his might, cursing me every time. "See how you like that one, Teacher."—lash—"Did you know this would happen, Prophet?"—lash. Still I hadn't said a thing.

I had taken over twenty-five lashes now in silence, and he was going to break me. Very quickly he went over and picked up a bucket of salt water and threw it on my raw back. It was like being on fire and then all of a sudden the fire becoming twice as hot. He picked up the whip again and the lashes continued. I thought I would explode.

All through this, I kept clinging to Him so that I wouldn't give in,

"I will praise you, Lord, for you have saved me from my enemies."—lash. "You refuse to let them triumph over me."[32]—lash. "Lord, I trust in you alone. Don't let my enemies defeat me."—lash. "You are my Rock and my Fortress"—lash. "Pull me from the trap my enemies have set for me."—lash. "You alone are strong enough."[33]—lash.

Towards the end of my flogging the man with the whip became very quiet, but started hitting me faster with less time for recovery between lashes. It was his last trick. I was finding out that despite the pain I could hold on to my Father's words even though I thought I was going to faint.

"They that wait upon the Lord"—lash—"shall renew their strength"—lash. "They shall mount up with wings like eagles"—lash. "They shall run and not be weary"—lash. "They shall walk and not faint."[34]

And finally it was over. I had won the second round. I had not uttered a word.

The third round started very quickly. They cut me loose and I fell in a bloody heap and lay there for a minute. Then they lifted me and dressed me in a purple robe, rubbing it into the weeping, bleeding wounds on my back to make sure the robe stuck and pulled everytime I moved. The soldiers took me to a bigger room. One of them came up to me with a crown of thorns and jammed it down on my head until the thorns lacerated my scalp and forehead. Blood was running into my eyes, but I could not wipe the blood away because my hands were tied behind me.

Next they blindfolded me and began playing the game called "Circle of

Eight." Eight Roman soldiers surrounded me, and as they walked around me, one of them would hit me in the face. Then they would take the blindfold off while each one continued to walk around me and I was supposed to guess which one had hit me. If I didn't get it right, which of course no one ever did, they blindfolded me for another round. How they relished the cruel game!

The entire time they ridiculed me, particularly the man with the whip who had made sure that he joined the circle. "Tell us who hit you, Prophet! Are you helpless, oh, Great One? Where is your mighty Father?" I was prepared not to retaliate, but to submit to this for the world's sake. The pain was almost overwhelming. I didn't know how much longer I could go on. My head ached, my face and the thorns in my scalp. My back was one great raw nerve. And then there was the taunting!

I didn't have long to think clearly because I was always between blows. As soon as my head stopped spinning from the last one, the blindfold would be off and they would be walking around me very fast; screaming at me, taunting me, spitting on me, pulling my beard. I was losing concentration with all this movement and pain. It was so difficult to concentrate on what I was doing that I was tempted to strike out at them. I remember at one point, with my head still reeling, thinking that they had just broken my jaw. But I had His promise that no bones would be broken. I persevered.

When they removed the blindfold, the man with the whip was standing there, shaking his fist in my face and screaming, "You think your Father is greater than this!" I remember for just a second wanting to break my hands loose, (and I could have done it anytime) and grab his fist, smash it in his face and then ask the others if they had any questions about my Father.

I quickly put those thoughts out of my mind by thinking about who I was and what I was doing. I would tell myself, "You are the lamb of God that taketh away the sins of the world. Take it, take it." Or, "He was wounded for our transgressions, He was bruised for our iniquities. It will be over soon. Do it for them."

I continually reminded myself, "not much longer. This time tomorrow it will be finished. This is only one day. I'm going to see the Father." Then another blow and I would have to search once more for His words. Of all my Father's words that I recalled, I clung to those in the middle of the 50th chapter of Isaiah. I knew them well because that was one way I had prepared myself for this moment.

> "I gave My back to those who strike Me, My cheeks to those who pluck out My beard; I did not cover My face from humiliation and spitting. Therefore, have I set My face like flint and I know that I shall not be ashamed."[35]

I fixed my mind on those words, lived them out, and won the third round even though I was wobbling like a drunkard. *(He started laughing here.)* I was the most beat-up champion you ever saw.

They brought me back to Pilate one more time, and I was a sight to see. Pilate immediately brought me out to the crowd that was still gathered and shouted to them,

"Behold the man!"[36]

I was just barely recognizable. My face had swollen grotesquely and one eye was almost shut.

Pilate was obviously saying to them, "Isn't this enough?" I'll never forget standing there above the crowd on that "stage," beaten and bleeding, with my body in infinite pain, and hearing them answer louder than ever: "Kill him! Kill him! Kill him!"

You can prepare for pain. Thank God for that, but it still hurt. As they were chanting, one man called out above the crowd, "He calls himself the Son of God." You should have seen Pilate's eyes. He took me back inside and sat down on his chair as I stood there in front of him completely exhausted. I hadn't sat down in over twelve hours except for the moment I collapsed after they flogged me.

He asked me, "Where did you come from?" I didn't answer him, and he became furious. "Don't you realize I have the power to kill you or release you?" I told him, "You have no power but what my Father gave you, but those who brought me to you have the greater sin."[37]

When I said that, letting him know who was in control, Pilate became even more agitated and tried to release me again. He reminded the Jewish leaders and the crowd that neither he nor Herod had found any wrong-doing on my part. The crowd kept screaming, "Crucify him! Crucify him!" He argued with them, "Why, what has he done?" Again from the mob came the reply: "Crucify him! Crucify him!"

The Pharisees standing there told Pilate that any rebel who claimed to be king was no friend of Caesar's. Pilate could see that the Pharisees were manipulating the crowd and manipulating him, but he was also afraid of a riot. In the end, immediate fear won out over eternal fear. Finally, Pilate had them bring him a bowl of water. Before the thousands of people, he symbolically washed his hands of the matter and said, "His blood be upon you." The out-of-control mob shouted back, "And upon our children!"[38] *And it was!*

Then Pilate turned me over to his soldiers to be crucified. Pilate didn't want to do it and I didn't want to go. But I went in total justification. I had won another round.

Any joy over that victory was short-lived. The soldiers immediately took me into the armory and called out the troops. The ones who wouldn't join in before now did so freely, because they were sure that I was going to die. This time they put a scarlet robe on me and made a new crown for me from longer thorns and jammed it further down on my head. They then placed a stick in my right hand to symbolize a scepter, and all kneeled down and began to mock me. "We praise you, Oh, King." Several of them came up and spat in my face. The saliva mixed with blood ran down my forehead, into my eyes.

They meant that to be a bad experience, but my Father used it momentarily for good. As I looked upon them while they were kneeling on the ground and looked at the scarlet robe they had placed on me which was so different from the white robe that was mine, I thought of the verse,

"Though your sins be scarlet, they shall be white as snow."[39]

I was wearing the sin of the world, but the message from my Father was clear even in their mocking. "You are a king, but not of this world."

The soldiers took my "scepter" from my hand and on the way out began to mock me and beat me over the head. Such bravado against the helpless!

Then you got your cross?

It was happening just as my Father said it would. They had flogged me, spit on me, and pulled my beard. I knew what was coming next. My cross. And yet it's strange what comforts you at a time like this. I took comfort knowing that they wouldn't break any of my bones and that I was to have a sign on that cross.

One of the most difficult things about the crucifixion was the constant temptation to rid myself of pain. I could have stopped it at any moment. I was prepared to submit for the world's sake, prepared not to retaliate. But the pain demanded relief. My head was bursting and every step jammed the thorns further into my scalp. Several of my teeth were loose. My face was bleeding, also my back, which felt like hot coals. I grew weaker and weaker as the trials progressed. I still hadn't had a drink of water since supper and now from the bleeding I reached a point where physically I expected to collapse. That's when I got my cross. That's usually when we get it. There's a verse in Scripture which says that the Lord never lays on us more than we can bear.[40] Sometimes you wonder if His scale and yours aren't vastly different. This was one of those times.

They gave me my cross to carry out of the city and up the big hill that now seemed like Mount Everest. It was unbelievably heavy. Whatever else any one tells you, my cross seemed to be made of lead. I had to drag it behind me, pulling it down the road on my shoulder. It helped that I had been a carpenter and knew some ways of dragging a big load, but still I had to use my back and my shoulders which were bleeding and weeping from the flogging. My robe stuck to the wounds, and now the cross was pressing down on them, rubbing against them. I couldn't take a step without making the pain worse.

I remember another thought that passed through my mind when I got my cross. "I have worked with wood all of my life, and here is the one piece I've been waiting for." Even though I had never seen it until that moment, I had been married to that cross my whole life—"bone of my bone, flesh of my flesh."

When I was a carpenter, I used to think about the cross from time to time as I was working with wood. The wood was a symbol of me; once alive, now dead. And I would think, "But one day you're going to live again." At the same time, wood, though dead, was incredibly strong—it gave strength in many ways to virtually every household, just as my being dead would do. As I went up the hill with my cross I couldn't think of anything for very long, but I tried to battle the pain all the way with my Father's words.

"The Lord is my strength and my salvation. Whom shall I fear?"[41]
"He is my defense; I shall not be moved."[42]
"Weeping may endure for a night, but joy cometh in the morning."[43]

I was determined to hold on to those words, and also determined not to cry out.

"He was oppressed, and he was afflicted, yet he opened not his mouth."[44]

I kept telling myself, "This is why you came into the world. Think about tomorrow. Think about tomorrow and the Father. You will see the Father."

As the cross bore down on my back, getting heavier and heavier, I kept thinking of Isaiah's words,

"He bare the sin of many, and made intercession for the transgressors."[45]

I went over and over those words, trying to get my mind to focus on nothing but them.

"Surely he hath borne our griefs, and carried our sorrows."[46]

I would think of that cross as carrying their sorrows. All the work I had spent in training my mind was helping despite the pain.

I would then take another step. I would stumble. And the pain would so overwhelm me that I would think of nothing else for a moment. It got more and more difficult to concentrate. I kept fighting. If I could have had some water it would have been easier. All the way up the hill, I kept holding on as to why I was doing this, "I was bruised for Peter's iniquity, I was wounded for John's transgressions, my mother's chastisement was upon me, by my stripes my father Joseph was healed. Death will cease to exist."

I kept trying to think of all of the people I loved, for whom I was doing this. My disciples—this was for them. It was for my brothers and sisters. How innocent they seemed at first, and yet how they had gone their own way. This was for them.

To keep my mind focused I would vary my thoughts, and sometimes I would think of my past glories on earth. I would dwell on my discovery at twelve, the gold box, my Baptism, the Transfiguration, and Palm Sunday. I would think too of my future glories. My mother kept coming to mind. I thought of all that she had done for me and all that she had been through for me. All would live in peace because of me. Then I would stumble again, and the jolt would send another round of pain through my body. The thorns would dig deeper. My swollen head would throb. The cross would feel like a mountain of sandpaper on my raw back. It sometimes took me a minute to bring my mind back to my thoughts. "What was it . . . Peace . . . Prince . . . Prince of Peace . . ."?

"Blessed are the peacemakers: for they shall be called the children of God."[47]

The pain was always there. With every step it would battle me, make me focus on my body and my incredible hurt, and I would think how much this was really costing. If only they knew. There were other dark thoughts, "And the worst hasn't even begun yet. There will be bones out of joint, hands and feet pierced. I will be gasping for breath." Those thoughts were almost as bad as the physical pain. The task seemed impossible. I kept telling myself, "Take one step at a time. You made it this far. Soon it will be over. He is my strength."

I suffered the stares. The road up the hill was packed with people. I felt as if all the eyes of the world were on me, watching me stumble and writhe in pain, but nobody would look me in the face. Every time I looked up they were horrified, and shook their heads, repulsed. I could hear the comments when they saw my face. Sometimes it was a child crying, "Look at His face!" Or again it would be a woman crying out, "Oh, no!" when she first saw me. At times, just that one word, "Oh," came out uncontrollably when a person first saw me. My face was disfigured by now. It was so distorted that I didn't look like a human being, but like a hideous monster. I was so offensive that very few could bear to look at me for longer than a second. I was virtually unrecognizable.

Always there would be someone saying, "Look, look at his face." Of course, the Pharisees and "their boys" were just ahead, making sure that the crowd was at its ruthless best. It sounded like a sporting event all the way up the hill.

I was the enemy. The crowd particularly hated me, too, because I was a picture of their own vulnerability. I portrayed their own deaths as well as their consciences. They were looking in a mirror, even though they weren't aware of it. The reflections enraged them. I felt their jeers, and experienced their closing in on me as if I were a dying animal. The memories of ridicule which had almost overwhelmed me when I was a child in Nazareth came back. I was a spectacle.

(He paused here for a long time.)

Shame is hard to take. It must have been unbelievably difficult.

Shame is one of the worst things in the world. That was as difficult as the physical pain. But He had told me that it would be like this. I couldn't have made it unprepared. Listen to the 109th Psalm,

"My knees are weak from fasting: And my flesh has grown lean. I also have become a reproach to them; When they see me they wag their head."[48]

Here's what Isaiah said about me,

> "He is despised and rejected of men; a man of sorrows, and acquainted with grief: and we hid as it were our faces from him; he was despised, and we esteemed him not."[49]

My Father told me again through Isaiah that I would be disfigured.

> "His appearance was so disfigured beyond that of any man and his form marred beyond human likeness."[50]

And he told me in advance about the crowd. It was just as it said in the 69th Psalm,

> "Those who hate me without a cause are more than the hairs of my head."[51]

I felt the eyes, the backs turned to me, the ridicule, the horror on their faces, and the women weeping.

You still had some fight left in you at this point when you talked to the women and you told them,

> "Daughters of Jerusalem, weep not for me, but weep for yourselves, and for your children. For, behold, the days are coming, in which they shall say, 'Blessed are the barren' . . . and you will say to the mountains, 'fall on us.' "[52]

Destruction was on the way to them.

As much as I could when I was going through that horrible experience of being gawked at, I focused my mind on my future glory. I thought about another time my face had been changed—at the Transfiguration. And that's who I really was. Carrying such tremendous pain your mind works in snatches, and I could get brief glimpses of the future. I remember thinking about the wonder in my disciples' eyes on the Transfiguration mountain. I kept telling myself it wouldn't be long until I received that again.

The crowd and the cross kept distracting my attention. Five days ago crowds had been cheering me, and now some of the same people ridiculed me or wouldn't look at me. The contrast made the ridicule stronger, as we went out the same gate I had come through five days before. That's where all the people had gathered on what is now known as Palm Sunday shouting with one voice, His voice, "Hosannah, Hosannah." I focused on that day as long as I could. The glory that had lifted me up would be mine again soon. I would be back through those gates one day.

There's still a gate waiting for you. *

Yes, it will be until I return. I fought to look at that crowd through the screen of the future, the screen of the Father, the screen of the past.

I thought often of my Baptism. I could still hear those words beyond

---

*There is today an east gate to the City of Jerusalem which has been closed for years and which the prophet Zechariah predicted would be closed until Christ walks through it when he comes again. Several people have attempted to destroy the gate and that prophecy, but their efforts have failed. The gate still stands.

belief, "This is My beloved son." My beloved son. I thought how the voices of the angels after the temptation were so different from those around me now. Then my mind would grasp for the Transfiguration again _____ for the robe in my hand so bright, for Moses and Elijah and the Voice. I recalled the other walk home with my parents from Passover at twelve, the time "I met the Magi" and received that gold box.

I had a treasure full of memories. My Father had made sure of that. Yet they were nothing compared to my forthcoming glory. I already had a glimpse of it, but I couldn't see any of those memories for very long.

Final Steps

The further I went the heavier the cross became, and the more difficult it became even to think. Sometimes all I could do was react. At several of those moments, I would just pray, almost beg, for a friendly face who would look at me. Usually I would find one. There would be someone who would hold my gaze even though it was obviously painful for them or someone who would say simply, "Lord." Once I looked at a lady who said everything through the tears of compassion rolling down her cheeks. She made no effort to wipe them away. She just looked at me with love. I know who those people were in that crowd, and I will be looking for them in heaven.

I would stumble again, or the pain would grab me, or the soldiers would push me, or someone would insult me—and it would start all over. My legs were weak, and my rational senses were going. Reflexively I was hanging on to my Father's words to me,

"With His stripes we are healed,"[53]
"The Lamb of God which taketh away the sin of the world."[54]

Sometimes I would cling to a brief thought: "I am the Lamb of God—the Lamb of God." When I would reach those points, the few words that meant the most to me were, "My beloved son." I was hoping that some of their reality could penetrate the fog of the moment. "Remember who you are; remember you can do it." If my Father hadn't prepared me, I couldn't have done it.

In a way He had to leave me, but in another way His words were there moment by moment. At the same time that He saw me as the most despicable person in history and judged me, He also saw me as performing the greatest deed in history. Imagine the mystery of how God could react so passionately both ways at the same time. I kept telling myself, "Don't take it personally. This is your job. That's why you're on this planet." Every time I would think I couldn't take it, I took it.

By now I was staggering with every step. I didn't have enough strength even to lift my head occasionally. My eyes were almost closed from the swelling. It seemed as though I had been walking under that load forever. I was so thirsty.

Finally, at one point my strength totally gave away, and I fell to the ground face down with the cross pinning me to the earth, knocking the breath out of me. I had dirt in my mouth, dirt covering my hair and my wounds. I was breathing dust into my mouth and nose, and I couldn't get up. Not even when one of the soldiers kicked me and hit me with his whip could I rise. I wanted to die right there, and at the same time I was afraid that I might.

The first thing I heard when I came to my senses was a man with the most evil laugh I've ever heard sarcastically saying, "So, you're going to raise yourself from the dead and you can't even get off the ground." And he laughed that laugh again and said, "Your Father is so powerful." What a temptation it was. I wanted to use my power, to show him my Father's strength. All I had to do was say the word, and I would be off that ground and that man would be dead. But I didn't retaliate. While on the ground a verse from Isaiah came to me,

"I the Lord thy God will hold thy right hand, saying unto thee, Fear not."[55]

It was interesting how God gave me different passages of Scripture at different times. I had prepared my mind for that journey, and my mind, living on His words, didn't let me down. I didn't give in to the scorner. I accepted my helplessness. I had won another round.

One of the soldiers conscripted a man named Simon of Cyrene to help me carry my cross. From that moment, one of my burdens was gone. My cross was no longer heavy. Simon scarcely said a word to me. He could have let me bear most of the weight of the cross, but he didn't. He took it from me. That encouraged me. At that moment Simon was a symbol of my Father.

By the time we got to the top of the hill, I had almost reached the point in which I had been in pain so long that I was beginning to feel numb. They ripped off my robe which had been stuck to my back, as if searing me with a flame. They cut off my under-garments and I was totally nude.

Just before they nailed my hands and feet to the cross, a soldier put up a sign in three languages, Latin, Greek, and Aramaic, above it that read: "Jesus of Nazareth, King of the Jews." It was just as God promised. It was as if my Father were picking me up, telling me, "Remember who you are. You are the king." He was saying to me, "I, the Lord God, am putting a sign on this cross that no one will ever take down." Even though my Father had to leave me in a real way to judge me, He made sure I was comforted.

When the Pharisees saw the sign they were enraged, and demanded that Pilate change the sign to read, "He says he's the King of the Jews." For once Pilate stood up like a man, and said that the sign should stay just the way it was.

The Hanging

Two soldiers held my feet and my arms while two others hammered iron spikes through my wrists and my feet. The pain was incredible. I couldn't believe how sensitive my hands and feet were. I became weaker, and then finally nauseous. Sweat broke out on my forehead because of the pain. That was nothing compared to the moment when they stood the cross upright and all my body weight rested solely on the nails in my hands and feet. It was as if thousands of volts of electricity were surging through me, pain. I had to shift my weight up and down to get a good breath. With every breath, there was a fresh dose of pain.

The crowd stared at my nakedness and agony. As they did, I thought of the snake Moses held up for everyone to look at so they would be healed—

"But I, when I am lifted up, will draw all men to myself."[56]

With each wave of pain I would lose my train of thought. It was getting more difficult to concentrate on anything but the pain and the ridicule. Between breaths I tried to keep my thoughts more brief so that I could remember where I was. And I was so thirsty.

The temptation to come down from the cross was so strong at first. I kept repeating my Father's words to me,

"The Lord is my defense, I shall not be moved."[57]
"With His stripes we are healed."[58]
"The Lord is my light and my salvation."[59]

The pain was all encompassing and I was doing everything I could to combat it. I tried thinking of the future.

"Thy throne, O God, is for ever and ever."[60]

Pain makes you twice as sensitive to noise and I could distinctly hear even the priests calling me names, daring me to come down, screaming blasphemies at me. To counteract them I kept going back to the words at my Baptism, "This is My beloved son, in whom I am well-pleased"—my beloved son. Those were the words I had lived on in the wilderness for forty days. Those were words that were so powerful that I never failed to remember them. I would recall all the beautiful names that my Father had called me in the first part of Isaiah, and I repeated those names over and over to myself.

"For unto us a child is born, unto us a son is given: and the government shall be upon his shoulder: and his name shall be called "Wonderful—Counsellor—The mighty God—The everlasting Father—The Prince of Peace."[61]

I would get through those words and then start again. Other times I would quote to myself complete Psalms from memory, one after the other. I did anything I could to combat the pain. I had won another round.

You were prepared.

I became more aware of what a spectacle I was. This got worse later. I had never been nude in front of a crowd. As I looked down at them, particularly at the people I knew, I shamefully was embarrassed. When I wasn't completely overwhelmed by the physical pain, I was painfully self-conscious.

I saw my mother with my aunt on one side of her and my disciple John on the other. Next to them was John's mother and Mary Magdalene, the former prostitute out of whom I had cast seven demons. I looked at each one of their faces and began to tell myself, "This is part of why you're doing it; for them, for the people you love." My mind was fading in and out, and on one occasion for several minutes all I could do to comfort myself was just to look at those five people who loved me and for whom I was doing this.

The Pharisees and others continued to berate me. I felt like a criminal. Here I was surrounded by two criminals, hanging on a cross like a guilty man, being ridiculed by a mob. It's impossible not to feel it when people degrade you, even if it isn't true. Once I thought of other people who had unjustly treated John the Baptist, and of Joseph who was betrayed by his brothers, unjustly accused by his boss' wife, and thrown in jail to rot. Isaiah was sawn in two for telling the truth. David was chased by Saul for years, and continually accused of being a traitor.

At the moment when I was thinking about those heroes, I looked down and saw the Roman soldiers throwing dice to see who would get my robe. I remember thinking, "Well, Joseph, they got my robe, too, didn't they?" How close that made me to Joseph at that moment, and here I was at the same time going over and over David's words in all the various psalms I kept quoting to myself. How ironic it was that these two men who had enabled me to get through my suffering at an early age because they, too, had suffered when they were young, were now once again a source of strength. Joseph and David were still with me on that cross. They had comforted me all my life.

The scoffers continued. These people were telling me hundreds of times in hundreds of ways, "You are evil. You are vicious. You are deceitful. You are egotistical, you are blasphemous, violent, and criminal for misleading the people." It's impossible not to feel it when people degrade you, when they constantly, hour after hour, place all their evil in you.

Truly I became sin for the world, and it was terrible. Everything about sin was offensive to me. I was honest and pure and loving and kind. Never once did I want to hurt without being extremely provoked. I hated evil and I hated all the evil that they were giving me.

The 69th Psalm had told me I would feel like this:

"I am come into deep waters, where the floods overflow me. I am weary of my crying: my throat is dried: . . . They that hate me without a cause are more than the hairs of mine head: . . . Because for thy sake I have borne reproach; shame hath covered my face."[62]

It was terrible. And just as the 69th Psalm said, I was up here on the cross taking all this evil for one reason—because I loved my Father and His truth and I had told the truth to the people.

> "For the zeal of thine house hath eaten me up; and the reproaches of them that reproached thee are fallen upon me."[63]

I was up here because of zeal for my Father, because of loving God. Resentment was trying to creep in to my mind, but I kept looking at my friends and going over my Father's words. I would tell myself, "You have to get through this for them or they are lost." I would think, "Give me your evil. Give it to me. I've got to take it away." I had to prove that good and love were stronger than evil. I had to show that love did not retaliate, but absorbed evil. I did just as Isaiah had prophesied that I would do,

> "He will swallow up death forever. The Lord God will wipe away all tears and take away forever all insults and mockery against his land and people."[64]

I was able to see that evil was absolutely blind and that I was the world's only hope. Only I could swallow death and live.

I kept telling myself, "This is your glory. This is why you came into the world. You are the Lamb."

I also thought of all the people I loved but had never yet met—Adam, Moses, Abraham, Jacob, Joseph. Samson, Ruth, Esther, David, Samuel. Daniel, Solomon, Jeremiah, and Isaiah. And all the people who would live after me who would be just as great as those before. They would be people such as Paul, Barnabas, Luke the Physician, Timothy, Augustine, John Wesley, Martin Luther, John Calvin, and Charles Spurgeon.

I knew that all of these people, as great as they were or would be, could never be reconciled to my Father without me because they all had that terrible evil disease—sin. I knew that any one of them under the right circumstances could be in the crowd below me expressing the evil side of his nature. There were people exactly like them in that crowd. People who didn't realize what they were doing to me, people who would one day be great followers of mine if I were to forgive them. In fact, my future apostle Paul was in that crowd. But he was on the wrong side then.

Last Words

As these thoughts were passing through my mind, I listened to the prisoner on my right direct a string of profanities at the Romans. What else could they do to him? He figured he may as well get in his licks.

I looked at him and thought that he needed to be rescued from his anger, too. All these people could be reconciled with my Father entirely and spend eternity with us if I would take away their evil from them. And I wanted to.

I thought back to that Last Supper and to my disciples; God knew how much I loved them. If it was my task to bring about reconciliation, I was going to do it like a champion.

Even during those horrible moments on the cross I was filled with the most indescribable love for my people. I wanted to bring them and my Father together. I would do anything to bring about that oneness. This was my glory —to accomplish that reconciliation. That was when I looked down upon the crowd and I prayed,

"Father, forgive them; for they know not what they do."[65]

That was the first thing you said to the crowd from the cross. It was one of seven brief statements you made while you hung there.

I would think, "Father, punish me for their sins. Accept my suffering in place of theirs." My Father took that opportunity fully to judge me. He did it in such a way that He was the one who put the nails in my hands and my feet and He was the one who beat me. In a real sense, I became the most evil person in history. Paul was wrong. I was the Chief of Sinners.*

I was more determined than ever to go through with it even though I was still barely hanging on. My weakness increased the thirst. My tongue was so dry it was literally sticking to the roof of my mouth. I felt less and less able to cope, and the taunts hadn't let up.

All this had been going on for a long time then. It was past two in the afternoon.

Most of my bones were out of joint because of the continual weight I was putting on them. Every time I thought it was impossible for one man to suffer more pain, something else would happen. Whenever I moved, not only did the muscles in my back and legs hurt, but there was the most excruciating pain imaginable in my joints, particularly in my shoulders. I kept saying to myself, "It will not be much longer; not much longer. Most of the prophecies have been fulfilled. There aren't many left." The only thing that made me move was my shortness of breath, but I didn't know how long I would last. The Scriptures had been of some comfort, saying,

"I, the Lord thy God will hold thy right hand, saying unto thee, Fear not:[66] . . . weeping may endure for a night, but joy cometh in the morning."[67]

That verse particularly came to mind when the sky had suddenly turned as dark as night. The darkness was a message from my Father. It was a warning that without me everything would be dark forever. Hell will be darker than you can imagine. I felt as if I were in it.

I kept fighting to keep my head above the pain, but I was so exhausted I kept sinking deeper and deeper. Finally, I reached the point almost of irresponsibility. All I could hear was the ridiculing, and all I could feel was the pain. I couldn't hear my own voice. I couldn't speak.

---

*Paul the Apostle at one point in the Book of Galatians, stated that he had been the Chief of Sinners prior to his conversion.

Suddenly, the man on the cross to my left cursed me, "So you are the Son of God. You can't even save yourself. Prove you're the Messiah. Save yourself and us, too. Prove it. Prove it if you can." It was too much, the last thing I had expected. I had known that the crowd and the Pharisees and the Romans would ridicule me. I had known that my disciples would leave me, but ridicule from a criminal who was guilty was almost unbearable! I was speechless. But the criminal on my right defended me.

"Don't you even fear God when you are dying? We deserve to die for our evil deeds, but this man hasn't done one thing wrong."

Then he looked at me and said,

"Jesus, remember me when you come into your Kingdom."[68]

I looked at him briefly as we were both getting a breath, wincing in pain. You can't imagine what that man had in an instant done for me. He had picked me up. He had given me strength. He had carried me on, and it thrilled me to say to him: "This day you will be with me in Paradise." Even on a cross between two criminals, my Father had found a way to comfort me.

Satan had gotten his man into that drama. He was trying to get me to step outside my Father's will, to "jump down" as he had tempted me to do before. And once again, he had used the subtle word "if." But in the unfolding drama, my Father had also gotten His man in next to me. He always does. And now this "useless" criminal had given me my second wind. I was once again reminded that it was worth it. Heaven would be full of people who stood up for me.

I looked at John standing there with my mother and I told him,

"Behold, your mother!"[69]

I wanted him to take care of her.

By now my thirst was so great that finally I said aloud,

"I thirst."[70]

They offered me some wine to kill the pain, and I refused. As much as I wanted relief, I refused because I was God and I was accomplishing salvation not by numbing the pain but by accepting the pain.

My chest was heaving. The pain was now wearing me down more than ever. And I was constantly short of breath and so thirsty.

It was extremely dark. It was past three in the afternoon by then, and I had been on that cross for more than three hours. Everywhere I turned, there was no relief. There was no relief even in thinking about all the memories— the Last Supper, the Transfiguration, the miracles, or even my Baptism. I could no longer hear those words "My beloved Son." They all seemed too far away, as if they had never happened. It was so hard to concentrate. Thinking about my future glory seemed too far away. I felt suspended in time as if I had been there and would be there forever. The pain was unbelievable. The staring and the mocking never let up. "So you trust the Lord. Why? Is He really looking after you? Healer, heal yourself." "Why don't you come on down, Prophet?"

I was defenseless. My mother and John my friend were too far away to comfort me. I looked at the man on my right, and at that point he wasn't any help. He was in as much in pain as I was. It was like looking in a mirror. Frighteningly, my Father's words had no comfort for me now. "The Lord is my strength." But I had no strength. His words seemed as dry as my mouth. That had never happened before, and I felt a terrible panic. I waited a minute and went back over His words. But it was only worse.

It became blacker and blacker for me. I was squirming like a worm on the end of a hook with all of my enemies watching me squirm and enjoying it. I was totally alone. And now my Father was gone, too. I was nude, dangling there disfigured. Gasping for air, writhing in pain, I was totally helpless. I wondered how much longer this would go on. Would it be forever? Time was standing still. The oppression was horrible. Hell couldn't be worse. I did not believe this much pain was possible. Every time I would try to get back up that mountain, "Think of your glory, think of why you are doing it, the Lord is my strength"—nothing—I would just fall back again. No comfort from His words. I wanted to run, to get down—but He was still my Father—but now he was gone. My head was pounding, blood and sweat were in my eyes, my back and legs were rubbed raw, my hands and feet were on fire, my joints were throbbing, all out of place; I was constantly short of breath and I was suffing incredible thirst. I couldn't take it anymore. Suddenly I screamed:

"My God, my God, why have you forsaken me?"

When that came out of me something happened. I was back at the beginning of the 22nd Psalm, and almost reflexively, I began to quote it from memory. Now I was back home. First that Psalm went through all my experiences on the cross. My strength poured out like water. My bones out of joint. My dry mouth, the mockery, and the gambling for my robe were all part of it. Then the Psalm comes to that great part,

"I will declare your name to my brethren. . . ."

There they were. I could see some of them. My spirit began to lift, and then came the next part of the Psalm as though He were reading my mind:

"For He has not despised or disdained the suffering of the afflicted one; He has not hidden His face from him, but has listened to his cry for help."

My Father had heard me and His voice was getting louder.

"All the ends of the earth will remember and turn to the Lord, and all the families of the nations will bow down before him, for dominion belongs to the Lord and he rules over the nations . . . posterity will serve him; future generations will be told about the Lord. They will proclaim his righteousness to a people yet unborn—for he has done it."[71]

He was telling me that I had done it. When I got to that place I began to feel an ecstacy. Good was greater than evil. I had done it! I had accomplished my task! I had given every last ounce of strength I had and the fight was over. I was the winner, the champion: son of God, reign forever.

I looked out on the crowd. I knew I'd taken their evil away from them and not given it back. Justice had been done. I had conquered fear. I had conquered hatred. I had overcome all evil.

The fight was over. I was still very thirsty, but I could wait for a drink because in just a few seconds I was leaving and where I was going I could have anything I wanted. But in fulfillment of prophecy, someone offered to quench my thirst. Typical of the world, all they could ever offer me was bitterness. I drank sour wine, vinegar. They passed the vinegar up to me on a sponge and I drank it. It was one final way of saying, "I take into me your bitterness."

Appropriately, that prophecy was from the 69th Psalm. That bitter Psalm which had haunted me all my life, the Psalm which had told me that I was to suffer unmercifully as a child and even more unmercifully as an adult on a Roman cross, that psalm whose every painful word I knew completely and had carried with me for years, now I could finally lay to rest. By drinking that cup, I was also saying one more time for everyone to hear, "Thy will be done. In the face of all the world's bitterness, to God be the glory."

Then I looked at the crowd and said,

"It is finished."[72]

I suffered not one second longer. With the power of the Son of God, I showed them that I gave my life, and nobody took it from me. I chose the moment of my death. For a few seconds, I intentionally paused and held my head particularly high as I looked out over the crowd to let them know I had conquered their shame. Finally, I looked up towards my Father in heaven, took as deep a breath as I could, and shouted that glorious verse from the 31st Psalm that I had waited for all my life,

"Into Thy hand I commit my spirit."[73]

And I left with my head up. It was over.

Burial

Right after you died, a Roman centurion who had witnessed the entire event spoke for all of us. He had watched how you had reacted the whole way—through your flogging, on your journey up the hill with that huge cross on your back, and then on the cross when the world had thrown everything at you. He observed that you handled it all like a king. He watched your struggle up that hill in complete silence without a complaint. He heard you utter only seven brief statements from the cross; and in three of them, he heard you comfort your mother, comfort the dying man next to you, and above all, comfort the very people who were killing you. He was convinced that you were the King of men. On that spot the Roman soldier proclaimed for the whole world to hear what he thought of you, "Surely he was the son of God."

I really did conquer the Romans as my people wanted me to do. I just did it in a way they didn't expect. My Father and I didn't have to overcome the Romans. Those we wanted came to us.

What happened next?

After it was over, all the other events happened just as He said they would, even down to the fact that, despite the usual custom of breaking a prisoner's legs after a crucifixion, mine were not broken.* Scripture had to be fulfilled. After I died, Joseph of Arimathea, one of the few Pharisees who had been a secret disciple of mine, came forward in a great act of courage and asked Pilate if he could have my body to bury it.

Pilate was shocked that you had died so quickly.

Pilate knew something was happening, but he couldn't quite figure it out. He couldn't control me *(laughingly).* If the truth were a snake, it would have bitten him. It was so obvious that I was God and he wasn't. I chose when to die, and my Father picked the circumstances. Pilate checked with his soldiers and they confirmed that I had died; so he gave Joseph my body.

So two men named Joseph took care of you from the time you were born until the time you died.

Joseph of Arimathea, who was not a big man physically, got a ladder and with his big, beautiful robe on, in front of all of the people including his peers, went up that ladder, got my body and brought it down over his shoulder with my blood and dirt staining his clothing. Nicodemus, another Pharisee who believed in me and who had once sneaked out in the middle of the night to see me so that no one would know, now made his own courageous stand as well.

That's what my crucifixion will do for you when you understand it. Nicodemus started out being afraid to let people even know that he was interested in me. But he kept listening to me and believing me until one day I was his Lord and he could say that in front of the whole world. He came with Joseph to the cross and brought embalming ointment made from myrrh and aloes. Together, in front of all of those people, they carried my body to the tomb and wrapped it in a long linen cloth and saturated it with those spices. Once again I was being wrapped in swaddling clothes.

The uniformity of the Scriptures never ceases to amaze me. You came into the world wrapped and went out wrapped. Through all his different co-authors, God continually puts down markers as if to say, "See how it all fits together."

---

*Often they had to break a prisoner's legs on the cross to hasten death, because the crucifixion was a long-drawn-out cruel torture. Broken legs prevented a person from pushing up or breathing. Both men who were crucified with Jesus had their legs broken and thereby expired.

The body that they were wrapping had no broken bones in it. One more time my Father was saying the same thing He said in the third chaper of Genesis, "You can bruise My son, but you can't break him." He was also telling everyone that His framework will prevail. You can't break it. He's too strong. That was the message, over and over again.

It was almost sundown, and the Sabbath was just beginning.* As Mary Magdalene and Mary the mother of James and Joseph watched, my body was taken to Joseph of Arimathea's personal tomb which was nearby. Joseph, who was a rich man, had a large tomb. As always, that fulfilled the Scriptures,

> "And he made his grave with the rich in his death because he had done no violence, neither was any deceit in his mouth."[74]

I was taking another man's tomb because I took his place on the cross. I died with the poor on the cross and was buried with the rich. I died for every man.

The Pharisees, in their usual manner, were going to stop God; so they got the Romans to put a big stone at the entrance to the tomb and seal it.

Several theologians say that it was not your physical death that really was important on the cross. They say that it was not really the source of the Atonement, but the important thing at the crucifixion was your spiritual death when God separated Himself from you spiritually and, in some way we can't understand, laid on you the sins of the world. That was the point when you were the most troubled on the cross because you, being perfect, were so offended by this stench of sin.

In a real way He laid the sins of the world on me through my humanity. These people separate my spiritual nature from my human nature as if I were not one person. My human experience was in a significant way the means He would use to judge the world.

I told you what went through my mind in Gethsemane. He was judging me in every way human beings can be judged for every crime they have committed. By having those crimes committed against me, I felt every one of them. That was the offense. None of those crimes was who I was, and none of them did I deserve. It was a tremendous offense to me physically, emotionally, and spiritually. It violated my integrity in every way.

These people who say my human suffering was not important don't have a high enough estimation of humanity. They think my taking human punishment was not really important because they don't think being a human being is really important. They don't understand the Incarnation. Everyone will understand more later.

How would you summarize what happened on the cross?

All your sins were destroyed on that cross. I acquired certainty for you. No one had ever conquered death before, even though I had prolonged the life

---

*The Sabbath runs from sundown Friday until sundown Saturday, and the Jews were not to do any work on that day.

of a few people for a few more years. You now have someone who has made it through. It was my purpose to get there. I had to prove that love was greater than evil.

During your trial and persecution, even though you were being judged by your Father, yet His words were with you. And He was with you, as you attested when you gave your life.

Not for one second did He quit empathizing with me. In the midst of my pain, He felt every blow. But at the same time, He judged me. His ability to do that is what made salvation possible. Without that greatness everyone would be damned. It's amazing that a personality can be that dichotomous, can feel two powerful emotions at the same time and be fully conscious of both. He was pouring all that rage out on me, and yet every second, He felt it with me.

As He judged me, He thought of every person in the world. When He had me called names, He thought of everybody who had ever called anyone a name, anyone who has ever gossiped. When He had me physically abused, beaten up, He thought of everyone who had ever been abused physically or ever thought about abusing. When He had them persecute me and kill me, He thought about all the dictators who had ever persecuted people. He thought of all of the parents who have abused their children and all the neighbors who have abused each other. Whoever you are, He judged you when He judged me. And I can testify, you were judged. It was a tremendous judgment. It was so much so that His great sense of justice was satisfied forever.

My Father is so much greater than you know even now. You will be shocked when you get to heaven, because of the wonders to be revealed. You are given glimpses of Him here. Imagine a personality so patient that He can wait thousands of years to carry out His plan. Before He started on "this project," He knew exactly how long it would take, down to the last second. You have no idea how omniscient He is.

There is something tough about your Father. He insisted that the price for justice be paid in full by you. Also, as you read the Old Testament, He repeatedly says, "Don't ignore me. If you do, you will pay an extreme price."

He's stern but intrinsically fair. Don't think that you can ever take advantage of Him. Don't think that everything doesn't count with Him. He's too important and, in His image, He made you important, too. God will have you be who He made you to be, or He will turn you over to yourself. Then you can be your own god. Never think that you can take advantage of God.

The Jews who weren't believers were still worried about you after you died. They had heard your claim that you would be back that you would rise from the dead. So they talked the Romans into putting a huge stone at the entrance to your tomb and placing Roman guards around the tomb so that your disciples wouldn't steal your body.

It wouldn't have made any difference to them if they had watched me walk out of the grave. They weren't going to believe me, no matter what. They were such liars. They insisted on "reality" being their way. They never told the people the truth about what happened next. It's the same story today. Some people will do anything to deny my resurrection, even to spending years writing books about how it didn't happen. That is some of the most wasted labor in history. It's right up there next to the Roman soldiers who rolled the stone over my tomb.

Two days later your body was resurrected. What happened? And how did it feel coming back from the dead?

No one visited my tomb the day after I died because it was the Sabbath. Early Sunday morning, long before daylight, Mary Magdalene came by herself to visit my grave. She had been unable to sleep that night because she was so grieved. Since she was lying awake and the Sabbath was over, she thought she would go out and visit my tomb, even though later that morning she had planned to come to my tomb with several other women including Salome and my Aunt Mary, my mother's sister. Caring not for her own life and thinking only of me, Mary walked all the way to my grave alone in the darkness.

Just before she got there, an angel suddenly appeared at my tomb. There was a great earthquake. Then the angel rolled back the stone from the tomb and sat on top of it. With his face brightly shining and his robe a brilliant white, he stared down at the Roman guards. They were so terrified that they fainted.

When they recovered and saw the huge rock still rolled aside and that the tomb was empty, they decided that their true friend was the chief priest, and not their superiors. They ran to the Temple and told the priest what had happened. The priest paid them secret bribes to say that my disciples had come in the middle of the night and stolen my body while the guards were asleep. The priests promised these guards that if the story got back to the Governor, they would take care of it and the guards would not get into any trouble.

By the time Mary Magdalene got there the first time, all she saw was an empty tomb and my grave clothes. She ran to get Peter and John, and didn't yet comprehend that I was alive.

Immediately Peter and John ran to my grave. John got there first, but he wouldn't go inside. As usual, when Peter got there he didn't hesitate. Unfraid, he walked inside the tomb. There he found the linens from around me unwrapped and left lying in a neat bundle. A napkin that had been around my head was lying to one side by itself. The angel had done that to let everyone know I was completely unwrapped. I was free of the tomb.

Did you really need the angels to unwrap you when your body came back to life?

Of course I didn't need them to do it. I gave them something to remember. They'll talk about that moment forever.

As I was telling you, Peter and John saw the same signs that Mary did, but they didn't know exactly what to make of them either. They returned to Jerusalem not yet being complete believers.

After telling Peter and John what she had seen, Mary Magdalene waited to meet the other women as she had planned. Just before daybreak, she headed back to the tomb with these women. Mary didn't want to upset the other women who had gone to great trouble and expense to buy spices for my burial, and she didn't want them to know she had gone ahead of them. So she didn't tell them that she had already visited my gravesite.

All the way to the tomb, the other women worried about how they were going to get the great stone from the doorway. Mary said very little, clearly upset. Salome and my Aunt Mary thought she was just grieving over my death.

When the three women got to the tomb, there was an angel sitting on top of the stone who told them not to be afraid. He knew they were looking for me, but he told them I was risen. He told them to go inside and see where "the Lord lay." Mary Magdalene was in complete shock by then and didn't understand that this was an angel. She thought the angel was just a man, and that he meant that my body had been moved somewhere else. The other two women went inside.

It was a large tomb, about fifteen by twenty feet, carved out of rock, and there were three angels there, two standing up wearing shining robes and a third angel sitting off to their right in a long, white robe. The women bowed down out of fear, and the angels asked them why they sought the living among the dead. The angels told these two followers that I was not there. I had risen from the dead just as I had promised. Then Mary and Salome remembered my words.

Finally the third angel told them to go tell the disciples that I would see them in Galilee. Quickly, Mary and Salome ran out of the tomb, consumed by joy. Since she had already been in the tomb and thought someone had moved my body, Mary Magdalene had been walking around my tomb looking for the place where my body might have been put. As they ran out of the tomb, the other two women couldn't find Mary and started back to Jerusalem without her. Later Mary Magdalene would catch up with them on the road.

When Mary Magdalene finally came back to the tomb, she stood at the door weeping and looked in to see the three angels. Mary Magdalene was with three angels but was totally unimpressed as she stood there sobbing. The other women had been afraid, but Mary was hurt.

I had been watching all this take place, and suddenly I appeared behind her and asked her why she was crying. She glanced over her shoulder at me thinking that I was the gardener, and told me, in fact almost scolded me,

> "Sir, if you have taken Him away, tell me where you have put Him, and I will go and get Him."

At that point, all I said was,

> "Mary."[75]

She knew that voice. And you should have seen the joy, unspeakable joy, that came over her face. The joyful smile, the radiance—that was my reward. You asked me how it felt to be resurrected. If you could see just one face like Mary's, if you could know that you had brought someone that much joy, it was worth it all. It was the same face I saw over and over again when I appeared to each of my disciples. Literally and figuratively, that tomb had been a womb for the greatest single event in history.

Remember, all my disciples except Judas were in the midst of grieving, and a tremendous change occurred in them when they saw the one who they thought was dead and for whom they were grieving walk into the room. It was overwhelming—the surprise, the awe, the excitement, the hope, the love! How different these faces were from the ones that surrounded me during my crucifixion. This was the joy for which I endured the pain of the cross. These were the kinds of faces that you will see in heaven—forever.

I told Mary that she couldn't touch me because I hadn't yet ascended unto the Father in Heaven. Then I left and appeared to Mary and Salome who were running down the road. When they recognized me, there were the same faces again, just like Mary Magdalene's. They fell at my feet. I told these women to go and tell my disciples what they had witnessed, and to tell them to meet me in Galilee.

Of all the people in the world, you appeared first to these women to announce your resurrection. Why was it to them?

Those were the ones who honored me. Who else arose early on the Sabbath to come to my grave? Since Mary Magdalene arrived first, she was the first to see me. These women understood loyalty, and loyalty has great rewards.

Did you see your Father after that?

I did. You should have seen it when I first walked into Heaven lined with angels shouting for joy and my Father in His glory as I walked to Him dripping in blood. That moment was preserved forever, and one day you will get to see it. That's all I can tell you. Read the book of Revelation if you want to know more.

But let's get back to the story. The women who had seen me on that Resurrection Sunday found the eleven disciples as soon as they got to Jerusalem and told them what they had witnessed. As usual, these men, destined to be world-famous apostles, didn't believe them. Not even Peter and John believed, who had already seen that the stone was rolled back and that the grave was empty. Some of them ran out to the tomb again, but they still didn't believe that these women had seen an angel. After all, they reasoned, if an angel were going to appear, he would certainly visit the apostles first and not "just" women. Besides, who could really believe that Jesus was alive?

The disciples ignored my instructions to go to Galilee, and they remained in that room, filled with fear, as their once-dead leader roamed the world. Peter, however, being the man that he was, had a bit more courage because of the light that had been given to him at this point in the day. In daylight with his life in greater jeopardy because of what he believed the Pharisees would do to him if he were caught, he returned once more to the grave alone. You don't think I would miss a chance to honor that kind of faith, do you?

Peter was the fourth person to see you that day.

After I appeared to Peter, I met two followers of mine. One was Cleopas, an uncle by marriage. His wife was my Aunt Mary, who had already seen me. These two men were walking to the village of Emmaus, about seven miles from Jerusalem. They were talking about my death as I came up beside them on their walk, disguised as just another traveler. They were obviously distraught and I asked them why they were so sad.

They couldn't believe that I hadn't heard about the death of Jesus whom they had thought was the Messiah before he was killed. These two men told me they had talked to Jesus' disciples that morning, and had heard the women's story that Jesus had appeared, that he was risen from the dead. The disciples themselves had substantiated that the tomb was empty, but who could believe it? Who could believe hysterical women, even if one of them did happen to be your own wife?

I told them that they were very foolish. I wondered why it was so hard to believe what the prophets had written. Wasn't what the women were saying predicted in the Scriptures? Then I began at the book of Genesis and went through the Scriptures quoting them passage after passage from the prophets and explaining to these two men what they meant. By the time we got to Emmaus, they had learned, much more than they had bargained for. But they were tremendously encouraged by the Scriptures and they begged me to go home with them.

You must have been an extremely comforting resurrected man. Even when you rebuked them, they still wanted you to come home with them.

So I did. And as we sat down to eat, I asked God's blessing on our food. And I took a small loaf of bread and broke it and began passing it to them. That was when they recognized who I was. As soon as they did, I disappeared.

Why did you appear to those two followers who didn't appear any more spiritual than the eleven disciples? Why did you come to two men who weren't in your "inner circle"? Two men of whom we never heard, one whose name we don't even know?

They weren't unknown to me. To this day I know both of them. I came to the whole world. That's what I was trying to say.

You appeared to your followers five times that day alone, not counting your journey to Heaven. As I read the story, it's as though you are saying to the world over and over in your typically subtle way, "See what I've done? I died for you —all of you."

The resurrection is the heart of it all. I'm glad you got the message.

Your fifth and last appearance of the day was to your disciples that night in Jerusalem.

It was Sunday night, and they continued to be frightened, in shock, still hiding out in that room. Peter and the two men I had walked with to Emmaus, as well as Mary Magdalene and the other women, had told them that they had seen me, but the disciples couldn't believe it yet. They had had one shock after another. Judas had betrayed me. I had been publicly declared a criminal and killed, and Judas had committed suicide. Then they had heard that my tomb was empty and that I had appeared. They had visited the tomb and had seen nothing, and they were still too afraid and confused to believe.

Suddenly I walked through the walls and appeared in their midst. As I looked around the room, I was instantly reminded of our last meal together. It was so good to be back with them, and this time I was free. But they didn't share my joy immediately. If you've ever been the ghost ten men think they're looking at, you'll know how I felt. I had seen it two other times before. So I said to them,

"Peace be unto you."[76]

That just frightened them more. The ghost could talk. Then I said to them,

"Why are you frightened? Why do you doubt that this is really I?"[77]

"Look at my hands, my feet, even my side. Touch them to make sure I'm not a ghost. Ghosts don't have bodies."

I held out my hands and not one of them would touch me. They were so different from the two women I met on the road who wouldn't let go of me. The disciples just stood there paralyzed, half full of joy and half full of fear.

Finally I asked them if they had anything to eat. With his hands trembling, Nathaniel handed me a piece of broiled fish, and all ten of them watched me eat it, uttering not a word. At this point, my disciples were just beginning to believe. Joy was starting to win out, but they still didn't know what to say or do. I reminded them,

"Don't you remember my telling you that everything written about me by Moses and the prophets and in the Psalms must all come true?"[78]

I looked around and I could see that finally I had reached them. I continued, "Long ago it was written that the Messiah must suffer and die, and on the third day rise again from the dead. Then this message of salvation was to be taken from Jerusalem to all the nations of the world. There is forgiveness of sins for everyone who turn to me.[79] You, my friends, have seen these prophecies come true. You are eye witnesses. And now, just as my Father promised, I will send the Holy Spirit upon you."

I told them not to leave Jerusalem yet. They would know when they had all their power from the Father. I looked around the room again and said to them,

"Peace be unto you. As my Father hath sent me, even so send I you."[80]

I then breathed on each of them, and gave them their authority,

"Receive the Holy Spirit. If you forgive anyone's sins, they are forgiven. If you refuse to forgive them, they are unforgiven."[81]

The look on their faces was impossible to describe. One day you'll see a most beautiful painting that captured that moment exactly, and that piece of art will hang in Heaven forever. The First Supper with my men on this side was so different than the Last Supper on that side. I no longer had to walk by faith. The anxiety, the uncertainty that faith demands was over. I had done it, and I knew they would, also. Nothing could stop my church now.

As I walked through the wall and left them there that night, I remember thinking: "One day they will have a body like this, too."

Thomas wasn't there that night, as you told us before. As the Scriptures record, afterwards when he heard about your visitation, he refused to believe the other disciples. He told them, "Unless I see the nail wounds in his hands and touch them with my own finger, and touch the hole in his side, I won't believe it."

Doubting Thomas was no different than the other men in the room who had heard from Mary Magdalene and the other women that I was alive. Those ten didn't believe I was alive even as I stood there before them.

But one week later, again on a Sunday with Thomas present this time, I appeared to all of them together a second time. The first thing I did that night was speak to Thomas. Thomas was strong-minded and bold. He wouldn't believe me until he touched me. He was the only one not afraid to touch me, including Peter. As soon as he did, true to Thomas, he held nothing back and fell to his knees in total devotion.

Fishing and Forgiveness

After your second appearance to your disciples in Jerusalem, your next appearance was not until several days later when your men were out in a boat fishing on the Sea of Galilee.

They had gone back to their trade temporarily to earn some money. Once again Peter and the rest had spent a long night fishing with nothing to show for their labor. I appeared as a man walking on the shore and called out to them to cast their nets on the other side. They did what I told them and, in just a few minutes, they had a superabundant catch. By this, I was telling them: "I meant what I said. I'm going to make you fishers of men." They caught one hundred and fifty-three large fish and the nets weren't broken, which again was my way of telling them my Father and I have great plans for them and that they would will be successful. Nothing would fail.

One of my favorite stories is what happened afterwards when you had a talk with Peter.

When they all recognized who I was, who do you think dove out of the boat and swam as fast as he could to me? It was Peter. He came the same way he came the first time I called him from the shore when I was starting my ministry. Peter, the disciple who had every reason to shy away from me because he had just failed me, swam to embrace me with his big heart. That made the rest of the disciples more comfortable. This time no one else dared to ask me who I was. They knew.

I had a fire going and breakfast ready. Once again I served them bread and fish, which brought back all the memories of the times in the wilderness when I fed thousands of people the same meal. That made the disciples feel even more comfortable around me.

Then I went over and sat down by Peter, who, knowing himself about as well as a human being can, had assured me on the evening before my death that he would do anything for me, even give up his life if he had to. I promised him at that time that he was about to deny me three times. This he did.

He had started out loyally after my arrest. He was one of only two disciples who followed my captors into the city. The trial was at the High Priest's house and the pressure became too great for Peter. All the religious power got to him. He was standing around the High Priest's courtyard and a servant girl asked him if he weren't one of my disciples. He replied, "Absolutely not." Eventually Peter was allowed inside the courtyard, and, as he was warming himself around the fire with some officials and servants, another servant girl said to everyone there as she pointed Peter out, "This man was with Jesus of Nazareth." Peter said forcefully, "I don't know the man," this time also swearing as he denied me.

Then another of the High Priest's servants, who was also a relative of the man whose ear Peter had cut off and who had seen Peter commit this impetuousity, came up to Peter, accompanied by several other servants and said, "I saw you in the olive grove. Your accent gives you away; you are from Galilee." Finally, swearing loudly again, Peter replied, "I told you I have never known this man, Jesus." As I had predicted, the third time he disavowed any connection with me whatsoever, the cock began to crow. Peter was ashamed. He was devastated.[82]

For Peter to be afraid was a failure for him. This was a man you would want next to you if you were ever cornered by a gang in a dark alley. He had been the disciple who came to meet me on the water. He had been the disciple who was not so awed, when he saw me transfigured and when he saw Moses and Elijah, that he couldn't help but offer to contribute something to the occasion.

He offered to build all three of you a temple.

He was a man of action. Like everyone else, he had to learn his limits.

He never thought that he had been afraid of another man in his life. Yet there he was, a coward, and the worst kind at that. He denied the one person he loved the most. The way he did it bothered him almost as much. It was not just a casual "no." He had been vehement about it even to the point of swearing. He couldn't stand up to three people's accusations of his knowing me, two of whom were servant girls.

It was a blow to him to think, "I—Peter—am a coward." But that's the end of the rope to which everyone must come. I knew that Peter was deeply ashamed, and that his shame haunted him. I knew that because I knew Peter.

When I sat down next to Peter the morning after my resurrection, I asked him

"Peter, do you love me?"

And he looked at me:

"Yes, Lord."

Then I asked him a second time,

"Peter, do you love me?"

He looked at me and said with a puzzled and hurt look on his face,

"Yes, Lord."

I waited just a few seconds and finally asked him a third time,

"Peter, do you love me?"

He hadn't caught on yet, and he said, very humbly, without his usual forcefulness,

"Lord, you know that I love you."

I looked at him and said to him,

"Peter, feed my sheep."[83]

You gave him three more chances to answer the way he really wanted.

Later I gave him some real opportunities to feed my sheep.

Peter didn't know it then, but a great revival was coming soon, just as the book of Jonah indirectly predicted. In Jonah's day, an entire ruthless foreign nation turned to God when they saw a bleached white prophet wash up on shore after the huge fish had spit him out. Now another prophet had come back from the dead. Only this time his disciples would be doing the preaching and Peter was to be one of them.

The next thing I told Peter was that he was going to die for me. He was finally going to get his wish. I was going to enable him to die as a brave man, to look death in the face and this time to stand up for me. As usual, Peter didn't hesitate to say what was on his mind. He wanted to know if John would be killed, too. I had to tell him that it was not his business to worry about John.

(This incident with his disciples and with Peter in particular makes me realize how much our lives are like the widow's mite. None of us has very much to offer, but Jesus takes it and blesses it, and it becomes a great deal. The same idea predominates in Scripture. From the little boy Jesus took the small meal, and fed thousands. A woman took all her savings and bought a bottle of precious ointment and gave it to Jesus, pouring it over his head before his burial. Jesus accepted it and told her story around the world for centuries, thereby giving hope to millions of people who have only small gifts to give.

All the disciples, including Peter, had to learn the lesson that in ourselves we have little to offer God. Peter the braggart, the coward, the loudmouth, offered Jesus his "piddling" life. Jesus took it and blessed it and Peter became the dynamic preacher, the brave martyr, the rock of the church. This disciple who was once renowned for his cowardice was later to be given the job of writing the classic Christian text on suffering. God even let Peter put his own name on it as the author. It was the book of First Peter.

It was the same for all of them. Matthew, renowned for his greed, became the famous apostle. John, one of the Sons of Thunder who once wanted to call down fire upon his neighbor, who once wanted to be exalted above all the other disciples and sit on Jesus' right hand, a selfish, angry man, became known as the Apostle of Love. To this day, all these limited followers continue to bear fruit for Christ and thus to reveal how great Christ's promise of "success" to his men was despite their faults.

It was the same way in the Old Testament. Ten of the twelve heads of the tribes of Israel, men whose tribes bore their names, were traitors —Joseph's brothers. Christ himself chose to come out of the tribe of Judah, not out of one of the tribes of the favored Joseph or Benjamin. Indeed, Jesus intends to honor his people.)

The Finale ... The Commencement

Over the next forty days, another one of those increments of forty, you appeared to your disciples only a few more times that we know about. And you appeared to five hundred of your followers at a special gathering. You also appeared to your half-brother James on at least one occasion but the Scriptures don't tell us the reason. Why was it to James?

James was like Peter. He had failed me terribly on two occasions. The first time he joined my peers when I was just a young boy and ridiculed me for "being illegitimate." The second time occurred as I was making my public claim to be the Messiah. After he had already witnessed my performing several miracles, he had come with the rest of my family to rebuke me.

I had grown up with James, and I knew how hard he would be on himself for failing me. The same kind of "strength" he showed in confronting me would now be turned on himself. You see, he had really called God Himself a bastard, and he knew it. He was my brother, and I had to comfort him. I couldn't leave him with that on his conscience.

I knew that if I could rechannel his strong will, he would be quite a Christian as my followers came to be called. It worked. He became the leader of the church in Jerusalem. Several years later, at a crucial point in church history when the Jewish Christians were trying to ostracize Paul and the Gentile believers, rather than taking sides and ridiculing the Gentile believers as everyone in Jerusalem was pressing James to do, he brought unity to that situation. A unity which has lasted to this day.

James had learned his lesson in humility so well that he spent so much time on his knees in prayer asking God for the wisdom and power he didn't have, that he developed callouses on his knees and became known as "old camel knees."

A few years later I made my last appearance on earth. It was to Paul, the future apostle. Like James, he had been my enemy. Unlike James, Paul came to the point of persecuting and killing people for believing in me. When he realized what he had done, he was, of course, filled with remorse. For Paul to be the kind of leader in the church I wanted, I had to appear to him to reshape his strong will. I had to shape it away from the Law on the one hand and away from self-condemnation on the other.

Remember that Paul did not have the Scriptures which emphasize grace and forgiveness to fall back on. He wrote them. I wanted a man who needed to understand grace and forgiveness himself to write those books. I had to have a man who had a heart for sinners.

(In choosing Paul and Jesus' half brother James to be leaders of the early church, along with Peter, John and Matthew, God continues His pattern of selecting utter failures to carry His message of grace to a fallen world. As always, each messenger carries the message he himself had failed to hear at first. All had utterly failed their Lord initially. Obviously Jesus wanted forgiven people to deliver his message of forgiveness.)

After your resurrection, the Scriptures always refer to your manifestations as appearances and not arrivals. It's as if they are saying that now you don't arrive anywhere, you are already there. You just appear.

At this point, I was manifesting my omnipresence and omniscience.

Several modern critics attack historic Christianity by saying that your disciples plotted to perpetuate the myth that you had risen.

The other thing these critics say is that somehow my disciples were fooled. They claim that my body was moved, or something to that effect. These are the two basic ways they attack my resurrection. The answer to both lies, regarding my disciples, is very simple. Only certainty gives courage. The only way my disciples and other followers could have withstood the sword that came down upom them for the first three centuries that the church existed, a time of persecution beyond comprehension, was to have unwavering certainty that I was alive. Only that assurance gave them the courage they needed, just as the certainty that my Father was alive gave me the courage I needed. Otherwise, as Pascal observed, my disciples, being the fickle creatures men are, would have crumbled in five minutes under the pressure.

There was no reason on this earth for them to perpetuate a lie. Only persecution lay ahead for those who said I was alive. Who would live a lie to be persecuted? But then, the resurrection can't be contained. It has no capacity for secrets. My resurrection radiates power to anyone, even to a coward like Peter. That's why he was so different after my return.

If someone is having a difficult time standing up for you, would you say to them, "Look at my resurrection?"

If you look at my resurrection long enough, it will give you the same strength that brought me out of the grave.

The last speech you gave that we know anything about, you made to your eleven disciples on a mountain in Galilee. In it you gave them their task which has come to be known as "The Great Commission."

I told them to meet me at this particular mountain. After they had been there awhile, I appeared to them. Some of the disciples by then were getting accustomed to my new power and reacted ecstatically when I appeared. But others still doubted that it was really I. They still thought I was a ghost. The critics who paint my men as easily-duped fools are far from the truth. My disciples came fighting the whole way.

As we were eating supper, I confronted them about their own belief. I talked about their stubborn refusal to believe me, the Scriptures, and the women who had seen the angels. They were just like modern men and women who can't believe in miracles. I asked them what it would take for them to believe me. The prophets had told them what would happen, I had told them myself, and it had occurred exactly as we all predicted. Now I was sitting with them. They could touch me, again, just as we all had predicted. I wanted to know what it would take for them to trust me.

I let them think about that. We finished the meal in silence.

Finally, as they were looking around at that beautiful view from the mountain, I told them what I wanted them to do,

"All power is given unto me in heaven and in earth. Go ye therefore, and teach all nations, baptizing them in the name of the Father, and of the Son, and of the Holy Ghost: Teaching them to observe all things whatsoever I have commanded you: and, lo, I am with you always even unto the end of the world."[84]

Then I told them that they would each have unique powers just like the ones they had had the time they had gone out before in pairs. They would be able to cast out demons and heal the sick in my name. Poison of any kind, including snake bites, would not be able to harm them. They would speak in tongues. John the Baptist had baptized only with water, but they would baptize with the Holy Spirit. As the Father had sent me with a difficult task to perform and yet with great authority, so I was sending them.

I had completed the first part of the mission. I had died for everyone. And now the second part was partially their responsibility. They were to let the people of the world know what I had done. Of course, I would help the disciples with their mission, just as my Father had helped me.

(It was so like Jesus after he had sternly rebuked his men to give them a chance to redeem themselves with a great task. Again it was so like him to bless them undeservedly by giving them great powers just at the moment they had failed him. To the end, he remained their loving but demanding saviour.

Once again as he told this story, I felt an excitement that the disciples surely must have felt, too. As a believer, I was going to do things in the name of the Father, and of the Son, and of the Holy Spirit.)

Apparently, following that talk you walked with your men back from Judea, near Jerusalem, to the Mount of Olives just outside Bethany, and there ascended to your Father.

Just as I had had the advantage of talking with someone—the angels—from the other world before I began my mission, my disciples had the advantage of talking with me. They had many questions on that walk to Bethany. Many of them were the same ones I had had before. "When will we use our power? How will we know what to say? What should we do? Do you think we can handle that much power without abusing it? When will we see you again? When will you make your Great Return?"

I told them what I had learned and said that their Teacher, the Spirit, who had been my Teacher would show them the rest. They were not to know specifically when I would return. That was only for the Us to know. But I had given them the signs to look for when my return was near. On that walk together, I could see their spirits picking up. I could see their boldness growing. It became so strong that in the next few weeks after I left, they would all go back to the Temple in Jerusalem this time unafraid to declare publicly their faith in the Living God.

When we arrived at Bethany, I gathered them around me and, just like at the Last Supper, I told them I had to leave. I was going to the right hand of my Father and would sit down at my place on His right hand. I promised them that one day I would return to the very spot on which they were now standing, the Mount of Olives.

I looked around one more time, touched each of them one last time, and blessed them. Then I began ascending into Heaven. As I looked down at them, I knew what Elijah had felt when he left the prophet Elisha in the same way, and what the angels felt as they left me after my temptation. I knew certainty. I knew my men would do it. The gates of Hell would not prevail against them, against my church. They were bold now and they were one.

(The disciples waited in Jerusalem as Jesus told them to do and sixty days later at Pentecost, one hundred days after their leader's "great defeat" at Passover, the promised Holy Spirit descended upon them with great power. It was a magnificent event. A sound like the roaring of a mighty wind filled the room in which the disciples were staying. A flame like tongues of fire was above each of their heads anointing them. They all began speaking in foreign languages they had never known before. That same day, Peter, in possibly the greatest single sermon any man ever preached, led three thousand Jewish people from all cultures to declare publicly their faith in Jesus the Christ. God had given Peter a thousand converts for each time Peter had denied his Lord.

Thus began the movement which within a few short years had so much impetus that, as Luke records, it turned the world upside down. The deeds which were to provide the power for this movement, whether for two thousand or two hundred thousand years, were the life, death and resurrection of Jesus, the God-man.)

Afterword

In the introduction to her book about the life of Christ, *The Man Born to be King,* Dorothy Sayers said that it is impossible for an author to do justice dramatically to the story of Jesus Christ, for such is the greatness of his character. One man, human and divine. Yet in the same book, Miss Sayers felt that an author should try to tell the story if one was as honest as he or she knew how to be. Miss Sayers insists that the artist must present the divine Christ as really becoming a man. Specifically, one test that she insisted upon was that theology must meet the demands of drama,

> "there is no more searching test of a theology than to submit it to dramatic handling; nothing so glaringly exposes inconsistencies in a character, a story, or a philosophy as to put it on stage and allow it to speak for itself . . . As I once made a character say in another context, 'Right in art is right in practice;' and I can only affirm that at no point have I yet found artistic truth and theological truth at variance."[1]

Unquestionably then, according to Miss Sayers' definition of living with the pressures of human existence, I think the Scriptures give evidence that Jesus led, from beginning to end, the most dramatic life that a human being has ever lived. "Tempted in all things as we are," as the Epistle to the Hebrews reveals (4:15, NASB). Thus, according to Miss Sayers, since I have written a story about this unique One, I have attempted the impossible. Although I might not have gotten it exactly right, the book is as right as I can make it.

Some will raise questions: Is this work valid? Is it scriptural? Is it consistent with church history? Even those who espouse the doctrine of "fully man, fully God" regarding Christ are not in agreement here as to how the two natures interface. Some people in the church take the position that at times Christ operated out of his human identity and at times out of his divine identity including his complete omniscience, vascillating back and forth at will. While claiming to be in agreement with the most important and last major church council on this subject (Chalcedon, 451 A.D., in which Christ was declared to be "fully God and fully man". Two natures, human and divine, in one person. Two natures united without mixture or division, confusion or separation.), this position of alternation functionally denies Christ's complete humanity.

To help clarify the issue, at any given point when Christ the man is allegedly using his omniscience, ask the question, "is he now fully man?" Those who assume he alternated natures forget that a major victory at Chalcedon was won by those who were insisting on a humanity as complete as his deity. Better a formulation which leaves Christ fully functional as a man and at the same time retains his deity. Yet there is this dilemma: How did he

---

[1]William B. Eerdmans Publishing Co., Grand Rapids, Michigan, 1943, p 3.

maintain his deity and become one of us? Above all, we must be most careful with his deity.

At the same time, it is crucial to understand the battle that has gone on in the church for the last two hundred years. The church has suffered significant damage over this issue from within its own ranks. These detractors have repeatedly attacked Christ's full deity *because* of his humanity. "If indeed he was human, he couldn't have been fully divine," they contend. These thinkers have shaped many of our seminaries and hence our pulpits. Never has a clearer answer regarding Christ's humanity been needed from those who maintain his deity. Never has the question been louder. Human and divine—irrational say the detractors. Deity is omniscient, omnipotent, and infinite; and humanity is finite and ignorant; and never the twain shall meet. Or will they?

The last dozen or so years have witnessed a tremendous expansion in the awareness of the horizons of the human subliminal mind, although this is not yet fully appreciated. And now, very possibly, we are near the answer to our theological dilemma.

Man—little man, limited man—is far more gifted and glorious than anything he imagined! For man possesses a subliminal mind which has observed and recorded in remarkable detail every moment of his life, beyond anything a computer or video-camera can do, a subliminal mind which has come to striking individual (separate from the conscious) conclusions based on its observations.

In essence, man has a vast mind, processing incoming information simultaneously on two tracks, conscious and unconscious, with the subliminal track possessing, for the most part, by far the greater abilities. To communicate its observations, this great subliminal mind, as it were, attempts to splice messages from the second track (the subconscious) at intervals in a coded fashion onto the first track (the conscious). In other words, when a person is communicating a message consciously on the first track, seemingly in response to his conscious observations, at the same time there is often concealed a second message, "on a second track," unbeknownst to him or her consciously.

To put it more simply, a person can communicate two separate messages at one time with the same words. Hence, educated or uneducated, every person possesses the capacity to be a brilliant unconscious observer and communicator beyond his or her wildest dreams.

The psychoanalyst who primarily discovered the vast perceptual ability of this unconscious mind said in amazement recently as he viewed clearly the unconscious mind of a patient during a case presentation, "it's like being in the room with an omniscient being."*

Now it is, in one sense, only one short step to the Incarnation. By analogy of course, but a very impressive analogy. If man himself possesses an "almost omniscient" nature, both knowing and not knowing simultaneously, is it not conceivable that Jesus the man could have possessed Jesus the God at the same time?

*Seminar with Robert Langs, M.D., New York, NY, 1985.

Now with our present understanding of the human mind what once seemed beyond belief is fully possible. Could not the divine Christ have chosen to truly become one of us in such a unique way that maintains the integrity of both natures as well as the unity of one person. Would not the existence of two distinct but united natures, and hence two distinct but united minds, similar to the way our own conscious and unconscious minds interface, meet fully the stringent criterion of Chalcedon—two natures united without mixture or division, confusion or separation. The theologian J.O. Buswell thought so, interestingly choosing the exact analogy of the conscious and unconscious mind as a picture of the Incarnation. Buswell states,

"It has been shown that there is no contradiction in the statement that the Son (in his human nature), at the time of the Olivet discourse, did not know the day and the hour of His Second Coming (divine nature), and yet He (in His person) retained, in the Incarnation, all the attributes of His eternal deity (divine nature), including His omniscience (divine nature). There is no contradiction, I say, because it is a fact that even in human psychology there are different levels of consciousness. It is not a contradiction to say that a person may know something which he does not know. In one sense of the word, he knows it, in the sense of the power of recall. In another sense he does not know it—he does not hold it in his active consciousness. Prior to the Incarnation the eternal second Person (divine nature) of the Trinity chose when He (divine nature) became flesh, to operate in a normal horizon so that He (human nature) might literally have common human experience. Thus, though omniscient He (divine nature) chose not to have in His active consciousness (human nature) at this time, the knowledge of the day and hour of His return (divine nature)."[1]*

Now we can understand how Christ could have been tempted in all things as a man and at the same time was actively Lord of the universe.

The implications for Christians viewing the Incarnation in this way are significant. While some may initially feel that Christ's veiling his omniscience detracts from him, further reflection reveals that this position would actually make things more difficult for him: for example, not to know consciously which event or temptation was coming next.

Ultimately this makes his life and great accomplishment, the Atonement, much more dramatic and far greater. He then would in truth "wear our shoes." Thus the crucifixion becomes not just an event endured by a superman, but unquestionably the greatest deed in human history. Furthermore, if Jesus limited his access to his own omniscience and had to learn about himself (as Luke in his gospel makes plain) and his Father just as we do, this exalts the Scriptures even further. Our Lord studied them, too. If, indeed, Jesus Christ himself submitted to the necessity of studying the Scriptures and to their authority, how much more should we?

Even further, what dignity our Lord brings to us as humans if he really chose to step within our boundaries and live life as it should be lived. What

[1]J.O. Buswell, *A Systematic Theology of the Christian Religion,* II, p.406.
*Parentheses used inside quote are the author's interpretation.

compassion for us. What courage he offers us as he himself faced the very worst possible of human conditions, and rose above them yet never once denying the pain. In essence, how loved we would be if he truly became one of us and one with us—as loved as the Son was by the Father. We could love one another in the same way. The beloved could then take the message around the world to the ignorant, the pagan, the poor, the crippled, the homeless, the sick, the prisoners, the rebels and the outsiders.

As I have pondered the subject of Christ's humanity and deity, I am reminded of a friend who once said, with great feeling, that the crucifixion would have meaning to him only if he knew that Christ thought of him when he hung on the cross. Before I understood what I now know about the human mind, I would wonder how it could be possible for a man to think of every individual in the world in one afternoon, particularly a man who was engulfed with unspeakable pain. As a physician I had seen many people in great pain and in those moments they could think of little else but the pain. And yet I realized that my friend was saying something profound, seeking in reverent anguish personal recognition from a personal God at the moment of crucifixion.

Now, some years later, I understand. I believe that Christ the man in his conscious mind was engulfed by pain and suffering, almost overcome by it, and yet united with his human unconscious mind, Christ the all-knowing God thought of every single person for whom he was making this sacrifice. As he screamed in pain from the cross, He thought of you and He thought of me, and I am convinced that He will tell us that one day face to face.

Andrew G. Hodges

Footnotes

Section One:

	PAGE	REFERENCE*		PAGE	REFERENCE
1.	7	Luke 1:42–45,TLB	37.	47	Psalm 40:6–8
2.	10	Psalm 69:7–8, 10–12, NIV	38.	49	John 8:12
3.	11	Luke 2:34–35,TLB	39.	50	Psalm 22:1–2,6–8,12–18,
4.	11	Luke 1:32–33,TLB			TLB
5.	15	Psalm 89:35–36	40.	50	Psalm 23:1–4
6.	15	Psalm 72:10 (implied)	41.	51	Psalm 24:7–9
7.	15	Isaiah 11:2,NASB	42.	51	Psalm 25:2
8.	18	Psalm 132:11–12,NIV	43.	51	Psalm 27:1
9.	18	Psalm 121:1–2	44.	52	Psalm 27:14
10.	18	Psalm 122:1	45.	53	Psalm 27:1
11.	18	Psalm 122:6–8,TLB	46.	53	Psalm 34:4,NIV
12.	21	Numbers 6:24–26	47.	53	Isaiah 53:7,NIV
13.	22	Isaiah 11:2,NIV	48.	53	Psalm 118:6,KJV
14.	23	See Daniel 11:3–4	49.	53	Jeremiah 1:8
15.	23	Psalm 89:4 (implied)	50.	54	II Peter 1:4,NIV
16.	23	Galatians 4:4 (implied)	51.	54	Matthew 7:23
17.	27	Luke 2:48,TLB	52.	55	Psalm 139:23–24
18.	27	Luke 2:49 (implied)	53.	55	Romans 1:18–19,NIV
19.	28	Luke 1:38	54.	58	I Corinthians 13:4–8,NIV
20.	28	Luke 1:47–48,TLB	55.	58	Matthew 24:35
21.	29	Luke 2:10–12	56.	59	Psalm 45:7,NASB
22.	29	Luke 2:14	57.	60	Psalm 16:5,TLB
23.	31	Luke 2:29–31,TLB	58.	60	Psalm 56:8a,TLB
24.	35	Isaiah 7:14,NAS	59.	61	Job 22:21
25.	38	Isaiah 53:5,12	60.	61	Psalm 30:5
26.	39	Psalm 121:1	61.	61	Zechariah 4:6
27.	40	Psalm 121:2	62.	61	Psalm 91:15
28.	41	Psalm 16:10,TLB	63.	62	Psalm 55:22,NASB
29.	45	Luke 2:52	64.	67	John 10:10 (implied)
30.	45	John 2:4,NIV	65.	68	Matthew 7:3 (implied)
31.	45	Psalm 121:4	66.	68	Jeremiah 17:9
32.	46	Hebrews 2:14b, TLB	67.	69	Psalm 49:14,TLB
33.	46	Matthew 4:4,NASB	68.	69	Colosians 2:2,3
34.	46	Isaiah 8:17,NIV(Hebrews	69.	72	Psalm 34:19
		2:14b)	70.	72	Isaiah 43:2, NASB
35.	47	Philippians 2:5–8,NAS	71.	74	Genesis 3:19 (implied)
36.	47	Phillipians 2:9,NASB			

Section Two:

	PAGE	REFERENCE		PAGE	REFERENCE
1.	81	John 1:29,NIV	3.	84	Deuteronomy 8:2–3,NIV
2.	82	Matthew 3:17	4.	84	Isaiah 11:1,2

	PAGE	REFERENCE		PAGE	REFERENCE
5.	85	Matthew 16:23	28.	109	John 4:50,TLB
6.	87	Matthew 4:4	29.	110	Luke 4:18–19,NIV
7.	87	Psalm 91:11–12,NIV	30.	110	Luke 4:21,NIV
8.	88	Deuteronomy 6:16	31.	112	Isaiah 9:2,NIV
9.	90	Matthew 4:7	32.	113	Luke 9:50,NASB
10.	90	Matthew 4:10,NIV	33.	114	John 1:45–46,TLB
11.	94	Hebrews 12:2	34.	114	John 1:47,TLB
12.	94	Hebrews 2:18	35.	114	John 1:49,TLB
13.	95	Matthew 5:11–12,NIV	36.	115	John 11:16,TLB
14.	95	Matthew 5:5	37.	115	John 14:6
15.	96	Genesis 1:26	38.	115	John 20:28,NIV
16.	96	Isaiah 9:6	39.	121	Psalm 41:9 (implied)
17.	99	Luke 2:14	40.	124	Psalm 89:9,TLB
18.	100	John 2:4,NIV	41.	124	Mark 4:39
19.	100	John 2:5,NIV	42.	127	Matthew 20:28,TLB
20.	104	Psalm 69:9,NASB	43.	127	Hebrews 12:2 (implied)
21.	107	John 4:10,NIV	44.	127	Luke 7:13,TLB
22.	107	John 4:13,NIV	45.	127	Luke 7:14,NIV
23.	107	John 4:15,NIV	46.	128	Luke 8:48,TLB
24.	108	John 4:19–20,NIV	47.	130	Luke 17:19,TLB
25.	108	John 4:26,NIV	48.	133	Matthew 9:2,NIV
26.	108	John 4:35,NIV	49.	134	Matthew 9:5–6,NIV
27.	109	John 4:48,TLB			

Section Three:

	PAGE	REFERENCE		PAGE	REFERENCE
1.	140	II Chronicles 27:14	24.	154	I Kings 10:23,TLB
2.	141	Luke 7:41,TLB (implied)	25.	155	I Kings 10:6–7,9,TLB
3.	142	Matthew 22:16–17,TLB	26.	156	Matthew 16:18 (implied)
4.	142	Matthew 22:21	27.	156	Luke 12:49–50,TLB
5.	142	Luke 20,42–43,TLB	28.	157	Luke 13:34,TLB
6.	143	Luke 11:45,TLB	29.	157	Matthew 6:34
7.	143	Luke 14:5,TLB	30.	158	I Corinthians 15:55
8.	143	Luke 13:12,TLB	31.	158	Isaiah 53:5,7
9.	144	Luke 13:14,TLB	32.	159	Matthew 24:2,NASB
10.	144	Luke 18:10–12,TLB (implied)	33.	162	Mark 3:34–35,TLB
			34.	165	Matthew 5:5,9–12,NIV
11.	145	Mark 10:18,TLB (implied)	35.	166	Proverbs 18:24,NASB
12.	146	See John 3:14 (implied)	36.	166	Psalms 40:5,NASB
13.	147	John 2:19	37.	166	Ecclesiastes 11:1
14.	147	John 8:7,NASB	38.	168	Psalm 45:4,NASB
15.	147	Luke 4:8	39.	169	John 6:31,TLB
16.	147	Matthew 19:19	40.	170	John 6:35,TLB
17.	147	John 6:35	41.	170	John 6:47–51,TLB
18.	150	I Corinthians 2:9	42.	170	John 6:53–54,TLB
19.	151	John 7:17 (implied)	43.	171	Zechariah 13:7,TLB
20.	152	I Corinthians 1:27	44.	173	Isaiah 42:6,NASB
21.	153	Psalm 119:99–100,NASB	45.	173	Isaiah 49:23,TLB
22.	153	Matthew 12:42,NIV	46.	173	Isaiah 49:25,TLB
23.	154	Ezekiel 16:13–14,TLB	47.	174	Jeremiah 33:3,NIV

PAGE		REFERENCE	PAGE		REFERENCE
66.	279	Isaiah 41:13	75.	287	John 20:15–16,TLB
67.	279	Psalm 30:5	76.	290	Luke 24:36
68.	280	Luke 23:40–42,TLB	77.	290	Luke 24:38,TLB
69.	280	John 19:27,NASB	78.	290	Luke 24:44,TLB
70.	280	John 19:28	79.	290	Luke 24:47–49 (implied)
71.	281	Psalm 22:1,22:27–28,	80.	291	John 20:21
		30–31,NIV	81.	291	John 20:22–23,TLB
72.	282	John 19:30	82.	292	Luke 22:56–62 (implied)
73.	282	Psalm 31:5,NASB	83.	293	John 21:15–17 (implied)
74.	284	Isaiah 53:9	84.	297	Matthew 28:18–20